WILLIAM RUSH, AMERICAN SCULPTOR

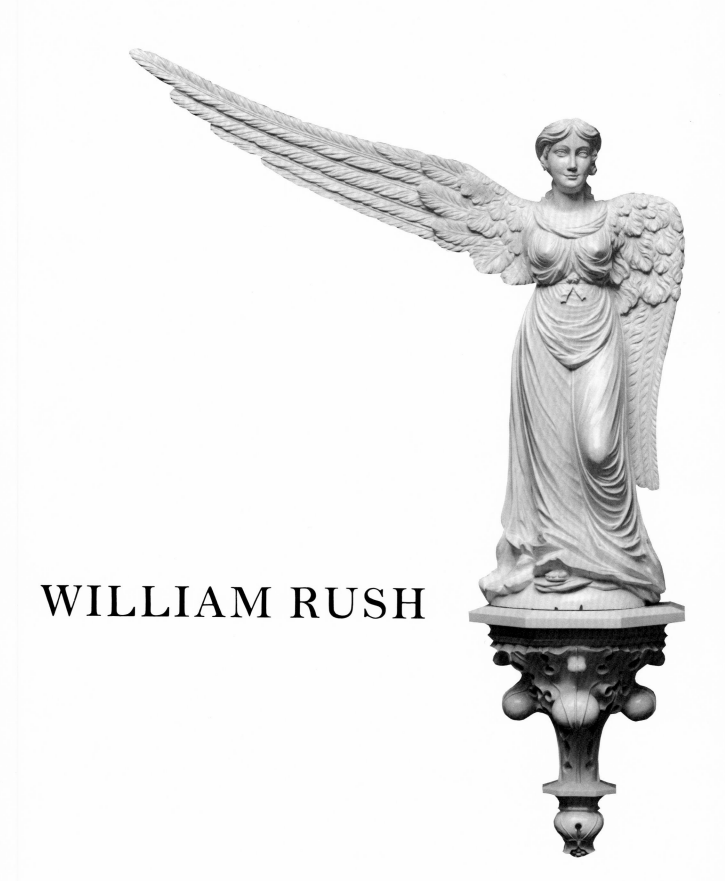

WILLIAM RUSH

AMERICAN SCULPTOR

PENNSYLVANIA ACADEMY OF THE FINE ARTS MCMLXXXII

William Rush, American Sculptor was organized by
the Pennsylvania Academy of the Fine Arts, Philadelphia,
and shown from June 20 to November 21, 1982. The exhibition
and catalogue were supported by grants from the National
Endowment for the Arts and The Pew Memorial Trust.

COVER: William Rush, *Self-Portrait*, c. 1822 [90]
FRONTISPIECE: William Rush, *Cherubim*, 1820–21 [82]

Library of Congress Cataloging in Publication Data
William Rush, American Sculptor
  Catalog of an exhibition.
  Bibliography: p.
  1. Rush, William, 1756–1833—Exhibitions.
I. Pennsylvania Academy of the Fine Arts.
NB237.R8A4 1982   730'.92'4   82-80636
ISBN 0-943836-00-X   AACR2

Printed in the United States of America

CONTENTS

FOREWORD AND ACKNOWLEDGMENTS

The Constellation should be represented by an elegant female figure characteristic of indignant Nature, at the period of the American Revolution, determined on the forming of a New Creation, from that Chaos of Ignorance, Vice and folly, which she had long been burdened with. . . .

William Rush to naval architect
Joshua Humphreys, April 30, 1795

"An elegant female figure characteristic of indignant Nature . . ." was part of a suggestion Rush made to Joshua Humphreys for a proposed figurehead for the *Constellation*. William Rush was a celebrated ship figurehead carver then, but within his lifetime he became known as America's first native sculptor.

Rush is notable for making the transition from the craft of wood carving to the art of sculpture. However, despite the appellation of first native sculptor and his listing in the official histories, this exhibition is the first comprehensive presentation of the work of William Rush since Henri Marceau's pioneering effort, *William Rush: The First American Sculptor*, shown in 1937 at the Philadelphia Museum of Art (then known as the Pennsylvania Museum of Art). In the preface to his catalogue, Marceau called it a catalogue raisonné, yet he further indicated that "although the list of works which follows may surprise some by its extent, it should not be considered complete. Much remains to be discovered. . . ." Linda Bantel, the organizer of the Academy's exhibition, has indeed discovered much new information, and her catalogue more nearly approaches the notion of a catalogue raisonné. The catalogue essays also go far beyond those of 1937 in presenting technical information about Rush's working methods and use of materials, the result of Sculptor Conservator Virginia Naudé's work in the Academy's laboratory from 1979 to 1982.

It is entirely fitting that the exhibition should take place in Philadelphia in this year of her Tricentennial Celebration. Philadelphia is a city with a rich sculptural tradition, a city, in fact, that could be called the birthplace of American sculpture and which, today, boasts more public sculpture than any other city in the United States. Philadelphia was also William Rush's home.

In addition, it is appropriate that this exhibition is organized by the Pennsylvania Academy of the Fine Arts, of which Rush, along with Charles Willson and Rembrandt Peale, was one of the founders. Sculpture has always been central to the Academy's school curriculum, and early on, the Academy began to assemble a collection of "statuary" for its museum. One of the great assets of this collection is the work of William Rush, of which the Academy owns seven important examples.

Any exhibition, especially one as thorough as this, is a massive undertaking. It requires the talents, skills, and generosity of the many people who are called upon to organize, implement, and support it. The people and organizations who have been willing to lend their valuable works are crucial. One of the most important loans, seven significant examples of Rush's work, comes through the generosity of the Grand Lodge of the Free and Accepted Masons of Pennsylvania in Philadelphia. Without these sculptures, originally commissioned for the Masonic Hall on Chestnut Street between Seventh and Eighth which was dedicated in 1820, this exhibition would be seriously lacking. To the Masons, along with the other generous lenders, our sincere thanks.

Our thanks also to the members of the Academy staff and the guest scholars who helped organize the exhibition and who contributed their insights to the catalogue: Linda Bantel, the chief organizer of the show, whose knowledge and perseverance pushed it to completion, with the able assistance of Susan James-Gadzinski, who is an astute and careful researcher, Elizabeth Owen, Nina Purviance, Joyce

Adelman, and Martha A. Diano; to Frank H. Goodyear, Jr., the Academy's Curator of Collections, who provided the initial idea and inspiration; and to the following who contributed their expertise in writing the essays: D. Dodge Thompson, National Gallery of Art, Washington, D.C.; Virginia Naudé, Pennsylvania Academy; and William H. Gerdts of the City University of New York. On behalf of the Academy, the following people have contributed much to the realization of this exhibition: Theodore T. Newbold, Chairman of the Academy's Collections and Exhibitions Committee; Janice Stanland and Gale Rawson, the Academy's Registrars; Catherine Stover, the Academy's Archivist; Elizabeth Romanella, the curatorial department; Marcela de Keyser, the director's office.

Virginia Naudé would like to thank Philadelphia Museum of Art conservators Andrew Lins and Thomas Robinson for sharing their expertise with us, guest conservators Wendy Stayman and Brent Hile for undertaking special conservation projects in our laboratory, and the Academy's team of conservation assistants, especially Steven Pine and Karen Molleson. Carol Olsen generously shared her knowledge of ship figureheads.

Linda Bantel would like to express her gratitude to the staffs of the Philadelphia libraries and institutions which have so graciously helped her in her research. Particular thanks to Edgar P. Richardson, the American Philosophical Society; Darrel L. Sewell, the Philadelphia Museum of Art; Kenneth Finkel, the Library Company of Philadelphia; and Peter Parker, the Historical Society of Pennsylvania.

Assembling a catalogue of this complexity requires the cooperation, dedication, and creativity of several people. Linda Bantel especially wants to thank Rick Echelmeyer for much of the photography and his help in interpreting his X-radiographs, and Klaus Gemming, a designer of flawless taste and efficiency, who designed and coordinated the production of this catalogue.

Special thanks to the National Endowment for the Arts and the Pew Memorial Trust, whose generosity made the exhibition possible, and to the Honorable William J. Green, Mayor of Philadelphia, a city whose Three Hundredth Birthday this exhibition celebrates.

Richard J. Boyle
Director

William Rush, Esq.

LINDA BANTEL

For the use of wooden statues we have classical authority. Daedalus, the first of the Grecian statuaries that acquired distinction, made all his figures of wood. Some of these were highly prized by the Athenians. There was one wooden statue in particular, in the temple of Minerva Polias, which was regarded with the highest veneration. The old Greeks said it fell from heaven: but this part of the story we do not believe. It was made by the William Rush of Greece,—by the first Athenian statuary. Athens had existed a thousand years, before she produced those beautiful specimens of the arts which have been the admiration of all succeeding ages. We cannot hope that Philadelphia will, one hundred and forty years after her foundation, rival Athens. We must proceed gradually towards excellence, after the manner of the Athenians. It will be our own fault, if we do not proceed more rapidly.[1]

At the time of the American Revolution, three-dimensional artistic expression was limited to crafts like carving gravestones, furniture ornaments, and shop signs.[2] As the shipbuilding industry grew, however, there were increasing opportunities for more ambitious wood-carvers to create ship's ornaments, which were America's first large-scale public sculptures. The War of Independence created an atmosphere sympathetic to the introduction of sculpture as a fine art and provided nationalistic subject matter. The development of sculpture was nurtured by an influx of imported works and then by the adaptiveness of native craftsmen (see William H. Gerdts, "Sculptural Genius or Inspired Artisan?"). Philadelphia's William Rush (1756–1833) was the most skilled of a new generation of wood-carvers (fig. 1). His career paralleled and was enriched by the ascendancy of his native city, which became a political, economic, scientific, and cultural center.

For most of the last quarter of the eighteenth century, Philadelphia was the seat of the United States government. During this period the city had emerged as the principal shipbuilding and mercantile center south of New England, her economy maintained by exports of flour derived from fertile farmlands to the west. British occupation of Philadelphia during the Revolution disrupted business only temporarily, and their evacuation in June 1778 created a minor shipbuilding boom to replace ships destroyed by the British. There was another surge of shipbuilding after peace was declared in 1783, when merchants built new larger vessels to transport abundant goods which Americans had lacked during the war. American merchants prospered with expanded trade routes to China and India and profited from the European markets which France and England were neglecting because of escalating Napoleonic Wars in the 1790s.

Rush's father, Joseph, was a ship carpenter,[3] a middle-class profession that was hereditary. Rush began in his youth "cutting out ships from blocks of wood," but also showed an early proclivity for "drawing figures in chalk and paints."[4] In his early teens, he was apprenticed to Edward Cutbush (c. 1735–1790), formerly of London and called the "best carver of his day."[5] None of his figureheads has been discovered.[6] William Dunlap, who knew Rush, recorded that within three years the student had surpassed his master.[7] Based on this information, Rush's twentieth-century biographer Henri Marceau postulated that if Rush entered Cutbush's shop about 1771, at the age of fifteen, he would have been on his own by 1774.[8] The American Revolution interrupted his career for a time. On September 9, 1777, Rush was commissioned an ensign in Captain Philip Wagener's Company of the Fourth Regiment of Foot of Lieutenant Colonel Wills's Philadelphia Militia.[9] The nature of or length of time of this service is unknown. On December 14, 1780, Rush married Martha Simpson Wallace, and two years later his first son, John, was born. He would become a shipcarver like his father (see "A Revised Genealogy of William Rush").

During the Revolution Rush did some unspecified work for the Pennsylvania state navy,[10] but for over a decade thereafter he worked primarily on merchant vessels. His participation in Philadelphia's Grand Federal Procession held on the Fourth of July, 1788, to celebrate the anniversary of the Declaration of Independence and the ratification of the Constitution by ten of the thirteen states, indicates that Rush was by now considered a leader of his profession. In the mile-and-a-half long parade of some five thousand people, including military figures, dignitaries, and representatives from all the trades, Rush marched with the carvers and gilders and conceived and executed their contribution to the pageantry, a "federal car" which Francis Hopkinson (1737–1791), the chairman of the Committee of Arrangement, described as follows:

The carvers and gilders exhibited an ornamental car, on a federal plan, being thirteen feet by ten on the floor, on which were erected thirteen pilasters, richly ornamented with carved work, the heads of ten gilt and labelled with the names of the several states arranged as they came into the federal union; the remaining three left partly finished; about three feet above the floor, a level rail united to the pilasters, denoting the equality of the subjects. In the centre a column, with a twining laurel running in a spiral form to the capping, which was ten feet high, on the top of which was placed a bust of general Washington crowned with a wreath of laurel, and dressed in the American uniform, with the thirteen stars on a collar; the whole supported by ten tight stays, leading from the finished pilasters to the cap of the column, from whence hung three slack stays, leading to the unfinished pilasters; over the general's bust, the American standard was displayed.

In the centre of the front, the head of Phidias, the most eminent of the ancient carvers, with emblematic figures supporting it; inside of the front rail a large figure for the head of a ship, richly carved and painted; the whole outside of the car decorated with the figures of the seasons, the cardinal virtues, and other devices in carved work. Before the car walked the artists of the several branches, preceded by mr. Cutbush, ship-carver, and mr. Reynolds and mr. Jugiez, house, furniture, and coach carvers, with young artists going before, decorated with blue ribands round their necks, to which were suspended medallions, blue ground, with ten burnished gold stars, one bearing a figure of Ceres, representing Agriculture; another Fame, blowing her trumpet, announcing to the world the federal union; the middle one carrying a Corinthian column complete, expressive of the domestic branches of carving. In the car was a number of artists at work, superintended by mr. Rush, ship-carver, who planned and executed the car with its principal ornaments.[11]

While Rush surely worked for more of Philadelphia's merchants than we know about, his association with Stephen Girard (fig. 2) is the longest and best documented.[12] Girard (1750–1831) was born in Bordeaux, France, and settled in Philadelphia in 1776, a month before the Declaration of Independence. By the early nineteenth century he had accumulated a fleet of over thirty merchant vessels. His records indicate that during an almost forty-year period, 1784–1823, he paid Rush for at least twelve figureheads [1, 8, 9, 11, 12, 16, 26, 27, 28, 30, 44, 91], representing one-quarter of Rush's known ship work. The earliest, in 1784, was for the brig *Two Brothers*, the last, in 1823, a Hercules for the *Superb*.

The large profits to be gained in merchant shipping were made with considerable risks. Almost twenty-five percent of American exports of dried and pickled fish, wheat, flour, and South Carolina rice went to Mediterranean ports. However, since the seventeenth century the Straits of Gibraltar had been controlled by Barbary pirates who would guarantee safe passage only to vessels which paid tribute. Before the Revolution, American merchants were subsidized by the British, but after Independence they lost this subsidy. Their refusal to pay the tribute brought harassment from Moroccan, Algerian, Tunisian, and Tripolitan ships, and in 1793 alone eleven American vessels were captured and over one hundred American sailors taken prisoner. Meanwhile, in the conflict between England and France, neutral American vessels were attacked or captured by ships of one country as they were bound for the ports of the other, and American seamen were taken for impressment.

Because of these assaults, on March 27, 1794, Congress authorized establishing a navy by appropriating $690,000 for six new frigates.[13] Congressional leaders had resisted this expense, but in the 1790s a nation's prestige and power rested on the ability of its navy to defend its shores and its mercantile investments on the seas. For an independent nation coming-of-age, the decision to build a navy was inevitable.

Joshua Humphreys (1751–1838), a leading shipbuilder in Philadelphia, was appointed the first naval constructor or architect. Because of limited funds, Humphreys (fig. 3) designed frigates, small warships carrying only thirty-six to forty-four guns, unlike the great British Royal Navy ships of the line with up to a hundred cannon each. Humphreys envisioned a highly maneuverable vessel that could fight easily or rapidly run. Only the *United States* [15] was built under his personal supervision at his

Fig. 1. Attributed to Rembrandt Peale (1778–1860). *William Rush*, before 1813. Oil on canvas, 23½ × 19½ in. (59.7 × 49.5 cm.). Independence National Historical Park Collection, Philadelphia. By 1813, this portrait of Rush, which depicts him in his mid-thirties to late forties, was part of the portrait collection in Charles Willson Peale's Philadelphia Museum.

Fig. 2. Bass Otis (1784–1861). *Stephen Girard*, c. 1832. Oil on panel, 29½ × 24 in. (74.9 × 61 cm.). The Rosenbach Museum and Library, Philadelphia. Girard's merchant fleet is depicted in the background.

Fig. 3. Thomas Birch (1779–1851). *Preparation for War*, 1800. Engraving, 9⅛ × 11⁷⁄₁₆ in. (23.2 × 29.1 cm.). The New-York Historical Society, New York City. The figure in the foreground wearing a tricorne is thought to be naval constructor Joshua Humphreys supervising construction of the frigate *Philadelphia* in his Southwark shipyard.

Southwark shipyard in Philadelphia. The *Constitution* [14] was built at Boston, the *Chesapeake* [21] at Norfolk, the *Constellation* [20] at Baltimore, the *President* at New York, and the *Congress* [22] at Portsmouth.

The War Department left the whole matter of the selection of figureheads and their carvers up to the shipbuilders and merely cautioned that the carvings not be too "tawdry or expensive."[14] Humphreys apparently selected Rush since he provided him with a preliminary list of names (Rush chose *Revolution* for the *Chesapeake*) and requested from him suggestions of appropriate subjects for figureheads and stern ornaments. In the following letter to Humphreys on April 30, 1795, Rush detailed for each vessel an elaborate, symbolic group:

As the REVOLUTION of America was a struggle for freedom, and gave birth to a great Republican Empire, it ought to be an Elegant Figure, representing the Genius of America binding the fasces with her right hand, and raising the emblem of Liberty out of the top of the fasces with the left, the bottom of the fasces resting on a rock, the Emblem of firmness and Independence, the American Eagle Darting upon and Destroying the Vitals of Tyranny, with the shackles of Despotism, etc.—and hurling them under the feet of the Genius of America.

As the UNITED STATES is a great Empire of Liberty, founded on Law and Justice, it should be represented by the Goddess of Liberty, supported by the figures of Law and Justice; and designated by the American Arms, Peace, Commerce, Agriculture, etc., etc., resulting from her.

As the CONSTITUTION of the Empire is the result of the Union of the States, and Union begets Strength, it ought to be represented by an Herculean figure, standing on the firm rock of independence, resting one hand on the fasces which was bound by the Genius of America, and the other hand presenting a scroll of paper, supposed to be the Constitution of America, with proper appendages, the foundation of Legislation.

The American Constitution having a President, Congress, etc., for its Government; and as no one hath been thought so fit for the Political head of so great a Republican body, as Washington let the President be the figure and likeness of him, in the Act of Delivering his address at the Opening of the Legislature, with Suitable emblems to express the great office of that Magistrate etc.—and the result of the Administration, supported by Justice and Prudence.

Congress being the great Legislative body on which the Majesty of the Republic alone can rest, it ought to be represented by the Goddess of Wisdom, in the Character of Democracy, reclining upon a pedestal, supported by the Cardinal Virtues—on top of which should be a Number of Volumes, supposed to be the laws framed by the Legislature. In her right hand should be the Constitution, Elevated so that the figure should be looking up to it—the Consequences flowing from the Law under a Wise Administration might be represented by the emblems of the Arts, Sciences, Industry, peace, plenty and independence, etc.

The Constellation should be represented by an elegant female figure characteristic of indignant Nature, at the period of the American Revolution, determined on the forming of a New Creation, from that Chaos of Ignorance, Vice and folly, which she had long been burdened with—She should have a flaming torch in her right hand, setting fire to the bursting World under her feet, with the emblems of Tyranny, Superstition, Folly, etc. issuing from it, and thrown into Confusion and fermentation, her left arm resting on the altar of Liberty. The American Eagle in the act of flight; a Sphere resting on his pinions with the Constellation inserted; soaring to heaven with one more great offering of Nature—or to adorn the new political firmament with light and Glory, to serve as a light to the Nations that have long Wandered in Political Darkness; and to Strike with Wonder and Surprise the Wise men of the East.

The contents are first thoughts, probably much better ideas may offer before it is Necessary to commence the Business.[15]

Rush's iconography is characteristic of the ideals of the young republic and his own staunch patriotism. Yet his use of language and the complexity of the scheme is evocative of and surely inspired by similar English figurehead groups, popular from the 1760s until the end of the eighteenth century, on first-rates, the largest and most prestigious war vessels. The 1790 figurehead for the *Queen Charlotte*, for example, was described as follows:

On the Larboard side of the head piece the principal figure is a large woman figure representing Victory, dressed in drapery and the head crowned with laurels proper, and with one hand holding a branch of laurels cut clear and through, and with the other hand supporting the bust of His Majesty; with one foot trampling down rebellion, represented by a Hydra with five heads, the whole scaled and the heads worked very clear resting on rich contrast scrolls and foliage leaves. At the upper part behind the figure Victory is a flying figure representing Fame, with one hand holding a trumpet as sounding forth our victories, and in the other hand holding a branch of palms denoting peace attending on victory;[16]

Since none of Rush's figureheads for the frigates have survived, their appearance must be gleaned through contemporary descriptions, ship portraits, or drafts. Comparison of Rush's "first thoughts" with newspaper accounts of the actual carvings indicates that Rush realized most of his ideas, but in the case of the *Constellation*, for example, the complicated iconography required extensive explanation. Pictorial sources for the figureheads are less reliable and only rarely relate to the written descriptions. Moreover, it is not unusual for two views of the same ship to show different figureheads, implying that the figurehead was replaced (not uncommon because of loss or damage at sea), or that the vessel had changed owners, or that the artist did not know what the figurehead looked like, as his source must often have been a ship draft, which seldom included the ornamental carvings.

No contemporary view shows the most familiar early American frigate, the *Constitution*, with her Hercules figurehead designed by Rush and carved by John and Simeon Skillin, Jr., of Boston. But since Hercules was such a common subject among figurehead carvers, both in America and abroad, one has a fairly good idea of what it looked like (see fig. 4). Rush himself used the subject again about 1799 for the publicly-funded frigate *Philadelphia* [24]. This is one of the few instances in which a draft (fig. 98) and a contemporary watercolor (fig. 5) clearly show the same figurehead—and probably the *Constitution*'s Hercules was similar.

Rush devised his own emblematic scheme for the ornamental carvings on the U.S. Navy frigates, but it was more common in the late eighteenth century for the ship-owner to choose the subject and sometimes even provide the carver with a graphic source. Most of Rush's subjects were obvious and specifically American, such as Indians [3, 44, 95] or national heroes—*General Washington, John Adams, Benjamin Rush, Benjamin Franklin* [4, 23, 72, 73,

Fig. 4. John Perriman and J. W. Edy. *Perspective View of the Valiant*, London, 1791. Aquatint, colored, 20 × 21⅜ in. (50.8 × 54.3 cm.). The Mariners Museum, Newport News, Virginia. A Hercules figurehead straddles the cutwater of this English man-of-war.

80]. *Columbus* [77] of 1791 is the only instance we know that Rush was encouraged to find a print source for his image,[17] but we can assume he did the same for other historical figures, such as *Sir Walter Raleigh* [81] or *Captain John Smith* [89].

For four of Stephen Girard's ships, which were named after French philosophers, and which are even today considered among the finest merchant vessels ever constructed in the United States, Rush carved either busts or full-length figures. Girard, always sympathetic to his native France, named the first ship, launched in 1795, after his favorite philosopher, *Voltaire* [11]; it was followed in 1801 by the *Rousseau* [27], in 1804 the *Helvetius* [28], and finally in 1806 the *Montesquieu* [30].[18] Rush himself may have admired these learned men, since in 1809 he gave marble busts of Voltaire and Rousseau to the Pennsylvania Academy.[19]

Lions were universally popular subjects for figureheads in Europe during the first half of the eighteenth century, but by the 1790s they were almost never used.[20] Rush revived this old form for three frigates [17, 18, 19] being sent as tribute to the Dey of Algiers, whose religion prohibited three-dimensional representations of human figures. This was part of a peace treaty passed by the Senate on March 2, 1796, in which free passage in the Mediterranean was guaranteed in exchange for annual payments to the Dey. Since that document resolved the major threat to American economic well-being, arming for war no longer seemed crucial, and construction of the three remaining frigates—the *Chesapeake*, the *Congress*, and the *President*—was halted. (All were completed by 1799 during America's struggle with France.)

Documentary evidence suggests that many of Rush's early figureheads were polychromed; the *Lions* [18, 19], the *Indian Trader* [3], and *Liberty* [12] were said to be painted "to life." Practices varied, however. Some European figureheads were polychromed, others were gilt or simulated gilt. Of Rush's three surviving figureheads, *Peace* [29] has traces of polychrome, but it has not been possible to determine how much is of Rush's period (see Virginia Norton Naudé, "Toolmarks and Fingerprints," note 17); *Benjamin Rush* [72] lost all its paint; and the *Benjamin Franklin* [73] for the naval ship of the line has several layers of white paint.

Fig. 5. Artist unknown. *U.S. Frigate Philadelphia*, c. 1800. Watercolor on paper, 11⅝ × 15¼ in. (28.3 × 38.7 cm.). The New-York Historical Society, New York City. The *Philadelphia*, carrying Rush's *Hercules* figurehead, is shown captured by Tripolitan corsairs. She was subsequently rescued but then burned by the Americans to keep her out of enemy hands.

According to John F. Watson, one of Philadelphia's most reliable early chroniclers and one of Rush's admirers and acquaintances, Rush was the first American figurehead carver to adopt the "walking attitude," which was popular with French carvers toward the end of the eighteenth century. Before the Revolution, American figureheads straddled the cutwater (the upright post of the bow), but Rush's seem to stroll forward with a foot raised, generally supported by a scroll-like ship's ornament. Watson claimed that Rush saw such a figure on a foreign vessel and that he "instantly conceived the design of more tasteful and graceful figures than had ever before been executed," and that his carvings excited as much attention abroad as at home. When the *William Penn* bearing the figurehead *Indian Trader* [3] docked in London, "the carvers there would come in boats and lay near the ship, and sketch designs from it. They even came to take casts, of plaster of Paris, from the head." At the sight of Rush's *River God* on the *Ganges* [10] the "Hindoos came off in numerous boats to pay their admiration and perhaps reverence to the various emblems in the trail of the image."[21]

Rush's figureheads also earned accolades from the highly critical and sometimes irascible English immigrant and architect Benjamin Henry Latrobe. In his discussion of the development of the fine arts in the United States presented in an 1811 lecture to the Society of Artists, he observed that America rivaled Europe in portraits and in engravings. "Commerce," he said, "has called for beauty in the forms and decorations of her ships, and where in Europe is there a Rush. . . . [He is] at the head of a branch of the arts which he himself has created. His figures, forming the head or prow of the vessel, place him in the excellence of his *attitudes* and *action*, among the best sculptors that have existed."[22]

The recent discovery of *Peace* [29] of about 1805–10, Rush's only full-size figurehead (fig. 6) known to have survived, allows us to appreciate Watson's and Latrobe's appraisals. Its dynamic conception and execution clearly distinguish it from the more naive and unremarkable works attributed to better-known contemporaries of Rush, such as Samuel McIntire or the Skillins in Massachusetts.[23] It has a graceful and naturalistic motion, a quality Latrobe particularly admired.

To appreciate this achievement one must understand the design restrictions imposed on the figurehead because of its vulnerability to wind and

Fig. 6. William Rush. *Peace*, c. 1805–10 [29]. Pine, painted white.

weather. For durability the figure was best designed and carved out of one log with projecting limbs or other elements kept close to the body (see Naudé, "Toolmarks and Fingerprints," for detailed technical discussion).

Rush's first documented association with Philadelphia's art community was on December 29, 1794, when he was among a group of about forty artists (including the Peales—Charles Willson, Rembrandt, Raphaelle, and James—the engravers William Birch and John Vallance, and the father and son sculptors Johann and Frederick Eckstein, Prussian-born and just arrived in Philadelphia), each of whom signed a pledge to organize one of the earliest American art academies, later named the Columbianum.[24] Its Constitution and Bylaws, adopted on February 17, 1795, followed the general organization of European academies. The objectives were to form a collection of old master paintings and plaster casts after antique models for study by young artists, to establish a class for "drawing from the living subject," and to inaugurate annual six-week art exhibitions.[25] Rush seems to have been as active as Charles Willson Peale in the founding of the Columbianum. He attended early organizational meetings, participated in framing the Constitution and Bylaws, and was a member of the Committee of Correspondence. One of his first duties in this last capacity was to invite naval architect Joshua Humphreys to join the Columbianum.[26] At its first exhibition, which opened on May 22, 1795, Humphreys showed a model of a 74-gun ship, and drafts of a 44-gun and a 36-gun frigate which were "building for the American Navy."[27] After this one exhibition, the fledgling academy, founded to encourage the development of the arts in America, disbanded because of internal controversy over use of the live model in the drawing class.[28] This dissension among artists foreshadowed a bitter dispute between the Pennsylvania Academy of the Fine Arts and the Society of Artists, over a decade later, in which Rush was an unhappy participant.

That the Columbianum, a society of professional artists, included Rush among its founders attests to the stature of shipcarving in the art community at that time. In fact, Rush's only known non-ship work before 1800 is the wood portrait bust of *Benjamin Franklin* [2], carved as a shop ornament for the New Haven bookstore and publishing house of Isaac Beers.

The bust was taken from life shortly after Franklin's return to Philadelphia from Paris in 1785. Rush's characterization differs from the more popular and widely reproduced European images of Franklin such as those by Jean Jacques Caffieri (original terracotta, 1777, Bibliotheque Mazarine, Paris) or by Jean Antoine Houdon (original terracotta, 1778, the Louvre, Paris):[29] Rush made no attempt to create a universal symbol of an aged, aristocratic, and somewhat aloof statesman for veneration by subsequent generations. Rather, his portrayal is forthright and accessible. While the sagging jowls of the eighty-year-old statesman are described, the face has a youthful and exuberant quality because of its simply modulated planes, broken by only a few crisply incised, almost decorative lines that define wrinkles on the brow and the chin. The wide-eyed gaze is directed upward—like a bust to be mounted on the stem of a ship—and enlivened by a few spirited chisel marks at the corners of the eyes; bushy eyebrows are a series of dancing lines self-confidently rendered with a small chisel. This treatment of the eyes and the distinctive iris of incised circle with scooped-out pupil are hallmarks of Rush's later portraits in both wood and terracotta. It is curious that in light of this vigorous characterization Rush did not exhibit a bust or a figurehead at the Columbianum, entries which would certainly have been in keeping with Humphreys's contribution.

By 1800 the nation's government had left Philadelphia to build a new capitol along the mud flats of the Potomac, under the direction of Benjamin Henry Latrobe. Philadelphia maintained her cultural hegemony, however, and this was especially the case in the field of natural history, a new science which was then considered a branch of medicine. One of its principal early enthusiasts and promoters was Charles Willson Peale. In his museum founded in Philadelphia in 1784, he exhibited his oil portraits of heroes of the American Revolution, interspersed with his collection of natural specimens which he classified according to a system established by the Swedish botanist and physician Linnaeus [56].

Rush's introduction to the scientific community seems to have been encouraged by Peale's activities. Rush collaborated with Charles Willson Peale and his son Rembrandt in carving missing bones of the mastodon exhumed by the Peales in New York State in 1801 [25]. The mastodon was then reconstructed under the guidance of Dr. Caspar Wistar, a board member of Peale's Museum, professor of anatomy

Pl. I. William Rush. *Plan for North East or Franklin Public Square*,
Philadelphia, 1824 [92]. Watercolor and pen and ink on paper.

PLATE I

Pl. II. William Rush. *George Washington*, 1815 [68]. Wood, painted white.

at the University of Pennsylvania, and a specialist of vertebrate paleontology.[30] In 1808, also under Wistar's supervision, Rush again collaborated with Peale in constructing what must have been the first of his large-scale anatomical models [33], the human throat and windpipe, for use in the medical-school classrooms of the University of Pennsylvania, which at that time boasted the most distinguished medical faculty and research facilities in America. Peale noted in his autobiography:

Doctor Wistar being desirous to have large models of the human throat and wind pipe, that the pupils at a distance could see the form of them, applied to Peale to make them, which he did some in papier mache and with wax, of an immensely large size; and his son Raphaelle modelled the brains also in a large size, to complete that part of the head Mr. Wm. Rush carved in wood the outer part; the whole a curious and interesting work, very important to illustrate the anatomical structure of the human head.[31]

Rush continued carving anatomical models until 1820; after Wistar's death in 1818 the project was completed by Wistar's colleague Dr. Philip Syng Physick, who is considered the father of American surgery. Rush immortalized both of these famous physicians in terracotta and plaster [58, 60].

During the early years of the nineteenth century, Rush not only became involved in Philadelphia's scientific and medical communities but also appeared increasingly as a leader in civic and cultural affairs. On October 16, 1801, he was elected to the Common Council of Philadelphia and served on it or the Select Council until 1826.[32] In 1805 he was a founder of the Pennsylvania Academy of the Fine Arts (fig. 7) and, with the exception of one year (June 1807–June 1808), was a stalwart director until his death in 1833.[33]

In 1810 Rush was elected by the artists of Philadelphia to be the first president and a Fellow of the Society of Artists, which was organized independently of the Pennsylvania Academy,[34] and in 1811 he was appointed professor of sculpture.[35] In addition to some impractical but remarkably visionary goals,[36] the Society had hoped to form a union with the Pennsylvania Academy of the Fine Arts. From the Academy's point of view, the main objection to this proposal was that, while members of the Society of Artists might enjoy some Academy privileges, they could not have the privilege of voting for directors or disposing of property without buying shares for $50 apiece and paying an annual two-dollar fee.[37] Many artists resented this because,

Fig. 7. Benjamin Tanner (1775–1848). *The Pennsylvania Academy of the Fine Arts*, 1809. Engraving, 4⅝ × 6⅜ in. (11.8 × 16.2 cm.). Pennsylvania Academy of the Fine Arts, Philadelphia; John S. Phillips Collection.

although they wanted full membership privileges, they felt they should not have to bear this extraordinary expense. One irate observer wrote to *The Democratic Press* on December 11, 1811:

It has indeed, we have heard, been insinuated, that the artists, if received, might perhaps outvote, and even put down the directors; to which, for our parts, we should reply, so much the better, as we have no doubt the artists are in every way better qualified than those who shut the door in their faces—But this, we presume, has been, if at all, urged only as an argument at a shift, and the real as well as the ostensible difficulty arises out of the additional subscription demanded. Now in a case of this sort, where excellent talents and slender means are on one side, on the other a board of controul, we have a spirit of insubordination in us, that impels us to intermeddle, and endeavor by a newspaper article, to aid the bees against the drones.[38]

The differences between the two organizations became increasingly strained and unresolvable, and finally on March 4, 1812, Rush, in obvious exasperation, sided with the Academy and resigned from the Society of Artists, along with Thomas Sully, Rembrandt Peale, Gideon Fairman, Talbot Hamilton, and John and Frederick Eckstein.[39] The following winter, in a conciliatory effort to regain "some of the most distinguished artists in the various branches of the arts," the members of the Society urged these defectors to rejoin the artistic community and to "consider themselves members of its body and cordially cooperate with [them] in promoting the advancements of the arts throughout this country."[40] Rush declined on March 10, 1813:

I have maturely considered the note you were so polite as to present me with your owne hands dated Febr^y 12, 1813 containing a resolution of the Columbian Society of Artists and am highly sensible of the honor & good will the Society contemplate conferring on me by becoming once more a member of their Society but to differ in thinking is the nature of the mind of man and as it respects the present question I can assure gentlemen whenever it occurs affords no pleasure. The reasons which caused me to resign my membership still continues in such strength as forbids me unpleasant as it is I cannot accept or consider myself a member again.

With the most sincere desire for the welfare of every member of the Society and prosperity of the fine arts in this our beloved country.[41]

In a letter to Benjamin West on March 22, 1815, Rush explained that he had resigned from the Society of Artists because the constitution was in "many points very objectionable" and that he "could not prevail on the Society to abandon their visionary projects, that they were determined on a charter, that Thos Jefferson must be their Pres^t and that without previously consulting him, he was contrary to the rules of order, made a member and president, and altho he accepted, yet from his answer (which I saw) the society could not expect any thing like patronage from him, his advanced age with many other objections were his plea . . . but this was done to facilitate its [the Society's] way to a Charter. . . . I resigned with many others, all pretentions to membership for ever with the Society."[42]

In March 1812, the Pennsylvania Academy had organized a group of Academicians, perhaps in response to the challenge of the Society of Artists whose Fellows gave special commendation to professional artists. The Academicians were limited to forty sculptors, painters, architects, and engravers, and only those "distinguished by the merit of his own original works" were admitted. Rush's name appeared first on the listing, followed by the most esteemed artists of his day: Thomas Sully, Rembrandt Peale, Charles Willson Peale, Gideon Fairman, John Eckstein, Thomas Birch, Benjamin H. Latrobe, John Jarvis, Washington Allston, John J. Vanderlyn, Benjamin West, John Singleton Copley, John Trumbull, and Robert Mills.[43] Rush, still one of only two artist-members of the Academy's board (the other was Rembrandt Peale), was subsequently elected a member of the Council of Academicians, the liaison between the Academicians and the Board of Directors.[44] Within the next year the Council of Academicians formed the Academy's first "life class."[45]

The confluence of Rush's role in these cultural institutions—especially the Pennsylvania Academy—and his position on the City Council would shape the rest of his artistic career. Rush served on a myriad of City Council committees over the next quarter-century, but he seems to have had the greatest emotional commitment to and the greatest pride in his role on the Watering Committee which was charged with the responsibility of overseeing the Philadelphia Waterworks, first at Centre Square and later at Fairmount. The waterworks were founded at the end of the eighteenth century in response to the prevailing theory that yellow fever epidemics could be forestalled by providing people with potable water. Yellow fever epidemics punctuated the 1790s, and the death toll, at times ranging up to ten percent of the population, left few Philadelphia families untouched. In 1793, the year of greatest human devastation, as much as fifty percent of the population evacuated the city,[46] and Rush's friend and teacher Joseph Wright succumbed to it. In his heartfelt plea to the Select and Common Councils in 1831, Rush urged them to resist the proposed encroachment of wharves and buildings along the Schuylkill, because such improvements would interrupt the natural flow of the river and threaten navigation and the future operations of the Fairmount Waterworks. His greatest fear, however, was that during hot weather the filthy, narrow, and poorly ventilated alleys between the buildings would promote "pestilential epidemic." When the summer wind blew properly, he wrote, it could "waft [the pestilence] on its wings till it penetrated the City, and spread the horrors of '93 again amongst us."[47]

This letter illuminates Rush's fervent belief in the importance of the waterworks, a belief which dated back to 1801, when he was first appointed to the Watering Committee and was responsible for the first waterworks at Centre Square, Benjamin Henry Latrobe's Pump House, which was built between 1799 and 1801 to pump pure water from the Schuylkill River and distribute it to city dwellings. In 1809 Rush carved as an ornament for the grounds in front of the Pump House the fountain *Allegory of the Schuylkill River* [35]. He is said to have used as his model Louisa Vanuxem, daughter of James Vanuxem who was then chairman of the Watering Committee. Subsequently, particularly during 1819–22, Rush was on the committee that oversaw the expansion of the waterworks at Fairmount, with new construction designed and directed by Fred-

Fig. 8. George Lehman (died 1870). *Fairmount Waterworks*, 1833. Lithograph, 9⁷⁄₁₆ × 12⁷⁄₁₆ in. (24 × 31.6 cm.). The Library Company of Philadelphia.

erick Graff, Latrobe's former assistant. In 1825 Rush, with his son John, carved the *Allegory of the Schuylkill River in Its Improved State* and *Allegory of the Waterworks* [96, 97] as ornaments over the millhouse entrances (fig. 8). These later works celebrate man's ability to direct nature for his own benefit and express confidence that pure Schuylkill water would finally free the city from the scourge of yellow fever.

Rush also served on the City Council committee which organized the festivities in Philadelphia for Lafayette's 1824 visit during his triumphal tour of the United States. The highlight of the decorations was William Strickland's Grand Civic Arch crowned with Rush's statues of *Wisdom* and *Justice* [61, 62]. While much of Rush's fame is based on the quality and originality of these statues and the waterworks allegories, less familiar are his park plans which also evolved out of his City Council committee work. He drew up at least two, one in 1824 for the North East or Franklin Square [92], and another in 1827 for Penn Square [98]; only the former has been located (pl. 1). It was colored by the English-born landscape painter Thomas Birch who was the Pennsylvania Academy's keeper, or curator, from 1813 to 1816. Though naive in execution, the plan is visually attractive, its axial symmetry relieved by gently curving paths. The grounds are dotted by a variety of trees: evergreens and weeping willows are recognizable. The design must have been regarded as successful for it was executed after Rush's death, and its general scheme still exists. This park plan is another example of the kind of versatility typical

of the artists of this era and of Rush's willingness to explore areas outside the realm of sculpture.

Rush's transition from ship-carving to architectural sculpture was motivated as much by his artistic interests and ability and civic activities as it was by the current political and economic situation. As hostilities between France and England escalated in the first decade of the nineteenth century, each continued to impose trade restrictions, and England continued to seize American vessels to impress seamen thought to be British. In retaliation, President Thomas Jefferson responded by signing, on December 22, 1807, the Embargo Act which denied France and Britain access to American goods and markets. This prohibition of American exports, the mainstay of her prosperity since 1790, was an economic catastrophe. The Philadelphia shipbuilding industry came to a halt. Within a year the unpopular embargo was replaced by less stringent restrictions, but the outbreak of the War of 1812 interrupted any permanent economic recovery. Joshua Humphreys, writing in 1813, reflected on the impact of the embargo on the maritime industry:

The average price of wages has been for several years two dollars per day but at the time of the Embargo and the present time wages was and is down to 150 cents/per day and many workman out of employ, many have left this place for Washington and others have gone into the country.[48]

Not surprisingly, Rush's shipcarving business suffered. From 1807 through 1813, Rush is known to have carved only two figureheads, *Fingal* in 1810

Fig. 9. Photograph, c. 1876, of the posthumous bronze cast of William Rush's wood fountain *Allegory of the Schuylkill River* [35] in Fairmount Park. Courtesy of the Philadelphia Museum of Art.

[36], and an Indian figurehead for the *North America* in 1811 [44]. It seems more than a coincidence that in 1808, the year the embargo was begun, Rush carved his first architectural statues, *Comedy* and *Tragedy* [31, 32], for the second-story niches on the facade of the Chestnut Street Theatre, recently remodeled by Benjamin Henry Latrobe.

Architecture must have been of more than passing interest to Rush: he was often on the Pennsylvania Academy's Building Committees and the City Council's Watering Committee. Architectural sculpture must clearly have offered him artistic, intellectual, and technical challenges for which ship-carving had prepared him well. Though figureheads were artistically limited by their function and had unique technical requirements, they nevertheless shared similarities of scale and subject matter with architectural sculpture. Rush carved a figurehead of *Commerce*, for example, for an English vessel about 1790 [5], a subject he used again for the Market

Street Bridge in 1821 [51], for the Penn Street Bridge in 1816 [75], and for William Strickland's Philadelphia Custom House erected in 1818–19 [40].

In addition to the economic forces which encouraged Rush's career shift at this late stage in his life, there was a growing taste for sculpture as neo-classical architectural embellishment. The most influential architectural books of the period, such as James Gibbs's *Book of Architecture*, first published in London in 1728, or Robert and James Adam's *The Works in Architecture*, the first volume of which was published in London in 1778, called for sculpture as part of the scheme. These books were widely available and referred to by American architects. The contemporary attitude about use of sculpture on public buildings was expressed by the influential English architect and teacher William Chambers in *A Treatise on the Decorative Part of the Civil Architecture*, first published in England in 1791. To Chambers, architecture was indebted to sculpture for a great part of its magnificence:

As the human body is justly esteemed the most perfect original, it has been customary, in all times, to enrich different parts of buildings with representations thereof. Thus the ancients adorned their temples, basilicas, baths, theatres, and other public structures, with statues of their deities, philosophers, heroes, orators, and legislators; and the moderns still preserve the same custom; placing in their churches, palaces, houses, squares, gardens, and public walks, the busts and statues of illustrious personages, or bas-reliefs, and groupes, composed of various figures, representing memorable occurrences, collected from the histories, fables, or traditions of particular times.[49]

Rush's most familiar sculptures—*Comedy*, *Tragedy*, *Wisdom*, *Justice*, the waterworks allegories and the bridge ornaments—fall into these civic and cultural categories. The extent of Rush's involvement with the architects in charge of these projects, however, deserves further investigation.

For commissions such as those meant to ornament neoclassical buildings, it is certain that Rush was influenced by and aspired to the ideals of antique statuary. Its importance to the education of the aspiring artist must have been impressed upon him in his role as a board member of the Pennsylvania Academy. One of the first priorities of the Academy was acquiring casts after the antique, and by spring of 1806 Rush was on a committee appointed to superintend placement of those casts in the gallery for their first display to the public.[50] Among the full-length figures were the *Apollo Belvedere*, the *Laocoon*, the *Venus de' Medici*, the

Borghese Gladiator, the *Crouching Venus* (called *Venus of the Bath* or *Accroupie*), *Castor and Pollux*, *Ceres, Mattei Ceres, Silenus with the Infant Bacchus*, *Capitoline Antinuous, Apollino*, the *Farnese Hercules*. Notable among the twenty-five antique busts were *Diane Chasseresse* (called *Diana, of Versailles*), *Caracalla*, and head of *Niobe*.[51]

Thus it is not surprising that Rush's later sculpture shows his awareness of the antique. Liberated from the self-contained poses and walking attitudes required for figureheads, for his public statues Rush adopted classicizing postures; he moved the arms out into space and frequently incorporated a column which, unlike its counterpart in classical marble sculpture, was unnecessary for structural support and served only as an artistic element. Dress was generalized and reminiscent of the antique, and Rush particularly excelled in rendering a variety of pseudo-antique hairstyles.

Almost all of Rush's public sculptures were painted white to simulate marble, enhancing the antique effect[52] so successfully that many of his contemporaries simply assumed he worked in marble. Frances Trollope, for example, the feisty English traveler who visited Philadelphia in August of 1830, wrote rhapsodically about Rush's *Water Nymph and Bittern*, which by that time had been moved to Fairmount (fig. 9):

a portion of the water in its upward way to the reservoir, is permitted to bring forth in a perpetual *jet d'eau*, that returns in a silver shower upon the head of a marble *naïad* of snowy whiteness. The statue is not the work of Phidias, but its dark, rocky back-ground, the flowery catalpas which shadow it, and the bright shower through which it shews itself, altogether make the scene one of singular beauty . . .[53]

While Rush's statues echo the antique, they do not transmit its austere mood. The figures of *Praise, Exhortation, Wisdom, Justice*, and *Washington* [53, 52, 61, 62, 68] are posed in relaxed attitudes with tranquil expressions on their faces, but their serenity is offset by the profusion of rhythmic detail which Rush clearly delighted in carving: curls, braids, feathers, scrolls, spirals, curlicues, pages of books. Where the neoclassical theorists stressed the importance of contour in sculpture,[54] Rush was more interested in creating surfaces that were unusually rich texturally, with a provocative movement that forced the eye to race from one part of the sculpture to another. It is this nervous sensibility—the legacy of Rush's shipcarving background—that he never abandoned. By taking from the antique only that

which he found useful, Rush retained his individuality and expressed his originality.

In the years following the embargo, Rush also received commissions to carve ecclesiastical subjects for the interiors of some of Philadelphia's most prestigious churches.[55] Between about 1810 and 1812, he carved crucifixes for St. Augustine's and St. Mary's churches [41, 47]. Since both have been lost their appearance is unknown. St. Mary's may yet be found, but St. Augustine's was destroyed during the anti-Catholic riots of 1844. It was called Rush's "chef d'oeuvre" and particularly admired "for the accuracy of its delineations."[56] These carvings are the most serious of Rush's known ecclesiastical work and surely intended to inspire spiritual devotion. The other religious works that have survived are in a more ornamental vein. The allegorical figures *Praise, Exhortation*, and the *Cherubim Encircled by a Glory* [53, 52, 54] have joyful and uplifting associations appropriate for their decorative function, originally for the organ case at St. Paul's Church. In 1830 they were moved to the organ case at St. Peter's (see fig. 10).

More didactic in intent are the seven quasi-religious pieces—*Virtue* [42], the *Cherubim* [82, 83], *Faith, Hope*, and *Charity* [84, 85, 86], and *Silence* [87]—which Rush carved for Philadelphia's Masonic Hall, then on the north side of Chestnut Street between Seventh and Eighth Streets. By 1730, within a dozen years of the founding of the Grand Lodge of London, its provincial counterparts were established in Philadelphia and elsewhere in the colonies. After the Revolution, the Provincial Lodge of Pennsylvania severed relations with England and founded the Grand Lodge of Pennsylvania, with over forty regular lodges under its jurisdiction. The goal of this fraternal and benevolent organization, which has its roots in the philosophical and educational ideals of the Enlightenment, is to foster international brotherhood. Through a variety of symbols it teaches universal moral principles and social virtues. While many of its allegorical symbols were derived from traditional Christian iconography, they were used in a way that was unique to the Masonic Brotherhood. Virtue and silence are major Masonic tenets and after 1787 appeared as mottoes on the seal of the Grand Lodge. Other symbols such as the cherubim, though based on biblical history, were more specific to Masonic ritual. The general iconography of armless angels, each with an outspread wing which spans an arch, relates to

Fig. 10. Interior of St. Peter's Church, Philadelphia, with William Rush's figures *Exhortation*, *Praise*, and *Cherubim Encircled by a Glory*, 1812 [52, 53, 54], installed on the organ case.

a special category of Masonry (see fig. 118).[57]

Membership in the Masonic Brotherhood during its peak in America, from 1775 to about 1825, included the most influential and progressive-minded men. While Rush himself was not listed as a member, many of his immediate circle were, including Stephen Girard, Benjamin Henry Latrobe, William Strickland, and Charles Willson Peale. Among the famous men Rush portrayed, those who were Masons were Benjamin Franklin, George Washington, Andrew Jackson, Oliver Hazard Perry, Benjamin Rush, and Lafayette.

Traditionally it was thought that Rush carved the Masonic figures in 1811 for the Hall when it was first dedicated. However, the building was gutted by fire in 1819, and we now know that Rush carved all the pieces, with the exception of *Virtue*, in 1820–21 for the rebuilt hall. With their redating [see 82-87], and the possibility of redating *Wisdom* and *Justice* [61, 62] to about 1812, there emerges

a stylistic sequence for Rush's full-length figures. His first, *Comedy, Tragedy, Water Nymph and Bittern* [31, 32, 35], were created within a year of one another. Rush was in his early fifties and at the zenith of his shipcarving career, so it is not surprising that should be apparent in these statues. They project vigorous energy, particularly *Comedy* and the *Water Nymph*, because of the way Rush described the drapery, which zigzags, folds, wrinkles, bulges, curls, and immodestly flares at the hemline revealing a shapely leg below the knee. Such movement is appropriate for figureheads intended to express speed and wind, but discordant for sculptures related to reserved neoclassical buildings. Indeed, that exuberant quality was seen as a major shortcoming by Latrobe, who otherwise so admired Rush's figureheads. In his 1811 oration delivered before the Society of Artists, Latrobe made the criticism that "ashore, [Rush's] figures want repose, and that which is his highest excellence afloat, becomes a fault."[58] These remarks must have been directed toward *Comedy, Tragedy,* and *Water Nymph and Bittern*, Rush's only known public sculptures existing at that time, and all three associated with buildings Latrobe designed.

Perhaps in response to Latrobe's views, Rush seems in his works shortly after 1811 (*Praise, Exhortation, Justice, Wisdom* [figs. 11, 12]) to have attempted to convey the more restrained mood of the antique by moderating surface movement through simplification of drapery patterns. With less dramatically windblown drapery, the hemlines of the skirts are more earthbound and cling to the ankles, possibly also in recognition of the chasteness required for ecclesiastical and civic sculpture. In addition, Rush introduced classical elements such as columns and "diagonally draped Grecian mantles" and alluded more self-consciously to antique statuary.

In the 1820s, the decade Rush carved statues for the Masonic Hall and the Fairmount Waterworks, there is a perceptible stylistic change. This may be partly explained by the reclining poses of these figures, unrepresented in his earlier statues, but used for his bridge ornaments and certainly for stern carvings. In addition to the consideration of pose, however, the works lack the verve of Rush's earlier statues. Female facial features are less individualized, hairstyles less energetically detailed, and drapery folds flatter and more schematic, particularly in *Faith* and *Hope*. In *Allegory of the Schuylkill River in Its*

Improved State [96], the male figure is surprisingly ill-proportioned: the head is too large for the body, the torso unnaturally short for the elongated legs. Such obvious anatomical inconsistencies appear nowhere else in Rush's work. There are also stylistic details such as the little flags crowning the head which are clumsy and unconvincing and lack the finesse of Rush's chisel. On the other hand, some of the rest of the carving is well done, particularly the stones, the chain, and the feathers of the glowering bald eagle—which, according to contemporary accounts, is about to soar angrily away because of the encroachment of the arts into its territory.

These anatomical inconsistencies raise the question of the extent to which Rush used a life model for his full-length statues. The story of Louisa Vanuxem posing for the *Water Nymph* [35] is often cited as proof that he did. In addition, his reliance on nature is documented by Dunlap, who related that Rush advised his assistants: "When I see my boys bungling in the carving a hand, I tell them look at your own hands—place them in the same

position—imitate them and you must be right. You always have the model *at hand*."[59] Rush's commitment to the use of the life model is most strongly confirmed by his role in initiating and overseeing the Pennsylvania Academy's first life class in 1813. One wonders whether in fact he consistently used a life model, since while facial features of the earlier allegorical works are varied and distinctive, in the later ones they are more uniform and bland.

These problems, as well as other stylistic shortcomings of the *Allegory of the Schuylkill River in Its Improved State*, raise the provocative question of the extent of involvement by Rush's assistants, particularly in the 1820s when the sculptor was approaching his seventies. The evidence is conflicting. One old shipcarver, a friend of John Rush who never worked under William Rush but claimed to be one of his disciples and knew one of his apprentices Millard, said that Rush "did it all by himself," and relied only on assistants to rough out the general figure.[60] That is unlikely since many of Rush's known apprentices went on to become carvers in their own

Fig. 11, (left). William Rush. *Justice*, after 1812–by 1824 [62]. Shown painted, in a niche at the Fairmount Waterworks. Photograph, c. 1876, courtesy of the Philadelphia Museum of Art.

Fig. 12, (right). William Rush. *Wisdom*, after 1812–by 1824 [61]. Shown painted, in a niche at the Fairmount Waterworks. Photograph, c. 1876, courtesy of the Philadelphia Museum of Art.

right and were surely given more ambitious opportunities to carve than this account suggests.

The Millard whom the old carver mentioned may have been Charles Millard, listed as a carver in the Philadelphia Directories from 1818 to 1820. Marion V. Brewington lists a Thomas Millard working in 1795 and a James Millard working from 1833 to 1856,[61] clearly a family of shipcarvers that warrants investigation.

In addition, Brewington lists sixteen other carvers working in Philadelphia between 1765 and Rush's death in 1833. Of these Rush was associated with at least seven. The first, Edward Cutbush, was his teacher. The second, John Merriam, seems to have collaborated briefly with Rush in 1793 when they billed Stephen Girard for work on the ship *Two Brothers* [9]. Merriam, on December 29, 1794, was one of the signers of the pledge to organize what would become known as the Columbianum.[62] The third, Benjamin Rush, who was working in the 1790s, is most likely William's half-brother since William's son of that name was not born until at least 1800. This Benjamin Rush was listed as a carver in 1783 at 221 North Front Street,[63] and also worked occasionally on Girard ships.[64] The fourth is an assistant known only by the name of Bids, who was apparently in Rush's employ in 1797 and was sent to do some of the carpentry work on the *Constellation* [20], then being built in Baltimore.[65] The fifth, John Brown, was a carver active in Baltimore from 1789 to 1804 and was said to have been "a pupil of mr Rush."[66] The sixth, Daniel Train, seems to have been Rush's best pupil of the 1790s since he went on to set up a shop in New York, and in 1799 is credited with doing ornamental carving for the *John Adams* [23], a ship for which Rush carved the figurehead.[67] Train carved the figurehead and other work for the 44-gun U.S. frigate *President*. The head was a bust of the "late President Washington supported by two female figures, Truth and Justice, standing on a rock, an emblem of strength."[68] The low-relief stern carvings were emblematic of national virtues like much of Rush's work.

The number of assistants who graduated from Rush's shop over a productive career that spanned more than fifty years was surely greater than this meager sampling. That Rush's pupils went on to other cities where they continued to rely upon their association with their master even after his death is indicative of Rush's fame and influence. Moreover, it explains the existence of such obviously derivative

work as *Pocahontas* (fig. 128) and *Music* (fig. 132) and their former attributions to Rush.

The most complicated aspect of the role of Rush's assistants, however, is his son John (fig. 13). By Rush's own testimony, John was an "equal partner" by 1819 when they worked together on the *Columbus* [88]. In addition, bills for the Masonic Hall and Fairmount Waterworks figures are from "William Rush & Son" [see 82-87, 96, 97]. John, first listed in the Philadelphia directories as a carver in 1815, seems to have been the only son to have followed his father's profession, although his younger brother Thomas was for a time in the related field of coachmaker.

About John, little has been discovered. Because we know of only one authenticated piece by him (fig. 138), carved many years after his involvement with his father, it is impossible to assess his contribution to his father's work in the 1820s. One cannot avoid speculating, however, that some of the obvious awkwardness of William Rush's late carving is directly related to John's increased involvement.

John probably lacked the intellect and personality of his father since his name appears in none of the same cultural organizations. For the most part, his career seems to have been overshadowed by and in many cases dependent upon his father's fame. This is certainly true of his first two documented works. In 1835 he carved an eagle for the pavilion overlooking the dam of the Fairmount Waterworks (fig. 137). The following year, he attempted to secure and perhaps later got the commission to execute his father's designs drawn up in 1824 for the *Pennsylvania* [93]. The only extant work of indisputable authorship for which John was responsible independent of his father is the *Goddess of Liberty* statue (fig. 138) which he carved about 1840 for the Berks County Court House. It is telling that even then, seven years after William Rush's death, the local papers referred to John, then in his late forties, as the "younger Rush."[69]

Most of John Rush's known works were the result of a major commission from George W. Carpenter (1802–1860), who accumulated a vast wealth in the drug and railroad businesses. A well-read and multi-talented man, Carpenter designed about 1840 a Georgian-style house in Germantown, Pennsylvania, called "Phil-Ellena." He decorated it in the eclectic fashion of mid-century, combining rococo, Greek, and Gothic styles with ceilings painted after the old masters.[70] He commissioned John Rush to carve eight full-length allegorical figures to ornament the grounds and buildings—*Flora*, *Ceres*, *Minerva*, *Eloquence* (fig. 140), *Diana*, and *Neptune*. Two were similar to works by William Rush: *Mercury*, and "A youth in a shivering position seated on blocks of ice," the description of which closely corresponds to William Rush's *Winter* [44]. It is curious and perhaps to John Rush's credit that this wealthy patron, who could have afforded to go to Europe for the best in marble statuary, chose instead a local woodcarver.

William Rush, besides working with apprentices and his son, may also have worked with Philadelphia cabinetmakers by carving three-dimensional figurative ornaments for furniture,[71] as did such carvers as John and Simeon Skillin, Jr. No bills or documents have been discovered to support this theory, but Edward Cutbush, who is said to have done some furniture carving,[72] could certainly have passed this skill on to his apprentice. Indeed, certain ship's ornaments, such as cat faces, are small-scale and relate to ornaments on furniture. This theory is corroborated by the recent discovery of Rush's *Commemorative Statuette* [34] carved in 1809 in cherry, with applied silver plaques engraved by William T. Kneass, and perhaps ultimately it will be possible to identify and attribute to Rush other furniture ornaments. The skill with which the figures and details of this 16½-inch statuette were realized (fig. 14) indicate that this was certainly not the first time Rush ventured into this related craft, nor can we possibly believe it was the last. Its general form, with figures surrounding and leaning on a central pedestal or sarcophagus crowned by an urn, is reminiscent in miniature of eighteenth-century English tomb monuments. The formula was used by the English sculptor John Bacon (1740–1799) as seen, for instance, in his monument to Ann Whytell of 1791 in Westminster Abbey.[73]

In March 1815, a few months after the signing of the Treaty of Ghent ending the War of 1812, Rush wrote to the painter Benjamin West in London:

[I] congratulate you on the return of peace, between Great Britain and the United States, its happy effects can only be appreciated by the blasting affects of the war a war of folly and madness, without the least object of interest to . . . either party—the fine arts have felt its baleful effects in the United States, as well as many of the more useful ones.

Fig. 13. Artist unknown (formerly attributed to John Neagle). *John Rush* (?), n.d. Oil on canvas, 30⅛ × 26 in. (76.5 × 66 cm.). National Gallery of Art, Washington, D.C.; Gift of Chester Dale.

He then noted that he was sending to West at the Royal Academy:

a plaster cast taken from a clay model, of Do Rush . . . as my common business has been much contracted, I have employed considerable part of my time in modeling several busts viz Do Physick, Do C Wistar, the Venerable Charles Thompson, Commodore Perry, and several others.[74]

Four years before, in the First Annual Exhibition at the Pennsylvania Academy of the Fine Arts, Rush took his first opportunity to exhibit his works publicly. He entered the allegorical work *Winter* [45] (in a general pose recalling the *Crouching Venus*)[75] and two portrait busts, one in wood, *A Citizen* [46], and one in terracotta, *Joseph Wright* [38]. At the Second Annual Exhibition, he showed seven wood pieces, including the portrait busts *Henry Ernest Muhlenberg* [55], *Linnaeus* [56], and *William Bartram* [57], and the allegorical figure *Agriculture* for the Schuylkill Permanent Bridge [50], and *Exhortation*, *Praise*, and *Cherubim* [52, 53, 54]. Thereafter, with the exception of his full-length wood

George Washington, he exhibited only portrait busts in clay, terracotta, or plaster. With these, Rush was one of the earliest American sculptors to respond to the widespread vogue for busts of soldiers, statesmen, scientists, and other great men. At the time, a middle-class gentleman's library was considered incomplete without a row of busts gazing down from atop bookcases, and that the busts portrayed the heroes of the young republic was inextricably bound up with America's new sense of nationalism. Benjamin Henry Latrobe's appeal in 1811 was one of several which expressed such sentiments:

Let the national legislature honour the hero or statesman of the revolution with busts; and sculptors will not be wanting.—The genius which under exotic influence has given so high a rank to the American pencil of a West, Copley, Trumbull, and Vanderline would, under domestic patronage, not refuse to inspire the American chisel.[76]

Like many other artists of the period, Rush seems to have done his portraits from life or at least from memory. According to his 1815 letter to Benjamin West, he went so far as to measure the head of Benjamin Rush, claiming that while "the size of the cranium appears large . . . the whole of the head, and profile is correct from actual measurement."[77] The only subject whom Rush did not meet or see was the Swedish botanist Linnaeus [56] for whose portrait he must have had to rely upon an engraving (see fig. 108).

In wood, Rush's most ambitious portrait was the posthumous full-length statue of George Washington (pl. II), which he first exhibited at the Pennsylvania Academy in 1815 in hopes of obtaining at least twenty subscriptions for plaster casts (see fig. 15). When this scheme failed, he produced a bust-size image in clay, probably thinking that plasters from this would be more easily marketed. Two years before his death in 1833 Rush claimed that he had modeled Washington from life on several occasions [see 68]. Around 1858 and close to the end of his life, Rembrandt Peale, in defense of the quality and accuracy of his own portraits of Washington, noted that: "No eye could be more critically nice in the observance of Character than that of the Philadelphia Sculptor, Wm Rush, who after saying of my Portrait of Washington—'I think it the best likeness of him, when in the vigour of life, I ever saw on Canvass'—goes on to say

I had many opportunities of seeing and observing his person, and particularly his face and features, in the time of the Revolution. I have been in battle immediately under his command—I have viewed him walking, standing, sitting—I have seen him at a game of ball, for several hours; exhibiting the most manly & graceful attitudes I ever saw. I have seen him dismount from his horse, a few hours after the Battle of Princeton, . . . reviewing with great anxiety his little band, which had just taken the British 17th Regiment . . . At that moment of crisis . . . his likeness was worth more guineas than the British would have given for his person.

In the fall of 1799 . . . I dined with Washington, by invitation from himself at West Point. After the War I had the honor of his visits at my House, to view my Works;—so that if any man can form a just idea of his person, I humbly think that I can. I have modeled him as large as life, and in miniature, in wood & in clay. . . .[78]

From a terracotta original Rush made a plaster piece mold from which he produced numerous plaster casts. He followed the practice of his contemporaries such as the French sculptor Jean Antoine Houdon, who would produce as many plaster replicas of his more popular portrait busts as the market would bear.[79] Like Houdon, Rush first exhibited a unique portrait in terracotta and then awaited public or private subscriptions for plaster replicas, just as painters of grand history pictures or city views made them with an eye for the potential of print subscriptions, a practice which made art more widely accessible.[80] Indeed, for a time Rush's plaster replicas of the terracotta busts were his bread and butter. In his letter to Benjamin West, Rush noted that he was selling the plaster casts of Dr. Rush and Dr. Physick for ten dollars apiece and that "within a few days fifteen hundred dollars were subscribed."[81] The whereabouts of only a fraction of these plasters are known today, but the variations among them suggests that they were made at different times and that each was individually finished, presumably by Rush himself (see Naudé, "A Technical Discussion"). The only instance in which he exhibited a plaster instead of a terracotta was the bust of Andrew Jackson [79]; the piece mold may have been made from an unfired clay, or the terracotta may have been too kiln-damaged to exhibit. Rush never worked in the more costly and durable material of marble which would have been the goal of most European sculptors (see Gerdts, "Sculptural Genius or Inspired Artisan?"). Presumably this was because he did not undertake to learn a new and complicated technique late in life when he ventured into sculpture more as a result of economic necessity than as a long-term career goal. According to Dunlap's correspondent, one of Rush's sons, probably

John, Rush's "time would never permit or he would have attempted marble."[82]

In Rush's earliest terracottas such as that of his teacher Joseph Wright, or his daughters Elizabeth and Mary Simpson Rush [38, 39, 40], the portrayals have a naive charm but they seem dull and the facial details tentatively defined. But by 1812–13, when Rush modeled the portraits of the doctors Benjamin Rush, Philip Syng Physick, and Caspar Wistar, he had mastered his medium and his technique and was able to capture a virile sense of character. These busts project a dignity and grandeur that is partially the result of their self-absorbed, averted gazes which create an effect of great seriousness of purpose. This is enhanced by the decorative treatment of the drapery which covers their clothes, frames the lower perimeter of the busts, and alludes to Greco-Roman sculpture. The spirit of the era, according to Houdon, required sculpture "truthfully to preserve the form and render imperishable the image of men who have achieved glory or good for their country."[83] This was the ideal Rush strove for—and achieved.

While some classical elements can be found in Rush's portraits, just as in his allegorical works, the portraits as a group are marked by their diversity. Much of this individuality is the result of Rush's close attention to details of dress and character of the subject: a fur collar for Dr. Physick, a gaudy uniform for Winfield Scott, a disarmingly direct stare from Lafayette. One of the most touching and subtly naturalistic details appears on the bust of Wistar, whose shirt collar button is left undone, affectionately suggesting that the portly doctor was unable to fasten it.

Like sketches for oil paintings, Rush's terracottas retain a freshness, vitality, and individuality that intimately reveal the artist's hand. The best are distinguished by their dynamic and rich textural surfaces. Rush's perpetual taste for a profusion of sinuous lines to recreate strands of hair or folds of clothing was given fuller expression in the more pliable medium of clay than in his wood shipcarvings and allegorical works. This technique reached its peak in his remarkable *Self-Portrait* of 1822 [90], in which more than half the surface is an exuberantly conceived and multi-faceted pine knot, from which emerges the noble head of the sculptor. Like Rush's portrayals of the doctors, this head projects sober dignity and commands veneration. That Rush chose to immortalize himself in this manner is a testimony

Fig. 14. William Rush. Detail, teacher's head, of *Commemorative Statuette*, 1809 [34]. Cherry.

to his self-perception. This bust stands out as one of the most compelling self-portraits produced in American art of this period. More than that, its vigorous characterization combined with the virtuoso deception represents a thematic summation of the artist's life-long artistic and professional concerns.

Rush's last years were marked by his continued interests in numerous civic and artistic projects. After 1820, coal replaced shipbuilding as Philadelphia's major industry, and Rush did only a few shipcarvings during the decade. His 1824 stern and figurehead designs for the U.S. Navy ship of the line *Pennsylvania* [93] was one of his last shipcarving commissions, and they were not executed during his lifetime. Although he was not reelected to City Council after 1826, he maintained a fiercely protective interest in the Fairmount Waterworks until the end of his life, offering continuous advice on its maintenance as well as on matters related to the projected buildup of a wharf area along the Schuylkill.[84] And in an angry letter to the *Philadelphia Gazette*, January 8, 1830, he expressed dismay that Joseph S. Lewis, a colleague on the Watering Committee, was gaining the major recognition for originating the idea of the Fairmount Waterworks and bringing it to completion. Rush pointed out that Frederick Graff had done all of the models and drawings for the waterworks and that, in any case, the credit should go to the Watering Committee as a whole, not to one man.[85]

Rush's only new interest was a brief association with the Franklin Institute, established in Philadelphia in 1824 to promote and encourage manufacturers and mechanics. Rush was among the founding members which included, in addition to manufacturers and mechanics, artisans and people friendly to the mechanical arts such as William Strickland, William Kneass, and Roberts Vaux.[86] In the Franklin Institute's first annual exhibition held in 1824 Rush exhibited his bust of Lafayette [94] in the fine arts category. The categories were purely commercial and included such other products as paints, iron and steel, dyed articles, musical instruments, cotton goods, cutlery, hats, combs and brushes, books, and stationery.[87] During the second annual exhibition Rush, along with the architect John Haviland, was listed as one of three judges of the "marble work" category.[88] After 1826 Rush's name no longer appears in connection with this institution.

Until his death Rush continued to be a member of the board of the Pennsylvania Academy of the Fine Arts although his attendance became increasingly sporadic. And as late as 1825 he was accorded the professional recognition of honorary membership in New York's American Academy of The Fine Arts.[89]

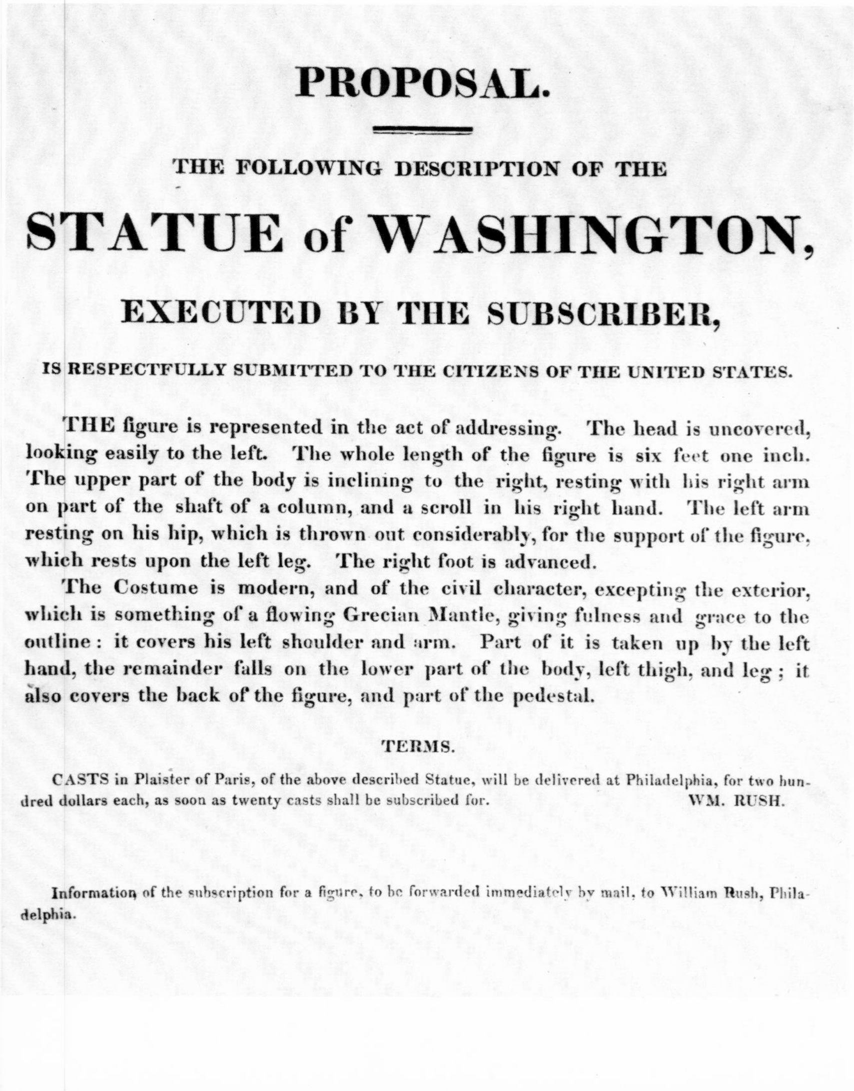

Fig. 15. Broadside advertising Rush's proposed plaster casts of his statue of Washington, 1815. Historical Society of Pennsylvania, Philadelphia.

PROPOSAL.

THE FOLLOWING DESCRIPTION OF THE

STATUE of WASHINGTON,

EXECUTED BY THE SUBSCRIBER,

IS RESPECTFULLY SUBMITTED TO THE CITIZENS OF THE UNITED STATES.

THE figure is represented in the act of addressing. The head is uncovered, looking easily to the left. The whole length of the figure is six feet one inch. The upper part of the body is inclining to the right, resting with his right arm on part of the shaft of a column, and a scroll in his right hand. The left arm resting on his hip, which is thrown out considerably, for the support of the figure, which rests upon the left leg. The right foot is advanced.

The Costume is modern, and of the civil character, excepting the exterior, which is something of a flowing Grecian Mantle, giving fulness and grace to the outline : it covers his left shoulder and arm. Part of it is taken up by the left hand, the remainder falls on the lower part of the body, left thigh, and leg ; it also covers the back of the figure, and part of the pedestal.

TERMS.

CASTS in Plaister of Paris, of the above described Statue, will be delivered at Philadelphia, for two hundred dollars each, as soon as twenty casts shall be subscribed for.　　　　WM. RUSH.

Information of the subscription for a figure, to be forwarded immediately by mail, to William Rush, Philadelphia.

Fig. 16. John Haviland (1792–1852). *Pennsylvania Institution for the Deaf and Dumb* (now the Philadelphia College of Art), 1824–25. Watercolor and pen and ink on paper, 28¾ × 20 in. (70.3 × 50.1 cm.). The Athenaeum of Philadelphia. According to this watercolor, Haviland's original design incorporated figures of the Abbés de L'Epée and Sicard for the niches of the facade. Despite encouragement from Rush five or six years later, there is no evidence that statues were ever put in place.

Ultimately all discussions of Rush's sculpture boil down to a debate of whether wood and plaster rather than marble were acceptable mediums for true art. As Rush reached his seventies, the first generation of American neoclassical marble sculptors was emerging, and American taste for marble statuary was developing, foreshadowed by Rush's carved-wood sculptures painted to simulate that stone. In the early 1830s his portraits continued to be successful, however, and he advertised the availability of busts of Jefferson, Madison, Washington, and Lafayette recently sculpted "for a gentleman in Covington, opposite Cincinnati, and a bust of Dr. Benjamin Rush, for a gentleman in New York. They may be seen for a few days, at [William Rush's] shop on Front Street near the Lehigh Coal Yard. . . ."90

By July 20, 1830, the indefatigable Rush was still trying to gain public commissions. In a poignant advertisement in *The Philadelphia Gazette, and Daily Advertiser*, he expressed awareness of the de-cline of wood carving, a tradition to which he had devoted his life:

Our ancient and respectable fellow townsman, WILLIAM RUSH, is very desirous of employment in the way of his profession. He is the father of American Sculptors; and it would be very agreeable to his feelings if he could leave behind him in his native city, a few more specimens of his art. As a number of our buildings require the embellishment of statues, we hoped his wish will be gratified. In the facade of the Jefferson College, there is a niche which ought to be filled with a statue of the author of the Declaration of Independence. The niches in the Deaf and Dumb Asylum, were intended to receive statues of the Abbes Sicard and De L'Epee [see fig. 16]. In front of Christ Church are two niches, which were certainly intended for statues of some description. In front of the Arcade and of the Walnut street Theatre are empty niches. All these buildings must appear incomplete, till the niches are filled agreeably to the original designs of the architects.

We pretend not to say that wooden statues are as elegant as marble. The contour may be as graceful, but there is a fineness in the lines of a marble figure which give it a great superiority. Wooden statues are, however, well adapted to the present state of the country, and seem perfectly appropriate in a Sylvan state. They cost only one-twelfth as much as marble statues: and will last quite as long as the buildings they are intended to ornament.[91]

In the essays which follow, Rush's particular artistic contributions and his working methods, as well as his treatment in the history of art, are discussed in detail. Of the man, the picture that emerges shows an extremely gifted craftsman and self-taught artist. Although he never went abroad and rarely ventured outside Philadelphia, he was nevertheless, through his extraordinary personality—a healthy mixture of idealism and practicality—able to participate in and influence many aspects of the artistic and civic growth of Philadelphia. His dynamic figureheads led early United States merchant and naval vessels over the seas. His public sculptures and portrait busts, well carved and modeled, were sought after for decades. And his congenial temperament combined with his ability to persuade helped him realize his artistic projects. As one of the only continuously active board members of the Pennsylvania Academy who was a professional artist, he played a crucial role in forming and shaping the Academy, particularly in his support of the annual exhibitions, and the life and antique drawing classes for aspiring artists which are still cornerstones of the Academy's curriculum.

The Public Work of William Rush: A Case Study in the Origins of American Sculpture

D. DODGE THOMPSON

THE STUDY of the origins of American art, which initially expended so much energy on the justification of a national school, has only recently turned to the more interesting examination of sources, context, and process. For example, the relationship between the sculpture of Georgian England and Federal America has never been systematically explored.

In 1937 Henri Marceau wrote of William Rush that "to attempt an appreciation of Rush's work one must necessarily place oneself in the spirit of that time. One must recall the total absence of models both in the form of sculpture and as represented by engravings or in books."[1] While heeding Marceau's admonition to study Rush in the spirit of his age, the art historian must at the same time test Marceau's contention that Rush evolved as a sculptor in the "total absence" of models. The following look at Rush's outdoor sculpture for public buildings and monuments will show that his artistic sources demonstrably included casts from the antique; graphic works including books and engravings; works of sculpture imported into America by contemporary European artists—originals, replicas, and casts; and sculpture by foreign-born artists working in America.

Rush was by no means unusual among his American contemporaries in his reliance on the images of earlier masters in the composition of his art. Waldron Phoenix Belknap, Jr., documented the extensive use of English mezzotint prototypes in colonial portraiture.[2] Jules Prown has discussed the use of prints of historical and mythological subjects in the early work of John Singleton Copley, and James Thomas Flexner identified the engraved source, in America, for Benjamin West's earliest neoclassical composition.[3] Similarly, the source of the works of American architects, from Peter Harrison to Charles Bulfinch, can frequently be traced to specific plates of English architectural books.[4] Native American

cabinetmakers as a matter of course took their inspiration from the pattern books and directories of English and French craftsmen.

Marceau recognized that Rush may have used engraved sources, such as *The Artist's Repository, or Encyclopedia of the Fine Arts* (London, 1808), as reference in his work.[5] In addition, in 1805 Rush, as a board member of the Pennsylvania Academy of the Fine Arts, must have been instrumental in obtaining through Nicholas Biddle, secretary to General Armstrong, American minister to France, plaster casts of antique sculpture for the Academy. However, in Rush's sculpture there is not to be found a direct one-to-one copying of any earlier work. By attempting to identify Rush's far-ranging artistic sources, and the process by which he assimilated them, we can more fully appreciate the nature of his achievement and the growth of an American sculptural tradition.

Comedy and Tragedy, 1808

The source for William Rush's first public sculpture may have been original drawings supplied for the purpose by England's leading painter of theatrical scenes. The story of Rush's commission illustrates the continuing dependence of Federal period artists on English prototypes.

William Rush found his niche, so to speak, when he was fifty-one years old. The vehicle for his earliest public sculpture was the Chestnut Street Theatre in Philadelphia (pl. III). The opportunity for Rush to carve the allegorical figures of *Comedy* and *Tragedy* [31, 32] was fortuitous and tied to the fluctuating fortunes of this important theater.[6]

Before the American Revolution the Quakers, Methodists, and Baptists in Philadelphia agreed on little, but they did unite in 1774 to prohibit all dramatic activity. At the time of the Constitutional

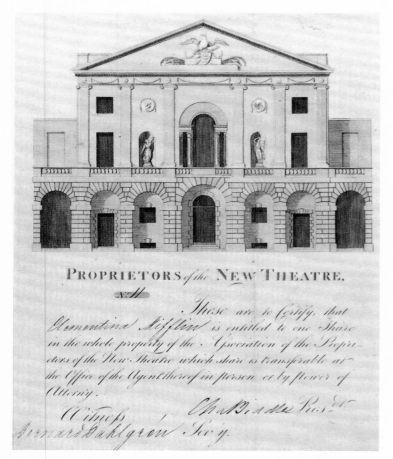

Fig. 17. Artist unknown. *Stock Certificate for Chestnut Street Theatre*, 1791. Engraving, 11⅕ × 7⅗ in. (28 × 19.3 cm.). Historical Society of Pennsylvania, Philadelphia.

ably supplied to Bulfinch by the managers, because some aspects of the program—including the sculpture—were not completed. Bulfinch's description of the Philadelphia theater, a building from which he borrowed generously for his design of the Boston Theater of 1793–94, is worth quoting at length:

The new theatre at Philadelphia is 134 feet long, 64 wide, 12 feet from the cellar to the ground line, 50 feet from the ground line to the top of plate. The principal front is on Chestnut Street, which is composed of Ionic pilasters, supporting a pediment of its order, the whole extent of the building in which will be placed the Eagle, and the Arms of Pennsylvania, designed by Charles Catton, Esq. Royal Academician. On each side of a large Venetian window are niches, containing whole length figures of the Tragick and Comick Muse, designed by Mr. Smirk [*sic*], R. A. who likewise composes the stage frontispiece with an emblematical ornament of American Freedom, depictured by the Bald Eagle sheltering the Genius of the Drama. The frieze will be ornamented with pattaras and swags of drapery. Over the niches are circular emblematical ornaments in basso relievo, all of which ornaments are manufactured of artificial stone, a composition equally durable to the much esteemed Portland. The whole of the front is completed by a range of seven rusticated arches, crowned by a balustrade, which by projecting ten feet from the main body of the building, shelters the avenues leading to the different parts of the theatre. On each side will be a wing which will form an arched passage to the whole length of the building for the convenience of the inhabitants in the northern parts of the city.
The stage is upwards of 70 feet in length, the audience part is a portion of a circle terminating in right lines on each side of the stage—subdivided into boxes for the reception of different parties. There are two ranges in the centre, and three on each side—these boxes are separated by columns composed of thirteen reeds bound by a ribband. The front of the gallery (which ranges with the upper tier of boxes, and which will contain near 800 persons) is composed of a gilt ballustrade. The pannels forming the front of the other boxes will be painted a beautiful lealock [lilac]. The stiles a delicate straw colour, and the whole of the mouldings will be gilt. The light will be conveyed from cut glass chandeliers, suspended by gilt chains and brackets.
The Theatre contains upwards of 1800 persons.
This magnificent building is the design of John Richards, Esq. Secretary of the Royal Academy, London, who stands unrivalled as a Theatrical architect and painter.[9]

John Inigo Richards, R.A. (died 1810), was a foundation member of the Royal Academy, principal scene-painter at the Theatre Royal, Covent Garden, from 1777, and architect of the interior renovation of that theater in 1782.[10] Robert Smirke, R.A. (1752–1845), was a well-known English painter of dramatic and literary subjects, a contributor to Boydell's *Shakespeare Gallery*, and a scene-

Convention there was considerable agitation for a theater in the city, but plans did not materialize until Philadelphia became the nation's capital. In 1791 Thomas Wignell and Alexander Reinagle, an English actor and a musician respectively, who had arrived in America shortly before the prohibition of drama, formed a company to sell stock to finance a playhouse. Wignell and Reinagle issued a stock certificate (fig. 17) which promised a handsome Adamesque facade, reassuringly similar to the Theatre Royal, Drury Lane, of 1775 by Robert Adam himself.[7]

Little would be known about the origins of the design for the proposed Chestnut Street Theatre, except that a twenty-nine-year-old aspiring architect and architectural reporter for the *Massachusetts Magazine*, Charles Bulfinch, submitted a report on the theater for the September 1792 issue of that publication.[8] The details of the theater were prob-

Pl. III. William Strickland (1787–1854). *New Theatre, Chestnut Street*, 1808.
Watercolor on paper, 25½ × 33½ in. (64.8 × 85.1 cm.). Signed and dated, lower left:
William Strickland pinx! 1808. Pennsylvania Academy of the Fine Arts, Philadelphia;
Gift of Mr. and Mrs. William Jeanes. The earliest known representation
of Rush's *Comedy* and *Tragedy* in situ.

PLATE III

Pl. IV. John Lewis Krimmel (1789–1821). *Fourth of July in Centre Square*,
1812. Oil on canvas, 23 × 28¾ in. (58.4 × 73 cm.). Pennsylvania Academy of
the Fine Arts, Philadelphia; Academy Purchase from the Paul Beck Estate. Rush's
Allegory of the Schuylkill River is shown in its original location in front of Latrobe's
Centre Square Pump House. The sculpture was painted white to resemble marble.

PLATE IV

painter at Covent Garden.[11] Smirke was also the father of the architect Sir Robert Smirke (1781–1867), whose first major project was the rebuilding of Covent Garden Theatre after its destruction by fire in 1808.[12] Charles Catton, R.A. (1728–1798), was a foundation member of the Royal Academy, official coach-painter to George III, and an ornamental painter at the Drury Lane Theatre.[13] It might be difficult to imagine the participation of such distinguished English artists in the Chestnut Street Theatre project—except that John Inigo Richards was Thomas Wignell's brother-in-law. Thus, it is entirely possible that Richards, Smirke, and Catton submitted designs to aid the infant theater in Philadelphia. This view is corroborated by a remarkable notice which appeared in *The Pennsylvania Gazette* on June 20, 1792:

NEW THEATRE

Monday arrived in this city from London, by way of New York, the model by which the new Theatre of Messrs. Wignell and Reinagle, in Chestnut-street, is to be erected. The plan has been pronounced by European Architects and persons of taste and judgment, to be better calculated for a building of convenient and elegant accommodation, as well with respect to the performers and audience, than any other Theatre of equal dimensions, hitherto constructed—The model will in a few days be exhibited for the gratification of the curious.[14]

The model from London of the proposed Chestnut Street Theatre must have been in part an ingenious marketing strategy devised by Wignell and Reinagle to promote the sale of stock in the project. The model was tangible proof of the London origins of the Philadelphia theater, and indicates the ambitious scale of the managers' undertaking.

At first Wignell and Reinagle encountered puritanical opposition in their attempt to purchase a site for the theater. However, they deceived John Dickinson of Wilmington, celebrated author of *Letters from a Farmer*, by persuading a third party to offer him £6000 for his plot on the north side of Chestnut Street above Sixth without divulging the intended use of the site.[15] In the end, Philadelphians readily purchased stock in the theater and the project appeared to be a great success.

The building was opened on February 17, 1794, but in spite of the considerable expenditure of $135,000, the decorative scheme planned for the Chestnut Street facade was dramatically reduced.[16] An engraving of 1800 by William Birch shows that although the Palladian window, pediment, and niches were retained, the original rusticated porch was eliminated (fig. 18). A rough wooden porch or shed was substituted to protect the spectators. Perhaps the managers had run short of funds, or possibly

Fig. 18. William Russell Birch (1755–1834). *Congress Hall and New Theatre in Chestnut Street, Philadelphia*, 1800. Engraving, 8½ × 11⁵⁄₁₆ in. (21.5 × 28.7 cm.). Historical Society of Pennsylvania, Philadelphia.

Fig. 19. Giuseppe Jardella (active c. 1795–1803). *Drama*, c. 1795. Stone, 36 × 72 in. (91.4 × 182.8 cm.). C. Carpenter Batchelder, Philadelphia.

Fig. 20. Giuseppe Jardella. *Music*, c. 1795. Stone, 36 × 72 in. (91.4 × 182.8 cm.). C. Carpenter Batchelder, Philadelphia.

they felt that a protective porch was necessary to shelter their customers from the inhospitable North American climate. In any case, about this time they hired a talented young English architect, Benjamin Henry Latrobe, to develop a scheme for an extended porch and otherwise to complete the theater.[17]

Latrobe's addition, a sixty-foot colonnade of Corinthian columns flanked by two fifteen-foot wings, was not completed until 1806.[18] The architect's scheme was a handsome and economical solution to the managers' program. Latrobe attempted to return to the facade some of the surface decoration which had been eliminated by financial exigencies. When he learned that the grandiose, uncompleted mansion of the bankrupt Robert Morris on the south side of Chestnut Street between Seventh and Eighth Streets was to be demolished, Latrobe salvaged the sculpted allegorical relief panels of *Drama* and *Music* (figs. 19, 20) to incorporate into the theater facade.[19] In the absence of native stonecarvers, architect Pierre Charles L'Enfant had brought Giuseppe Jardella from Italy about 1794 to embellish "Morris's Folly," and Latrobe ingeniously adapted the abandoned product of this early effort at high-style carving in Philadelphia.[20]

There is no documentary evidence whether it was Latrobe who encouraged William Rush to carve the two allegorical figures for the facade of the Chestnut Street Theatre; a bill or invoice would have been lost in the conflagration of 1820.[21] Latrobe's contention to President Jefferson in 1805

that there were no qualified stonecarvers in America, and that the decorators for the U.S. Capitol must be sought in Italy, is well-known.[22] However, the ingenious suggestion to use carved pine, painted to look like white marble from which it would be indistinguishable at the height of the niches of the theater, might well have been Latrobe's idea. Certainly the public praise which Latrobe subsequently accorded Rush shows that he approved of his efforts.[23]

Rush's fellow Philadelphians were also evidently pleased. On April 2, 1808, Poulson published in the *American Daily Advertiser* the following lines:

William Rush, Esquire, of this city, has recently compleated two elegant figures (Comedy and Tragedy) for the proprietors of the Philadelphia Theatre, to be placed in the niches in front of that building on Chestnut street. In the execution of this work, the genius of the artist is truly pourtrayed; he has done himself honor, and added to that of his country.[24]

One of the major questions remaining about Rush's debut as a sculptor of public monuments is whether he worked from preparatory designs by Robert Smirke. Smirke did indeed design for sculpture. The diarist Farington quoted Royal Academician Nathaniel Marchant as saying that the prolific English sculptor J.C.F. Rossi, R.A., "could do nothing without Smirke's designs."[25] And it was Rossi who carved the allegories of *Comedy* and *Tragedy*, similarly accompanied by their identifying masks, for niches in the facade of Smirke, Jr.'s influential Theatre Royal, Covent Garden, of 1808–09.[26] However, the evidence is inconclusive. Not enough study has been made of Smirke, Sr.'s designs for sculpture to make a meaningful stylistic comparison. Rossi's sculptural pair is severe and conscientiously classicizing, befitting the first great statement of Greek Revival architecture in England, whereas Rush's realization is playful and rococo. It is possible that Rush was working from Smirke cartoons from around 1791 when Wignell and Reinagle first announced their scheme. The cartoons might well have been brought to Philadelphia from London with the architectural model. Stylistically, there is little question that Rush was working from some rather sophisticated graphic image.

The question of whether Rush worked from cartoons by Robert Smirke may never be resolved, because on Easter Sunday night, April 2, 1820, the Chestnut Street Theatre was destroyed by fire. Scharf and Wescott recorded that little was saved except

an old eight-day clock, an antique mirror, and the old sick-chair which was used in the business of stage. . . . The wardrobe destroyed included the principal part of Lord Barrymore's private wardrobe, court costumes, and costly dresses. The beautiful drop-curtain, which was the admiration of every artist and connoisseur, was lost. It was the work of Wignell's brother-in-law, the celebrated Richards, and was commonly called "Richard's Drop." The subject was a Grecian triumphal arch, with a most exquisitely-wrought Italian sky in the perspective, relieved with variegated foliage.[27]

Fortunately, the allegorical figures of *Comedy* and *Tragedy* by William Rush were also saved from the fire.[28]

Allegory of the Schuylkill River or *Water Nymph and Bittern*, 1809

Between 1791, when the Chestnut Street Theatre sculptural program was conceived, and 1809, when Rush carved the first figural fountain in America, a new type of source material became available to him: plaster casts of antique sculpture. While there was a cast from the antique in Philadelphia as early as 1783, it was only with the arrival of Nicholas Biddle's shipment of plaster casts in 1806 that Rush could readily study the form and variety of antique sculpture.

Like his first pair of public sculpture, Rush's fountain at Centre Square was related to a project of the architect Benjamin Henry Latrobe. No patron gave the infant art of sculpture in America more encouragement than Latrobe. When Latrobe was unable to find a native stonecarver worthy of his vision of the nation's new Capitol in Washington, he approached the greatest sculptor of the age, Antonio Canova, about the commission for a large figure of Liberty.[29] For the decoration of the Capitol Latrobe imported from Italy two of the few accomplished carvers of their generation to come to America, the figurative sculptor Giuseppe Franzoni (1786–1816), and the decorative carver Giovanni Andrei (1770–1824).[30] Latrobe through his own work encouraged the ornamentation of architecture; and to this end he promoted the cast-stone architectural ornament of Coade and Company, London, whose designers included John Bacon the elder, Thomas Banks, John Flaxman, J.C.F. Rossi, and Benjamin West.[31] In 1804 when the managers of Pennsylvania Hospital acquired from an English country estate a life-size lead sculpture of William Penn variously attributed to John Bacon the elder or John Cheere, Latrobe submitted designs for its installation.[32] And certainly Latrobe must have encouraged William Rush to attempt his first public sculpture, the allegories of *Comedy* and *Tragedy*, for his renovation of the theater on Chestnut Street.

For his controversial scheme for the Philadelphia waterworks in 1798, Latrobe proposed a fountain *for every street*.[33] Not only would the waterworks be "rendered an ornament to the city," Latrobe argued, but the spray of the fountains would be cooling and cleansing. Although Latrobe's proposal for public fountains was initially attacked as "a confused and enormously expensive project of 'aerial castles,'"[34] a commission for a single fountain in Centre Square was given by 1809 to William Rush ([35], pl. IV). Marceau suggested that Rush derived his inspiration for the fountain from no less than the most vaunted image of classical antiquity, the *Venus de' Medici*.[35] Rush could have copied the *Venus de' Medici* from a volume of *The Artist's Repository*. However, Rush did not purchase his edition until 1812, and there existed at close hand a more tangible source. In 1783 when the painter Robert Edge Pine arrived in Philadelphia from England to paint the portraits of American patriots, he brought with him a plaster cast of the *Venus de' Medici*. Judge Joseph Harrison recalled that Pine "brought with him a plaster cast of the Venus de Medicis, which was *shut up in a case*, and only shown to persons who particularly wished to see it; as the manners of our country, *at that time*, would not tolerate a public exhibition of such a figure."[36] In 1794 when Rush, Charles Willson Peale, and friends founded their art academy, the Columbianum, "the cast of the Venus de Medici was resurrected from the surrounding mass of rubbish in which it had been left by the family of Pine. . . . This cast and a composition figure given by James Trenchard and a few battered antiques, were the only models from which the students of the school had to draw from."[37] The Columbianum lasted little more than a year, but Pine's cast of the *Venus de' Medici* survived to the founding of the Pennsylvania Academy of the Fine Arts in 1805 by Rush and Peale, and served its early classes of students. In 1806 the *Venus de' Medici* was joined by the other antique casts of Biddle's shipment.

Rush did not slavishly copy the *Venus de' Medici* in the composition of his fountain. Certainly in its left arm, Rush's figure would have reminded the educated viewer of the right arm of the classical model which chastely conceals her upper torso, and in the graceful contrapposto of the composition. Rush's figure also evoked other classical sculpture which would have been known to the artist through plaster casts at the Pennsylvania Academy and through illustrated books. For example, Rush's sculpture is in many respects closer to the *Celestial Venus*, also called the *Vénus sortant du bain*, which has been on view at the Uffizi Gallery since 1664 (fig. 21).[38] The inventory of plaster casts of sculpture at the Pennsylvania Academy in 1811 lists several versions of the Venus of the Bath, and the similarity of the upraised arm and the interest in drapery argue for Rush's consciousness of this famous classical composition no less than the *Venus de' Medici*.

In addition to classical sculpture, Rush may have modeled his fountain figure on the daughter of a fellow member of the Watering Committee. Gordon Hendricks has reiterated the known facts and restored some proportion to the story of Rush's use of Louisa Vanuxem as a model for the fountain figure, much romanticized by Thomas Eakins in his painting *William Rush Carving His Allegorical Figure of the Schuylkill River* (fig. 63).[39]

Marceau preferred the title *Water Nymph and Bittern* and dismissed the view of Eakins and others that the fountain at Centre Square was an allegory of the Schuylkill River.[40] However, there is sufficient evidence to restore Eakins's alternate title. Every other public work of sculpture by Rush has an overtly allegorical connotation. In this respect Rush was striving to emulate the convention of English

Fig. 21. *Celestial Venus (Vénus sortant du bain)*. Hellenistic. Marble, height 56¹³⁄₁₆ in. (144 cm.). Uffizi Gallery, Florence.

sculptors of the period. The most influential document of the fashion of English sculptors toward allegory was George Richardson's *Iconology; or A Collection of Emblematic Figures . . . Moral and Instructive; in Which are Displayed the Beauty of Virtue and Deformity of Vice* (London, 1779). This sumptuous two-volume folio edition served as a pattern book for English painters, sculptors, and architects. James Cox, the English drawing master who established a painting and drawing school in Philadelphia as early as 1790, and whose valuable book collection was sold to the Library Company of Philadelphia, owned a copy. Two aspects of Richardson's *Iconology* are relevant to the consideration of Rush's intent at Centre Square. First, in Richardson's work, illustrations of birds accompany the figurative allegories in seventy instances, and the adjacent narrative explains the specific bird as an appropriate attribute.[41] Second, in Richardson's allegory of the river god Thames, the author goes to great length to point out the novelty and propriety of including a swan as an attribute of the English river.[42] Thus it seems that Rush, by including the indigenous bittern in his fountain at Centre Square, and later the eagle in his *Allegory of the Schuylkill River in its Improved State* (1825), to represent the Schuylkill River, was merely subscribing to an accepted tradition of allegory.

Centre Square is located halfway between the Delaware and Schuylkill rivers, and the choice of the source for Philadelphia's drinking water was a matter of considerable debate in Latrobe's original proposal. Latrobe sensibly insisted on Schuylkill water, while other self-serving entrepreneurs argued for the Delaware. Latrobe won the debate, and Rush may have been emphasizing the virtue of the decision by presenting an allegory of the Schuylkill River.

The invoice for Rush's work, dated August 11, 1809, is preserved in the Philadelphia City Archives:

> The Corporation City Philada.   Dr.
> Wm. Rush
> to carving figure for fountain at Centre Square
> to Collecting stone for Ditto and
> Superintending the Erection thereof
> and painting figure $200[43]

Latrobe must have been pleased with Rush's picturesque sculpture. On November 1, 1809, he wrote to Philadelphian William Jackson and claimed that his Italian protégé, Franzoni, was the only sculptor worthy of the name in the Untied States—except for William Rush.[44]

Wisdom and *Justice*, after 1812–by 1824

The imagery of Rush's most ambitious project can be identified with a specific graphic resource, the most influential of all pattern books for eighteenth-century sculptors, James Gibbs's *Book of Architecture* (London, 1728). The manner in which Rush adapted Gibbs's imagery, and the remarkable history of the project, illustrate Rush's ingenuity in utilizing available graphic sources.

In 1976 this author asserted that "it is certain that Rush did not originally intend the *Mercy* [*Wisdom*] and *Justice* for the Grand Civic Arch, but rather for another project which was never realized. It may be that Rush intended the pieces for niches on the garden side of the State House [Independence Hall]. . . ."[45] My thesis was based on the suggestion in 1774 by Benjamin Franklin that the statue of William Penn, now at Pennsylvania Hospital, "would well become a Niche in some part of the Statehouse next to the Garden."[46] Also, I cited the "internal evidence" that the two figures had been excavated in the back, thus obviously not meant to be seen in the round as they were displayed on the temporary triumphal arch, but rather frontally, as in niches.

Happily, Linda Bantel recently discovered proof positive of this hypothesis: Robert Mills exhibited at the Pennsylvania Academy in 1812 drawings for improvements to the State House including "the removal of two blank windows under the portico, and putting in their place niches for the reception of the statues of Wisdom and Justice."[47] This documentation pushes back the date of conception of the sculpture more than a decade, and is more consistent with the stylistic evidence of the sculptor's evolution. It remains to be determined at what point during the dozen years between the exhibition of Mills's drawings and the well-documented debut of the two allegorical figures during the visit of Lafayette in 1824 Rush actually carved the sculpture [61, 62]. There is no known reference to *Wisdom* and *Justice* after 1812, until the great celebration in 1824.

The Marquis de Lafayette, comrade-in-arms and friend of Washington, hero of Monmouth and Yorktown, had expressed a desire to return to America after forty years' absence. In January 1824, Congress passed a resolution instructing President Monroe to communicate to Lafayette "the assurances of grateful and affectionate attachment still cherished for him by the Government and people of the United States."[48] Lafayette's year-long triumphal tour included visits to all twenty-four states, from New Hampshire to Virginia. He was met everywhere with ceremonial parades, banquets, balls, and illuminations. Philadelphia, where the young French nobleman had received his honorary commission of major general from the Continental Congress a half-century earlier, was not to be surpassed in its appreciation.

Fig. 22. Artist unknown. *General Lafayette's Arrival at the State House [Independence Hall], Philadelphia,* 1824. Lithograph, 2¼ × 7¼ in. (5.7 × 18.4 cm.). Free Library of Pennsylvania, Philadelphia.

On Monday, September 27, Lafayette with Governor Williamson of New Jersey crossed the Delaware River at Trenton, where he was met by Governor Schulze of Pennsylvania. They were met by some 10,000 troops, which accompanied the retinue to the State House where the crowds were estimated to be from 100,000 to 200,000 persons. They passed through thirteen triumphal arches designed by architect William Strickland, aided by his pupil Samuel Honeyman Kneass. The final arch, the Grand Civic Arch, was the most elaborate of Strickland's designs, and received extensive description in the press (fig. 22):

This arch displayed great taste and judgment in the design, and skill in the execution. It was constructed of frame work covered with canvas, admirably painted in imitation of stone. The plan was derived from the triumphal arch of Septimus Severus at Rome. Its dimensions were forty-five feet front, by twelve in depth—embracing a basement story of the Doric order, from which the principal arch springs to the height of twenty-four feet above the pavement. The spandrels, or abutments on each front were decorated with figures of Fame, painted in basso relievo, having their arms extended, and mutually holding a civic wreath over the key-stone of the arch. The wings on each side of the centre, were of the Ionic order, being decorated with niches and statues representing liberty, victory, independence and plenty—each having appropriate mottos, inscribed in corresponding pannels. The whole of the building was surmounted by an entablature, thirty-eight feet from the pavement and supporting a flight of steps in the centre, upon which were placed the arms of the city, executed in a masterly manner by Sully. On each side of the arms were placed the statues of Justice and Wisdom, with their appropriate emblems, sculptured by Mr. Rush, in a very superior style. They had all the beauty and lightness of drapery, of the Grecian school; and so excellent was the workmanship, that it was not until after positive assurances, that a spectator would give up the belief that they were executed in marble. The arch was designed by Mr. Strickland, and executed under the direction of Messrs. Warren, Darley, and Jefferson, scene painters of the new Theatre. The superficial surface of painted canvas amounted to upwards of three thousand square feet.[49]

No preparatory drawings for the Grand Civic Arch are known to exist, but Strickland wrote a commemorative hymn to Lafayette which was published with an engraving of the triumphal arch. The sheet music was issued by G. E. Blake of Phila-

Fig. 23. After William Strickland. *Come Honor the Brave!* Detail of engraved sheet music, copyright September 6, 1824. New York Public Library.

Fig. 24. Attributed to Thomas Sully (1783–1872). *Arms of Philadelphia*, c. 1824. Oil on canvas, 56¼ × 56 in. (142.9 × 142.2 cm.). Independence National Historical Park Collection, Philadelphia.

delphia, copyrighted September 6, 1824, and according to a note with the engraving, the arch was already under construction (fig. 23).

The Grand Civic Arch was appropriately named, for its program included a symbolic, almost heraldic, image of City and State. In the spandrels were two Fames supporting "a civic wreath over the keystone of the arch," an allusion to Pennsylvania which even then was known as the Keystone State.[50] Flanking Thomas Sully's Seal of Philadelphia, which survives in a large copy (fig. 24), were the two Rush figures, traditionally known as *Wisdom* and *Justice*. In fact, although never recognized in the contemporary press, the Rush figures are also an allusion to the State, for they bear the attributes of its first proprietor, William Penn. Rush derived the attributes for *Mercy* and *Justice* from the 1770 engraving of Penn by Pierre Eugène du Simitière (see fig. 25), which was itself based in part on plate 118 of James Gibbs's *Book of Architecture*. More importantly, Rush also referred to plates 111, 116, and 118 in Gibbs's well-known work in establishing his sculptural types (figs. 26, 27).

The influence of Gibbs's *Book of Architecture* on eighteenth-century English sculpture was enormous. As Margaret Whinney has observed, "For many English craftsmen, it would seem that the appearance of Gibbs's *Book of Architecture* in 1728, in which many designs for monuments were included, was even more influential than the sculpture produced by the foreigners by that date. Sometimes a design is fairly closely repeated; more often a Gibbsian frame encloses a somewhat naive arrangement of figures."[51] Helen Park identified thirteen copies of Gibbs's volume in America before the Revolution, and a copy was recorded in the Library Company of Philadelphia catalogue of 1789.[52] The designs by Gibbs, as engraved by Elisha Kirkall and George Vertue, remained vital and memorable for Rush in spite of their origin in English graphic art almost a century earlier.

Fig. 25. John Hall (1739–1797), after Pierre Eugène du Simitière (c. 1736–1784). *William Penn: First Proprietor and Founder of Pennsylvania*, 1773. Engraving, 4¾ × 3¹⁵⁄₁₆ in. (12.1 × 10 cm.). Historical Society of Pennsylvania, Philadelphia.

Fig. 26. James Gibbs (1682–1754), engraved by Elisha Kirkall (1682–1742). Detail of *A Design for a Monument for His Grace the Late Duke of Buckingham.* Pl. 116 in *A Book of Architecture* (London, 1728). Engraving. Philadelphia Museum of Art.

Fig. 27. James Gibbs, engraved by Elisha Kirkall. *A Monument for a Noble Lord and Lady, executed with some variation.* Pl. 118 in *A Book of Architecture* (London, 1728). Engraving, 14⅝ × 8¾ in. (37.2 × 22.2 cm.). Philadelphia Museum of Art.

Certainly Rush was instrumental in developing the symbolic program for the Grand Civic Arch. The attributes of William Penn, "Mercy" and "Justice," were clearly spelled out on the coat of arms by du Simitière. What about Robert Mills's alternative title, *Wisdom* for *Mercy*, which was reiterated in the popular press at the time of Lafayette's visit? Mills or Rush ingeniously related the attributes of William Penn to the two corresponding wings of the State House. Thus *Wisdom / Mercy* represented old Congress Hall, the legislative wing to the west, and *Justice* stood for the Supreme Court, the judicial branch to the east.[53] Eventually, *Wisdom / Mercy* and *Justice* were geographically associated with their appropriate branches of state government: in 1829 the allegorical figures were placed on opposite sides of Independence Square on pedestals in the garden.

Rush must not have been altogether pleased with this placement of his sculpture or the reception ac-corded it. The sculpture was placed on freestanding pedestals which required that linen be tacked to the back to hide the excavation. The pieces were originally meant to look out together from Independence Hall; they were now forced to face each other uncomfortably across the square. On September 5, 1829, the *Saturday Evening Post* published the following humorous report which serves as a colorful document of the situation:[54]

INDEPENDENCE SQUARE, better known as the State House Yard, has lately been *embellished* (after the fashion of primer-makers, who embellish their works with wood-cuts,) by the erection of two wooden figures, on opposite sides of the principal walk, intended to represent *Justice* and *Wisdom.* These figures were carved some years ago, we believe, by Mr. Rush, and were originally destined to fill niches at a considerable elevation. Until lately, however, no use had been made of them, and it was reserved for the gentlemen who have charge of the public squares at present, to exhibit their beauties to the public gaze and admiration. This they have done by causing them to be placed on pedestals, 3 or 4 feet high, in the most conspicuous part of the State House Yard, where they attract daily some dozen of boys, who seem wonderfully delighted with their surpassing elegance. Their backs, which, as they were intended to be placed in a niche, are of course rough and unshaped, are covered with folds of canvas, so puckered as to resemble drapery. This circumstance has given rise to several squibs, and among others to that which will be found annexed to this paragraph. . . .

HARD TIMES

Hard times, hard times, are these, no doubt,
Wisdom and Justice both turned out,
   To call on passers by,
And ask a penny from each purse,
To keep their clothes from getting worse,
   Or better ones to buy.

Their linen is of canvas made,
And stitched together by the trade,
   Of hammer, and of nails,
So, *Tailors*, mind your P's and Q's,
Or else the gentry will refuse
   To patronise your sales.

Tho' once united in the laws,
They're now opposed in ev'ry cause,
   For diff'rent sides they take;
They're kept within a magic ring,
Or some such curious kind of thing,
   Like martyrs at a stake.

Tho' this, by some, is counted hard,
From ancient rights to be debarr'd,
   And e'en from shelter driven;
If they reflect, the reason's plain,
That they may their redemption gain,
   By looking up to Heaven,

                  E.

In 1848 *Wisdom* and *Justice* were placed in the Assembly Room of the Fairmount Waterworks, below the present site of the Philadelphia Museum of Art, where they were shown for the first time in niches (figs. 13, 14). There they remained until 1937 when the Museum's director, Henri Marceau, gave William Rush his first retrospective exhibition and elevated him from the ranks of ship carver to his due consideration as America's first native-born sculptor of distinction.

Allegory of the Schuykill River in Its Improved State and Allegory of the Waterworks, 1825

The source for Rush's famous pair of river gods has been a point of speculation for scholars. However, there is visual evidence that Rush was looking at a source which has hitherto gone unrecognized, imported casts in artificial stone of work by a contemporary Georgian sculptor.

The allegorical river god was a common pictorial device of Georgian sculptors and architects. This neoclassical tradition descends directly from the excavation in 1512 of the pair of Roman sculptures, *Nile* and *Tiber*, which today recline in the Braccio Nuovo of the Vatican Museum and in the Louvre respectively.[55]

For Georgian London it was John Bacon the elder, R.A. (1740–1799), who gave currency to the image of the symbolic river god. Between 1778 and

Fig. 28. Artist unknown. *A View of the River God THAMES 9 feet Figure & 4 SEASONS as placed in the Kiln, for Burning, so as to represent Stone, at the Lythodipyra at Lambeth,* 1786. From the *European Magazine,* London. Engraving. Courtesy of the Greater London Council.

1789 Bacon designed and supervised the sculptural program for Somerset House, which centered on the bronze group of *George III and the River Thames* in the courtyard.[56] The Somerset House *River Thames*, with its attribute of a cornucopia, is ultimately based on the Louvre *Tiber*.

Bacon's popular image of the *River Thames* was reproduced at full scale by the Coade Artificial Stone Manufactory in Lambeth.[57] In 1786 the *European Magazine* published a view of Mrs. Coade's kiln at Lambeth, illustrating a cast of Bacon's river god (fig. 28). The engraving also reproduced a Coade keystone with a grotesque mask of the type applied to the William Bingham mansion in Philadelphia (see fig. 33) and an allegorical group of *Four Seasons*. These female allegorical figures were produced in large number by the Coade factory, and possessed conveniently interchangeable attributes (fig. 29). The *River Thames* appears as item number 1 in the widely distributed Coade sales catalogue of 1784, nine feet in length for 100 guineas. Examples of the Bacon-Coade river god survive at the Terrace Gardens at Richmond and at Ham House, Surrey (fig. 30). American architects, as we shall see, admired and imported Coade manufactures.

The freestanding river god was probably introduced to the United States in 1800 by John McComb, Jr. (1763–1853), the architect with J. F. Mangin of New York City Hall. It is identified here that it was McComb who designed the mu-

Fig. 29. After design, c. 1784, by John Bacon the elder (1740–1799). *Pomona*, c. 1788. Cast Coade stone, over life-size. Heveningham Hall, Suffolk, England; photo courtesy of Alison Kelly.

Fig. 30. After design, c. 1784, by John Bacon the elder. *River God*, c. 1800. Cast Coade stone, length 108 in. (274.3 cm.). Ham House, Surrey, England; photo courtesy of Alison Kelly.

nicipal reservoir at Collect Pond in New York City for the Manhattan Company. McComb proposed to the corporation a tetrastyle Tuscan frontispiece on Chambers Street, surmounted by a reclining river god (fig. 31). The figure, *Oceanus*, was in fact the official logo of the Manhattan Company and represents one of the earliest American trademarks.[58] A watercolor of 1825 shows the Tuscan porch and river god installed at the reservoir.[59] It is likely that the Manhattan Company's *Oceanus* at the Collect Pond was a variation of John Bacon's popular river god, and purchased from the Coade factory about 1800.

At the same time that Alexander Hamilton, Aaron Burr, and their fellow New Yorkers formed the Manhattan Company to supply water to that city, the Common Council of Philadelphia initiated its own scheme to provide water to the burgeoning population of the new capital. Benjamin Henry Latrobe was put in charge of the design of the Philadelphia waterworks, and was assisted by Frederick Graff, chief draftsman. Latrobe visited New York at this time to study McComb's Manhattan waterworks project.[60] The solution of Latrobe to Philadelphia's need for water is summarized in the previous section, "Allegory of the Schuylkill."

By 1812 Philadelphia had already outgrown Latrobe's water system, and the design and transfer of the new waterworks from Centre Square to the banks of the Schuylkill River at Fairmount became the responsibility of Latrobe's former lieutenant, Frederick Graff. Early elevation drawings by Graff at the Franklin Institute show that he initially envisioned a single entry to the millhouse of the Fairmount Waterworks. Graff, who knew at first hand McComb's decorative solution for the Manhattan reservoir, originally suggested crowning the millhouse pediment with a single, allegorical river god (fig. 32). When Graff finally proposed two symmetrical millhouses to punctuate the long river facade of the waterworks, a second river god was required (pl. v).[61]

William Rush needed little encouragement to accept the commission to carve the two new allegorical figures of the Schuylkill. Not only was his *Allegory of the Schuylkill River* (*Water Nymph and Bittern*) an integral and popular element of the earlier waterworks, but Rush was one of the most active members of the Watering Committee of the Common Council, and his son Samuel was secretary and registrar of the Watering Committee. Rush began the *Schuylkill Improved* and the *Waterworks* [96, 97] when he was almost seventy years old; he was assisted by another son and partner, John.

Marceau and all subsequent writers have traditionally referred to Rush's allegories of the Schuylkill River as *Schuylkill Chained* and *Schuylkill Freed*, without contemporary documentation.[62] Charles Coleman Sellers in 1974 established the dating for the sculpture by publishing Rush's bill of March 1825.[63] The bill itself suggests the more accurate, if less euphonious, titles for the pieces adopted here:

Fig. 31. John McComb, Jr. (1763–1853). *Elevation of a Reservoir of 100,000 Gallons*, 1800. Pen and ink on paper, 24½ × 21¼ in. (62.2 × 54.6 cm.). The New-York Historical Society, New York City. Reproduced for the first time, McComb's drawing shows the architectural frontispiece for the Manhattan Reservoir, Chambers Street, New York City, erected 1800. The allegorical figure, *Oceanus*, was the logo of the Manhattan Company, the predecessor of the Chase Manhattan Bank.

Fig. 32. Frederick Graff (1774–1847). *Doorway to Mill House at Fair Mount*, n.d. Pen and ink and watercolor on paper, 10¾ × 15 in. (27.3 × 38.1 cm.). The Frederick Graff Collection, The Franklin Institute Science Museum, Philadelphia.

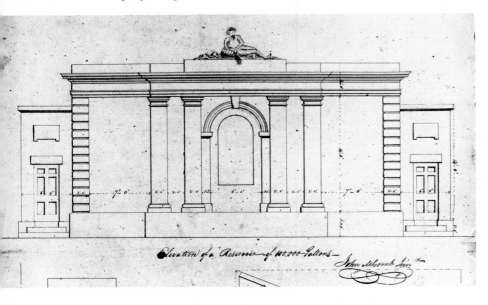

Corporation City Philada.   Dr.
Wm. Rush & Son.
to carving two figures for water work fair Mount
One male figure Emblematic river schuylkill in its
improved state
One female Ditto Emblematic of the water works
$450[64]

Rush's terse description was elaborated in a contemporary account of the symbolism:

The male figure represents the Schuylkill in its present improved state, no longer running uncontrolled, but flowing gently from dam to dam, and passing through artificial canals by locks and gates. The female figure personifies the waters, a work unequalled in its kind throughout the world.

The male figure is recumbent on a bed of rocks, the water flowing in several directions from him. It represents Old Age, the head covered with flags, a long flowing beard, the body covered with water-grass, etc., and a chain attached to the wrist, intended to emblemise the neutralized state of the Schuylkill by locks and dams. A bald eagle at his feet with wings opening is about to abandon the banks of the Schuylkill in consequence of the scene which art is introducing.

The female figure is represented as seated near the pump which pours water into the reservoir. On the left side is represented a water-wheel; her left arm gently waved over it is indicative of the water-power; her right arm or elbow, rests on the edge of a large vase, representing the reservoir at Fairmount. On the side of the vase a pipe represents the ascending main. Water gushes out of the top, falling into the vase, and, to make it more picturesque, but not appropriate, overflowing the vase and falling down its sides.[65]

Fig. 33. Charles Bulfinch (1763–1844). *The Mansion House of William Bingham*, 1789. Pen and ink on paper. The Library of Congress, Washington, D.C.

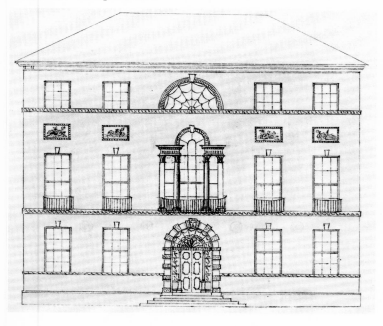

As Dorinda Evans has pointed out, as sculpture the figures are strangely inconsistent.[66] The figures do not seem to be conceived as a formal pair like *Comedy* and *Tragedy* or *Wisdom* and *Justice*. The male figure is emotional and expressive in his Promethean captivity; the female figure is serene and classical in her effortless occupation. The paired Schuylkill allegories appear to be derived from different sources. Rush's *Schuylkill Improved* may be a direct descendent of the Georgian model of John Bacon. But what about the reclining female figure personifying the *Waterworks*? It has been suggested that the type of classical female figure was in such general use that it does not have a specific source.[67] However, a visual source was known to Rush, a source so prominent that it must be given consideration.

The Mansion House, about 1788, the residence of millionaire William Bingham at Third and Spruce Streets, was considered by many to be the grandest house in America (fig. 33).[68] The exterior decoration consisted of Coade stone architectural elements including four impressive relief plaques above the second-story windows. These plaques, illustrated in the Coade factory's catalogues after 1777, employed an all-purpose reclining female figure which was made to symbolize any profession or virtue required simply by substituting attributes.[69] While the Bingham mansion plaques disappeared when the house was razed about 1850, a similar set from the Bank of Montreal has survived (figs. 34-37).[70] The scale of the casts—almost four feet long by two-and-one-half feet high—would have interested Rush as life-size sculpture beyond mere architectural ornamentation. The stylistic and formal similarities between, for example, the Coade allegory of *Arts and Manufactures* and Rush's *Waterworks* is unmistakable in the draperies and the general effect of the profile. Even the uncomfortable and artificial relationship of Rush's *Waterworks* figure to her attributes suggests an origin in the interchangeable nature of the accoutrements of the Coade allegories. Who was the sculptor of the Coade plaques which Rush so admired? None other than John Bacon the elder.

Mercury, 1829

The image of Mercury surmounting a temple or pergola was a common form of English garden ornament dating from the first half of the eighteenth

Fig. 34. After design, 1770s, by John Bacon the elder. *Commerce*, 1819. Cast Coade stone, 30 × 46 in. (76.2 × 116.8 cm.). Bank of Montreal, Canada.

Fig. 35. After design, 1770s, by John Bacon the elder. *Arts and Manufactures*, 1819. Cast Coade stone, 30 × 46 in. (76.2 × 116.8 cm.). Bank of Montreal, Canada.

Fig. 36. After design, 1770s, by John Bacon the elder. *Agriculture*, 1819. Cast Coade stone, 30 × 46 in. (76.2 × 116.8 cm.). Bank of Montreal, Canada.

Fig. 37. After design, 1770s, by John Bacon the elder. *Navigation*, 1819. Cast Coade stone, 30 × 46 in. (76.2 × 116.8 cm.). Bank of Montreal, Canada.

century. The picturesque vantage point of William Rush's *Mercury* [99] is illustrated in J. T. Bowen's lithograph of the waterworks of 1838 (fig. 38).

As Wayne Craven has observed, the image of Mercury possessed a certain popularity in this country even before William Rush's version [99].[71] A wood *Mercury* once crowned the summer house of Isaac Royall in Medford, Massachusetts. The Skillins carved the *Mercury*, 1792, that identified the Post Office in Boston and now resides in the Old State House (fig. 39).[72] Franzoni and Andrei carved a large *Mercury* in relief for the Commercial and

Farmer's Bank of Maximilian Godefroy, about 1813, and that architect exhibited a watercolor or elevation drawing of the facade that year at the Pennsylvania Academy of the Fine Arts.[73]

The form of the flying Mercury derives from the much-copied model of Giovanni da Bologna. Rush's *Mercury* deviates from the locus classicus in one notable respect: while Boston and Baltimore tolerated a nude Messenger of the Gods, the Philadelphia version is prudishly arrayed in classical armor. Rush never chose to represent the nude male figure in his public sculpture; the torso of the *Schuylkill in Its Improved State* is likewise concealed by its flowing beard. On the other hand, Rush's treatment of the cuirass of *Mercury* allowed him great play with the surface decoration. To *Mercury*'s antique helmet, Rush attached wings derived from his famous American eagle—that noble bird with which William Rush will always be identified for his development of a heroic symbolism in sculpture for the young Republic.

Although Rush is often represented as an unlettered ship carver, if perhaps the most accomplished on either side of the Atlantic, his surviving works give clues as to how considerable was his acquired respect for traditional artistic methodology and pedagogy. This examination of an important segment of Rush's production—the outdoor works for public buildings and monuments—illustrates the ingenuity of the "first native American sculptor" in adapting available artistic sources. In the larger sense it is a case study of the transfer of a sculptural tradition from England to the United States.

Fig. 39. John Skillin (1746–1800) and Simeon Skillin, Jr. (1756/57–1806). *Mercury*, 1792. Wood, height 38 in. (96.5 cm.). The Bostonian Society, Old State House, Boston.

Fig. 38. John T. Bowen (active 1834–1856). *A View of Fairmount Waterworks with Schuylkill in the Distance Taken from the Mount*, 1835. Lithograph, uncolored, 21¾ × 14⅝ in. (55.2 × 37.2 cm.). The Library Company of Philadelphia.

"Tolerable Likenesses":
The Portrait Busts of William Rush

FRANK H. GOODYEAR, JR.

THE WORK of William Rush has won the attention of art historians as much as that of any other early figure in American sculpture. A catalogued exhibition devoted exclusively to his work was organized in Philadelphia in 1937. Histories of American sculpture, both early and more recent, pay tribute to Rush's importance. In all of these studies, including Marceau's catalogue for that 1937 exhibition, the authors have consistently given far more attention to Rush's carved work than to his modeled oeuvre. The wood carvings have not only been studied more, they have even been called "more important."[1]

Perhaps this emphasis on William Rush's wood carvings is only natural—they are physically larger, there are more of them, and they have thus been more conspicuous. The wood carvings were made as public sculpture and are intimately linked with the history of early nineteenth-century architecture and commerce in Philadelphia. Additionally, the emphasis continues the popular perception of Rush in his own day, when he was recognized first and foremost as a carver. Despite this, and notwithstanding the fact that Rush came to modeling portrait busts at a relatively late stage in his career and that his portrait oeuvre was small, Rush himself would have preferred to have been known as a sculptor. He seems to have been an ambitious man, for in his many professional associations and close friendships with artists in Philadelphia, it was obviously important to him to seem to be on equal footing with his peers.

It was through his modeled portrait busts that Rush achieved this status of artist, and it is in the few surviving terracottas that Rush also realized his greatest artistic successes. These works particularly allow us to measure Rush against the emerging neoclassicism as manifested in contemporary European and American sculpture. In fact they are best interpreted against the backdrop of neoclassicism, for to label them "representative of an American vernacular style"[2] is not only to diminish their quality, but to overlook their origins.

When exactly Rush began modeling portrait busts in clay is open to conjecture. William Dunlap recorded that Rush "commenced modelling in clay about the period at which I introduce him to the reader."[3] That would have been in 1783 when Joseph Wright, painter, sculptor, and son of Patience Wright, a modeler in wax, first came to live in Philadelphia. Since Dunlap also records that Rush himself "said that Wright taught him to model,"[4] it may be that Dunlap, knowing of Wright's presence in Philadelphia as early as 1783 (until April 1785), chose that date as logical. There is no reason to question the accuracy of Dunlap's record that Wright taught Rush to model (although others may have taught him as well). However, it seems more likely that if Wright did teach Rush to model, it happened during Wright's second sojourn in Philadelphia between 1789 and 1793, when he died of yellow fever.

Several factors suggest that Rush's familiarity with modeling in clay early in his career involved learning only the rudiments, and were it not for Dunlap's overall reliability, one might question Rush's involvement with modeling in clay at all until the early years of the nineteenth century. This involvement was almost certainly not serious until then; otherwise why did not Rush, one of the founders of the Columbianum, use the opportunity to show his work at the Columbianum's first, and only, exhibition held in the State House in Philadelphia in 1795. Perhaps he was hesitant to show his portrait busts in terracotta, if they existed at all, in the illustrious company of sculptors like Giuseppe Ceracchi. He unquestionably realized that his carved busts, made as figureheads, were inappropriate for an art exhibition.

It therefore seems likely that the terracotta portrait busts as we know them today did not exist in Rush's oeuvre in the eighteenth century. The two portrait busts of daughters Elizabeth (born 1801) and Mary (born 1803), which on the basis of the subjects' ages seem to date about 1808–10,[5] must be interpreted as Rush's earliest surviving modeled works. Technically, and this is particularly true of the bust of Elizabeth, these busts are experimental;[6] their modeling is even less sophisticated than the posthumous bust of Joseph Wright which almost certainly dates about 1810–11.

Rush seems to have turned to a serious involvement in modeling portrait busts at the very time that his work as a figurehead carver was jeopardized by the collapse of the maritime industry in Philadelphia.[7] He must also have been inspired by the example of other sculptors—Jean Antoine Houdon, Giuseppe Ceracchi, Giuseppe Jardella, George Miller, and his close friend Charles Willson Peale—in Philadelphia to raise his sights above those of the skilled craftsman. As a practical man, he recognized the possibility of considerable personal profit from the sale of plaster replicas taken from his terracotta busts of famous men—heroes like George Washington, his second cousin Dr. Benjamin Rush, the Marquis de Lafayette, Commodore Oliver Hazard Perry, General Andrew Jackson. He was also taking advantage of the new galleries of the Pennsylvania Academy of the Fine Arts, where he could be assured a public forum for the display of these busts.

In extending his oeuvre into portraiture, Rush was also acting out his patriotic sentiments (like his peers John Trumbull, Gilbert Stuart, Charles Willson Peale) as well as fulfilling the obligations, as he understood them, of the neoclassical artist. He naturally wanted to honor the first men of the republic, and he understood the function of the portrait bust as a symbol of honor. He also appreciated the moralizing responsibilities of art for the neoclassicist. It is not too much to say that Rush's portrait busts, sometimes individually but certainly taken as a whole, underscore definite political and philosophical ideas. In the true spirit of neoclassicism, he saw himself and those around him as participants in the building of a new world. His friend Charles Willson Peale must have served as a constant reminder to Rush of his own ideals; as Charles Coleman Sellers has said of Peale, "His hope was to see a new world born from the lessons of nature."[8] Rush's hopes were not so different, and it is not surprising that he chose as his portrait subjects great patriots of the young nation—botanists, prominent physicians, educators, ministers, statesmen, and military heroes. He saw vested in these subjects the ideals around which to build this new world.

Rush's determination to work as a portrait-bust sculptor was undoubtedly stimulated by the example of other sculptors; one is impressed in reading newspaper advertisements of the 1790s by the large number of foreign artists, many of whom remain obscure, settling in Philadelphia, albeit temporarily. Rush's own perceptions about sculpture must have been heightened by their presence. He also must have been influenced by classical statuary, either from marble and plaster copies which were increasingly available for Rush's inspection in late eighteenth-century Philadelphia or as interpreted by neo-

Fig. 40. Charles Willson Peale (1741–1827). Detail of *The Peale Family*, c. 1770–73 and 1808. Oil on canvas, 56½ × 89¾ in. (143.5 × 228 cm.). T. J. Bryan Collection, The New-York Historical Society, New York City.

Pl. V. Thomas Doughty (1793–1856). *View of the Waterworks on Schuylkill—Seen from the Top of Fair Mount*, 1826. Oil on canvas, 16¼ × 24 in. (41.3 × 61 cm.). Private collection.

PLATE V

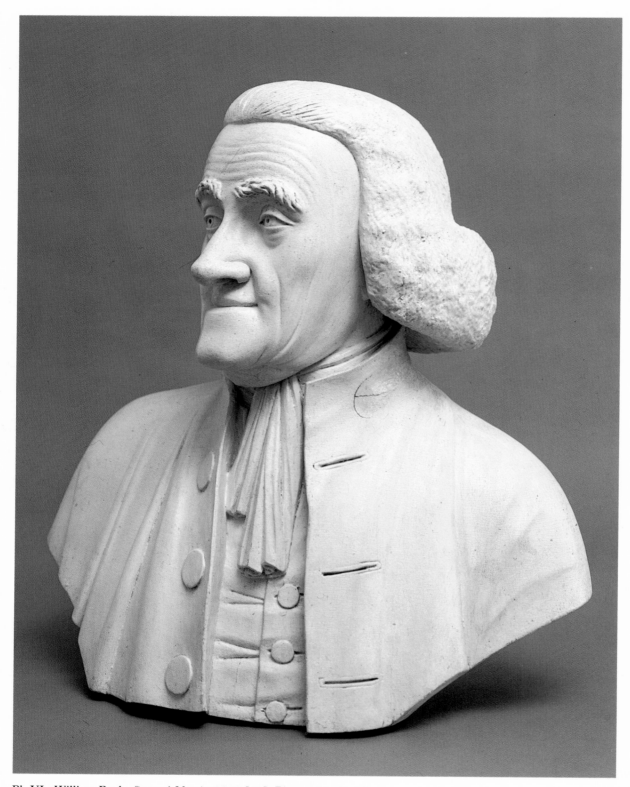

Pl. VI. William Rush. *Samuel Morris*, 1812 [48]. Pine, painted white.

PLATE VI

Fig. 41. William Rush. *Joseph Wright*, c. 1810 [38]. Terracotta.

classical sculptors like Ceracchi. Finally, and most importantly, Rush followed his own instincts in developing his portrait oeuvre—he looked to nature. These instincts—to base art on the study of nature, which it was the duty of the artist to ennoble—were in basic conformity with the tenets of neoclassicism.

The influence that other sculptors had on Rush's sculpture is open to conjecture; research has not so far revealed anything substantive on this score although reasonable conclusions can be posited. Peale and Rush were close friends and frequent collaborators. They shared the life of Philadelphia for over fifty years. Their artistic viewpoints were similar: both valued likeness, both saw art as a means to honor great men and events, both understood its public function. One can imagine Peale, in need of portrait busts for his museum, urging his friend Rush to provide them for him—and Rush offering new likenesses as soon as they were available.

Peale's role may have been more that of the en-

courager than the actual teacher, for sculpture played but a small part in his oeuvre (see fig. 40). Charles Coleman Sellers is probably more accurate to suggest "a Peale influence in the emergence of Rush as a portrait sculptor"[9] than Peale's active hand as instructor to Rush in the art of sculpture. It seems more probable, given the evidence in Dunlap, that Rush learned the craft of sculpting from Joseph Wright, although it also seems certain that it was not until some fifteen years after Wright's death that Rush took up sculpting seriously. By this time (about 1808–10), his knowledge of sculpting materials and his skill as a modeler were still unsophisticated. During the next few years Rush so perfected his modeling technique that, based on records thus far discovered which do not indicate any other teacher, one can reasonably argue that he should be considered self-taught. However, the fact that he chose to model a posthumous portrait of Joseph Wright, a work that was exhibited at the Pennsylvania Academy in 1811 (this seems to be the first time Rush ever publicly exhibited a terracotta), strengthens the supposition that Rush felt indebtedness to his teacher and wished to honor him (fig. 41).

Rush may also have learned some techniques in modeling clay from the Italian sculptor Giuseppe Ceracchi (1751–1802), who was in Philadelphia in 1791–92 and again in 1794–95. Ceracchi was certainly known to Rush for in the fall of 1791 Ceracchi exhibited in Philadelphia a large and elaborate terracotta model for his *Monument Designed to Perpetuate the Memory of American Liberty*, which received extensive newspaper coverage. He also set about "modelling the bust of every man in Philadelphia who he considered influential enough to advance his plan."[10] During Ceracchi's second stay in Philadelphia, when he rented a house at 214 Second Street, Rush would have become reacquainted with Ceracchi through the Columbianum exhibition of 1795. Rush did not himself exhibit in the Columbianum, but as one of its principals he would have been in contact with Ceracchi who showed a portrait bust in marble of David Rittenhouse (fig. 42).

Fig. 42. Giuseppe Ceracchi (1751–1802). *David Rittenhouse* (1732–1796), 1794. Marble, height 19¾ in. (50.2 cm.). The American Philosophical Society, Philadelphia.

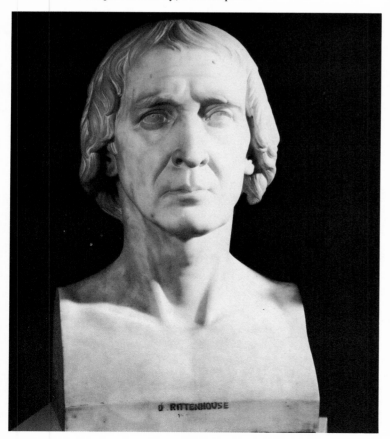

It would seem natural that Rush, who by the 1790s had probably already articulated ambitions beyond those of a figurehead carver, would seek the help of a sculptor of the rank of Giuseppe Ceracchi. A comparison of Rush's later, finer portrait busts with those of Ceracchi's made in America, however, indicates that Rush rejected the severe classical style of Ceracchi in favor of a more restrained classicism. While he embraced the neoclassical ideal to praise famous men, to treat them as heroes, he wanted them to be seen as contemporary men. In this respect, Rush was reflecting on the precedent established in the painting *The Death of General Wolfe* of 1770 when Benjamin West, in a radical departure from theretofore accepted practices, chose to portray the hero Wolfe in contemporary, rather than classical, dress. Rush's portrait busts display less emphatic classical references and are less universal, less ideal than much of neoclassical sculpture. They are even less classically oriented than many of his full-length carved allegorical figures, but they nonetheless embody the simplicity, strength, dignity, and truth which characterize neoclassicism.

Rush respected the classical tradition, but he also wanted to instill in his work a more naturalistic character. Whether this preference was his own or reflected the tastes and aspirations of his sitters is hard now to decipher. As Sellers has said of Charles Willson Peale, "his aim was not immutability but present persuasion,"[11] and Rush shared Peale's aims. His portrait busts reveal a greater individuality of expression than was otherwise generally common in sculpture at the time. This emphasis on greater naturalism was the legacy of the great French sculptor Jean Antoine Houdon. No other sculptor seems to have had so profound an effect on Rush's sculpture, particularly the portrait busts and the full-length figure of George Washington. Notwithstanding, Rush probably never met Houdon, who came to America but once, in 1785 in the company of Benjamin Franklin with the express purpose of making preparatory studies for a statue of George Washington commissioned by the Assembly of the State of Virginia. Houdon arrived in Philadelphia by mid-September, was at Mt. Vernon from October 2 to 19, thereafter returned to Philadelphia, and thence to Paris on December 25, 1785. At this time, Rush, twenty-nine years old, was at the beginning of his career as a carver.

When Rush was first exposed to Houdon's work is unknown. It is also uncertain what exactly of

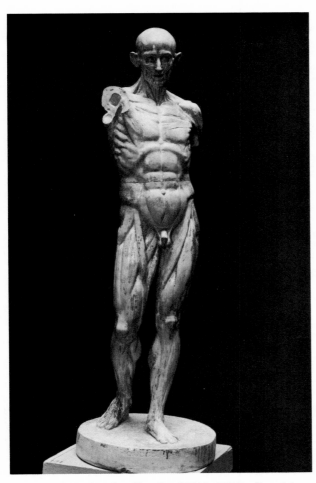

Fig. 43. Jean Antoine Houdon (1741–1828). *Ecorché*. Plaster after Houdon by P. P. Caproni, Boston, c. 1890–1900; height 69 in. (175.3 cm.). Pennsylvania Academy of the Fine Arts.

ultimately have seen the sculptures, probably plasters, which Houdon left in Philadelphia in 1785 in the care of Robert Edge Pine, to be sold, among them the plaster bust of Benjamin Franklin given to the American Philosophical Society in 1800 by Colonel Jonathan Winters, and one of at least eight plasters of John Paul Jones taken from the 1781 marble bust owned by the U.S. Naval Academy.[12] In spite of the dearth of existing documentation, which may suggest that Rush's exposure to Houdon was limited, the influence of Houdon's work on Rush must have been considerable.

Houdon had an expert knowledge of anatomy. Rush did too; he may, in fact, have referred to Houdon's *The First Set of Muscles* at the Academy for anatomical instruction. He may also have studied anatomy with Dr. Caspar Wistar, who deemed Rush competent enough in anatomy to commission anatomical models carved in wood and painted, for use in his own anatomy classes. Houdon employed inherently practical working methods, as did Rush. Neither Houdon nor Rush seemed to work from drawings of their portrait subjects, although Hou-

Fig. 44. Jean Antoine Houdon. *Joel Barlow* (1754–1812), c. 1804. Plaster, 23 × 20 × 12½ in. (58.5 × 50.8 × 31.7 cm.). Pennsylvania Academy of the Fine Arts.

Houdon's work he actually saw. Did Rush ever see, for instance, the full-length marble *Washington* that was shipped to America in the winter of 1796? Or did he only know of it from written descriptions or engravings? Had he ever seen any of Houdon's terracottas? Certainly, he must have seen Houdon's now famous écorché, or *The First Set of Muscles in the Human Subject*, as it was listed in the 1807 catalogue of statues in the collection of the Pennsylvania Academy (fig. 43). He undoubtedly also saw the few other pieces, some of which were plaster casts, that Houdon exhibited at the Pennsylvania Academy: in 1811 a bust of Voltaire; in 1812 busts of George Washington, Benjamin Franklin, and Joel Barlow (fig. 44). It also seems likely that Rush would

Fig. 45. William Rush. *Benjamin Rush*, 1812 [49]. Terracotta.

Rush, like Houdon, was most involved in "see[ing] the figure," no matter what its ultimate material. He obviously prided himself on his acute observational powers, which he often was forced to rely upon in unfavorable conditions. For instance, his *Marquis de Lafayette* is said to have been modeled on the strength of Rush's studying his subject's features during one of several official dinners celebrating Lafayette's visit to Philadelphia in the fall of 1824. Several other portrait busts were done from memory. Rush clearly valued the specific information he garnered from close observation and prided himself on good likenesses. One senses that satisfaction in a letter Rush wrote to Benjamin West in London in which he comments on the "tolerable" likeness of his portrait of Benjamin Rush (fig. 45):

By the ship Electra Capt Williams, I expect you will receive for the Royal Academy, a plaster cast taken from a clay model, of Dr. Rush, which I executed about 8 or 9 months before his death. The likeness you may judge must be tolerable, when in a few days fifteen hundred dollars was subscribed principally for him, some for Dr. Physick at $10 per cast. . . .[14]

As if to anticipate West's criticism of the piece, Rush justified the size of the cranium of *Benjamin Rush* in a particularly revealing remark:

the size of the cranium appears large, but that, with the Whole of the head, and profile is correct from actual measurement.[15]

Rush undoubtedly preferred a captive sitter; he certainly followed his own advice to his studio assistants, whenever it was possible, to imitate nature "and you must be right."[16] Note, for instance, the difference between *Caspar Wistar* (fig. 48), whom Rush modeled from life, and *Joseph Wright* (fig. 41), done posthumously, with the end result considerably more schematic.

During the period that Rush exhibited at the Pennsylvania Academy, specifically from 1811 to 1832, he showed nineteen portrait busts in terracotta or wood and the full-length carved-wood and painted statue of George Washington. He never exhibited the carved bust of Samuel Morris nor the modeled busts of two of his children, Elizabeth Rush and Mary Simpson Rush, nor the bust of the Marquis de Lafayette. In all, this production numbers at least twenty-four, of which we know that seventeen were in clay fired to terracotta, five carved in wood, at least one unfired clay, and the full-length *Washington* in wood. Other than experimental

don occasionally employed life and death masks, a technique Rush is not known to have used. Both are known to have measured their subjects carefully. Both were consummate students, innately sensitive and deeply concerned with the personalities of their subjects.

Rush never worked in marble and, of course, Houdon did; his marbles were, for him, the ultimate sculptural form. Rush seems to have made little of the fact that he did not work in marble. Dunlap records that "[Rush] used to say it was immaterial what the substance was, the artist must see distinctly the figure in the block, and removing the surface was merely mechanical."[13] Rush's response seems to be an honest, consistent one, to a question that may have been put to him in an accusatory tone.

pieces—made after the busts of his daughters and before the bust of Joseph Wright, for there must have been some of these, and not including carved busts intended to serve as figureheads and other ship carvings—this accounting probably represents a high percentage of Rush's lifetime portrait-bust production. Of these works, eleven survive in wood or terracotta; there are also numerous surviving plaster casts, some taken by Rush from the terracotta, and some cast later, presumably even from other plaster casts.

Rush's bust of his daughter Elizabeth, one of the two earliest surviving modeled works, is made of a coarse mixture of clay, indistinguishable from brick clay, fired to red. Its surface is full of irregularities although its modeling is more sophisticated than the bust of Mary, made from a higher grade clay, which was probably made about the same time. Both are best described as experimental: technically unsound, unsophisticated, schematic in the way the facial forms were executed. They are, notwithstanding, real likenesses at the same time that they embody a universal expression of youthful charm. They point to Rush's ability to engage in personalities.

When Rush executed these busts of his two children he was still a carver. By the time he made the bust of Joseph Wright his understanding of the material and his skill as a modeler had advanced considerably. The very fact that he allowed the piece to be subjected to public scrutiny at the Pennsylvania Academy's First Annual Exhibition in 1811 meant that he had some confidence in it. Based on the memory of his mentor, now dead for eighteen years, reinforced perhaps by painted or engraved images of Wright, it is not surprising that Wright's likeness is somewhat schematized also. It reveals a hard, linear quality, relying heavily on simplified surfaces, emphasizing contours. The modeling lacks the naturalistic subtleties that characterize Rush's finest busts to come.

Rush also carved at least five portrait busts during the period of about 1810–12. Four of these, along with several carved allegorical figures, were exhibited at the Pennsylvania Academy: in 1811, *A Citizen* [46]; and in 1812, *Linnaeus* [56], *William Bartram* [57], *Henry Ernest Muhlenberg* [55]. The carved-wood *Samuel Morris* [48] was installed at completion in the Castle of the State in Schuylkill. Only two of these five busts are located today, *Linnaeus* and *Samuel Morris*.

Marceau suggested that the *Linnaeus* bust must have been an "ideal one" since Linnaeus never visited America.[17] It surely derives from an engraving, of which there must have been numbers in Philadelphia as the celebrated Swedish botanist was then a popular figure. Charles Willson Peale, for instance, named one of his children Linnaeus, and by the early nineteenth century there was a Linnaean Society in Philadelphia. It may have been Peale who encouraged Rush to carve the bust of the young Linnaeus, with the idea of using it in his museum. (Rush also carved a companion bust of the American botanist William Bartram at the same time.) Rush chose to memorialize Linnaeus as a young man of high intelligence, with classical features and an assured, determined mien; he is wearing a wig. Surely, Linnaeus must have represented to Rush the ideals of the Enlightenment.

The bust of Samuel Morris, whom Rush met on numerous occasions, was done shortly after Morris

Fig. 46. William Rush. *Mary Simpson Rush*, c. 1810 [40]. Terracotta.

Fig. 47. Charles Balthazar Julien Fevret de Saint-Memin (1770–1852). *Samuel Morris*, 1800–10. Engraving, published in *The History of the State in Schuylkill*, 1883. Courtesy of the Historical Society of Pennsylvania, Philadelphia.

died on July 7, 1812 (pl. vi). Even though Rush knew Morris, and thus could work from memory, he may have relied on a miniature in mezzotint of Morris by Charles Balthazar Julien Fevret de Saint-Memin, probably done between 1800 and 1810 (fig. 47). Rush showed Morris as a thoughtful, kindly old man, with his head slightly turned to intensify the character of the eyes, a subtlety that adds drama to the whole carved composition. Like Linnaeus, Morris is wearing a wig (a prominent feature also in the Saint-Memin mezzotint), which Rush further articulated by layering a gesso composition over the carved surface, all of which was painted white.

Except for ship figureheads, *Samuel Morris* may be the last carved-wood portrait bust that Rush ever made. None survives that can be dated after 1812, and with the exception of the full-length statue of Washington, Rush did not exhibit a portrait in wood at the Academy after 1812. Rather he turned to clay for the busts, which he fired at a low temperature to make terracotta, or "clay burnt" as it was then referred to. As he became proficient as a modeler, he must have come increasingly to recognize the limitations of wood carving for his portrait bust oeuvre. He could do so much more with clay to achieve the subtleties of naturalistic modeling that he valued. He must also have realized that in the eyes of the world he would never be considered more than a skilled artisan if he remained only a carver. There was a certain prejudice against wood as proper material for the sculptor, even among laymen, when it came to high-style art. For instance, when Giuseppe Ceracchi requested the favor of a Mr. Williamson to sit for his bust, Williamson tellingly replied:

Mr. Hugh Williamson is much obliged to Mr. Ceracchi for the polite offer of taking his bust. Mr. Williamson could not possibly suppose that Mr. Ceracchi had offered such a compliment by way of a bribe; for the man in public station who could accept of a bribe, or betray his trust ought never have his likeness made except from a block of wood.[18]

Rush understood this prejudice.

Rush had fully mastered the modeling of clay by the time he turned to making the busts of Benjamin Rush [49], Philip Syng Physick [60], and Caspar Wistar [59], each taken from life in 1812 or 1813. The busts of these three highly distinguished Philadelphia physicians represent a major advancement in Rush's portrait oeuvre. He must have realized this for he chose to exhibit them exclusively at the Pennsylvania Academy's Annual Exhibition of 1813[19] and regularly thereafter during his lifetime.

The three doctors' busts are best distinguished by their naturalistic detail; one feels the sitter's presence, witnesses in each Rush's ability to endow the features with far more surface subtlety than in his previous works. They bear the dignity, intelligence, compassion, and determination of the doctors. They are portraits of American patriots, democrats, men of science, and for Rush they represented both friends and heroic ideals.

With these works, Rush, who seems to have retained the original terracotta busts for his own uses during his lifetime, first realized the potential of replication—of making money and extending his reputation through the sale of plaster casts for which there was some public demand. To facilitate production of the plasters, which were made up from piece molds taken from the originals, the terracottas were fired without some of their protruding parts, particularly the collar tips and jabots. Once the casts were made, the missing parts were added. Consequently, these "made-up" parts on the plasters conform neither to each other nor to the terracottas (see figs. 81-91). The plasters of William Rush remain an important area for further study.

The idea of replication, of making multiple casts in plaster, may have had something to do with the subtle change in Rush's choice of subject matter. This change is first manifested around 1814 by his decision to carve a full-length statue of Washington, and to sell plasters from it. Rush probably expected to realize a bonanza from these sales, based on Washington's tremendous popularity, for he was doing well selling plaster replicas of the three doctors. For the plasters to sell, they had to be of a timely subject. Subsequently, in choosing subjects like Commodore Oliver Hazard Perry, General Winfield Scott, and General Andrew Jackson, military heroes of national prominence, Rush was recognizing the popular market.

The full-length figure of Washington was begun in 1814; Rush recorded that it was completed after "the labour of nearly four months of my son and myself."[20] It was exhibited at the Pennsylvania Academy in the spring of 1815. Rush claimed in his later years (when few could or would want to challenge him) to "have modeled Gen. Washington in his life frequently, in *miniature* and *as large as life*,"[21] a claim which seems unlikely as Washington died in 1799 and Rush did not seriously begin modeling until more than ten years later. Therefore, if any of these studies did exist, it seems improbable that they would ultimately have served Rush years later. The *Washington* statue is a composite of what Rush knew about Washington. Compositionally it appears to have been influenced by the full-length marble of Washington made by Houdon in 1788 (fig. 51), which was the most celebrated statue of its kind in America. Notwithstanding the similarities of the two *Washingtons*, particularly evident in the treatment of the heads, their differences are substantial both in detail and in iconography. Houdon's *Washington* is taller and more erect and is articulated with more descriptive detail than Rush's, and the poses of the two are reversed. Houdon dressed Washington in regimentals whereas Rush's *Washington* is in civilian clothes. Houdon's *Washington* conjures up images of Cincinnatus, of the military hero and peacetime leader, whereas Rush's *Washington* appears the statesman.

Rush's hopes for the plaster market were never realized with the *Washington* statue; there was simply not enough interest in plaster replicas. This was a particularly cruel blow to Rush since it came at the very time that his regular (or "common," as he referred to it) business was declining. His subse-

Fig. 48. William Rush. *Caspar Wistar*, 1812–13 [59]. Terracotta.

Fig. 49. William Rush. *Philip Syng Physick* [60]. Plaster. The American Philosophical Society, Philadelphia.

quent venture in modeling a clay bust portrait of Washington, a far less successful likeness than the larger statue's head, for the purpose of casting plasters may have produced equally discouraging results since only one plaster made from Rush's terracotta has survived [76].

Rush's involvement in the modeling of terracotta portrait busts reached its peak during 1812 to 1817, though he continued to work, albeit sporadically, in this medium until the end of his life. Unfortunately, many are unlocated: *Samuel M. Fox* [67], *Charles Thomson* [71], *Oliver Hazard Perry* [64], *Alexander Contee Hanson* [69], *Joseph Stansbury* [66], *Winfield Scott* [65], and *Andrew Jackson* [79].

Two of Rush's finest portrait busts, which do survive, were made toward the end of his life: *Self-Portrait* of about 1822 and the *Marquis de Lafayette* of about 1824. The *Self-Portrait* [90] was first exhibited at the Pennsylvania Academy in 1822 as "Wm. Rush, Carver, modelled in Clay burnt." The catalogue notation and the *Self-Portrait* are interesting on several counts: first, the notation refers to Rush as a "Carver"; second, though modeled in clay the bust represents an obvious attempt to simulate the look of wood carving. That Rush would have preferred to call himself a carver (and surely he must have had something to say about it) when depicting himself in clay may have been the result of his own modesty. Or was it false modesty? The *Self-Portrait* seems to say, "You may think of me as a carver, but I am so skilled that I can model clay to fool you. I can make clay look like wood" (pl. VII). In fact, if there was a companion bust in wood to compare with the terracotta, and this seems unlikely, Rush's versatility would have been even more apparent.

None of Rush's portrait busts achieve to the same degree the dramatic effect of the *Self-Portrait*. Not only does setting the head at an angle intensify the expression of the eyes, it also adds greater movement. The finely finished head itself emerges from the rough surface of a pine log, draped with boughs and needles. It is a triumph of skill and genius.

The bust of the Marquis de Lafayette [94], executed between September 28 and October 5, 1824, when Lafayette was visiting Philadelphia, is the latest surviving example of Rush's portrait oeuvre, although he continued to model portrait busts up to the end of his life. It was done from observation and characteristically was completed over a short period of time—less than a week. It is a more formal portrait than others by Rush and overall slightly larger. Certainly it reveals Rush's innate sensitivity to personalities (pl. VIII).

Rush's portrait bust oeuvre, particularly the busts modeled in clay, represents a distinct body of work which is best interpreted against the backdrop of neoclassicism. Rush, an American neoclassicist, understood the public function of art, as well as the role of the artist in developing a timely, national heritage. For him the portrait bust stood as symbolic of public honor, and he wanted these busts to have a public life. Perhaps we cannot imagine today with what anticipation the public awaited their viewing.

Whenever possible, Rush based his art on the study of nature which he felt it was the duty of the artist to ennoble. He found his clients in sympathy with his aims; Philadelphians looked to Rush when they needed three-dimensional portraiture. William Rush, the famous carver of Philadelphia, was also its most "distinguished Sculptor"[22] in the early nineteenth century.

William Rush: Sculptural Genius or Inspired Artisan?

WILLIAM H. GERDTS

THE Father of American Sculpture is an appellation that has been assigned to a good many artists and artisans working in America over the century-long period from about 1725 to 1825. The term has been appropriated for such diverse figures as the Boston metalworker Shem Drowne; for Samuel Skillin, Sr. and Jr., early figurehead carvers; for Patience Wright of Bordentown, New York, and eventually London, who created wax effigies (more correctly, of course, "The Mother of American Sculpture"!); and for as late a figure as Horatio Greenough, who in 1825 inaugurated the procession of young American sculptor hopefuls traveling to Italy to acquire the experience and training that would allow them to compete with their European contemporaries, and to establish their places in a confraternity stretching back to Phidias and Praxiteles.[1]

What we recognize today as the practice of sculpture had existed for centuries before Greenough began his transatlantic pilgrimage, yet not Drowne's crude but amusing copper effigy of an Indian atop Boston's old Province House made about 1716 nor his gigantic grasshopper which still caps Faneuil Hall, nor the Skillins' attractive imagery in wood, nor Mrs. Wright's scarcely more imposing wax head and hand of William Pitt in the museum of Westminster Abbey (the rest of the effigy consists of robes and a wig, all supported by an iron armature) would seem to qualify as honorable descendants of the Olympian Zeus. On the other hand, William Rush, who has most continuously been recognized as the earliest American sculptor must be considered as fully, honorably, meriting that designation.[2] For Rush produced a multitude of monumental images, both portraits and ideal pieces, in a variety of mediums—some of it publicly exhibited and much of it for public edification—which were recognized by his contemporaries and applauded by them: *The*

Philadelphia Gazette of July 31, 1830, referred to Rush as "the father of American sculpture" in his own lifetime.

Commemorative images of imposing scale were already in several American cities in the early nineteenth century when Rush's monumental figures began to appear in public places in Philadelphia, but they were few and their makers were foreign artists. Those installed before the colonies rebelled against England were all by British sculptors and commemorated Englishmen. Among them, three were by one of the leading English sculptors of the time, Joseph Wilton, and were destined to survive unscathed for only a very few years. All three of these late baroque images were installed in 1770, two in New York, representing King George III and William Pitt (fig. 50), and another of Pitt in Charleston, South Carolina. In retaliation for the rebels' destruction of the equestrian George III, British troops mutilated the New York Pitt; fragments of both survive at the New-York Historical Society. Charleston's Pitt still stands but was damaged several times, first in the 1780 attack by the British during the Revolution. Likewise, Richard Hayward's statue of Lord Botetourt, the Royal Governor of Virginia, which had been installed in Williamsburg, was damaged by colonial patriots; it stands now on the grounds of the College of William and Mary.[3]

In the early days of the new republic, the major sculptural monuments to appear were also of foreign origin, but not, of course, commemorating British statesmen and rulers, and not, for the most part, by British artists. George Washington was naturally the most frequent subject for the renowned sculptors of Europe. The first of the Washington statues remained the most approved, that carved by Jean Antoine Houdon in 1788 for the State Capitol in Richmond (fig. 51), which he based on a life mask

Fig. 50. Joseph Wilton (1722–1803). *William Pitt*, 1770. Marble, life-size. Courtesy of the *News and Courier*, Charleston, South Carolina.

and a bust he modeled in clay at Mount Vernon in September of 1785.[4] North Carolina set out to rival her northern neighbor with a Washington commissioned in 1816 from the Italian neoclassic master Antonio Canova; his seated Washington, portrayed in the guise of a Roman general, was installed to great fanfare in 1821 but perished in the fire in the State Capitol in 1830.[5] About the same time, Massachusetts approached her expatriate artist-son Washington Allston to help secure a Washington statue from one of the leading English sculptors of the day, Francis Chantrey, but the Boston State House received its Washington only in 1826.[6]

The choice of foreign artists such as the French Houdon, the Italian Canova, and the English Chantrey to carve public monuments to the nation's leader was dictated by the well-founded belief that there were no native artists capable of rendering such images in a successful, professional manner. Not that there weren't professional sculptors active in

the United States by the time North Carolina and Massachusetts commissioned their Washington images, for in the post-Revolutionary years, a growing number of European sculptors of decided ability, if mostly of less than first rank, began to appear in the United States. Artists were enticed here by the recognition of the need for likenesses of and commemorative monuments to the military and political leaders of the Revolution, and in 1805 the construction of the new Federal Capitol in Washington required able carvers of both architectural elements and allegorical imagery.

Most, though not all, of these sculptors were Italian. The most prominent among them, Giuseppe Ceracchi, was also, in 1791, the earliest to arrive; he should never have left since he lost his

Fig. 51. Jean Antoine Houdon, (1741–1828) *George Washington*, 1788. Marble, height 74 in. (188 cm.). Virginia State Library, Richmond.

Fig. 52. Giuseppe Ceracchi (1751–1802). *George Washington*, c. 1796. Marble, 23¹³⁄₁₆ × 20⅞ in. (60.5 × 53 cm.). Carolina Art Association, Charleston, South Carolina.

head to the guillotine in France in 1802. Almost all of Ceracchi's American works were busts of important leaders of the Federal period, strong likenesses in the neoclassic mode, that of Washington appearing particularly in a classic, Roman manner, the most idealized and least transcriptional of all (fig. 52). He also conceived of a great allegorical monument to Liberty, but straightened finances in the new nation prohibited his conception from becoming a reality.[7] Two other Italian sculptors who were hired to work on the nation's new Capitol building, Giuseppe Franzoni and Giovanni Andrei, saw their work, including Franzoni's *Eagle* and plaster statue of *Liberty*, destroyed in the burning of the unfinished building in the War of 1812, although their allegorical sandstone relief of *Ceres and Neptune* of 1807 for the Union Bank in nearby Baltimore survives.[8]

A wide range of allegorical sculpture done by the mostly Italian carvers who came to this country

at the end of the War of 1812 remains in situ in the Capitol: from Giuseppe Valaperta's marble eagle of 1816, to the Rotunda reliefs by Antonio Capellano, Francesco Jardella, Enrico Causici, and Nicholas Gevelot (a Frenchman and the only non-Italian among the Capitol carvers of the period), all carved between 1824 and 1828. Jardella's work consisted of profile portraits of early discoverers, and most of the rest were historical reconstructions, but all were done in a combination of baroque allegorical flourishes and neoclassic ideality. The most ambitious of all such sculpture for the Capitol was the pediment over the East Portico with figures of *America* surrounded by *Hope* and *Justice* (fig. 53), created by Luigi Persico in 1825-28; his statues of *War* and *Peace* below the pediment were carved later, in 1834.[9] All except the last two of these were done during William Rush's lifetime and could have been seen by him on some undocumented trip to Washington.

Fig. 53. After E. Luigi Persico (1791–1860). *Justice, America,* and *Hope*, East Portico of the United States Capitol, 1826. Marble, height of each sculpture, 108 in. (274.3 cm.). Architect of the Capitol, Washington, D.C.

Several of them involve motifs, and others a general allegorical approach, that Rush had used or would use in his own work in Philadelphia.

Philadelphia herself was not without practitioners of the "plastic arts" in the post-Revolutionary days. The first public monument to be erected there was the statue of Benjamin Franklin commissioned from the minor Italian artist Francesco Lazzarini; it

Fig. 54. Attributed to John Cheere (died 1787); formerly attributed to John Bacon the elder. *William Penn*, 1774. Lead, painted black; height without base 79 in. (200.7 cm.). Pennsylvania Hospital, Philadelphia. For new attribution, see Phoebe Dent Weil, "Technical Examination Report and Proposal for Conservation Treatment . . . Prepared for the Pennsylvania Hospital," The Center for Archaeometry, Washington University, St. Louis, Missouri, December 1, 1980.

was installed in the facade of the Library Company of Philadelphia in 1792. Twelve years later a statue of William Penn, perhaps by the English sculptor John Bacon, was installed at the Pennsylvania Hospital, though it was an earlier work, of 1774 (fig. 54).[10] These were imported pieces, but foreign sculptors themselves began to appear in the last decade of the century, beginning with Ceracchi.

John and Frederick Eckstein, father and son, arrived in 1794. The father had been a sculptor of significance first in Prussia and then in England, although few of his works are known today, while his son's career is more properly associated with the beginning of sculptural achievement in Cincinnati.[11] Giuseppe Jardella from Italy, George Miller from Scotland, John Dixey from Ireland, and numerous other foreigners enriched the budding sculptural life of Philadelphia beginning in the late eighteenth century. And Rush's friend Charles Willson Peale had been involved in modeling portrait likenesses beginning in 1768 with a group of busts made in London.[12]

The work of all the artists so far mentioned and the sculptures imported from Europe are significant because they not only represented the ambitions of the new nation in establishing a sculptural tradition and a recognition that sculptural embodiment constituted the most significant and proper mode of commemoration. These works also laid the groundwork and provided examples for inspiration for further patronal encouragement and for artistic emulation. A subject that has not been studied to any degree is the availability to artists and connoisseurs of individual examples of European art that were not public monuments. Houdon's likenesses of a good number of Americans including Benjamin Franklin, Thomas Jefferson, Joel Barlow (fig. 44), John Paul Jones, Robert Fulton, as well as his busts of Washington constitute the best known group of such works, but there were other imported sculptures as well, such as Jean Jacques Caffieri's well-known likeness of Franklin, and not all of these were portraits. The most famous and perhaps the most notorious of ideal marbles seen in the early exhibitions of the Pennsylvania Academy would have been Bertel Thorwaldsen's *Venus*, which was shown in 1832. Most of the works by Canova and Chantrey that were seen at the Academy, however, were plaster casts. Even in plaster, ideal pieces by Canova and other contemporaneous sculptors would have been inspirational in defining the parameters of sculptural expression as well as providing exemplars of current stylistic approach.

Within this framework of sculptural expression in the late eighteenth and early nineteenth century, Rush was certainly the most significant native figure to produce monumental three-dimensional works, and such figures and busts as he made received contemporary recognition, but in a limited fashion—limited not only in the amount of notice, but in the nature of such recognition. Even the esteem of Rush's closest and most significant Philadelphia colleague and contemporary, the painter Charles Willson Peale, was tempered: we find the following description in the 1813 catalogue of Peale's Philadelphia Museum: "[William Rush] Has long been distinguished as a Carver, his ship figures being frequently purchased and taken off the American ships in Europe. He is the first American Sculptor whose works have decorated the public places."[13]

Nevertheless, Rush's involvement with Peale and Peale's Philadelphia Museum was particularly strong. In Charles Willson and his son Titian Peale's 1822 view of the Long Room of the museum (fig. 55), William Rush's busts of Drs. Benjamin Rush and Philip Syng Physick, of General Winfield Scott, and probably that of Andrew Jackson can all be identified; Peale purchased the Rush and Physick busts in December 1813, and the Jackson in January 1822. Rush's full-length wood statue of Washington was exhibited in Rembrandt Peale's museum in Baltimore when it was completed in 1815, and Rush was much annoyed in the spring of the following year that Peale had not lived up to his promise to paint the statue white, in imitation of marble. Peale and Rush, who had served in the same regiment of Philadelphia militia during the Revolution, worked together on such projects as the reconstruction of the mastodon skeletons [25] for the museum and the anatomical models for Dr. Caspar Wistar, some of which survive [33]. Stylistic and technical influences from one upon the other have been explored by Charles Coleman Sellers, who has pointed out that the description of Peale's transparency of *Silence*, painted in 1808, suggests similarity to Rush's surviving figure of the same subject carved.[14]

While Peale's notice of Rush in the museum catalogue can only be taken as a strong encomium, it is necessary to reflect on what it emphasizes and what it neglects. The qualitative emphasis is on Rush's artisanry, his ability as a carver of ship figureheads. In regard to his role as an artist in the field of public sculpture, it is his native primacy which is recognized, but the question does arise: was Rush truly a *sculptor* in terms of contemporary recognition of that branch of the Arts as representative of high cultural endeavor and achievement? We are accustomed today to viewing the history of native American sculptural development as originating with Rush, and at least until recently, few art historians would hesitate to praise Rush's vitality and originality over the twice-derivative marmorean imagery of Hiram Powers and the other neoclassicists ("twice-derivative," because of their combined homage to classical prototypes and traditions, and their allegiance to the already defined European aesthetic of neoclassicism). For Americans from the 1830s, however, Powers, Horatio Greenough, and others dominated American sculptural expression; Rush may not only have been regarded as an artist of an earlier, perhaps more primitive era, but may not have been thought of as an artist at all. Such an issue has tended to be obscured or, perhaps, ignored

Fig. 55. Titian Ramsay Peale (1799–1885). *Interior of Peale's Museum*, 1822. Watercolor on paper, 14 × 20¾ in. (35.6 × 52.7 cm.). The Detroit Institute of Arts; Gift of the Founders Society, The Director's Fund.

because of the aesthetic climate out of which our modern-day perception of Rush emerged.

It is not fortuitous that it was the work of William Rush, not Powers or such a later nineteenth-century artist as Augustus Saint-Gaudens, which was awarded recognition in the exhibition of 1937 at the Pennsylvania Museum of Art. This was a period of political isolationism and cultural emphasis upon national roots and national expression which found contemporaneous artistic relevance in the painting of the Regionalists, and made its most significant development in native art historical revelation in the new exploration and exposition of American folk art. For an audience thus primed for works of art which exuded crude but vigorous "Americanism" and eschewed European derivation, Hiram Powers offered little aesthetic reward, but William Rush's work gave a great deal.

Rush's contemporaries would seem to have re-

Fig. 56. Erastus Dow Palmer (1817–1904). *Peace in Bondage*, 1863. Marble relief, 30 × 25¾ × 1½ in. (76.2 × 65.4 × 3.8 cm.). Inscribed, lower left: E. D. Palmer Sc./1863. Albany Institute of History and Art.

garded him in a somewhat different light, however, and the generations immediately following remembered him, if at all, rather for his superb artisanry than for his primal place in the development of American sculptural expression. His work falls, as does the work of the later marmoreans, into two basic categories: portraiture and what were termed "ideal" representations. The former often represented more personal monuments, even if conceived for public places; the ideal pieces tended to be larger, more ambitious, and more demanding works and were, and are, generally the sculptures upon which an artist's reputation has been evaluated.[15]

In Rush's case, these ideal pieces such as *Comedy* and *Tragedy* [31, 32]; *Faith*, *Hope*, and *Charity* [84, 85, 86]; *Silence* [87]; *Peace* [29]; *Wisdom* and *Justice* [61, 62]; the *Allegory of the Schuylkill River in Its Improved State* and *Allegory of the Waterworks* [96, 97]; and the *Water Nymph and Bittern* [35] can often find thematic parallels in later American marble sculpture. Powers carved busts of the three cardinal virtues; Erastus Dow Palmer's finest relief is his *Peace in Bondage* (fig. 56); and both Joseph Mozier's and Augustus Saint-Gaudens's *Silence* are, like Rush's, a standing figure with a finger to the mouth. What is thematically unusual in Rush's art, however, is that *all* his ideal pieces are allegories. Allegorical representations are not, as we have indicated, unknown in later American sculpture and were prominent among the early sculptures carved for the Capitol, but they are not common in comparison with the number of historical, religious, literary, or even classical subjects. In general, allegorical art was not well received in America, and tended to be looked upon as inappropriate for American expression, perhaps because of its associations with Catholic and monarchical art, as well as its obscurant possibilities. Ironically, one of the strongest statements against artistic allegories was made by Benjamin Latrobe for two of whose buildings, the New Chestnut Street Theatre and the Centre Square Waterworks, Rush designed his best known allegorical figures. In 1819, Latrobe inspected the painting by Mme. Plantou of *The Peace of Ghent 1814 and Triumph of America* and concluded that, while the picture was well enough rendered, "its inherent sin, especially in America, is its being an allegorical picture." Latrobe went on to say that, "as to *allegory* generally it is a most difficult branch of the art of the painter & sculptor, & belongs rather to the poetical department."[16]

Proscription against allegory in American art remained strong in America and found perhaps its ultimate expression in 1856 in an article entitled "Allegory in Art." The author insisted that the office of art was with the visible world, or with ideality, but that "there is a degradation of the Art involved in making it the servant either of ethics or theology . . ." and went on:

There is a double danger in this mingling of the two elements of thought, the one, that of making Art secondary in the public estimation to the subject of allegory, and the other, that of leading the artist himself to forget, in his keen following out of some poetical idea, that his business is to see and to interpret what he sees. . . ."[17]

In truth, within the overall categories of ideal or historical art, allegorical representations in America were more common, and thus presumably more popular, in the eighteenth century and the early nineteenth than later. This was certainly due to the greater temporal proximity to the aesthetic standards of the Renaissance and baroque periods, with allegorical representations deriving from either precedent European work or from images taken from emblematic pictorial imagery. The point here is that Rush's art relates thematically more to its past than an American future, deriving more from baroque expression than leading to future American development. Thematically, his art is more a termination in a provincial backwater than the first soundings of republican sculptural representation.

Wood was the figurehead carvers' medium, and it is the one in which Rush most consistently gave vent to his genius. Yet carving in wood was very much the artisan's mode, one primarily associated, after all, with furniture and the *useful* arts; it was a trade learned in an artisan's shop and often in an apprentice system, rather than associated with art academy education. One of Rush's sons, possibly the sculptor John Rush, wrote to William Dunlap in 1833 that his father had said it was immaterial what substance the sculptor used, and that Rush would have attempted marble had the time permitted.[18] But Rush did not. There is much documentation that at least some of his wood pieces were painted white to imitate marble, and it is probable that all of them were so painted. Rembrandt Peale was to have painted Rush's full-length *Washington* [68], and Philadelphia's watering committee in 1825 paid to have the artist's *Schuylkill Improved* and *Waterworks* painted to simulate stone.[19] A writer in *The Port Folio* the year before praised Rush's *Justice*

and *Wisdom* for the excellent workmanship and lightness of drapery "of the Grecian school," noting the difficulty in convincing spectators that the statues were not executed in marble.[20] But these and many of Rush's allegorical pieces were seen at a height, not subject to close scrutiny, and not really meant to be objects of contemplation.

In 1815, William Tudor of Boston spearheaded an effort to establish an art organization in that city, and in an article in the *North American Review* of that year, Tudor listed the prominent artists resident there. The only sculptor he could mention was Solomon Willard. Like Latrobe writing of Rush, Tudor mentioned the freedom, grace, and harmonious design of Willard's ship carvings, but went on to admit that "it was impossible not to regret that his talents should not be exercised on more noble and durable materials . . . but it may be hoped that he will be hereafter occupied in higher branches of sculpture." In fact, Tudor went on to footnote the disparity of "nobility" and challenge presented by the two materials. He wrote:

Some may object perhaps that carving in wood is very different from sculpture in marble. A mere ordinary carver might be unsuccessful in marble, but real talent is wasted in working upon wood. The process of the sculptor is as follows: he first makes a drawing of the work he contemplates; he then models it in clay. This model he transfers to marble, the latter operation though of some nicety is merely a mechanical process. Mr. Willard observed to the writer that he could execute much better in marble, than in such a course [sic] material as wood; just, said he, as a man can write better on white paper than on brown.[21]

Rush did model in clay, a technique which he probably learned from Joseph Wright,[22] and which was preliminary to the plaster portrait busts he made from the baked clay, or terracotta "originals." However, in Rush's case, as he neither carved marble himself nor hired carvers to translate his clay or plaster pieces into stone under his supervision, the plasters were his final products. This was not consistent with contemporary aesthetic theory concerning true sculpture. In one of the earliest significant articles to concern itself specifically with American sculpture (and *more* specifically directed at the art of Hezekiah Augur who was just then making the transition from wood to marble), the unidentified author stated:

Plaster casts, beautiful as they are, are but sorry cadaverous representatives of the pure, *more* beautiful marble. Their opaque, rayless hue detracts very much from the charm which the purity of the material imparts to the original. An *artist* who has eyes to probe through to the centre and soul of a statue—be it plaster or marble—tough as porphyry, or black as bronze—might deem the criticism hypercritical. But it enters more than he imagines into the emotion of the beholder, and has much to do in winning a popular enthusiasm in behalf of the art. . . . There is in a fair specimen of statuary a translucency—a species of illumination among its particles, which is by no means a bad emblem of 'the light that is within us;' and which renders it a very fit tabernacle for so much in intellect, or heart, as may take up its abode therein. Indeed it does more. It exerts a sort of vestal rule in chastening and hallowing whatever of life the artist is fain to commit to it. The statue's spotless whiteness and mellow light become 'part and parcel,' of the attribute or virtue lodged there. Mind borrows from it dignity; and passion, purity. Nay, every representation of the gross or commonplace is incongruous and unpleasant. Michael Angelo, with the fidelity of an artist's fancy, thought, too, that the sinless marble was a better resting place for morals. . . .[23]

We note that the supremacy of marble lies principally in its physical embodiment of the moral purity that constitutes the justification of sculptural representation, but it also rewards the viewer through aesthetic satisfaction, as against the deadness of plaster. As such, Rush's plaster portraits could offer no more to the connoisseur of his time than transcriptional accuracy. His wood ideals, in turn, embodied a double incongruity. If allegory, either painted or sculptured, was looked upon as ill-suited to artistic representation, the wood medium, even if painted white in imitation of marble as we presume most of Rush's pieces were, could only present a travesty of the "attribute or virtue" lodged in "spotless whiteness and mellow light." And while the author of the article allowed an *artist* to work in either plaster or marble, even in "tough porphyry" and "black bronze," the artisan working in wood was obviously excluded.

Rush's methodology in clay and plaster was not, of course, totally inconsistent with that of the sculptor in marble, but it was only a partial approach. Daniel Fanshaw, in 1827, described a sculptor's process:

The sculptor's material is the soft clay, which he first moulds into the form which he has conceived; on this he employs his invention, and finishes it to the utmost of his power; he then calls in the plasterman to cast in plaster what he has just embodied in the more perishable clay; the plaster model, thus made, passes through the various classes of workmen to be blocked out and imitated by mechanical measurement; and when completed, so far as the mechanics in his employment can complete it, the sculptor, with his small chisel and mallet and the rasp, gives to it the last delicate touches and expressive marks. The *first moulding*, and the *last touching*, are the appropriate label of the real sculptor; all the intermediate process is performed by workmen, and of these the plasterman's duty is least laborious and least intellectual.[24]

Given this scenario for sculpture creation, written contemporaneously with Rush's activity, one can deduce that Rush would not completely qualify as a representative of the art. Whether he used a plasterman or did the plaster casting himself is not the issue. For Rush, the plaster was the end product of his clay pieces; Rush finished up with works whose outward appearances evoked the activity that was "least laborious, and least intellectual." His own activity in regard to the sculpture corresponded with approved, defined methodology, but it constituted only a beginning. He was not the master of the chisel, the mallet, and the rasp upon the marble, nor did he oversee the mechanic in his employment upon the stone.

Outside of the figureheads, almost half of Rush's known work consists of portraits—probably over half, if the replications of these in their various mediums were tallied. The exact sequence of these and their various purposes are partially, though not fully understood. The portrait busts were modeled in clay and then baked to terracotta in order to preserve them. This is distinct from neoclassic methodology where the original clay models were not preserved but were translated into the more permanent material of plaster. For Rush, as we have seen, the plaster portrait was usually the final product.

Rush also made portraits in wood. Few of these have been located and their histories, the located and the unlocated ones, are obscure. Since some of Rush's large ideal wood pieces such as *Comedy* and *Tragedy* and the various Schuylkill allegories and, of course, the figureheads were done as architectural and decorative adornments, it is possible that some of the wood portrait busts were similarly conceived, while the replicable plaster busts were made for private consumption. That is, Rush may have relegated most of his wood sculptures to the realm of "embellishment," while the plaster pieces (for which the terracottas were preliminary states) were his closest equivalent to marble sculptures—to "true" sculpture. What little present history is known of his wood busts, or speculation concerning them, does not contradict this. On the other hand, Rush's relatively limited exhibition record would suggest that the wood busts, which were shown in 1811 and 1812 and never later, by and large preceded the busts in terracotta and plaster which he began

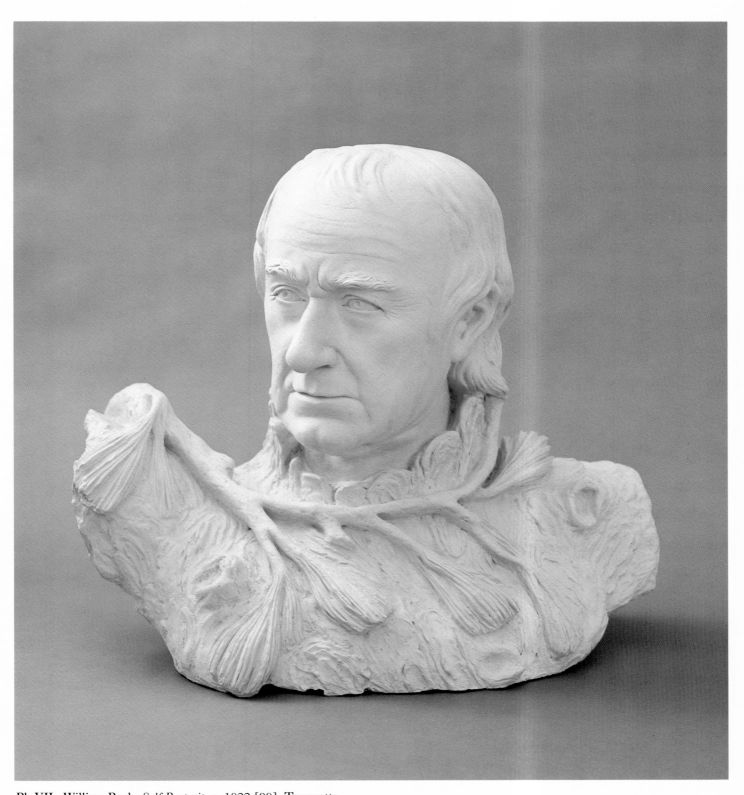

Pl. VII. William Rush. *Self-Portrait*, c. 1822 [90]. Terracotta.

PLATE VII

Pl. VIII. William Rush. *Marquis de Lafayette*, 1824 [94]. Terracotta.

PLATE VIII

to exhibit in large numbers in 1813.[25] This might even suggest that Rush's involvement in portraiture was confined primarily to wood likenesses until, in about 1813, he developed sufficient confidence to work regularly in clay, or that the opportunities provided by a regular, annual exhibition outlet at the Pennsylvania Academy brought the realization that lucrative commissions for replication of images of honored citizens were available. He could, of course, have made plaster replicas from wood busts and figures, as his unrealized plans for replicating his statue of George Washington attest. His letter of November 30, 1815, to President James Madison acknowledged the weak, unsatisfactory response to such a plan with only Madison and Governor Daniel D. Tompkins of New York subscribing to plaster replicas.[26] In fact, as he wrote Benjamin West that year, he even hoped to replicate the statue "in mettle."[27] However, the usual procedure was to make the plaster casts from clay, not wood originals. It is possible that Rush did, in fact, have a clay image of Washington based upon his carved pine, life-size, full-length statue which would have served as the basis for the unrealized plasters; he did exhibit at the Academy in 1817 his terracotta bust of Washington which is a variant of the upper half of his full-length statue. It is also possible that he was planning to resort to the more unusual methodology of plaster casting from wood because he was unable, or ignorant of the method, to create a full-length clay image that would not break or crack. A clay portrait bust was a compact mass; a full-length figure with dangling arms and legs would have been difficult to model, to hold together, and to cast.

Wood, clay, and plaster all have different qualities intrinsic to the material, as do marble and bronze in which mediums Rush did not work. It is difficult to know whether Rush conceived of his sculptures as aesthetically different when he varied his mediums, since only his portraits of George Washington and of Dr. Benjamin Rush are known in wood and also in terracotta and in plaster. And as indicated above, the *Washington* portraits, his most ambitious on several counts, may have necessitated unusual treatment and considerations; furthermore, the known plasters of Rush's *Washington* may well be castings made posthumously.

The most interesting of Rush's bust portraits from the aspects of medium, technique, and aesthetic, is, therefore, that of Dr. Benjamin Rush, known in terracotta, in plaster, and in wood. These busts are

Fig. 57. Hezekiah Augur (1791–1858). *Jephthah and His Daughters*, c. 1828–30. Marble, height with base 39 in. (99.1 cm.). Yale University Art Gallery, New Haven; Gift of the Citizens of New Haven.

similar but not identical. Rush's basic training in the artisan wood-carving mode is strikingly apparent in the wood bust of Benjamin Rush, with its sharp planes, deep undercarving, and broad surface areas. The clay and plaster busts are far more dependent upon the modeler's skills and confirm Rush's successful realization of the basic sculpture techniques. This is, for instance, in marked contrast to the sculpture of the younger Hezekiah Augur of New Haven, whose few known marble pieces, such as his busts of Alexander Fisher and Oliver Ellsworth, or the ideal two-figure group of *Jephthah and His Daughter* (fig. 57), all still suggest the hand of the wood-carver let loose with a basically unfamiliar and unsympathetic medium.[28]

Nevertheless, while Rush's portrait busts share with Charles Willson Peale's painted portraits a vigorous concern with individual identification and trenchant characterization, many of them, like his preference for allegorical themes, relate his work to the eighteenth-century past rather than the neoclassic present. In their vigorous animation in the intense expressions and the strong action in the turn of a head, Rush developed an aesthetic which we today find extremely attractive, but which was at odds with the staid decorum of his neoclassic period. We have only to read the contemporaneous writings of Thomas Hope in England to understand the ac-

Fig. 58. Thomas Crawford (1814–1857). *Armed Freedom*, c. 1855. Plaster model, height 234 in. (594.4 cm.). Architect of the Capitol, Washington, D.C.

ronistic; it would have as little relevance in its aesthetic as in its medium to the course of later American developments.

This is no less true of his large allegorical pieces, but with them we must also consider the functions for which they were made. Any definition which attempts to distinguish between art and artisanry must be deficient, since all artisanry involves aesthetic judgments and all art serves some function and usually several. Yet, a consideration of motivation does harbor a kernel of truth in establishing distinctions here. Rush's large ideal works, whether ships' figureheads or the later, extant pieces by which he is today best known, were functional sculptures. *Wisdom* and *Justice* were rendered in a more permanent medium than the painted, canvas-covered triumphal arch for Philadelphia's festivities in celebration of Lafayette's return visit to America in 1824, which they were carved to adorn. Although meant for more substantial settings, *Comedy* and *Tragedy* and the *Schuylkill Improved* and *Waterworks* were created to decorate buildings that are no more. The function of such works was symbolic, not practical, and the virtues and truths they em-

Fig. 59. Hiram Powers (1805–1873). *Eve Tempted* or *Eve Before the Fall*, 1842. Marble, 68⅞ × 29⅞ × 20½ in. (174.9 × 75.9 × 52.1 cm.). National Museum of American Art (formerly National Collection of Fine Arts), Smithsonian Institution, Washington, D.C.; Museum Purchase in memory of Ralph Cross Johnson.

cepted and acceptable procedure in presenting the bust portrait. After allowing for the possibility of action in the movement of the body or in the turn of the head in a full-length figure, Hope insisted that:

if a mere bust, which we may easily view in every possible aspect, by ourselves moving around it, in place of being allowed to leave this task entirely to the beholder, be made itself to turn its face away from our sight, though it have not a body, to account for this less easy and less usual position of the head, the portrait loses all claim to naturalness and truth; it forfeits the appearance of dignified simplicity which is so essential and so fascinating for an air of inane and pompous affectation; and it moreover, from the different direction given to the face and to the chest, can seldom be so situated as not to look ill-placed and awkward.[29]

Such an approach to portrait sculpture in plaster or in wood as Rush took, then, was basically anach-

bodied were respected as permanent, universal ones, but the motivation for the works themselves was intimately involved with the function of the structures which they decorated. This was not untrue of some later, neoclassic sculpture; for example Thomas Crawford's *Armed Freedom* (fig. 58) atop the United States Capitol relates to the nature of the government functioning in the building beneath it. But neoclassic ideal statues such as Hiram Powers's various *Eves* (see fig. 59) or his *Fisher Boy* were adornments of beauty, not didactic allegories; if they embodied truths, and they usually did, it was because truth was beauty and beauty, truth. Their function was more private delectation than public edification, their destination was the art gallery, and their ancestry lay in the aesthetic monuments of classical antiquity.

Almost all the professional sculptors of the two generations after Rush sought that inspiration from antiquity on the soil of Italy, and those who did not would probably have been better off if they had. The many reasons for the attraction of Italy have been discussed often elsewhere, but it is worthwhile to point out what the expatriates had left behind. It was not only a young nation with an inadequate training ground and a paucity of classical monuments for inspiration; it was a land where sculpture had been regarded as commodity. When Greenough, Powers, and Thomas Crawford shipped out for the destinations of Rome and Florence, they were demonstrating that they were no longer "in the trade." They were joining the aristocracy of artists, attaching themselves to an honorable pedigree known to all cultured persons. The proof of this is found in the roles they played once settled in Italy. Abroad, they were regarded as distinguished citizens, and a visit to the studios of the American sculptors was *de rigueur* for the ever-increasing hoards of wealthy Americans making the Grand Tour, as was cataloguing those visits in the near-obligatory travel memoirs as among the status-enhancing advantages of foreign travel. Reading these, one often wonders how the expatriate sculptors ever had time to model and oversee sculptural production at all, with the constant social pressures upon them to which it was incumbent that they attend. The prevailing neoclassic methodology established the hired workmen as the enlargers, plaster-casters, and actual carvers, with the sculptor himself only preparing the original small clay model, supervising the total operation, and perhaps adding some finishing touches. Given

the sculptor's role as a lion in expatriate society, with its very real opportunities for commissions, no other methodology would have been possible. These Italian-based Americans operated on all levels in a manner both literally and figuratively foreign to the earlier "honest wood carver," William Rush.

That is not to say that Rush and/or his public saw his work as totally divorced from the grand tradition. Rather, it seems more likely that Rush shared with Charles Willson Peale a very democratic, New World belief in the universality of both the arts and of artistic ability, one that eschewed the concept of "genius." Proper training and a sincerity of interest and of faith in one's cultural and political institutions were the basic ingredients of a productive career in any field. Rush obviously did not see the need, nor feel the compulsion to travel abroad and ally his art or artisanship with European models; if there were any such contact it was sufficient for him to find his inspiration, as has been suggested, in the examples of French figureheads adorning vessels in Philadelphia's harbor. And again we are reminded by his son, through Dunlap, that "it was immaterial what the substance was" in which he worked. Rush's attitude was that of the *artisan*; for the true *sculptor* of Rush's day, medium, like theme, had a recognized, prescribed hierarchy which Rush appears to have ignored.

Rush's dependency upon classical and other prototypes is undefined and must probably for the most part remain unspecific. Attempts have been made particularly to assign sources for both individual features and aspects of expression and even entire poses to models which appear in *The Artist's Repository, or Encyclopedia of the Fine Arts*, the four-volume, 1808 London edition of which Rush is known to have owned. However, Rush's copy is annotated as having been purchased in 1812, and he certainly had mastered expression and developed a set repertory of anatomical definition before then. Henri Marceau has suggested that Rush utilized an illustration of the *River Nile* (fig. 60) from this publication for the pose of his *Schuylkill Improved* which is not unlikely, but depending upon what other illustrated books of classical art were available to him, there were many alternatives. Pietro Bellori's *Admiranda Romanarum Antiquitatum*, of 1693, included as plate 6 another very possible model (fig. 61), while plate 21 (fig. 62) might have contributed to Rush's conception of the companion, the *Waterworks*. Actually, another, slightly earlier edition of

Fig. 60. *River Nile*, 1808 [vol. 1, pl. 107, fig. 2, *The Artist's Repository, or Encyclopedia of the Fine Arts*, London]. Engraving. The Library Company of Philadelphia.

the *Artist's Repository*, entitled *Artist's Repository and Drawing Magazine*, published in London between 1785 and 1794, reproduced as plate 6 in volume 4 a river goddess as "a figure in a cumbent attitude," a model exceedingly close to Rush's conception. And his figure of *Tragedy* is posed not dissimilarly from the Vestal Virgin depicted in Domenico de Rossi's *Raccolta statue antiche e moderne*, published in Rome in 1704, a copy of which was in the Library Company of Philadelphia. D. Dodge Thompson has also pointed out that Rush's *Wisdom* and *Justice*, perhaps more properly *Mercy* and *Justice*, relate to the attributes of William Penn as defined in an engraving of 1770 by Pierre du Simitière, itself based upon one or more plates from James Gibbs's 1728 *Book of Architecture*, either or both of which Rush could have known.[30]

But such pose and motif-chasing may ultimately prove unproductive. On the one hand, the possible sources for Rush's sculptures from engraved book plates and even casts available at the Pennsylvania Academy were too numerous for specific identification, and on the other, there were natural poses and positions as well as traditional ones that did not necessarily require prototypes. The question of sources may, at least in part, simply come down to this: given a conception such as a reclining river god, for instance, which entails traditional conventions of anatomical disposition, how many natural positions can be found for the alignment of body, head, and limbs?

Rush created sculpture as we conceive of it today,

but was he so recognized in his own time? And in historical perspective, was his role as our first sculptor regularly accepted? Rush was certainly a more talented artisan than his fellow figurehead carvers in the first years of the nineteenth century, such as the various members of the Skillin family or Joseph Wilson who carved dozens of polychromed figures of illustrious men and women from Biblical, American, and world history to adorn the grounds of "Lord" Timothy Dexter's house in Newburyport.[31] But even today, laudatory comments upon Rush's talents and his carvings, such as those by Wayne Craven in his 1968 *Sculpture in America*, recognize more the Philadelphian's aspirations to move from artisan to artist, and see his work as "the culmination of the native American wood carving tradition . . . representing the apex of this movement [yet] his work was also its swan song. . . ."[32]

In earlier times, testimonials to Rush's superior abilities at figurehead carving abound. Similar recommendations of his talents as a sculptor either of portrait busts or public monuments were, in his own lifetime and afterwards, relatively few and even so, often qualified. In 1807, just the year before Rush appeared in the guise of public sculptor with his *Comedy* and *Tragedy* for the New Theatre, George Clymer, the president of the Pennsylvania Academy, presented an address at the Academy to announce the acquisition of casts of the most celebrated statuary in Europe. While making mention of Benjamin West, John Singleton Copley, Gilbert Stuart, and John Trumbull, neither Rush nor Peale

Fig. 61. Giovanni Pietro Bellori (c. 1615–1696). Detail of *Iudaici Triumphi Pompa ac Ferculum cum Simulacro Lacus Genesar*. Pl. 6 in *Admiranda Romanarum Antiquitatum*, 1693. Engraving. The New York Public Library, Astor, Lenox and Tilden Foundations.

figured in Clymer's discourse; indeed Clymer pointed out in regard to the classical heritage of artistry embodied in the surrounding casts taken from the masterpieces of antiquity that:

some indeed, there are, among us, who have a professional acquaintance with such subjects—but these are few, and the rest, not particularly instructed, are, I trust, not inclined to supply the defect of science by the affectation of taste or the cant of connoisseurship: their business is not to offer the proofs of any present skill, but to lay the foundation, to furnish the means of the future attainment. . . .[33]

One presumes that if William Rush had occurred to Clymer as one of Philadelphia's "few" with professional acquaintance with the traditions embodied in such classical sculpture he would have been so mentioned.

Given his role in the founding of the Columbianum in Philadelphia in 1794, it is strange that Rush did not exhibit any of his sculpture in the one exhibition held by that organization the following year—if he saw himself in the role of sculptor. This suggests that even his bust of Joseph Wright [38] was modeled afterwards and was, therefore, a posthumous image, and that Rush did not regard his figureheads as "art" to be exhibited. With the placement of the *Water Nymph and Bittern* in Centre Square in 1809 and the inauguration of annual exhibitions of the Society of Artists at the Pennsylvania Academy two years later, Rush's works were more regularly visible, and offered to view as works of art, particularly during the years 1811 to 1817 when Rush participated quite regularly in the Acad-

Fig. 62. Giovanni Pietro Bellori. Detail of *Via Traiana*. Pl. 21 in *Admiranda Romanarum Antiquitatum*, 1693. Engraving. The New York Public Library, Astor, Lenox and Tilden Foundations.

emy exhibitions and with a good many works of various themes, portraits and ideal pieces.

The *American Daily Advertiser* took notice only of Rush's *Winter* in its review of the first annual exhibition held at the Academy as a work done in wood, "the material which he so happily models into every curve of female elegance for ship's heads."[34] While *The Port Folio* magazine did not review the first annual exhibition of 1811, Benjamin Latrobe's anniversary oration before the Society of Artists, of which body Rush was a founding member, was printed in the magazine that year. It is usually quoted to indicate the high contemporary regard for Rush's work and that, indeed, is contained therein. But the remarks need to be evaluated for Latrobe's meaning. Latrobe was speaking about American artistic accomplishment, and he boasted that "we already rival Europe in portraits and in engravings." Rather than make any similar, and therefore exaggerated claims for American sculptural achievements, he followed the above with: "Commerce has called for beauty in the forms and decorations of her ships, and where in Europe is there a Rush. Let the national legislature honour the hero or statesman of the revolution with busts; and sculptors will not be wanting—the genius which under exotic influence has given so high a rank to the American pencil of a West, Copley, Trumbull, and Vanderline [*sic*], would under domestic patronage not refuse to inspire the American chisel."[35]

Latrobe clearly distinguished here between true sculpture, works of national commemorative purpose, and the utilitarian, artisan decoration of commercial vessels in which field he among many acknowledged Rush as supreme. In fact, Latrobe appended a long footnote to his comments on Rush:

Mr. William Rush, of Philadelphia, is at the head of a branch of the arts which he has himself created. His figures, forming the head or prow of a vessel, place him, in the excellence of his *attitudes and action*, among the best sculptors that have existed; and in the proportion and drawing of his figures he is often far above mediocrity and seldom below it. The rules of design by which the figures of Mr. Rush are to be judged require a considerable latitude. The great object is general effect.—In this he succeeds beyond competition. High finish would be misplaced. The constrained attitude of a figure on the prow of a ship would appear an insuperable difficulty. With him it is nothing. In looking at his figures in general it would appear that his attitudes were those of choice; so little do they embarrass him. There is a *notion* in his figures that is inconceivable. They seem rather to draw the ship after them than to be impelled by the vessel. Many are of exquisite beauty. I have not seen one on which there is not

the stamp of genius. But his element is the water. Ashore, his figures want repose, and that which is his highest excellence afloat becomes a fault.—The ships'-heads of Rush, engraved, would form an invaluable work.[36]

Not only is there considerable qualification here in regard to Rush's Philadelphia public monuments, but it is suggested that the aesthetic of his figure-heads is exactly *in*appropriate for those public works—their breadth, their sense of movement and action, just as the prescription for proper bust portraits laid down by Thomas Hope was violated in Rush's examples of portraiture.

In the 1811 exhibition at the Academy, Rush showed his terracotta portrait of Joseph Wright, and two wood pieces, a bust of *A Citizen* [46] and *Winter* [45]. The following year his representation was much more extensive, his *Exhortation*, *Praise*, and the *Cherubim Encircled by a Glory* [52, 53, 54], all for St. Paul's Church; wood busts of Linnaeus [56], William Bartram [57], and the Reverend Henry Ernest Muhlenberg [55]; and the wood figure of *Agriculture* designed for the Schuylkill bridge [50]. Of this last, a reviewer in *The Port Folio* commented:

This subject is executed in bass [*sic*] relief, and produces a very bold and striking effect, and does much credit to this very meritorious and well known artist. In reviewing the works of this truly American sculptor, it is but fair to remark that he has been confined to a particular branch, namely, the figure heads of ships and other ornamental work in naval architecture, in the execution of which he has been limited, both as to time and price.—The nature of such ornaments require that they should be executed in a bold manner, so as to appear with their appendages to the best advantage, and we will venture to say that no man in any country has ever surpassed Mr. Rush in this department of sculpture. His works have travelled with American commerce, all over the world, and are justly appreciated abroad, as well as at home; and we have no hesitation in giving it our decided opinion that, if his studies had been directed to the higher branches of art, with proper opportunities, he would have rivalled the most eminent sculptors of the present age. We are gratified that Mr. Rush begins to employ his chisel on subjects more durable and more likely to perpetuate his fame, than those he has in general hitherto executed.[37]

Yes, his new subjects were, indeed, more durable, though it seems not the figure of *Agriculture*, which, along with its companion, *Commerce*, were destroyed in a fire in 1875 along with the bridge they decorated. But the praise is for the nature of his subjects, not a new and more appropriate approach to sculpture. The reviewer's highest commendation again is given in regard to Rush's work done for American commerce, defined as ornamentation and requiring a bold, not subtle, manner, one not compatible with "the higher branches of his art." For all its fulsome praise, the review was basically an apologia; a comment in the review concerned the works for St. Paul's, that they were done "in a very masterly style" and "are intended as ornaments for a splendid organ," again suggesting inspired artisanry, not sculptural genius.

In 1813, Rush exhibited only his three terracotta busts of noted Philadelphia doctors, Benjamin Rush [49], Philip Syng Physick [60], and Caspar Wistar [59]. *The Port Folio* reviewer, unfortunately, did not have time nor space to go into the art displayed in the Antique Saloon of the Academy to any length, and he dismissed the sculpture with: "There are two beautiful busts in marble by Ceracchi. Several excellent models by Rush."[38] Even so, there is a distinction to be noted here. Ceracchi's works are defined as busts, Rush's as models; the former are thus seen as completed works of art, the latter as at a stage toward becoming works of art. And as such each garnered an appropriate adjective: as models, Rush's pieces were "excellent," commendatory for Rush and the stage at which he had arrived. Ceracchi's busts (of Washington and Franklin) were "beautiful," an aesthetic evaluation of the works themselves and intrinsic to them.

During these same years, several Philadelphia magazines published articles on the progress of the fine arts in the United States. One, which appeared in 1810 in *The Port Folio*, was a published address delivered by George Murray before the Society of Artists, but neither Rush nor the art of sculpture are mentioned.[39] In a similar but longer article that appeared in the *Analectic Magazine* in 1815, again, painting, engraving, and architecture are mentioned, but the author was strangely silent in regard to sculpture.[40] Nor did the situation abate in the many published discourses that continued to be presented before the various art academies such as that by De Witt Clinton, delivered before the American Academy of the Arts in 1816, or those offered to the same body by Gulian Verplanck in 1824, by William Beach Lawrence and Richard Ray in 1825, or M. Charles Paterson in 1826. And Rush was not mentioned, or remembered either, in his native Philadelphia in the discourses of Henry D. Gilpin in 1826, George W. Bethune in 1840, or Henry Reed in 1849.[41]

Richard Ray's address of 1825 is particularly sig-

nificant for our treatment of the state of sculpture in America at the time because, after discussing classical sculpture, Ray went on to state:

Let us hope that our country too may soon produce native Sculptors, to delineate in marble or bronze the features of those who are arising, or have arisen, to serve it; that our cities may not want the decorations so classical and so useful in their associations to freedom—nor our young men, the powerful incentives to lives of virtue, in the prospect of similar honours.[42]

Ray's call for sculpture in the classical tradition, works carved in marble or cast in bronze, was just at that time being answered by John Frazee and then Hezekiah Augur at home, and by Horatio Greenough who, in that very year, made his first voyage to Italy to begin to create an art allied with the classical past and the neoclassic present. When reviewers and critics began to discuss the actualities of American sculptural achievements rather than the prospects of the future, it was to such artists as these that they looked. Daniel Fanshaw followed his aforementioned discussion of the nature of the sculptural process in the *United States Review and Literary Gazette* in 1827 with a discussion of several portrait busts exhibited at the National Academy by Frazee, Augur, and Washington Allston's disciple John Cogdell of Charleston, South Carolina, even while lamenting that "there is nothing in the present exhibition in the higher departments of sculpture," i.e., ideal representations.[43] Two years later, in May of 1829, in the *American Monthly Magazine* published in Boston, the earliest significant article on "Sculpture and Sculptors in the United States" was published as a preamble to an introduction to Hezekiah Augur, although the writer wrote in a footnote that: "Mr. Augur is as yet but in the outset of his pursuit, and in such distinction as he has attained to, cannot be said to be alone. Mr. Frazer [*sic*], so far as he has gone, is respected as an artist; and Mr. Greenough has, even thus early given high promise of successful talent. The latter gentleman is now in Italy."[44] But no mention of William Rush.

Rush was discussed briefly by William Dunlap in his momentous compendium on the history of American art, published in 1834, the year after Rush's death. Even there, Rush's son acknowledged to Dunlap that "it was always a source of regret that he had so little time spared him from his occupation in ship carving where he succeeded so admirably."[45] In addition to Rush's absence from the general discussions of the state of the arts in America in the various published addresses mentioned above, Rush's name is also absent in the first American histories of art (as opposed to histories of American art) which were inaugurated with Benson J. Lossing's *History of the Fine Arts* in 1840. Not surprisingly, these books began to appear when the inclusion of a historical American section was viable. Lossing, for instance, makes mention of Horatio Greenough, although Miss Ludlow in her volume of ten years later only speaks of American painting and architecture, and foregoes a discussion of sculpture in this country.[46] The first American book devoted solely to the history of sculpture was published by Pickering Dodge that same year, 1850, as a companion to his *Art of Painting* of 1846. Dodge concluded his tome with a discussion of sculpture in the United States, writing about the works decorating the United States Capitol and other public monuments, speaking of Greenough, Hiram Powers, and Thomas Crawford, and including a detailed discussion of the short-lived Shobal Clevenger.[47] Rush was ignored. Rather, Rush was to be found in print in the successive editions of John Fanning Watson's *Annals of Philadelphia*. Again, however, Watson found Rush deserving of commendation "as a ship carver. In his skill in his art he surpasses any other American, and probably any other ship carver in the world!" Watson repeated this encomium in the section of the *Annals* concerned with "Ships and Shipbuilding," stating that "we may justly congratulate ourselves on having had the ablest ship-carver in the late and aged William Rush, that the world has ever seen."[48]

Rush remained peripheral to serious historical consideration of American sculptural developments. Henry T. Tuckerman in 1867 noted Rush's modeling in clay after mentioning native sculptural involvement only in figurehead carving, but this was preliminary to extended discussions of the work of Frazee and Augur.[49] It was twelve years later, in *Harper's New Monthly Magazine*, that Samuel Benjamin became the first historian to consider Rush "a man of genius" rather than a talented wood-carver, and Benjamin was speaking not only of Rush's figureheads but also of his portrait busts and the *Water Nymph and Bittern*.[50] The date of these articles, 1879, is significant—Benjamin's series of articles on American art in *Harper's* were assembled into his *Art in America* published the following year—for Benjamin's was the first American art history survey

to appear after the Philadelphia Centennial with its retrospective and nostalgic look back into America's past.

One year earlier, Rush had been ignored in William J. Clark's *Great American Sculptures*, but far more significantly, his achievements and his history were enshrined a year before, 1877, in the first of Thomas Eakins's completed paintings depicting *William Rush Carving His Allegorical Figure of the Schuylkill River* (fig. 63).[51] It is not improbable that Eakins's picture and its subsequent exhibition in New York City at the first exhibition of the Society of American Artists in 1878 may have been the impetus for Benjamin's assessment of Rush and his singling out of the statue of the *Nymph*. The Society's exhibition catalogue had stated that: "William Rush, ship carver, was called on to make a statue for a fountain at Central Square, on the completion of the first Water Works of Philadelphia. A celebrated belle consented to pose for him, and the wooden statue he made now stands in Fairmount Park, one of the earliest and best of American statues."[52]

Eakins's involvement with the history and legend of William Rush is beyond the scope of this essay. Suffice it here to say that both appeared as artist-pioneers in their mutual native city; both were involved with sculpture, although Eakins was only peripherally so, and both had to battle opposition to their concern with the nude figure as a vehicle for artistic expression. In that regard, it may not be insignificant to Eakins's inspiration for the Rush theme that Louisa Vanuxem, Rush's model for the *Nymph*, died at an advanced age in 1874, the year before Eakins began to work on his painting. Eakins's picture is a late and very American example in the long series in Western art of painters and sculptors creating scenes from the lives of earlier artists whom they admired and emulated.[53] Eakins depicts Rush in elegant, rather than workingman's, dress of the Federal era, but shows him as humble craftsman. His workspace is an artisan's shop, not an artist's studio, and designs for ship carvings taken from a now lost sketchbook of the artist are included in the rear of the workroom. Eakins's lack of concern for historical accuracy can be demonstrated in his inclusion of Rush's later statues of Washington of 1815, and the *Schuylkill Improved* and *Waterworks* of 1825, while working on the earlier *Nymph* of 1809. Eakins here commemorates not only an illustrious predecessor but a significant moment in

Fig. 63. Thomas Eakins (1844–1916). *William Rush Carving His Allegorical Figure of the Schuylkill River*, 1877. Oil on canvas, 20⅛ × 26½ in. (51.1 × 67.3 cm.). Philadelphia Museum of Art; Given by Mrs. Thomas Eakins and Miss Mary A. Williams.

the history of art in Philadelphia when native crafts-manship became national sculpture. This was in part the retrospective message of the Philadelphia Centennial where Rush's own terracotta bust of Washington was exhibited, which confirmed the artist's own historic role.

Even with the pictorial notice by Eakins, fol-lowed by the historical appreciation of Benjamin, Rush was accorded scant consideration during the rest of the century. The earliest article specifically devoted to his life and career was written by E. Leslie Gilliams, a writer on early history, but not art history; this appeared in *Lippincott's Monthly Magazine* in 1893.[54] It would be almost thirty years later, in June of 1921, that another article would be devoted specifically to Rush, again written by a

historian of local Philadelphia issues, Wilfred Jor-dan, but by then such a disquisition on Rush would be published in an art journal, *Art and Archaeol-ogy*.[55]

Rush's rise to historical recognition in the annals of American sculpture is quite clearly traced in the writings of Lorado Taft, the important Chicago sculptor who was also one of the leading lecturers and historians on art at the turn of the century and an important figure in the popularization of the arts, particularly in the Midwest, through the Central Art Association in Chicago. Taft wrote on "Amer-ican Sculpture and Sculptors" in *The Chautauquan* in January of 1896 but did not deal with any early developments in this country.[56] Four years later, in *The Fine Arts*, a series of university lessons pub-

Fig. 64. Hiram Powers. *The Greek Slave*, 1843. Marble, height without base 65½ in. (166.4 cm.). Yale University Art Gallery, New Haven; Olive Louise Dann Fund.

lished in Chicago by the International Art Association, Taft wrote the section concerning "Sculpture of the Nineteenth Century." In dealing with "American Sculpture" in Lessons 10 through 12, he broadened his earlier treatment to consider a retrospective survey, but only back to John Frazee.[57] It was finally in his monumental and pioneering *History of American Sculpture*, published in 1903, that Taft considered Rush. While relying upon

Dunlap for his initial information, Taft presented detailed analyses of the *Water Nymph and Bittern* and the "pine-knot" *Self-Portrait* [90].[58] Taft did, however, distinguish between Rush's achievements and those of "professional sculptors" and, while admiring his talent, really concluded that Rush's influence counted for more than his art. That is, in his activities in founding several Philadelphia art organizations, in exhibiting contemporary, native sculpture at the Pennsylvania Academy, and in uniting artistic activity with public service, Rush defined the artist's role within the community.

Only with the publication of Taft's definitive volume was William Rush finally enshrined in the annals of American art, though often not without some condescension or disclaimer. Adeline Adams, in her 1923 *The Spirit of American Sculpture*, acknowledged that such works as Rush's "show Yankee ingenuity rather than Promethean fire. The inventive spirit is part of our pioneer heritage. . . ." She also perceptively noted that Rush's emphasis upon discerning the final form in the original block—in this case the piece of wood—conformed to "Michelangelo's Gothic creed, somewhat outworn among sculptors," but she observed that this creed had regained respect.[59] Certainly further explanation for the growing regard for and interest in Rush's work lay not only in the new concern for the medium of wood in the 1920s and 1930s, but also in the belief in direct carving—the "Gothic creed" described by Adams. Chandler Rathfon Post had two years earlier begun his American section of *A History of European and American Sculpture* with an introduction to Patience Wright and to William Rush, though rather than extolling Rush's "pioneer heritage" and "Yankee ingenuity," Post found that:

The production of these early American sculptors, Rush included, does not definitely belong to any school but is the result of the poor conglomerate artistic education that they could pick up in this remote country from prints, casts, or the very few examples of European sculpture that they chanced to see. They had to work out their own style but even in the United States they already fell more or less under the influence of the neoclassic movement. Rush's feminine allegorical figures are as neoclassic as they are anything, but the woodcarver's technique gives them a rococo "fussiness" and projection of the folds. The personifications of Tragedy and Comedy at the Actor's Home in the suburbs of Philadelphia, awkward in gesture and humorously unsuccessful in attempts at expression in the countenance, reveal what difficulties the sculptors had in offsetting the lack of that schooling which in European countries made it possible for even mediocre artists to produce tolerable statues.[60]

Adams and Post, in their contrasting treatment of Rush in the early 1920s, suggest the divergent points of view toward his art, that of nativist appreciation or cosmopolitan denigration. In the literature of the first three decades of the twentieth century, Rush was never acknowledged as a predecessor in American art in more specialized treatment of sculptural themes in which he had early participated—the creation of ecclesiastical monuments [41, 47], of angelic forms [52, 53, 54], or of fountain sculpture [35][61]—but in the abundant discussions of the figurehead, Rush is ever present.[62] Likewise, Rush figures prominently in several articles on early wood sculpture and portraiture which appeared in the late 1920s—again almost certainly stimulated, in part at least, by the revival of interest in the sculptural medium of wood.[63] And the aforementioned article on Rush by Wilfred Jordan, published in 1921, concludes with: "It is impossible to find in America better expressions of the woodworker's art than the work of this genius who may be truthfully called the earliest native-born American sculptor."[64]

Sixteen years later, at the Pennsylvania Museum of Art (now the Philadelphia Museum of Art), Henri Marceau organized the first exhibition of the work of William Rush, significantly repeating Jordan's identification in his subtitle, *The First Native American Sculptor*.[65] Rush was that, but only from a circumscribed viewpoint, at least in regard to contemporary conceptions of sculpture—what it was, how it was created, and the functions it was to serve and express. Rush's neglect for decades after his death and the hesitant approach to identifying his historic place until the modern era were not merely a matter of historic or aesthetic obtuseness. For the aesthetic goals and ideals of the several generations which followed his activity, Rush offered nothing of a role model, and his work could provide no inspiration at all. Whether this substitution of neoclassic idealism for native ingenuity was aesthetically desirable is really beside the point; it was a cultural necessity. Different generations with changing aesthetic preconceptions will evaluate these separate artistic directions and predilections variously, though we are gradually shedding the nativist ideology which enjoined even so perceptive a scholar as J. Meredith Neil to write recently of Rush that:

Consciously ignoring neoclassic dogma, his carvings should have planted the seed of a virile and truly indigenous American sculpture. Unfortunately, the public had already been too thoroughly indoctrinated with the notion that "Art" in sculpture could only be in marble, and so they failed to see Rush's work as an American version of the traditional art of sculpture. . . . Accordingly, several generations of would-be American sculptors sedulously copied the styles and subjects of Europeans, leaving Rush's example for those anonymous craftsmen who decorated circus wagons and carved cigar-store Indians.[66]

Horatio Greenough's marmorean *George "Jupiter" Washington* and Hiram Powers's *Greek Slave* (fig. 64) may, indeed, testify to stronger foreign influences and more complete absorption into the neoclassic aesthetic than does the *Water Nymph and Bittern*, but they bespeak the new nation's more complete cultural aspirations than does the work of the inspired Philadelphia wood-carver. The very controversies the former sculptures engendered, of classical appropriateness in national interpretation, or the question of the propriety of nudity, were as much or more germain to the ethos of the striving young republic than the enthusiasm of the dockside crowds for William Rush's figureheads. The latter were, and are, significant monuments of material culture; the former are "Art."

Toolmarks and Fingerprints:
A Technical Discussion

VIRGINIA NORTON NAUDÉ

WILLIAM RUSH was trained as a ship carver, and throughout his long career, he worked on figureheads and stern ornaments as well as sculptures for individuals and organizations in Philadelphia. Wood was his foremost sculptural material, but when he was fifty-five, he began exhibiting terracotta portrait busts, from several of which he made and sold plaster casts. As a founder of the Pennsylvania Academy of the Fine Arts, he was certainly aware of contemporary European work and probably well informed about the various materials and techniques available to sculptors at that time. He never worked in marble, and although at least once he considered casting in "mettle," the project never materialized.[1] That he worked in wood, terracotta, and plaster shows that these were his choices of mediums, the ones in which he felt most comfortable and in which he anticipated success.

The present technical study of Rush began at the Pennsylvania Academy in 1979 with the conservation of his work in the permanent collection. Since then his sculptures in other collections have been examined, and a number have been brought to the Academy for conservation. The observations are up to date, but investigations will continue during the exhibition and findings will be placed in the Academy's Archives. The following discussion is the result of the combined interests and participation of the Academy's curators, conservators, conservation apprentices, and sculpture faculty and students.

Wood

Rush used *Pinus strobus* (eastern white pine) for all of his carvings with only four known exceptions. This softwood was cheap, accessible, quick and easy to carve, and relatively light for its volume. The general American use of pine for figureheads follows the English custom: a Royal Navy Board order of 1742 required ships to ease superfluous weight, so pine replaced oak as the main wood for ship carvings. It was not very durable, however, and there are numerous recorded examples of pine ship carvings having to be replaced because of rot even after only twenty years of service.[2] It also explains the loss of so much of Rush's work over the years. He may have turned at the end of his career to *Cedrela ororata* (Spanish cedar) for the three figures at the Fairmount Waterworks because he had witnessed weather destruction of some of his own pine carvings. Then readily available in Philadelphia, Spanish cedar is in the mahogany family, a reddish hardwood native to tropical America and the West Indies.[3] It was considerably more expensive than pine but superior in its resistance to rot. It is lightweight but cohesive and easier to carve than pine because it is more finely ringed and even textured, is less resinous, and has a firm, non-splintering resistance to the chisel. The single known example of Rush's carving in a dense hardwood is the small, cherry *Commemorative Statuette* [34].

Ship Carvings and Other Outdoor Sculpture

Of the forty-three figureheads Rush is thought to have carved, only three are known to have survived. They are all constructed solid in the traditional manner: *Benjamin Rush* [72] is made from one piece of wood; *Peace* [29] is made from one large block with small additions in a few places where the design projects outward, such as the left kneecap and foot; the joinery of *Benjamin Franklin* [73] is masked by at least fourteen layers of paint but the object appears to be made of a large piece of wood in the center front with blocks of various sizes added at the sides and in the back. Strength of basic structure was the prime requirement of a figurehead that had to withstand the rigors of life at sea, which are indicated by the severely weathered condition of *Benjamin Rush*.

The figures Rush carved solid for display indoors are helpful in filling in the sketchy picture of his work in ship carving. Figures in the round, *Virtue* [42], *Exhortation* [52], *Praise* [53], and *Silence* [87], were conceived in large volumes with details that can be read at a distance. If the bases and backs had been worked differently, they could have served as figureheads. A high relief like the Academy's *Eagle* [37] could have been a stern ornament with only slight changes in the mounting. The relief carvings *Faith* [84] and *Hope* [85] could have been taken almost as they are and placed on a taffrail.

The three sculptures that Rush completed in the 1820s for the Fairmount Waterworks are also related to his work on ships because of their sturdy construction and surface treatment. *Allegory of the Schuylkill River in Its Improved State* [96], *Allegory of the Waterworks* [97], and *Mercury* [99] had to withstand all kinds of weather, and all were painted; a bill details the protective treatment the *Allegories*

received: "to Geo. Swope/May 7 1825 to Painting the figurs five Coats/$10."[4]

Maintenance of ship carvings and outdoor wood sculpture was obviously a problem. Ship figureheads were probably caulked, like the vessels themselves, with oakum and putty. Wood strips were probably used also for repairs, set into cracks with a putty made of whiting and linseed oil. White lead was often added to putty, as it was to various glues (casein, fish, and animal), to increase water resistance. White lead was also used in paint, and the objects were painted repeatedly.

Paint was clearly not enough protection for Rush's most famous outdoor monument, the fountain *Allegory of the Schuylkill River* [35]. The sculpture must have been drilled through to receive a water pipe leading upward into the beak of the bittern, so the wood was attacked both by moisture traveling inside the boring and by water on the surface. It is not surprising that the figure deteriorated badly; only the head survives and the sculpture is known today through a bronze cast taken in 1872.

Because of the few surviving examples of outdoor sculpture and ship carvings, the following discussion of Rush's working methods draws heavily on surviving examples which were conceived for display indoors or in the protected space of an architectural niche. The techniques he employed were probably very similar.

Joinery

Rush usually worked life-size or slightly larger. The figurehead of *Peace* [29] was taken from a solid pine block, six feet high by two feet in diameter. For figures such as *Wisdom* and *Justice* [61, 62], he used a central block the entire height and then added pieces of pine for arms which projected out from the body. Rush typically attached pieces of wood together with a simple butt join secured with at least three machine-cut nails or brads[5] driven in at different angles, as illustrated in the X-radiograph of the right arm of *Justice* (fig. 65). The nails were hammered below surface and the holes were filled. Glue was not used in the joins, but where the pieces of wood did not fit flush, a filler was used to even the surface prior to nailing. In figure 65 the density of the X-radiograph in the join area indicates the presence of lead in the filling composition. The Academy's *Eagle* [37] was constructed in a similar

Fig. 65. *Justice* [62]. X-radiograph of the right arm showing a typical Rush join filled with putty and secured with nails driven in at various angles and set below surface. A patch in the arm replaced faulty wood.

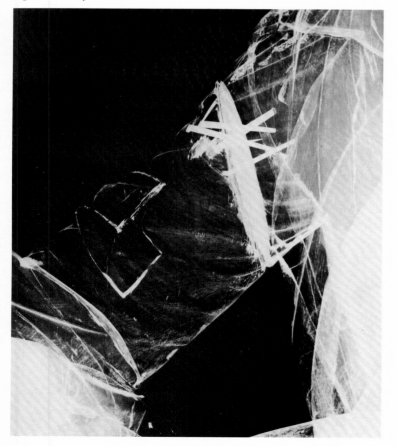

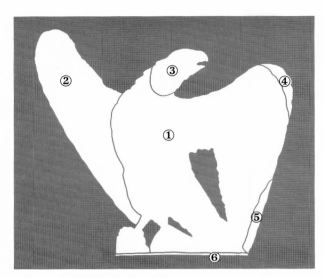

Fig. 66. *Eagle* [37]. Diagram showing the object's construction out of six pieces of pine. The central section, piece number 1, is 26½ inches high, 25 inches wide, and 6½ inches deep. Piece 6 stabilizes the delicate parts that are carved out of the massive block at a point where strength is essential. Piece 2 is attached behind the central section and pieces 3, 4, and 5 are placed forward from it.

manner (fig. 66), as was the sculpture of *George Washington* [68].[6] The only exception to the use of a flat butt join is found in *Mercury* [99] where a cap formed by the wood in the right shoulder protects the attached raised right arm, serving as a cleat to prevent movement. The join is secured with three nails.

Rush used hand-wrought nails, in addition to the machine-cut brad whose profile is clearly defined in figure 65. Nails were more expensive and sparingly used, probably saved for places where their superior clinching ability was required.[7] Rush used hand-wrought nails of all sizes in his various sculptures, and many are slightly bent, most likely either previously used or adapted for a particular application (fig. 67).

These nailed joins have not proven terribly strong, and many have had to be repaired over the years. Examples of repair can be found on the two shoulder joins to the body of *Wisdom*. X-radiographs show the shadows of dowels or pegs, and there is total absence of nails. Traces of putty have been removed to make a clean new mend. Henri Marceau noted that the arms of *Comedy* and *Tragedy* [31, 32] were attached by means of sockets and wooden pins.[8]

These sculptures have not been available for examination, but Marceau was probably describing a repair rather than an original join.

Many joins were not repaired as carefully as those on *Wisdom*. A quicker solution to a weak join was often found by driving in additional hardware, and a number of X-radiographs show a buried collection of hand-wrought nails, machine-cut brads, modern wire nails, and screws.

Patches

In figure 65 the outline of a wooden patch in the upper arm of *Justice* is clearly visible in the X-radiograph thanks to the outline formed by traces of lead white paint in the crevices. Rush made extensive use of patches to fill holes where knots or imperfections in the wood were removed. No patches were removed for examination but they, like the plugs in the heads of the figures, must have been set in with glue because the X-radiographs show neither nails nor the putty filler used in joins. Patches are usually, though not always, inserted with their grain running with the grain of the main block, but it is unusual for the patch to have the same quality

Fig. 67. Shadows of nails and screws recorded on X-radiograph film from (groups from left to right) *Eagle* [37], *Wisdom* [61], *Benjamin Franklin* [2], and *Anatomical models* [33]. The size of the shadow varies with the distance of the film from the metal. Broken lines indicate an interruption of the image on the film.

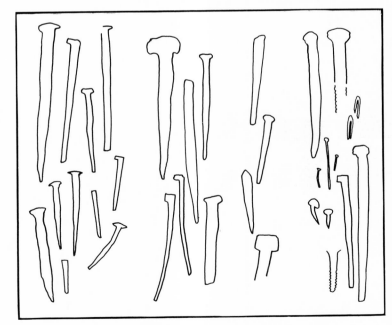

Fig. 68. Development of checks in cut timber. External cracks travel inward and heartchecks travel outward. Rush often prepared the logs he used for sculpture to avoid the problems of cracking.

and color as the wood around it. Thus visually disturbing rough areas on the sculptured wood surface, and patches not set entirely flush can be explained by the sculptor's anticipation that irregularities would be masked with gesso,[9] and painted for the final effect toward which he was working. His first concern in constructing the figures was the stability and durability of the blocked wood.

Excavation Techniques

Rush was capable of working in a much more sophisticated manner than the idiom of ship carvings required. He took pride in preparing timber so that over time the object would undergo minimal distortion and cracking. He wrote the following lines—the best surviving fragment of technical information from his pen—to President Madison to describe the life-size statue of *George Washington* [68]:

The figure is executed in wood well seasoned, the interior is all hollow, so that air circulates through the inside, and leaves nothing to ferment and rot, nor yet to rent, for it is not more than three inches on an average in thickness, is perfectly seasoned and saturated with oil—with such preparations it would (particularly under cover from the weather) stand the test of a century at least.[10]

We know of no other instance in which Rush carved a full-size figure in the round and hollowed it out. It was important for him to carve this piece in the round because he intended to make a mold from it and sell freestanding plaster casts.[11]

Many of Rush's monumental wood figures were excavated on one side of the log to prevent checking (fig. 68).[12] The two large horizontal figures for the waterworks [96, 97] have hollows underneath. Some vertical figures are three-quarters round (*Comedy* and *Tragedy* [31, 32], *Wisdom* and *Justice* [61, 62]) and are partially excavated on the back sides in a manner worked out so as not to interrupt the design. In the figures of *Wisdom* and *Justice* Rush took an additional precaution against checking by position-

Fig. 69. *Justice* [62]. Heartwood has been removed behind the head and the log has been deeply excavated.

ing the center of the log behind the head so that he could remove the heartwood (fig. 69).

When *Wisdom* and *Justice* were placed on top of the grandest of the triumphal arches erected for Lafayette's visit to Philadelphia in 1824, they were adapted for temporary display in the round by applying canvas over the excavated areas and presumably painting it white to match the surfaces of the sculptures; tacks which held the canvas are still there (see [61, 62]).

Plugs

Rush's preparation of timber for minimal distortion over time can be seen in his handling of the wood portrait bust of *Samuel Morris*, made for the Citizens of the State in Schuylkill in 1812 [48]. The bust is excavated from the back and the head is hollowed out. The head is centered on the heartwood, which was removed at the top of the head and a plug inserted (fig. 70). The plug was presumably secured by glue because no nails are present. The surface on top of the head was gessoed and painted so that traces of this procedure are scarcely visible.

Plugs are found also in the heads of the full-length *George Washington* [68] and the bust of *Benjamin Rush* [72]. The former must have been used to release heartwood tension or patch a fault. The latter, used on a solid object, is very shallow and may have repaired damage caused by a clamp that held the wood in place during carving. In discussions of American eighteenth- and nineteenth-century carving, it is often suggested that plugs in the head enabled oil to be routinely introduced inside the sculpture to preserve the wood. This was surely not the reason for the plug in *Samuel Morris* because the object is hollowed out and could have been treated from behind. In the case of the full-figure *Washington*, the joinery and filling methods that will be discussed shortly would not have produced an oil-tight container. Further, it is unlikely that oil would have been poured in and the sculpture then rolled around upside down in order to coat the cavity walls of the six-foot monument. Thus Rush appears to have used plugs in the head only to improve the surface or increase structural stability.

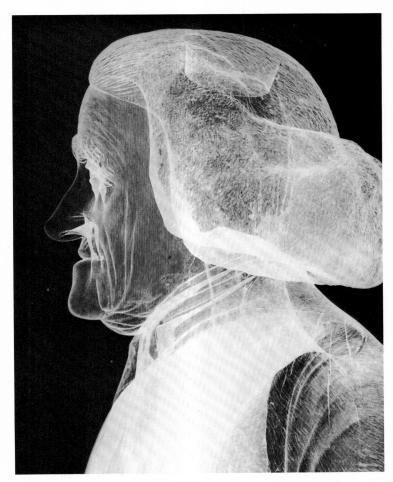

Fig. 70. *Samuel Morris* [48]. X-radiograph. A plug is inserted in the hole at the top of the head from which heartwood was removed to prevent checking.

Anatomical Models

During the conservation of two carved anatomical models [33], Rush's joinery and finishing techniques could be well studied. The general shape of each of the models, which were made for Dr. Wistar's use in lectures at the University of Pennsylvania Medical School, is elaborately constructed from small pieces of wood nailed together. A lime putty was used to fill gaps and define shapes, and the surface was gessoed and painted. A variety of other materials were also used: On the *Right maxilla*, a thin, weak area was strengthened by attaching a thin lead plate on each side. These are similar to three lead plates used on the life-size *George Washington*, one behind his left elbow and two on his left leg. However, Rush's use of linen saturated with animal glue and applied to strengthen wood parts which needed to be very thin is unique to the anatomical models, as is his use of leather and papier-mâché for creating the small parts that represent arteries, muscles, and nerves. The hardware is varied and inconsistent; Rush made little attempt to match the thumbscrews or the metal plates which guide and receive them. He appears to have used whatever was around in the shop, from springs through all different kinds and sizes of nails and screws, even to straight sewing pins. Inside the model of the *Left temporal bone* he left what may well be a sample from his workbench—loose wood shavings, metal filings, and pieces of putty. The *Temporal bone* was made with imagination and ingenuity, and also very quickly. There are no signs of reworking or adjustment during construction. Rush depended heavily on putty (chalk and limestone in oil) to fill gaps between wood blocks and to smooth down rough edges to form the anatomical contours. The putty is sometimes applied as thickly as five-eighths of an inch and takes on the character of a sculptural material in its own right.

Gesso and Paint

Rush customarily prepared his wood surfaces for painting by applying a gesso (whiting in a non-oil binder). On several objects the gesso is used thickly enough to add dimension to the carved detail on the surface, as on the hair of *Samuel Morris* or the feathers of the Academy's *Eagle*. The sculptural quality achieved by the gesso must have been a delightful aspect of much of Rush's sculpture, an aspect which has unfortunately been lost in past paint-removal treatments. The last few generations have come to know Rush's work without the gessoed and painted surfaces, a condition that would have seemed strange and probably disturbing to Rush. It was very important to him that his figures were painted,[13] but it was not important that he actually applied the paint himself.[14]

Although all but one of Rush's wood sculptures have traces of paint in the crevices, there is only a single example on which the original white paint has been preserved, the bust of *Samuel Morris* [48]. It has not changed hands since 1812, and there is no evidence of alteration to the surface. It was painted with two coats of white which differ slightly from each other. The top coat is finer and whiter; the undercoat coarser and slightly yellow.[15] It seems to have been common practice in house and ship painting at that time to use different paints for the first,

second, and even third coats with the relatively finest and most expensive pigment reserved for the last coat,[16] and there is no reason to believe that in 1812 sculpture was treated any differently. In recent work to restore the original white appearance to Rush sculpture previously stripped to the bare wood, it is the re-creation of the visual quality of this original Rush paint treatment, rather than the chemical composition, that has been attempted.[17]

Although it is known from contemporary comment that Rush's figures were painted not only white but also "to the life" [3, 18, 19], the only surviving polychromed example is the anatomical model of the *Temporal bone*, with the bones painted rose, the arteries and muscles red, and the nerves white, colors that are indeed true to life.

Commemorative Statuette

The absence of paint traces on this signed cherrywood object is only one of several technical details that set it apart from all the other known wood sculptures by Rush. Sixteen inches high, it is the only sculpture carved in dense hardwood on a small scale. Whereas on the life-size figures Rush established the planes with large bold chisel strokes, here he delicately defined them, presumably with small files. This statuette thus demonstrates Rush's ability to perfect the entire surface of an object without patching, filling, or preparing for a surface coating. Although stylistically consistent with Rush's other known works in wood, the piece was not made using the same working methods, is technically unique and cannot be compared to his other sculptures. Its quality suggests Rush's mastery of a skill that he must have used to make other small carvings yet to be discovered [see 34].

Working Methods and Installation

Rush appears to have been totally involved with the creation of many of his sculptures from the drawing stage through installation. He worked quickly, probably by natural inclination but also no doubt under pressure of deadlines and the next commissions. On the objects, one can imagine how rapidly his "Masterly Chissel"[18] cut out repetitive detail, such as the fringe on the shawl of *Peace* [29] or the beading on the crown of *Justice* [62]. Sharp, sure, single chisel strokes repeat the lines of ornament at slightly varying distances from each other.

Rush's ability to work surely and quickly shows up other places: he wrote that *George Washington* [68] was "the labour of nearly four months of my son and myself."[19] The figurehead *Goddess of Wisdom* for the ship *Congress*, commissioned April 24, 1799, was completed by June 7, 1799 [22]. *Samuel Morris* was finished in seventeen days [48]. The often quoted passage in Dunlap gives us the impression of the spirit in which Rush worked: "His time would never permit, or he would have attempted marble. He used to say it was immaterial what the substance was, the artist must see distinctly the figure in the block, and removing the surface was merely mechanical. When in a hurry he used to hire a wood chopper, and stand by and give directions where to cut, by this means he facilitated work with little labor to himself."[20] Another item often quoted is attributed to an anonymous ship carver: "And he did it all himself—except the first rough hewing of his bit of timber."[21]

The bill Rush tendered for the *Allegory of the Schuylkill River* indicates his involvement from design through installation: "Aug 11th 1809/The Corporation City Philad^a . . . to carving figure for fountain/at Centre Square/to Collecting Stone for Ditto and/Superintending the Erection thereof/and painting figure./$200."[22] Rush gave President Madison the following recommendation for installing *George Washington*: "to exhibit the figure to the best advantage it ought to be elevated on a pedistal, at least three feet & a half in hight, and to view it at least 25 feet distance, the light would be much the best from above—."[23]

In a letter to the Navy Commissioners in 1819, Rush discussed his work for the battleship *Columbus*:[24]

I am sorry that the trailboards should not fit—I gave Mr Humphreys the draught to get them prepared and I had not a doubt but that they would have come together compleately.
. . .

I am at present just making a finish of all the sternwork that was sent on, I think in the course of five or six days I shall have it cased up—I shall then have the top and bottom finishings of the quarter gallery, the droops for the windows and stars to do which will compleat all that I have hear to do— . . .

Permit me to suggest that whether it would not be better to have the whole work finish which I have to do hear first— and then my son can go on and take a journeyman with him—I shall also come on if I should be in health, especially as I have a strong desire to see the ship & as you speak of further orniments I shall be able to sketch them appropriately.

As the stern work consists of a great number of pieces I think it would be proper for the Carpenters who put them up, not to fasten any part till the whole is tacked up and every part in its place, if they will observe such a rule, I will engage provided the pencil marks which were made for my guide was correct, that it will fit compleatly.

The design of a ship's head and of the figure for it were part of a vessel's overall design, so the method of fixing the figurehead had to be established before the carver's work commenced. The solid form of the figurehead often included either a bracket behind or a stand below to facilitate installation. The figurehead of *Benjamin Rush* [72], whose original stand has been replaced, was probably attached resting on a platform created in the knee of the ship's head in the manner shown in a design for the figurehead *Hercules* for the *Pennsylvania* [93a]. The figurehead *Benjamin Franklin* [73] was similarly installed as is suggested in a sketch by Thomas Birch (fig. 112). On *Peace*, Rush's only extant full-length figurehead, there is good evidence of the way he worked the fittings (fig. 71). The sculpture was carved basically from one large piece of pine. This included the bracket of wood in back that was shaped to fit against the lacing[25] of the ship (fig. 72). A notch was cut into the center back heel of the figure, about eight inches deep and four inches high and wide. The notch was prepared to receive part of the knee of the head on which the figure would rest. Once stabilized on this platform, the bracket was brought closely in line with the lacing[26] and then affixed to it with iron nails driven in at an angle in an upward direction, one about every sixteen inches. A horizontal channel was drilled through the figure at the level of her left kneecap to prepare the path of a treenail or a copper or iron bolt that would attach the figure to the ship. The cap of *Peace*'s left knee is made of a separate piece of pine, presumably affixed after installation to protect the cavity in the wood resulting from the large bolt and also for aesthetic reasons. Metal fragments embedded in the left side of *Peace* may be remains of one of several hooks for further securing the object to the vessel with chains. The scroll on which *Peace* strides forward, although part of the carving, probably continued visually the curve of the knee of the head which had been interrupted in providing a support shelf.

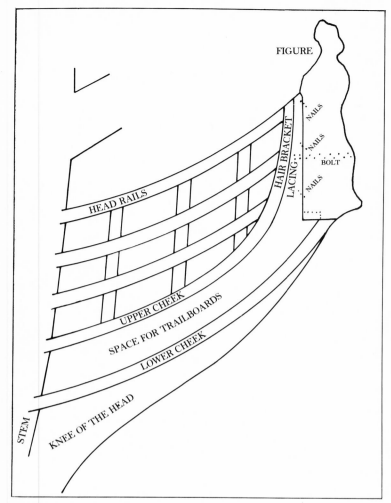

Fig. 71. Diagram of probable installation of *Peace* [29] on the head of a ship suggested by drawings of ships' heads during the period 1790–1830 and physical evidence found on the figure.

Fig. 72. *Peace* [29]. Side view showing bracket at the back carved to butt against the foremost timber of the ship's head.

Terracotta

We know from Rush's correspondence that he sketched ideas on paper. It was also a traditional and common practice for sculptors to sketch ideas in clay, and for someone who worked quickly it would have been an ideal way to establish the relative size and placement of masses to be finalized in wood. It is not surprising that Rush was familiar with clay and that he supplemented his carving commissions by executing portrait busts in terracotta or "clay, burnt," as the material was listed in the Pennsylvania Academy exhibition catalogues from 1811 onward.

Clay was widely available in Philadelphia, where brickmaking was a long-established and important industry. Clay is a naturally occurring sedimentary material. It is generally blue-gray but can also be

reddish where periodic exposure to air allows some of the iron content to oxidize. The most common material in clay is kaolinite, hydrated aluminum silicate. It is usually combined with quartz in the form of sand. Clay can also contain other chemicals which have an effect on the color when it is fired. Magnesia and alumina in the clay produce a buff color; calcium oxide (lime), a yellow or greenish color; and 5%-6% ferric oxide in clay produces the characteristic red color of brick that can be anywhere from pink to reddish black depending on the quality of the clay and the heat of the kiln, the higher temperatures producing the darker results.[27] The range of firing temperature for sculpture is between 600°C and 1200°C. All clay sculpture that has been fired hard, regardless of the heat of the kiln or the resulting color, is properly referred to as terracotta.[28]

There are nine surviving terracotta portrait busts

by William Rush, all of which we have examined: *Elizabeth Rush* [39], *Mary Simpson Rush* [40], *Joseph Wright* [38], *Benjamin Rush* [49], *Philip Syng Physick* [60], *Caspar Wistar* [59], *George Washington* [76], *Self-Portrait* [90], and the *Marquis de Lafayette* [94]. Except the bust of *Elizabeth*, they are all made of a clay that fired predominantly off-white, or bisque. A small amount of iron oxide made the clay of the *Self-Portrait* fire pale pink, and an increased amount is responsible for the strong pink color of *Lafayette*.[29] The portrait of *Elizabeth*, however, is made from a coarse mixture and fired brick red. Visually, the material seems no different from that of a building brick of fairly high quality. It is not surprising that we have no other examples of Rush's experimentation with brick clay for portraiture for the large particles in the clay must have made it hard to work, and it did not stand up well to firing. More satisfactory sculptural material is prepared by rinsing away soluble impurities in the clay and sifting out large foreign particles.

Clay sculpture can be made by building up forms directly onto an armature or by pressing clay into a mold.[30] It is believed that the Rush portraits are freely modeled because only a single example of each

bust is known in terracotta and because of the absence of cast marks. However, the finishing techniques would have been the same no matter which method was used to create the basic form.[31] The busts are hollowed out and have walls of fairly uniform thickness for safe firing; inside the heads and on the backs of the chest walls one can see traces of wire loops and finger trails where clay was removed and the inside surface made firm. The small portraits of Rush's daughters Elizabeth and Mary have very thin necks, and it may have been necessary to cut away part of the hair in order to remove clay from inside the head. Markings on the hair of *Elizabeth* indicate that the back of the head was cut out at one point, and there was no attempt to cover up the line of rejoining. From the inside of *Lafayette*, there are visible signs of a hole having been cut out at the top of the head for the same reason. All the busts are partially open in the back and rest on clay supports modeled and fired as part of the sculpture (fig. 73). The bottom of the support system is hollowed out to insure safe firing (fig. 74). This support system has proven to be easily damaged and there has been loss in this area in the cases of *Elizabeth Rush*, *Physick*, *Washington*, and *Lafayette*.

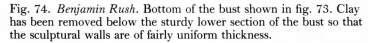

Fig. 73. *Benjamin Rush* [49]. Terracotta. Like all the clay portrait busts, this sculpture was hollowed out for safe firing, and the creation of a clay support at the back enables the object to stand freely.

Fig. 74. *Benjamin Rush*. Bottom of the bust shown in fig. 73. Clay has been removed below the sturdy lower section of the bust so that the sculptural walls are of fairly uniform thickness.

Clay shrinks both as it air dries to the leather stage and again when it is fired, and the total decrease in size from a wet clay model to final form is about ten percent. Rush allowed for this in order to produce the gentlemen's portraits that are indeed life-size. The portraits of his daughters seem small but the measurements could be correct for their ages at the beginning of the nineteenth century.

Building an object in clay by placing slabs or small pieces of clay one on top of the other results in a laminated product. In this additive process, moist air can be trapped between slabs of clay and can expand in the kiln, exerting steam pressure, and forcing the pieces of clay apart. This can occur whether the clay slabs are pressed into a mold or whether they are pressed on top of one another on a freely modeled object.

On three of the Rush terracotta portrait busts there appears to be kiln damage. On the brick-like portrait of *Elizabeth*, some of the surface of the face came away in large flakes and appears to have been reaffixed at that time with a water soluble material having the properties of unfired clay. The head of *Washington* [76] appears to have cracked in the kiln but the extent of damage is hard to evaluate due to later breaks and extensive repairs. The bust of *Physick* suffered dramatic kiln damage (fig. 75). During the modeling, slabs of clay that were added to the lower front part of the bust to form the drapery did not bond to the clay behind them, resulting in large, flat air pockets on both sides. During conservation

an unsatisfactory repair on the left side was taken apart and the residue of what appears to be shellac was found inside covering the area of the large flat break. There is a good chance that the sculptor himself used shellac to repair kiln damage. A similar large shallow air pocket that exists on *Physick*'s right side did not force the slab off during firing; it was weakly bonded on three edges and came away later. On this right side, there was evidence of the shellac-like substance having been introduced into the air pocket through a crack at the outer edge of the slab. Rush probably did this when he repaired the left side in an attempt to stabilize a potential problem he knew existed on the right.

There is no evidence that he painted his terracotta sculpture to simulate marble, although it is certainly possible as there was precedent for that practice in eighteenth-century England. However, during their history, almost all the portraits have been painted.[32] The only object that came into the laboratory still painted was the *Self-Portrait*, and although there were four layers of paint on the surface, where it was possible to mechanically lift away paint, a coating of grime was found on the terracotta surface which indicates that the untreated terracotta was acceptable to the sculptor, at least for a while after the piece was made.

The number and kinds of tools employed by early nineteenth-century clay sculptors were fairly limited.[33] The imprint of the claw chisel, so often seen on European works of this period, is not visible here.

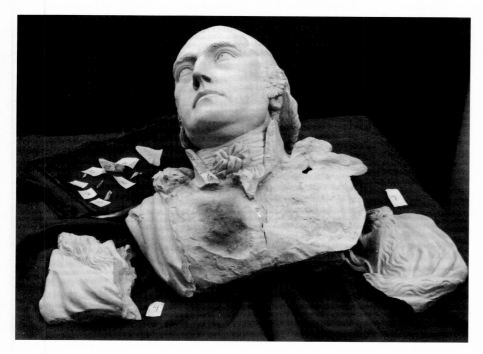

Fig. 75. Philip Syng Physick [60]. The terracotta bust suffered extensive kiln damage and was probably repaired and stabilized by the artist.

For excavation in back and for construction of the supporting walls, Rush appears to have used his fingers, wire loops, sticks, and knives.

He also used his fingers to work over the surfaces of the portraits. Following this, he used a strong pointed stick or metal stylus to deepen grooves on drapery, define buttonholes, texture the eyebrows and hair, and delineate the eye, which he always made by incising the circular line of the iris and removing a ball of clay from the center to form a deep shadow for the pupil. After working with the clay to build up the masses, Rush established the final details by removing clay, his tools acting in the same manner as the familiar chisels on wood. In fact his treatment of eyes was identical in wood and clay.

Particularly in Rush's later portraits of *Lafayette* and of himself, one finds evidence of the speed and urgency of creating that is referred to by Rush's contemporaries in discussing his carving. On these two busts one sees that he has not taken time to remove imprints of the woven covering cloth he used to keep the clay damp between work sessions (fig. 76). Particularly in his *Self-Portrait*, his speed and assurance is indicated by the lines of the fingers moving around the surface, and by such details as the small bit of clay which he placed underneath the bottom lip but did not return to smooth down completely (fig. 77). In the area of the pine cloak in the *Self-Portrait*, one sees the shallow, irregular, rounded grooves of finger pressure side by side with rapid use of a sharp instrument to define the pine needles. Rush used the sharp tool with a combination of sureness and speed which produced deep, crisp grooves, yet left burrs along the ridges (fig. 78).

Rush apparently intended to use the terracotta portraits of the three doctors, Rush, Physick, and Wistar, as models for plaster casts when he started to make them. All three portraits are fired without the narrow, high, protruding tips on the collars perhaps to facilitate making the molds and simplify the process of pulling plaster casts out of the molds. Scoring or registration holes on the places the collar was cut away was done at the leather stage to prepare for a good, accurate bond after the pieces had been fired (fig. 79). That one of the separate terracotta collar tips still exists for *Rush* indicates that similar pieces for the collars of all three busts once existed but are now lost.

In figure 79 *Wistar* is shown without terracotta collar tips or jabot. The clay in the area of the jabot

Fig. 76. *Self-Portrait* [90]. A woven cloth, used to cover damp clay during interruptions in work, left markings that were not removed from the surface before the clay was fired.

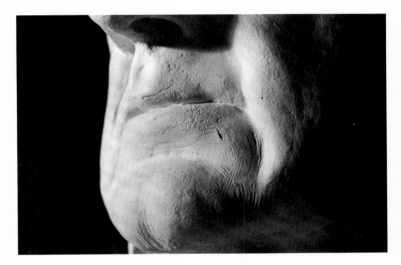

Fig. 77. *Self-Portrait*. Detail of lower part of face.

Fig. 78. *Self-Portrait*. Detail of pine ornament.

has been roughened and looks as though it was made ready to receive an additional piece of clay during the wet modeling stage. It is certainly worked in a different manner from the collars and does not suggest an intentional omission, as was the case with the collar. An original jabot must have come away during the drying or firing stage and has been lost, and he arrived in the laboratory with a plaster jabot plastered in place.[34] It is interesting that the plaster cast of *Wistar* belonging to the College of Physicians of Philadelphia was made from a model without a jabot; a separate jabot was affixed later.

If *Wistar*'s jabot were the only instance of a plaster addition to a terracotta sculpture it would not warrant discussion, but there is another example where the combination of materials seems to be intentional: the handsome and stylistically correct jabot on the terracotta portrait of *Washington* [76] is made of plaster. A plaster cast that appears to have been taken from this object, owned by the Art Mu-

Fig. 80. *George Washington.* Plaster. The Art Museum, Princeton University.

Fig. 79. *Caspar Wistar* [59]. The terracotta bust was fired without collar tips, but registration holes were set to prepare for joining separately fired pieces afterwards. An area was prepared to receive a clay jabot which is now missing.

seum, Princeton University (fig. 80), differs only in the placement of the jabot, presumably, again, a separate piece. The plaster was cast without a queue on the wig; that also was added later. The original terracotta was fired without a queue or lost it in the kiln. It is missing and there is no sign of breakage.

Plaster

The immediacy of Rush's involvement in the creation of his wood and terracotta sculptures makes it difficult to imagine him working with the same spirit in plaster where the final effect is not so directly controlled by toolmarks and fingerprints. It is debatable whether plaster casts can be considered unique artworks in themselves. The issue of originality in serial sculpture from Houdon's time onward is unavoidable. Arthur Beale has suggested a line of questioning that is appropriate and fair:

Our studies have shown that it was entirely possible in the nineteenth century to have more than one "original" work associated with a single subject. If this observation is valid, some of the questions to be asked as criteria for originality might be as follows. First, did the artist conceive this work as complete and appropriate in this material? Second, did the artist initiate a direct action which would realize the work in this material? Third, did the artist finish or approve the work himself?[35]

Fig. 81. *Benjamin Rush*. The Library Company of Philadelphia.

Fig. 82. *Benjamin Rush*. The College of Physicians of Philadelphia.

Fig. 83. *Benjamin Rush*. Pennsylvania Hospital, Philadelphia.

Fig. 84. *Benjamin Rush*. Collection of the late Andrew Oliver, Boston.

Fig. 85. *Caspar Wistar*. Pennsylvania Hospital, Philadelphia.

Fig. 86. *Caspar Wistar*. The American Philosophical Society, Philadelphia.

Fig. 87. *Caspar Wistar*. The College of Physicians of Philadelphia.

Fig. 88. *Philip Syng Physick*. Robert E. Jones, M.D., Philadelphia.

Fig. 89. *Philip Syng Physick*. The American Philosophical Society, Philadelphia.

Fig. 90. *Philip Syng Physick*. The College of Physicians of Philadelphia.

Fig. 91. *Philip Syng Physick*. The Library Company of Philadelphia.

Figs. 81–91. Known examples and locations of plaster casts from terracotta portraits of the three doctors.

Fig. 92. *Benjamin Rush*. Detail of fig. 83, a plaster cast probably taken from the terracotta original at the Pennsylvania Academy.

The answers to all three questions are affirmative when asked of Rush's plaster casts of the three doctors (figs. 81-91), of *Washington*, and probably also of casts of other subjects [79]. They were probably all made from plaster piece molds. Traces of the mold are still present on figures 82 and 88. The latter was cast in an open mold of approximately twenty-five pieces, not including the base. It is likely that the other casts were similarly made. In this case, the addition of the absent collar tips is very subtle, but in many casts, including the *Rush* at Pennsylvania Hospital, clear lines are seen, even through the paint, at the place of joining (fig. 92).

Although each cast must have received individual attention when it came out of the mold, at least to attach collar tips, the presence of fairly thick and disfiguring paint on most of the casts has made it

difficult to study the differences among them. However, the Pennsylvania Hospital cast of *Rush* has only one layer of paint and affords an excellent opportunity to compare it to the terracotta model. William Rush seems to have worked over the plaster after it came out of the mold to deepen the line between the lips, add definition to the hair, and suppress the buttonholes as a design element. When we compare the treatment of the left collar to the single extant terracotta collar, we can see that on the plaster the artist gave the collar a different relationship to the chin.

In these plaster busts, the heads are cast round and the front drapery is complete, but the backs are open so that the object cannot stand on its own. The busts were mounted on plaster bases of several different styles, at a variety of angles; some lean slightly forward and create an intimate effect. In X-radiographs the bases were seen to be both solid and hollow, but all of them support the busts by means of a wooden dowel reinforced with plaster.

Fig. 93. X-radiograph of base of fig. 87. Rush cast plaster busts open at the back and mounted them on plaster bases by means of a wooden dowel secured with fresh plaster.

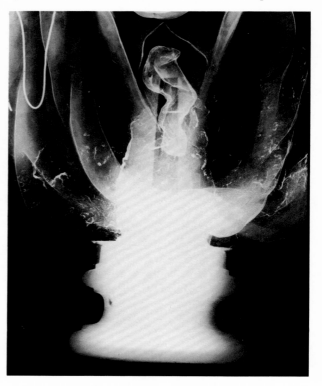

Some dowels have metal tacks in them to help the dowel key more securely to the plaster support material (fig. 93). However, even for busts that have been in the same collection since Rush's time, there does not seem to be a consistent mounting technique.

All the casts were coated at some point. Four busts are now painted black and six white, but whether the intention of using paint to imitate a bronze or marble bust originated in Rush's studio, we cannot yet say. The one bust that has a plaster surface is the cast of *Rush* owned by the College of Physicians of Philadelphia. Recent conservation, which included paint removal, revealed that the first of four coatings on top of the plaster was gesso, applied so thickly that it completely filled the incised lines of the iris and gave the eyes a blank stare. This bust must have left Rush's studio without any surface coatings. A pencil inscription found on the plaster (under the gesso) indicates the first owner, "Do^r John C Otto," Dr. Rush's protégé.

A "bronzed cast bust" by Rush of Andrew Jackson, owned by James Ronaldson, was exhibited at the Franklin Institute in 1825.[36] This confirms the existence of the bronze aesthetic for plaster during the period in which Rush was making the serial sculpture. The market to whose demands we have seen Rush willing to respond could have been content with raw plaster or could also have insisted on a patina that simulated a more costly sculptural material.

Investigation of Rush's treatment of the plasters is further complicated by the problem of *surmoulage*, a cast of a cast. It appears that there are at least two instances of *surmoulage* in the group of busts studied; two versions of *Physick* were not cast from a mold taken from the original terracotta, and their contours are not identical. The deeply overhanging sides of *Physick*'s wig in the cast illustrated in figure 88 are made separately and have been affixed to a simplified form of the original shape (fig. 94). On the cast shown in figure 91, a collar was never applied to the cast and the area prepared to receive a collar was cut back considerably from the corresponding position on the terracotta. Rush may have made either or both of these examples in an attempt to increase the efficiency of production, or add more

Fig. 94. *Philip Syng Physick*. Detail of fig. 88, probably a *surmoulage*.

variety to the individual pieces. It is also a possibility that the plaster casts of Rush's portraits continued to be made after his lifetime and that these two are among them. However, to resolve these questions, we would have to have more documentary material and access to information on the busts' plaster surfaces which are now camouflaged with paint.

In 1856, twenty-three years after Rush's death, a marble copy of the terracotta bust of Washington, now in the collection of the Historical Society of Pennsylvania, was made by J. A. Beck. Subsequently a number of plaster replicas of Washington were produced by Shaw & Co., based on the original terracotta, but the proportions were changed—the face was made narrower and the object was cast in one piece to include a high base so that the effect is very different from Rush's casts. Though these sculptures clearly have nothing to do with Rush's work itself, they represent a tribute paid to the man, a continued admiration for the forms he created, and a confirmation of his lasting popularity. It is ironic that works in materials suitable for mechanical reproduction, marble and plaster, served to keep alive a reputation earned in a medium and technique that cannot be successfully reproduced, wood carving.

Catalogue

BY LINDA BANTEL

with the assistance of
Susan James-Gadzinski
and Elizabeth Owen

Frequently Cited References

Brewington
> Brewington, M. V. *Shipcarvers of North America*. 1962; corrected republication, New York: Dover Publications, 1972.

DANFS
> *Dictionary of American Naval Fighting Ships*. 6 vols. Washington, D.C.: Navy Department, Office of the Chief of Naval Operations, 1959–76.

Dunlap
> Dunlap, William. *A History of the Rise and Progress of the Arts of Design in the United States*. 3 vols. 1834; reprint, New York: Dover Publications, 1969.

Girard Papers
> *Stephen Girard Papers*. Microfilm edition. Philadelphia: American Philosophical Society.

Marceau
> Marceau, Henri. *William Rush 1756–1833: The First American Sculptor*. Exhibition catalogue. Philadelphia: Pennsylvania Museum of Art, 1937.

Navy Records
> National Archives, Washington, D.C. Record Group 45, "Naval Records Collection of the Office of Naval Records and Library."

PAFA
> Pennsylvania Academy of the Fine Arts, Philadelphia. Exhibition history of William Rush's sculpture at the Pennsylvania Academy is compiled from Anna Wells Rutledge, ed., *Cumulative Record of Exhibition Catalogues: The Pennsylvania Academy of the Fine Arts, 1807–1870; The Society of Artists, 1800–1814; The Artist's Fund Society, 1835–1845*, Memoirs of the American Philosophical Society, vol. 38 (Philadelphia, 1955).

PMA
> Philadelphia Museum of Art; formerly Pennsylvania Museum of Art (until 1938).

Pinckney
> Pinckney, Pauline A. *American Figureheads and Their Carvers*. New York: W. W. Norton & Company, 1940.

Scharf and Westcott
> Scharf, J. Thomas, and Westcott, Thompson. *History of Philadelphia, 1609–1884*. 3 vols. Philadelphia: L. H. Everts & Co., 1884.

Watson, *Annals*
> Watson, John F. *Annals of Philadelphia and Pennsylvania in the Olden Time*. 1830; revised and enlarged to 3 vols. by Willis P. Hazard, 1887. Philadelphia: Edwin S. Stuart, 1905.

[2]

1 Figurehead

For the *Two Brothers*. 1784. Wood. Whereabouts unknown.

A bill dated May 15, 1784, indicates that Rush executed an eight-foot figurehead for this brigantine built by the Philadelphia merchant Stephen Girard (1750–1831), as well as assorted carved work including a pair of quarter pieces (ornamental carvings at the corners of the stern) and a taffrail (ornament at the upper part of the stern). These are Rush's earliest known documented ship carvings. The payment of £30.15 was apparently made in goods, according to the notation on the bill, "Contra C^r By Goods." In 1793 Rush executed a second figurehead for this ship [9].

Reference: Girard Papers, series II, reel 461, bill dated May 15, 1784.

2 Benjamin Franklin

1787. Pine. 20¼ × 16¼ × 13 in. (51.4 × 41.3 × 33 cm.). Yale University Art Gallery, New Haven (1804.4).

This life-size bust of Benjamin Franklin (1706–1790) is Rush's earliest known portrait. It shows the eighty-one-year-old statesman with sagging jowls and an alert gaze. The bust was first attributed to Rush in 1940 by Pauline Pinckney. In 1941, it was erroneously published in *Antiques* as the figurehead for the *Franklin*, which was launched from Philadelphia in 1815. That figurehead is now at the U.S. Naval Academy in Annapolis [73].

In Noah Webster's diary, an entry discovered by Charles Coleman Sellers indicates that the portrait of Franklin was executed in 1787 as an ornament or shop sign for the New Haven bookstore and publishing house of Isaac Beers (1742–1813). Webster was in close contact with Franklin after his return to Philadelphia from France in 1785, and Webster entered the following in his journal on February 9, 1787: "Wait on Mr. Rush, Carver, for a Bust of Dr. Franklin, for Mr. Isaac Beers, N. Haven" (quoted in Sellers, *Franklin*, p. 357). On April 14, Webster recorded "£26.10 Penns. currency dollars at ⅞" in payment for the bust.

The bust has been in the collection of Yale College since 1804. Mrs. Augustus R. Street, Isaac Beers's granddaughter and wife of the founder of the Yale School of Fine Arts, recorded the following in an undated listing of art objects owned by Yale College: "Bust of Dr. Franklin carved by Rush. This work of art, taken from life, was presented by Dr. Franklin to his friend Isaac Beers Esq. of N.H." (Sellers, p. 358).

References: Pinckney, pl. xv, pp. 117-18. "A Franklin Figurehead by William Rush," *Antiques*, vol. 39 (February 1941), fig. 2, pp. 83-84. "Yale Bust of Ben Franklin Found to be Work of Eminent Sculptor," *New Haven Register*, November 22, 1953, p. 2. Charles Coleman Sellers, *Benjamin Franklin in Portraiture* (New Haven and London, 1962), pp. 181, 357-58, pl. 38. Clarence P. Hornung, *Treasury of American Design and Antiques* (New York, 1976), no. 42, p. 26, no. 1551, p. 439. Helen A. Cooper and Jules D. Prown, "American Painting and Sculpture at Yale," *Antiques*, vol 117 (June 1980), p. 1294.

3 Indian Trader

Figurehead for the *William Penn*. c. 1789. Wood. Whereabouts unknown. M 63.

A particularly popular subject for American figureheads was the Indian. According to Scharf and Westcott, Rush's *Indian Trader* for the merchant ship *William Penn* was so remarkably lifelike that sketches and plaster casts were made by carvers when the ship docked in London right after the Revolution.

An 1828 article in the *American Daily Advertiser* credits Rush with having produced several variations of this theme, "prior to '93 and afterwards." It goes on to describe the different poses:

Placing him (the Indian) . . . in exact position, either, as drawing his arrow to the head, at the supposed bounding deer; flourishing his tomahawk . . . or else, in attitude of solemn thought, with his arms folded within his blanket drawn closely around him, and showing exactly, the countour of his brawny person and limbs. The frontlet of distinction fastened upon his forehead, and pinioned behind with the eagle's plume. The head closely shaved, leaving only the single tuft of black hair, to aid in the scalping. The eyebrows drawn closely together, under the compress of thought, emanating . . . from the "Great Spirit:" softening down within his eye of flame, the native savage fire of revenge, cherished by him as a virtue, into gentle pity for the devoted object before him; his faithful Dog . . . crouching at his heels.—Each figure head was so admirably brought out, from its original block of wood, and coloured to the life, by the Painter, under directions from the Sculptor.

Other examples of Rush's Indian figureheads are discussed in catalogue numbers 44, 95, and 107.

References: "Dry Goods," *Poulson's American Daily Advertiser*, Philadelphia, December 16, 1828, p. 2. Scharf and Westcott, III, p. 2337. Watson, *Annals*, I, p. 576. Marceau, no. 63, p. 64. Pinckney, p. 38.

4 George Washington

Figurehead for the *General Washington*. 1790. Wood. Whereabouts unknown. M 67.

An account book for the ship *General Washington* lists "William Rush's Bill/Carver/29.10.0" as an entry for December 13, 1790, but does not identify the type of carvings. At the time of the launching, *The Pennsylvania Journal* reported that "the bold and striking likeness of the President, on the 'General Washington,' . . . must give pleasure to every spectator. The artist who executed this, we hear is Mr. Rush" (quoted in Marceau, p. 65). A later account in the *American Daily Advertiser* describes Rush's work as a life-size figurehead of Washington holding a perspective glass in his left hand and pointing with his right. This work was greatly admired in London when the *General Washington* docked there.

The 250-ton *General Washington* was built by William Woodcock and launched at Wilmington, Delaware, on October 16, 1790, under the command of Captain Thomas Forte.

References: General Advertiser and Political, Commercial, Agricultural and Literary Journal, Philadelphia, October 27, 1790, p. 3. General Washington Account Book, 1790–92, Historical Society of Delaware, Wilmington. "Dry Goods," *Poulson's American Daily Advertiser*, Philadelphia, December 16, 1828, p. 2. Marceau, no. 67, p. 65.

5 Commerce
6 Figurehead

For two English vessels. c. 1790. Wood. Wherabouts unknown. M 64, M 65.

According to Watson's *Annals*, first published in 1830, Rush had executed two figureheads nearly forty years earlier to fulfill orders received from Eng-

land by Nicklin and Griffith. One of the figureheads was a female personification of Commerce.

Although Watson dated the pieces about 1790, he was apparently referring to the company's name after 1800, since the merchants Philip Nicklin and Robert Eaglesfield Griffith were not listed as a partnership in Stafford's Philadelphia Directory until 1801. The Philadelphia Directories from 1785 to 1800 listed the firm's name as Philip Nicklin and Co.

References: Scharf and Westcott, III, p. 2337. Watson, *Annals*, I, p. 576. Marceau, nos. 64, 65, p. 64.

7 Indian

c. 1790–1800. Wood. Whereabouts unknown. M 1.

An undated Philadelphia *Evening Telegraph* clipping entitled "An Appreciation—by a Ship Carver," in a scrapbook kept by William Rush Dunton, Jr. (and quoted in Fried, p. 18), documents a tobacco store Indian by Rush:

The figure in front of the cigar store on Third Street above Walnut is by Rush. . . . [It is] the somewhat grotesque little Indian in an iron frame over the door. The outstretched arm is a restoration. . . . The figure is a good specimen of Rush's early manner.

Frederick Fried speculates that the figure illustrated here (fig. 95) is the one referred to in that article. It is difficult to relate this figure stylistically to Rush's other works, particularly since it is unlocated and known only from an old photograph.

References: Marceau, no. 1, p. 23. Frederick Fried, *Artists in Wood: American Carvers of Cigar-Store Indians, Show Figures, and Circus Wagons* (New York, 1970, fig. 9, p. 18.

8 Figurehead

For the *Sally I*. 1791. Wood. Whereabouts unknown. M 66.

Stephen Girard owned a half share in this brig between 1791 and 1795. The following bill is the only evidence that Rush worked on this ship:

Received of John Ross Thirty three pounds fifteen shillings

Fig. 95. Possibly by William Rush. *Indian*, c. 1790–1800. Wood. Photograph courtesy of the Frederick Fried Archives.

9 Female figurehead

For the *Two Brothers*. 1793. Wood. Whereabouts unknown.

This brigantine was variously named *Kitty* (1786–87), *Two Friends* (1787–89), and *Virginia* (1789–93), and their French equivalents. Rush executed the ship's first figurehead in 1784 [1]. According to a bill dated July 25, 1793, Rush and another wood-carver, John Merriam, carved a "head Female figure £11.5," as well as assorted other work including a taffrail and a pair of quarter pieces, and repaired the figurehead, all for a total payment of £25.

Reference: Girard Papers, series II, reel 166, bill dated July 25, 1793.

10 River God

Figurehead for the *Ganges*. c. 1793. Wood. Whereabouts unknown. M 68.

According to Watson, and Scharf and Westcott, this East Indian ship bore a figurehead of a river god carved by Rush, which was greatly admired by the Indians.

Charles Willson Peale reportedly said of the figurehead: "Its beautifully proportioned moulding forms a face that seems 'petrified by the sentiment of the Infinite;' one is impelled to reverence" (Jordan, p. 246).

Marceau dated it about 1793.

References: Scharf and Westcott, III, p. 2337. Watson, *Annals*, I, p. 576. Wilfred Jordan, "William Rush: The Earliest Native-Born American Sculptor," *Art and Archaeology*, vol. 11, 2 (June 1921), p. 246. Marceau, no. 68, pp. 65-66.

in full for work done for ship Sally, Phila April 29th 1791. £33.15.0   [signed] William Rush

From the size of the payment, it is likely that Rush executed a figurehead for the ship, although the type of carving is not specified in this bill.

References: Dreer Autograph Collection, Architects and Sculptors II, receipt dated April 29, 1791, p. 22. Marceau, no. 66, p. 64.

11 Voltaire

Figurehead for the *Voltaire*. 1795. Wood. Whereabouts unknown. M 75.

This brigantine, the first of Stephen Girard's four ships that have become known as the French philosophers' series, was named for the Enlightenment philosopher Voltaire (1694–1778). It was launched

December 5, 1795 (Marceau, p. 71), under the captaincy of Ezra Bowen. According to Scharf and Westcott, Rush executed either a bust or a full figure of Voltaire. A bill dated November 23, 1795, indicates that Rush was paid £25 for carving "head figure Voltaire," as well as assorted carved work, including a taffrail and quarter pieces, for a total payment of £79. In December 1805 John Swain painted the ship's figurehead, and in August 1814 Rush was paid $5 for repairing the figurehead.

References: Girard Papers, series II, reels 317, bill dated November 23, 1795; 320, bill dated December 1805; series III, reel 37, disbursement dated August 5, 1814. Scharf and Westcott, II, p. 1066. Marceau, no. 75, p. 71.

12 Liberty

Figurehead for the *Liberty*. 1795. Wood. Whereabouts unknown.

The ship *Liberty*, owned by Stephen Girard, was launched on April 15, 1795, and first commanded by Captain Paul Post. According to a May 1795 bill, Rush was paid £56.15 for carving a figurehead of Liberty and assorted other work including a taffrail. William Fling, a painter, was paid in May 1797 for "putting head & Rails in Coulars." In February 1799 Rush billed £0.15 for carving a liberty cap, presumably as an attribute for the figurehead. The cap was gilded in 1807 by John Swain. According to three further bills made out to Girard, Rush repaired the figurehead in 1800, 1801, and 1808.

References: Girard Papers, series II, reels 171, bills dated May 26, 1795, and May 7, 1797; 172, bills dated February 6, 1799, and March 25, 1800; 173, bill dated May 5, 1801; 175, bills dated June 15, 1807, and June 22, 1808.

13 Figurehead

For a snow. 1795. Wood. Whereabouts unknown.

The only documentation of this figurehead is the following letter from John Murray, 4th Earl of Dunmore, written in Nassau, New Providence:

Sir—
I was a few days ago favoured with yours of the 20th . . . for which I am much obliged to you, and I with pleasure

take the earliest opportunity of returning you my sincere thanks for the trouble you have had with the Head for the Snow [a ship similar to a brig but with the addition of a trysail mast close behind the mainmast], which is really incomparably well done, and is the admiration of all that has seen it, and I shall be much obliged to you if you will thank Mr. Rush for the attention he has paid to it.

Reference: Letter from John Murray to Unknown Gentleman, April 1, 1795, Emmet no. 3831, Manuscripts and Archives Division, The New York Public Library.

14 Design for Hercules

Figurehead for the *Constitution*. 1796. Whereabouts unknown. M 76.

In September 1796, according to War Department correspondence, Rush was working on the design of *Hercules* for the *Constitution*. In October, the completed drawing was transmitted to the Boston carver John Skillin (1746–1800), whom Rush had recommended as "a qualified artist to undertake the carving." M. V. Brewington mentions a carving expenditure of $719.33 paid to the brothers "John and S[imeon] Skill[in]" for the *Constitution* (p. 124).

On May 31, 1797, the Reverend Dr. Bentley of Salem recorded in his diary: "saw the new ship . . . the Head called Constitution, finished by the Skillings. It is an Hercules with the fasces of the United States & the Constitution standing upon a rock & his batton lying beneath him" (quoted in Brewington, p. 124).

This 44-gun U.S. Navy frigate was designed by Joshua Humphreys and built in Boston by George Claghorn (1748–1824). The *Constitution* sailed on July 22, 1798, under the command of Captain Samuel Nicholson (1743–1811), who had supervised her construction. *Hercules* was damaged when the ship collided with the U.S. frigate *President* in September 1804 and was replaced by a billethead (Brewington, pp. 124-25). In combat with the British frigate *Guerriere* during the War of 1812, the *Constitution* earned an important victory for the United States and the nickname "Old Ironsides." She is presently docked in Boston.

References: Navy Records, Letters Sent by the War Department Relating to Naval Matters 1790–1798, M 209, letter to the Secretary of the Treasury, September 20, 1796, letter to Henry Jackson, October 18, 1796. Marceau, no. 76, pp. 71-72. Pinckney, p. 67. Brewington, pp. 124-25. DANFS, II, 1963, p. 173.

Fig. 96. Attributed to Samuel Lewis (active 1795–1817). *The United States Frigate Dressed with the Colors of Various Nations*, after 1797. Oil on canvas, 12½ × 15¾ in. (31.8 × 40 cm.). Warren Sturgis.

15 Genius of the United States

Figurehead for the *United States*. 1796. Wood. Whereabouts unknown. M 73.

In a painting showing the *United States* after July 1797, Rush's figurehead appears gilded (fig. 96). It was described earlier that year in the *American Daily Advertiser*:

The Genius of the United States: she is crest with a Constellation, her hair and drapery flowing. Suspended to the ringlets of hair, which fall or wave over her Breast and reclining in her bosom, is the portrait of her favorite son, George Washington, President of the United States; her waist bound with a Civic Band. In her Right hand, which is advanced, she holds a spear, suspended to which a Belt of Wampum containing the Emblems of Peace and War. On her left side is a Tablet, which supports three large volumes which relate to the three Branches of Government; the Scale, emblematic of Justice, blended with them. The Left hand suspends the Constitution over the books, &c on the Tablet; the Eagle with his wings half extended, with the Escutcheon, &c of the Arms of the United States on the Right, designates the figure. The attributes, Commerce and Agriculture, and a modest position of the Arts and Sciences.

The 1793–97 letter book of Joshua Humphreys contains an itemization of the frigate's building costs as of January 2, 1797, including an unspecified carver's bill of $1000. Pinckney wrote that Rush

was paid a similar amount (p. 66). Rush's figurehead must therefore have been completed in 1796, not 1797 as suggested by Marceau.

The 44-gun, 1576-ton frigate was constructed by Joshua Humphreys in Philadelphia and first commanded by Captain John Barry (1745–1803). Launched on May 10, 1797, she was the first of the six U.S. Navy frigates authorized by Congress in 1794 to approach completion. *Porcupine's Gazette* for July 22, 1797, reported that she was "equipping with the greatest expedition. Her lower masts are already in."

The *United States*, which survived numerous rebuildings, was sunk at Norfolk on April 20, 1861, raised in 1865, and broken up the following year (Chapelle, p. 556).

References: Joshua Humphreys Papers, Letter Book 1793–97, p. 252, Historical Society of Pennsylvania. *Claypoole's American Daily Advertiser*, Philadelphia, March 4, 1797, p. 2. *Porcupine's Gazette*, Philadelphia, July 22, 1797, p. 3. Scharf and Westcott, II, p. 1066. Navy Records, Lt. George F. Emmons, "United States Navy Ships Built at Philadelphia Prior to the Establishing of a Government Owned Navy Yard" (undated typescript), U.S. Navy, 1775–1900, AC–Construction of U.S. Ships, Philadelphia Navy Yard. Marceau, no. 73, pp. 69-70. Pinckney, pp. 65-66. Howard I. Chapelle, *The History of the American Sailing Navy: The Ships and Their Development* (New York, 1949), pp. 478, 556.

16 Figurehead

For the *Sally II*. 1796. Wood. Whereabouts unknown.

Stephen Girard owned this brig from 1795 until 1800, when it was captured by the British. A 1796 bill documents that Rush executed a figurehead and the following assorted carved work for the ship: a pair of quarter pieces, a taffrail, and quarter badges (ornamental carvings around the windows), for a total payment of £53.15.

Reference: Girard Papers, series II, reel 315, bill dated August 25, 1796.

17 Design for Lion

Figurehead, and stern carvings, for the *Crescent*. 1797. Whereabouts unknown. M 70.

The *Crescent* was intended as a "gift" to the Dey of Algiers to fulfill the terms of a peace treaty passed by the U.S. Senate on March 2, 1796. In a December 1796 letter to the War Office, the Secretary of the Treasury specified that, because of Muslim religious beliefs, the ship not be decorated with a human figure and suggested that a lion would be more appropriate.

The 36-gun, 600-ton ship was built by James Hackett in Portsmouth, New Hampshire, from designs by Josiah Fox. In October 1796 the keel was laid, and the frigate was launched on June 29, 1797.

The letter book of Josiah Fox contains a May 1797 document on an "Algerine Frigate," probably the *Crescent*, in which he specifies that "a Carver is to be furnished by Mr. Rush who has a Draught of the Stern and Will Design the Necessary figures. . . ." On June 7 Rush's designs were sent by the ship's captain, Thomas Thompson, to the War Office. The carving was to be done in Portsmouth, probably by William Deering, Jr. (born 1741). According to War Office correspondence, the ship's figurehead and other carvings were completed by August 15, 1797 (Marceau, p. 68).

References: Navy Records, Letters Sent by the War Department Relating to Naval Matters 1790–1798, M 209, letter to the Secretary of the Treasury, December 15, 1796. "Letters and Abstracts of Josiah Fox" (typescript), Letter Book III, vol. 2, no. 1009, Phillips Library, Peabody Museum of Salem, Massachusetts. *Porcupine's Gazette*, Phila-delphia, July 8, 1797, p. 3. Marceau, no. 70, pp. 67-68. Pinckney, p. 71.

18 Lion
19 Lion

Figureheads for two unknown frigates. c. 1797. Wood. Whereabouts unknown. M 71, M 72.

A Navy Department list of timbers destined for Algiers, to fulfill treaty obligations, includes the following items (quoted in Marceau, p. 68):

2 Lyons carved elegantly by Rush, for frigates, both of a size of the one carved for the CRESCENT, very airy &c different attitudes, one tearing a Fox to pieces, the other destroying a Tiger or a Lioness, Painted to the Life.

References: Marceau, nos. 71, 72, p. 68. Pinckney, p. 71.

20 Nature

Figurehead, and stern carvings, for the *Constellation*. c. 1797. Wood. Whereabouts unknown. M 69.

The following description of the completed *Constellation* figurehead, said by an unnamed correspondent to be in Rush's words, was published in the August 9, 1797, Baltimore *Federal Gazette*:

She [the female figurehead] is crested with fire, her waist is encircled with the zone and signs of the zodiac, her hair and drapery loose and flowing, her right arm and head elevated, her left arm lightly resting on a large sphere, on which the Constellation is rising, her feet on a rock, part of which is formed into a rude pyramid, allegorical of the rapid and natural Union of the States. . . . The Flame ascending from the top of the rock, is expressive of the fire, which gave energy to the Patriots; its water descending from the rock is an allusion to the Temperance peculiarly characteristic of the American Revolution; the scale and the mirror, at the foundation of the Pyramid, emblematic of the truth and justice of the cause; the figure of the Dove or bird of peace, resting in the cap of Liberty . . . the Herculean club encircled with laurel, is emblematic of that heroic Virtue that defended and obtained the cause; the broad Rock on which the figure stands, is emblematic of that Independence which was the ultimate end of the Revolution.

In the same paper appeared the following description of Rush's stern carvings:

The centre [of the stern] is a large sphere, with the Constellation inserted resting on a massy pedestal of an artificial form, with the fasces inlayed in the panel, emblematic of the Union. . . . Three large Volumes and a Scroll, representing the three branches of Government and the Constitution is reclining on the side of the pedestal and the Eagle and arms of the United States on the other; next are two of the cardinal virtues, Fortitude and Justice. . . . Next to the figure of Fortitude on the starboard side is the figure and emblem of Order, joined to the emblems of Industry and Agriculture; supported by Ceres, the goddess of agriculture, in the starboard quarter-piece. On the larboard side next to Justice is the figure and emblems of Science, joined to the arts of shipbuilding, navigation, &c., supported by Neptune, the god of the seas. . . .

The 36-gun U.S. Navy frigate was designed by naval constructors Joshua Humphreys (1751–1838) and Josiah Fox (1763–1847), although the plans were later altered by the builder, David Stodder. Captain Thomas Truxtun (1755–1822) supervised construction and was the ship's first commander. The *Constellation* (fig. 97), sister ship to the *Constitution* [see 14], was the second of six naval frigates authorized by an act of Congress on March 27, 1794. She was launched in Baltimore on September 7, 1797, and she left on her first trip in June 1798 at the outbreak of war with France. By 1854 the *Constellation* was in need of extensive repair and was subsequently modified and updated (DANFS, II, p. 171); Rush's carvings may have been removed at this time. The ship is presently docked in Baltimore.

References: Claypoole's American Daily Advertiser, Philadelphia, March 4, 1797, p. 2. "United States' Frigate Constellation," *Federal Gazette and Baltimore Daily Advertiser*,

August 9, 1797, p. 3. Scharf and Westcott, II, p. 1066. Marceau, no. 69, pp. 66-67. Pinckney, p. 66. Eugene S. Ferguson, "The Figure-head of the United States Frigate Constellation," *The American Neptune*, vol. 7 (October 1947), pp. 255-60. DANFS, II, 1963, pp. 170-71.

21 Revolution

Figurehead for the *Chesapeake*. 1799. Wood. Whereabouts unknown. M 74.

William Rush, in his "first thoughts" for figureheads for five U.S. naval frigates, the *Chesapeake*, the *United States* [15], the *Constitution* [14], the *Congress* [22], and the *Constellation* [20], described to Joshua Humphreys the idea that "the Revolution of America was a struggle for freedom, and gave birth to a great Republican empire. . . ." Thus when Humphreys presented Rush's figurehead suggestions to the Secretary of War (letter dated between May 28 and June 25, 1795; quoted in Marceau, p. 70), he wrote that because of the "difficulty of representing the Chesapeake, [Rush] has suggested that the Idea of calling on the Revolution as it is intended only to apply to our glorious Revolution, I should suppose it might be adopted without creating improper revolutionary principles. . . ."

According to Navy department records, Rush had finished the figurehead for the *Chesapeake* by June 26, 1799 (Marceau, p. 71). A treasury department entry for July 16, 1799, reports Rush was

Fig. 97. Edward Savage (1761–1817). *Constellation and L'Insurgent—The Chace*, 1799. Aquatint, 13⅞ × 20⅛ in. (35.2 × 51.1 cm.). The New-York Historical Society, New York City; Irving S. Olds Collection.

paid $917.37 for carving and painting figureheads and trail boards for the *Chesapeake* and the *Congress*.

The 36-gun *Chesapeake*, designed by Josiah Fox, was built in Norfolk, Virginia. Under the command of Captain James Barron (1769–1851), the frigate was launched December 2, 1799, and sailed on her first cruise June 6, 1800. She was captured in a confrontation with the H.M.S. *Shannon* on June 1, 1813, and after serving in the British navy, was sold and dismantled in Plymouth, England, in 1820.

References: Joshua Humphreys Papers, Correspondence 1775–1831, letter from William Rush, April 30, 1795, p. 23, Historical Society of Pennsylvania. Navy Records, Warrants Drawn on the Treasurer of the United States, 1798–1800, M 209, entry dated July 16, 1799. Marceau, no. 74, pp. 70-71. Pinckney, p. 68. DANFS, II, 1963, p. 95.

22 Goddess of Wisdom

Figurehead for the *Congress*. 1799. Wood. Whereabouts unknown. M 77.

This 36-gun U.S. Navy frigate, designed by Joshua Humphreys, was built in Portsmouth, New Hampshire, by James Hackett. The Secretary of the Navy wrote on January 15, 1799, to Jacob Sheafe, Naval Agent in Portsmouth, about the ship and a figurehead. The letter contained "hints suggested by Mr. Rush . . . also the copy of a letter from Mr. Joshua Humphreys naval architect. . . . The carver will observe Mr. Rush's observations applicable thereto." Further naval correspondence indicates that on April 24 Rush received the commission for carving the figure, and that by June 7 it was completed and ready to be sent to Portsmouth as soon as the paint was dry. An entry in the treasury department accounts for July 16, 1799, authorized a $917.37 payment to Rush for carving and painting figureheads and trail boards for the *Congress* and the *Chesapeake* [21]. *Congress* was launched on August 15, 1799, under the command of Captain J. Sever. The 1250-ton ship was outfitted in Portsmouth and Boston, and proceeded from Newport, Rhode Island, to sea soon after December 1799. In 1834, she was in extreme disrepair and was broken up at Norfolk Navy Yard. It is not known whether any carvings were salvaged.

References: Navy Records, General Letters Sent by Navy,

M 209, letter to Jacob Sheafe, January 15, 1799; General Letter Book of Navy, M 209, letter to William Rush, April 24, 1799; Warrants Drawn on the Treasurer of the United States, 1798–1800, M 209, entry dated July 16, 1799. Marceau, no. 77, pp. 72-73. Pinckney, p. 69. DANFS, II, 1963, p. 162.

23 John Adams

Figurehead for the *John Adams*. 1799. Wood. Whereabouts unknown. M 78.

The *John Adams* was a 544-ton U.S. Navy frigate named for the current President and funded by the citizens of Charleston, South Carolina, under a contract to the builder Paul Pritchard. According to Scharf and Westcott, her figurehead was "a life-like portrait-bust of John Adams . . . cut by Rush for the sloop-of-war bearing the name of that statesman."

The frigate was launched June 3 or 5, 1799, and sailed under the command of Captain George Cross about the first of October. An account in the June 5, 1799, *American Daily Advertiser* described the figurehead, "which is said to be a great likeness of the President of the United States arrived from Philadelphia some days ago, and is now placed on the frigate; it is from the masterly chissel of Mr. Rush of that city, whose elegant productions have long since placed him at the head of his profession."

During Lafayette's visit to Philadelphia in September 1824, illuminations were shown aboard the *John Adams*.

References: Claypoole's American Daily Advertiser, Philadelphia, June 5, 1799, p. 3. *Poulson's American Daily Advertiser*, Philadelphia, September 30, 1824, p. 3. Scharf and Westcott, II, p. 1066. Marceau, no. 78, pp. 73-74. Pinckney, p. 82. DANFS, III, 1968, p. 521.

24 Hercules

Figurehead, and stern carvings, for the *Philadelphia*. c. 1799. Wood. Whereabouts unknown. M 79.

Rush was paid $809.33 for "carved work" for the frigate *Philadelphia*, according to an undated memo in Navy department records (Marceau, p. 74). This presumably included the figurehead, which the *American Daily Advertiser* described before the

Fig. 98. Nathaniel Hutton (active 1791–1832). *Sail plan for the Frigate Philadelphia*, 1800. Pen and ink on paper, mounted on linen, 20⅛ × 29 in. (51.1 × 73.7 cm.). The Lenthall Collection, The Franklin Institute Science Museum, Philadelphia.

launching: "an Hercules with his attendant emblems, has lately been put up; a very handsome piece of sculpture—though we question the legitimacy of one of the emblems, which is the Roman fasces in the left hand of the figure, intended to represent the American union" (fig. 98).

The 36-gun U.S. Navy frigate (fig. 5), originally called *City of Philadelphia*, was funded by her citizens. Construction was begun in November of 1798 at Joshua Humphreys's shipyard. The 1240-ton vessel was launched November 28, 1799, and left on her first cruise April 5, 1800, under the command of Captain Stephen Decatur, Sr. (1752–1808). In October 1803, under the command of William Bainbridge (1774–1833), she ran aground off Tripoli, and the crew was taken captive. She was burned the following February by a volunteer party from the *Intrepid* led by Stephen Decatur, Jr. (1779–1820). Some carvings were said to have been removed from the vessel before her destruction, and at one time, they and the stern carvings were in the Museum of the U.S. Naval Academy, Annapolis, but their present whereabouts is unknown.

References: Claypoole's American Daily Advertiser, Philadelphia, November 8, 1799, p. 3. Marceau, no. 79, p. 74. Pinckney, p. 70. DANFS, v, 1970, p. 282.

25 Mastodon bones

1801. Wood. Life-size. Existence of original wooden bones uncertain.

The event Charles Willson Peale commemorated in *The Exhumation of the Mastodon*, painted between 1806 and 1808 (Peale Museum, Baltimore), was a milestone in his life as well as in the history of natural science—the excavation of "the great American incognitum." In the summer of 1801 Peale, with the aid of his son Rembrandt and others, unearthed the remains of three mastodons from the marl pit on John Masten's farm and from the morass on land belonging to Peter Millspaw and Captain Barry near Newburgh, in upstate New York. Peale was overwhelmed by the scientific implications of the discovery, and in consultation with Dr. Caspar Wistar and others, immediately began to prepare two of the most complete skeletons for exhibition. From Masten's farm came the best, "the Philadelphia mastodon," which was reserved for Peale's Philadelphia Museum and is now in Hessiches Landesmuseum, Darmstadt. The "Baltimore mastodon" (now owned by the American Museum of Natural History, New York) was the less complete of the two. It was reserved for Rembrandt Peale who would take it on a European tour, to share with the Old World the natural wonders of the New. Charles Willson and Rembrandt Peale and William Rush carved missing bones for both skeletons, modeling them on existing bones (fig. 99). The major piece reproduced in wood was a lower jaw for the Philadelphia mastodon. Peale reminisced in his autobiography (p. 312):

Very few bones were found wanting in . . . the skeleton obtained first . . . but getting a complete under jaw at Milspaws morass, was a very fortunate thing, as it enabled Peale with the aid of his friend the ingenious Mr. Rush . . . to complete that part of the skeleton, and who also assisted Rembrandt and his father to carve all the deficient parts of the second skeleton. . . .

Charles Willson Peale completed the head in papier-mâché and first exhibited his mounted eleven-foot-high mastodon in Philadelphia on December 24, 1801, at the Philosophical Society. Shortly

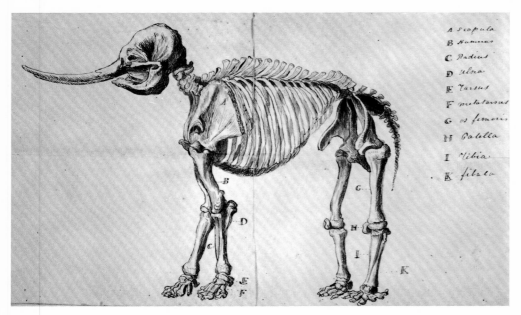

Fig. 99. Rembrandt Peale (1778–1860). *Mastodon Skeleton*, 1801. Pen and ink on paper, 15¼ × 12¾ in. (38.7 × 32.4 cm.). American Philosophical Society Library, Philadelphia.

thereafter, Rembrandt held a dinner party as a promotional event for his European tour. The thirteen guests, Rush among them, dined under the skeleton, and the evening was characterized by whimsical toasts followed by raucous singing to the accompaniment of John I. Hawkins on his newly patented portable grand piano.

References: Charles Willson Peale, "Autobiography," undated, transcribed by Horace Wells Sellers, pp. 312, 315, American Philosophical Society. George Gaylord Simpson and H. Tobein, "The Rediscovery of Peale's Mastodon," *Proceedings of the American Philosophical Society*, vol. 98 (August 16, 1954), p. 280. Charles Coleman Sellers, *Charles Willson Peale* (New York, 1969), pp. 298-302.

26 Quarter pieces

For the *Good Friends*. 1801. Wood. Whereabouts unknown.

The ship *La Bonne Amie* was purchased from Bordeaux, France, by Stephen Girard on September 29, 1792, and its name Anglicized. In June 1796, for the sum of £8, Rush repaired the ship's quarter pieces, and in April 1801 he received £15 for carving a new pair.

References: Girard Papers, series II, reels 140, bill dated September 29, 1792; 141, bill dated June 7, 1796; 144, bill dated March 9, 1801.

27 Rousseau

Figurehead for the *Rousseau*. 1801. Wood. Whereabouts unknown. M 80.

This ship, the second of Stephen Girard's French philosophers' series, was named for Jean Jacques Rousseau (1712–1778), influential political theorist, author, and composer. Marceau gave the launching date for the *Rousseau* as 1801 (p. 74).

Scharf and Westcott were uncertain whether Rush carved a bust or a full-length figure of Rousseau (II, p. 1066). Rush's bill, dated November 10, 1801, for the sum of £39.17.6, was for executing a figurehead as well as some carved details for the ship. In 1808 he charged $2.50 for repairing the figurehead. In October 1815 John Rush billed $5.00 for "Repairing figure Rousseau" and in May 1824, $8.00.

References: Girard Papers, series II, reels 336, bill dated November 10, 1801; 338, bill dated April 27, 1808; 340, bill dated October 1815; 343, bill dated May 5, 1824. Scharf and Westcott, II, p. 1066. Marceau, no. 80, p. 74.

28 Helvetius

Figurehead for the *Helvetius*. 1804. Wood. Whereabouts unknown.

This ship, the third of Stephen Girard's French

philosophers' series, was named for Claude Adrien Helvétius (1715–1771), who in 1758 published *De l'esprit* (*Essays on the Mind*), a work condemned by religious leaders for stating that all men are born with equal abilities and that distinctions arise from exposure to life's experiences.

A bill dated April 11, 1804, records that Rush charged £33.15 for carving the ship's figurehead, but it did not describe the size or the subject. Scharf and Westcott claimed that it was a full-length figure of the philosopher himself. A watercolor of the ship, painted by Jacob Petersen about 1810, shows a striding full-length male figure at the prow (fig. 100).

In January 1824 William Rush and his son John were paid $10.00 for repairing the figurehead, and in June 1828 John was paid $4.00 for repairing it. According to other bills, the figurehead was repainted in 1822 and 1829. The ship's history after 1830 is unknown.

References: Girard Papers, series II, reels 231, bill dated April 11, 1804; 242, bill dated November 8, 1822; 246, bills dated June 4, 1828, and December 1829; series III, reel 63, disbursement dated January 3, 1824. Scharf and Westcott, II, p. 1066.

29 Peace

Figurehead for an unknown vessel. c. 1805–10. Pine, painted. 70 × 24½ × 27½ in. (177.8 × 62.2 × 69.9 cm.), without base. Mr. and Mrs. Gerald S. Lestz.

Peace, known to Henri Marceau by 1960 and heretofore unpublished, is Rush's only full-length figurehead to come to light so far. The weather-damaged figure still has at its center back remnants of a projection, carved out of the same log to form a bracket for installation against the ship's stem. *Peace* was identified as by Rush because of its obvious relationship to *Virtue* [42], which is a similarly posed striding female figure with a fringed shawl. *Peace* was dated about 1805–10 because of stylistic affinities with *Comedy* and *Tragedy* of 1808 [31, 32]. In all three the drapery ripples in convoluted twists, cascades between the legs, and flutters around the feet, producing a kind of windswept effect.

The figurehead's original name and the name of the ship she adorned are unknown, but female figureheads of Peace and other allegorical subjects were commonly seen along Philadelphia wharves (see Marceau, p. 65, excerpt from the *Pennsylvania Journal*, November 23, 1791). In the twentieth century the figurehead has been variously titled *Mary* and, more recently, *Peace*. The dove is the embodiment of peace. In eighteenth-century iconography, however, the allegory of Peace was generally represented with a cornucopia of fruit and flowers, holding an olive branch in one hand, and setting fire to the emblems of war with the other. A dove with an olive branch and a lamb were more appropriately attributes of "Meekness" or "Humility" (George Richardson, *Iconology; or a Collection of Emblematic Figures* [London, 1779], II, figs. 245 and 374, pp. 31, 126-27).

Fig. 100. Jacob Petersen (1774–1854). *The Ship Helvetius of Philadelphia command^t by Captn Adam Baush*, c. 1810. Watercolor on paper, 19³/₁₆ × 21¹/₁₆ in. (48.7 × 53.5 cm.). J. Welles Henderson Collection, Philadelphia Maritime Museum.

For some time during the second half of the twentieth century, *Peace* was a garden ornament and suffered substantial water and flood damage and infestation by carpenter ants. In 1981 the figurehead was conserved at the Pennsylvania Academy. Areas where major aesthetically disfiguring losses had occurred—around the neck, at the top of the head, the forehead, the end of the nose, and the drapery fringe over the left foot—were reconstructed from fragmentary evidence on the sculpture itself, supplemented by visual clues from related Rush works. Evidence that led to the recreation of a white surface and technical information about the treatment is given by V. N. Naudé in "Toolmarks and Fingerprints: A Technical Discussion," note 17.

Provenance: G. B. Marrow, Lancaster, Pennsylvania, by c. 1935 to 1959; Mr. and Mrs. Gerald S. Lestz, from 1959.

30 Montesquieu

Figurehead for the *Montesquieu*. 1806. Wood. Whereabouts unknown. M 81.

Montesquieu (fig. 101) was the fourth and last of Stephen Girard's ships named after French philosophers, all of which Scharf and Westcott claim were ornamented with busts or figures of their namesakes. In *Spirit of Laws* (1748) Montesquieu (1689–1755) argued that powers of government should be separated and balanced to guarantee the freedom of the individual.

On April 3, 1806, Rush billed $90.00 for carving a figurehead for the ship, which was launched, according to Marceau, that year (p. 74).

References: Girard Papers, series II, reel 327, bill dated April 3, 1806. Scharf and Westcott, II, p. 1066. Marceau, no. 81, p. 74.

31 Comedy
32 Tragedy

1808. Pine (originally painted). Height of each without base, 90½ in. (229.9 cm.) The Edwin Forrest Home, Philadelphia. M 2, M 3.

Rush's first essays into public sculpture were the figures of *Comedy* and *Tragedy* for Philadelphia's New Theatre on Chestnut Street. Although they were not installed until 1808, similar allegorical ornaments were envisioned for the second-story niches in the original 1791 plan (see fig. 17), by the English architect John Inigo Richards, R.A., brother-in-law of Alexander Reinagle (1756–1809), one of the theater's founders. However, apparently because of excessive construction costs, the proprietors postponed such "frills." The theater's first regular season opened on February 17, 1794.

Seven years later the owners hired the English-

Fig. 101. Unknown Chinese artist. *Ship Montesquieu off the Harbor of Macao*. Oil on canvas, mounted on wood, 20¾ × 27 in. (52.7 × 68.6 cm.). The Stephen Girard Collection, Girard College, Philadelphia.

[31] Shown painted in 1926 photograph.
Courtesy of the Philadelphia Museum of Art.

trained architect Benjamin Henry Latrobe (1764–1820) to enlarge and modernize the Adamesque structure. Latrobe's principal innovations were to add wings and a porch supported by a Corinthian colonnade and to incorporate sculpture onto the facade. From Robert Morris's unfinished estate, he salvaged rectangular stone reliefs of *Drama* and *Music*, carved by the Italian sculptor Guiseppe Jardella (see figs. 19 and 20, and D. Dodge Thompson, "The Public Work of William Rush"), which by 1804 were installed over the arched wings. For unknown reasons, it was not until around 1808 that Rush's *Comedy* and *Tragedy* were placed in the second-story niches, flanking the large Palladian window (see pl. III). On April 2 the following notice in the *American Daily Advertiser* documents their installation:

William Rush, Esquire, of this city, has recently compleated two elegant figures (Comedy and Tragedy) for the proprietors of the Philadelphia Theatre, to be placed in the niches in front of that building on Chestnut street. In the execution of this work, the genius of the artist is truly pourtrayed; he has done himself honor, and added to that of his country.

When the theater was destroyed by fire on April 2, 1820, Rush's statues were saved. Another New Theatre, designed by William Strickland and built on the same site, opened on December 2, 1822, and *Comedy* and *Tragedy* were again incorporated into second-story niches flanking a recessed Corinthian loggia. When this building was torn down in 1855, the renowned Philadelphia thespian Edwin Forrest (1806–1872) acquired Rush's statues and displayed them in the garden of his estate, "Springbrook." After Forrest's death, the estate, by stipulation of his will, was converted into a retirement home for aged actors. *Comedy* and *Tragedy* remain in the collection of the Edwin Forrest Home.

In 1931, the several accumulated layers of paint were removed, and the figures were repainted gray. Nine years later this paint was removed and the pine was simply stained.

Provenance: The New Theatre, Chestnut Street, Philadelphia (destroyed by fire 1820); the New Theatre, Chestnut Street, Philadelphia (demolished 1855); Edwin Forrest, Philadelphia, after 1855; The Edwin Forrest Home, Philadelphia, after 1872.

Exhibitions: PMA, *Rush*, 1937 (cat.: Marceau, nos. 2, 3 [ill.], pp. 23-24). PAFA, *The One Hundred and Fiftieth Anniversary Exhibition*, 1955 (cat.: nos. 19, 20, p. 23). Whitney Museum of American Art, New York, *Art of the United States, 1670–1966*, 1966 (cat.: essay by Lloyd Goodrich;

p. 19 [ills.], nos. 351, 352, p. 11). National Portrait Gallery, Washington, D.C., *Portraits of the American Stage, 1771–1971*, 1971 (cat.: [cover ill.], nos. 94, 95, p. 196). PAFA, *Acres of Art*, 1972 (checklist: nos. 88, 89). PAFA, *Pennsylvania Academicians*, 1973 (checklist: nos. 51, 52). Whitney Museum of American Art, New York, *200 Years of American Sculpture*, 1976 (cat.: figs. 31, 32, p. 30; *Tragedy*, checklist no. 216).

References: Poulson's American Daily Advertiser, Philadelphia, April 2, 1808, p. 3. Christie, Manson & Woods, New York, *American Paintings, Drawings and Sculpture of the 19th and 20th Centuries*, May 22, 1980, lot no. 174 (withdrawn) (cat.: pp. 103–05 [ill.]).

33 Anatomical models

1808–20. Pine, leather, papier-mâché, polychrome. *Left temporal bone with inner ear structures* (M 4h), $21^{7}/_{8} \times 30 \times 23$ in. ($55.6 \times 76.2 \times 58.4$ cm.); *Right maxilla* (M 4i), $24^{5}/_{8} \times 25^{1}/_{4} \times 16$ in. ($62.5 \times 64.1 \times 40.6$ cm.). The Wistar Institute of Anatomy and Biology, Philadelphia. M 4a-i.

Rush's ingenuity is apparent in the design and construction of the anatomical models he created for the anatomy students at the University of Pennsylvania. These heroic—they are several times life-size—three-dimensional, anatomical parts were without precedent as medical-school teaching aids. Rush began making them in 1808 under the direction of Dr. Caspar Wistar [59]. After Wistar's death in 1818, Dr. Philip Syng Physick [60] oversaw completion of the project. Wistar undoubtedly helped Rush in decisions on the simplification of details and the degree of enlargement. In a lecture in 1831 to students at the University at Pennsylvania, Dr. William E. Horner recollected that Wistar had wanted to make up for the lack of anatomical specimens available to the medical students by "having a number of very large models in wood executed by Rush, with the view of giving every member of his class an equal opportunity for learning" (quoted in Marceau, p. 25). Figure 102 shows the page from Horner's 1824 "Report on the State of the Anatomical Museum of the University of Pennsylvania" which lists fifteen anatomical models made by Rush. All that remain are the *Maxilla* and the *Temporal bone*. In addition to these, Marceau catalogued the following seven that were extant in 1937 but are today lost:

[32] Shown painted in 1926 photograph. Courtesy of the Philadelphia Museum of Art.

13		Model of ventricles of Brain, by Rush, in wood				W.
14	Do.	basis	do.	do.	do.	do.
15	Do.	Eye		do.	do.	do.
16	Do.	Larynx		in clay		do.
17	Do.	do.		do.		do.
18	Do.	Thyroid Cartilage		paper		do.
19	Do.	Male organs of generation		in clay		do.
19–1	Do.	Chinese foot		do.		Chapman
20	Do.	First row of Carpus,	by Rush, in wood			P.
21	Do.	Second row of do.		do.	do.	do.
22	Do.	Radius		do.	do.	do.
23	Do.	Sphenoid Bone		do.	do.	W.
24	Do.	Upper Maxilla & Palate Bone	do.	do.	do.	
25	Do.	Lower Turbinated Bone		do.	lead	do.
26	Do.	Cellular portion of Ethmoid		do.	wood	do.
27	Do.	Ethmoid Bone		do.	do.	do.
28	Do.	Os Unguis		do.	do.	do.
29	Do.	Temporal Bone		do.	do.	do.
30	Do.	Labyrinth		do.	do.	do.
31	Do.	External Ear		in clay		do.
32	Do.	Temporal Bone		in wax		do.
33	Do.	Bones of Tympanum	do.			do.

Fig. 102. Page 10, detail, from William E. Hornor's "Report on the State of the Anatomical Museum of the University of Pennsylvania," 1824, listing Rush's models of anatomical parts.

a. Sphenoid bone, c. $4\frac{1}{2}$ times life-size.
b. Sphenoid bone, c. 7 times life-size.
c. Under surface of the brain, c. 4 to $4\frac{1}{2}$ times life-size.
d. Lateral ventricles of the brain, c. 4 to $4\frac{1}{2}$ times life-size.
e. Ethmoid bone, c. 7 times life-size.
f. Semicircular canals of the ear (osseous labyrinth) heroic model, detachable.
g. Temporal bone, c. 4 times life-size.

Wistar's own anatomical interests are evident in his selection of models; his particular contribution to practical anatomy was the clarification of the relationship between the ethmoid and sphenoid bones.

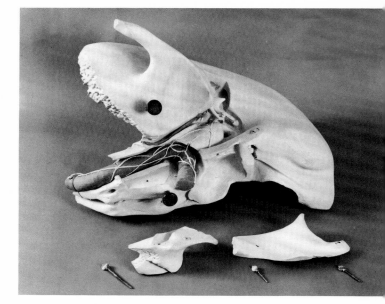

[33] Bottom view, left temporal bone, disassembled.

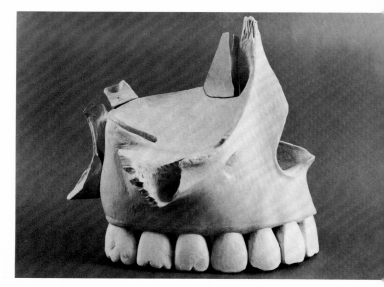

[33] Right maxilla.

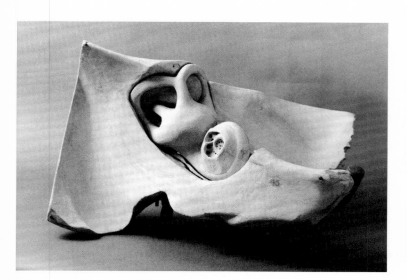

[33] Left temporal bone with inner ear structures.

[33] Undersurface of the brain and semicircular canals of the ear. Photograph from Marceau, no. 4.

The durability and accuracy of these models are attested to by their continued use as instructional tools at the University of Pennsylvania Medical School at least through the 1930s.

The model of the *Maxilla* shows the nasal cavity, the medial wall of the eye socket, the relationship between the upper teeth and the maxillary sinus and nasal cavity, and the route of tears from their duct near the eye into the nose. It is made of three pieces of pine attached to one another with metal thumbscrews which could be easily removed for demonstrations. The irregular wooden forms are defined by small blocks nailed together and then coated with thick gesso to model the appropriate shape. The surface was painted light ocher and then given a rose wash. The teeth were painted white.

The *Temporal bone* shows the inner ear which houses the hearing and balancing mechanisms. It is similarly constructed and painted, although it includes more complex and detachable elements. Attached to the main form are numerous bones, muscles, arteries, and nerves made out of wood, leather, papier-mâché, and string. The arteries and muscles were painted red, and the nerves were painted white. Two turned wooden knobs appear to have served as feet to support the model in one position during demonstration. Three brass feet support the model in a second position.

Exhibitions: PMA, *Rush*, 1937 (cat.: Marceau, no. 4a-i, pp. 25-26). PMA, *The Art of Philadelphia Medicine*, 1965 (cat.: nos. 85 [ill.], 86 [ill.], pp. 92-93). Birmingham Museum of Art, *The Art of Healing: Medicine and Science in American Art*, 1981 (cat.: by William H. Gerdts; p. 12; *Maxilla*, checklist no. 83).

Reference: Thomas G. Morton, *The History of the Pennsylvania Hospital 1751–1895* (1895; reprint, New York, 1973), p. 496.

[34]

34 Commemorative Statuette

1809. Cherry, silver, and brass. 16 × 9½ × 4¼ in. (40.6 × 24.1 × 10.8 cm.). Incised on book, beneath left figure: Wᵐ Rush Fect. Engraved on silver plate, lower left: Rush sculptor; lower right: Kneass Eng. Private collection.

This statuette, recently discovered and published here for the first time, is one of two known signed works by Rush; the other is the 1812 wood bust of Samuel Morris [48]. The statuette is unique among

Rush's works for its small scale and its relationship to furniture carving (see Linda Bantel, "William Rush, Esq."). According to its inscriptions, in 1809 this commemorative piece was commissioned of Rush and Philadelphia diesinker and engraver William Kneass (1780/81–1840) by Roberts Vaux (1786–1836), Quaker philanthropist whose major interest was prison reform.

The text of the inscription engraved on the silver plate at the front of the statuette reads: "DEDICATED by Roberts Vaux in Testimony of Friendship Ardent and Sincere commenced in Youth and CHER-

[34] Detail, showing signature.

ISHED IN MANHOOD." The brass plate on the back reads: "Club Inst. 1795 at Friends Pub. Sch! Found^d by Ch^{tr} of Wm Penn J.B. Thompson S.N. Lewis J. Thompson R. Vaux W. Morrison 1809." The statue shows a teacher and his pupil surrounded by attributes of knowledge: a globe for Truth, a lyre for Poetry, and books, a torch, a wreath, and an urn crowned by a flame finial.

In the 1790s James Beaton Thompson (1785–1818), Samuel Neave Lewis (1785–1841), Jonah Thompson (1786–1861), William Morrison (1785/86–after 1824), and Roberts Vaux attended the Friends' Public School in Philadelphia, at Fourth Street between Chestnut and Walnut Streets. Based on the inscription, the boys must have been nine or ten when they formed the club that was later commemorated by the statuette. We can find no information about it or the 1795 club in the Roberts Vaux Papers at the Historical Society of Pennsylvania, in the records of the William Penn Charter School (the school's later name), or in the Quaker Collection at Haverford College.

So far we do not know whether the statuette commemorates a specific occasion or why it was commissioned in 1809. We do know that in that year James Thompson was married, and Samuel Lewis married James and Jonah Thompson's sister, Rebecca Chalkley. By 1809 Roberts Vaux and three of his friends were successful merchants in their early twenties, and they may have met Rush through their shipping activities.

In the years following 1809, Roberts Vaux participated in the organization of several Philadelphia institutions, including the Academy of Natural Sciences, the Linnaean Society, the Franklin Institute, the Athenaeum, and the Historical Society of Pennsylvania, and from 1818 to 1831 he served as President of the Board of Controllers of the Philadelphia Public Schools.

References: D. G. Brinton Thompson, "John Thompson of Nether Compton, Dorset, and Philadelphia, Quaker Schoolmaster and Merchant, and His Philadelphia Descendants," *The Pennsylvania Genealogical Magazine*, vol. 23 (1964), p. 155, fn. 65.

35 Allegory of the Schuylkill River *or* Water Nymph and Bittern

1809. Pine (originally painted). Surviving fragment of the head, 10 × 9½ × 10 in. (25.4 × 24.1 × 25.4 cm.). Private collection. M 5, 5a, 5b.

The wood head and perhaps part of the bittern (now unlocated) are all that remain of one of Rush's earliest and most acclaimed public works, and his only fountain. Before it disintegrated completely, the full-size wood statue was cast in bronze, a material Rush never used. The story of Rush's creating this fountain dates back to the yellow fever epidemics of the 1790s.

A major civic concern resulting from widespread fatalities during recurrent epidemics was the development of wholesome water sources for drinking, cooking, personal hygiene, and cleaning the streets. To this end, Philadelphia's Councils sought the advice of a young English architect and engineer, Benjamin Henry Latrobe, recently arrived in Philadelphia. Latrobe's *View of the Practicality and Means of Supplying the City of Philadelphia with Wholesome Water* of December 29th, 1798 (Philadelphia, 1799), was radical and controversial. It proposed using two steam engines, one at the foot of Chestnut Street to pump water from the Schuylkill River (which Latrobe considered of "uncommon purity") through a tunnel to Centre Square, where a second pump would distribute it to subscribers by a gravity-feed system through wooden mains (see David Orr, "Centre Square Pump House," *Philadelphia: Three Centuries of American Art* [PMA, 1976], no. 153, pp. 188-89). The waterworks were formally opened as envisioned, on January 27, 1801. The round, delicately scaled Engine or Pump House in the form of a Greek temple crowned Centre Square and concealed the modern industrial machines. The project was a technological and architectural triumph, and

[35]

Centre Square quickly became a source of civic pride, and a popular and convivial gathering place. During the decade following its completion, trees were planted, and walks and benches were installed.

In a postscript to his 1798 proposal (p. 18), Latrobe acclaimed the cooling and hygienic benefits of fountains: "the air produced by the agitation of water is of the purest kind, and the sudden evaporation of water, scattered through the air, absorbs astonishing quantities of heat." To cool and adorn the grounds in front of Latrobe's Pump House, Rush, in 1809, designed and supervised installation of Philadelphia's earliest ornamental fountain built with public funds (pl. IV). Like Latrobe's Pump House,

Rush's sculpture combined beauty and function and was a critical and popular success. A writer in the *American Daily Advertiser* of August 28, 1809, hailed the fountain as elegant and "to the highest degree ornamental to our City." The nymph was placed on a picturesque bed of rocks "as nearly resembling nature as circumstances would admit," and from small lead pipes sprung streams of Schuylkill water in varying heights. From the waterfowl's beak issued a column of water about eight feet above the figure. *The Port Folio* of July 1812 noted the "fine and refreshing effect" produced by the new fountain and, while finding the bird wanting in grace, thought the "figure of the nymph . . . well executed."

Fig. 103. Posthumous full-length bronze cast of *Allegory of the Schuylkill River* or *Water Nymph and Bittern*, 1872.

The fountain also worked on an allegorical level. Although Rush's subsequent bills for other commissions usually specified his intended symbolism, his August 11, 1809, bill for the fountain did not. It was for $200 for "Carving figure . . . Collecting Stone . . . and Superintending the Erection thereof and painting." In nineteenth- and early-twentieth-century literature, the statue was variously called *Nymph and the Swan*, *Leda and the Swan*, or *Water Nymph at Fairmount*. Apparently one of the first critics to appreciate the sculpture's symbolism was the painter Thomas Eakins, who called it an "allegorical representation of the Schuylkill River." By 1937 the waterfowl had been identified as a bittern, and Marceau adopted the descriptive title *Water Nymph and Bittern* because he felt the fountain was so far from the Schuylkill that "it is more likely intended to symbolize *water* without any direct reference to its source." Both of these interpretations seem to have merit, although considering Rush's keen civic awareness and involvement, Eakins's was probably closer to the artist's intent. After all, Rush was himself a member of the Watering Committee at various times from at least 1802 on, and certainly in his own mind the statue must have been a kind of visual manifestation and celebration of the achievement of Philadelphia's highly touted water system, the controversial source of which was the Schuylkill. Rush specifically alluded to the river by including the bittern—a large wading bird in the heron family, known for its loud thumping cries—which was commonly found on that river's marshy shores.

According to Eakins and to Vanuxem family tradition Rush's model was said to be the lovely and socially prominent Louisa Vanuxem (1782–1874), daughter of James Vanuxem, a wealthy merchant and Chairman of the Watering Committee in 1809 when Rush carved the nymph. As other writers on this subject have observed, there are no contemporary accounts documenting the scandal that was said to have been created by Louisa's posing for the figure, the shape of which is so provocatively revealed under the clinging drapery. Apparently the myth was established by Eakins, in conjunction with research for his 1877 painting *William Rush Carving His Allegorical Statue of the Schuylkill* (fig. 63).

By 1812 the Centre Square Waterworks were inadequate to meet Philadelphia's water demands and a new and expanded waterworks were established on the Schuylkill at Fairmount. Around 1829, the Centre Square buildings were torn down, and Rush's fountain was reinstalled in the forebay opposite the Millhouse. Although Marceau wrote that the deteriorating wood statue was cast in bronze in 1854, it was not until 1872 that the city decided the fountain "was very much decayed and likely to become a complete wreck. As a relic of the first works supplying the City with water, it was thought desirable that it should be perpetuated" (*Journal of the Select Council of the City of Philadelphia*, 1873, Appendix p. 22). Robert Wood & Co., a Philadelphia firm, which from about 1866 to 1878 specialized in bronze statuary, was paid $1200 by the City of Philadelphia for casting the wood original (*Journal of the Select Council*, pp. 22, 97). According to Eakins's account, the "founders burned and removed the heavy accumulations of paint before moulding." The *Journal* records that "the dark color of the metal would naturally make it ineffective if placed against the rock in the position that it formerly occupied. It has, therefore, been mounted on a pile of large rocks in the centre of the marble fountain basin in the garden of the works, where it presents a fine appearance" (fig. 9). Scharf and Westcott gave the location as near Callowhill Street (III, p. 1868).

Eakins recorded that the original was then repainted and returned to the forebay of the waterworks. By around 1900 the wood nymph was almost totally disintegrated and moved inside to the attic of the Assembly Room of the waterworks (Marceau, p. 28). Shortly thereafter John S. Wurts (1876–1958), a great-great-nephew of Louisa Vanuxem, salvaged from the fragmentary remains the head and part of the bittern (PAFA, Minutes, April 17, 1913). Wurts had two bronze casts made of the head, both now in private collections.

Although Marceau listed Wurts as having presented one of those bronzes to the Pennsylvania Academy, the history of the version now in the Academy's collection is that it was given in 1913 by Edward H. Coates, the Academy's president from 1890 to 1906. Coates reported that he had the several layers of paint removed from the wood head, a plaster cast taken by the sculptor Charles Grafly, and a bronze made by Roman Bronze Works of Brooklyn, New York. He described its patina as "Gilt" (PAFA, Minutes, April 17, 1913, pp. 3-4); today its color is deep brown.

Posthumous cast: 1872. Bronze (originally not patinated artificially). Full-length, 90¾ × 19⅛ × 34⁵⁄₁₆ in. (230.5 × 48.6 × 87.2 cm.). Incised on base: Robert Wood & Co/Bronze Founders/Phila. The Fairmount Park Commission, Philadelphia (fig. 103).

Exhibitions: PMA, *Rush*, 1937 (cat.: Marceau, nos. 5, 5a [ill.], 5b, pp. 26-29). PAFA, *The One Hundred and Fiftieth Anniversary Exhibition*, 1955 (cat.: no. 22, pp. 21, 23). PMA, *La Première Pose: The Nude in Philadelphia*, 1975.

References: Committee on Water, Papers 1804–54, bill August 11, 1809, R.S. 120.42, City Hall Archives, Philadelphia. *Poulson's American Daily Advertiser*, Philadelphia, August 28, 1809, p. 3. "The Water Works," *The Port Folio*, vol. 8 (July 1812), p. 30. *Journal of the Select Council of the City of Philadelphia*, Appendix No. 13—"Annual Report of the Chief Engineer of The Water Department for the Year 1872" (Philadelphia, 1873), pp. 22, 23, 97. Thomas Eakins, "William Rush" (manuscript), c. 1878, Sartain Collection, Historical Society of Pennsylvania. Scharf and Westcott, I, p. 543; II, p. 1066, III, pp. 1868-69. Gordon Hendricks, "Eakins' William Rush Carving His Allegorical Statue of the Schuylkill," *The Art Quarterly*, vol. 31 (Winter 1964), pp. 382-403. Charles Coleman Sellers, "William Rush at Fairmount," in *Sculpture of a City: Philadelphia's Treasures in Bronze and Stone* (New York, 1974), pp. 8-10 (ills.).

36 Fingal

Figurehead for an unknown vessel. 1810. Wood. Whereabouts unknown. M 52.

Rush is mentioned by Scharf and Westcott as having carved a "head," probably a bust, of Fingal, the subject of a highly popular epic poem published by James Macpherson in *The Works of Ossian* (1765).

In 1810 the following article appeared in the *American Daily Advertiser*:

Admirers of the arts will find themselves gratified by paying a visit to the carving shop of Mr. Wm. Rush, were there is just finished a head of the celebrated ancient hero Fingal. The conception and expression of character as well as the execution of the work, in its line, has never been excelled in any country. We understand it is intended for a ship building in one of the eastern states.

References: Poulson's *American Daily Advertiser*, Philadelphia, June 15, 1810, p. 3. Scharf and Westcott, II, p. 1066. Marceau, no. 52, p. 59.

37 Eagle

c. 1810. Pine, painted. 30⅜ × 32 × 12⅝ in. (77.2 × 81.3 × 32.1 cm.). Pennsylvania Academy of the Fine Arts, Philadelphia; Gift of Wilson Mitchell (1922.12). M 54.

[37]

Marceau attributed this eagle to Rush. Although it was given to the Academy in 1922 with no recorded history, it bears a close stylistic relationship to Rush's eagle at St. John's Church [43]. Its feathers are also similar to those of the angel's wings of *Exhortation* [52] and *Praise* [53]. In addition, the butt joins and the way the nails were used are consistent with Rush's working technique. This is the only one of the three eagles Marceau listed under "Attributed works" which seems certainly by Rush.

Provenance: Wilson Mitchell, to 1922.
Exhibitions: PMA, *Rush*, 1937 (cat.: Marceau, no. 54, p. 60). The Art Institute of Chicago, *From Colony to Nation: An Exhibition of American Painting, Silver and Architecture from 1650 to the War of 1812*, 1949 (cat.: no. 100, p. 66). The Denver Art Museum, *Life in America*, 1951. PAFA, *The One Hundred and Fiftieth Anniversary Exhibition*, 1955 (cat.: no. 11, p. 23).

38 Joseph Wright

c. 1810. Terracotta. 19¾ × 16½ × 10 in. (50.2 × 41.9 × 25.4 cm.). Pennsylvania Academy of the Fine Arts, Philadelphia (1813.1). M 10.

Born in Bordentown, New Jersey, Joseph Wright (1756–1793) was the only son of Patience Lovell Wright (1725–1786), the noted modeler of wax portraits. From 1772 to 1782, Wright resided in England with his widowed mother, who taught him clay and wax modeling while he also studied painting with Benjamin West. After a brief visit to Paris in 1782 where he painted his famous portrait of Benjamin Franklin (replica, Yale University Art Gallery, New Haven), Wright returned to the United States. He was in Philadelphia from 1783 to 1786, and there he painted and modeled George Washington from life. Wright was in New York from 1786 to about 1789 and then returned to Philadelphia where in 1792 he was appointed the first designer and diesinker of the United States Mint. He died in the Philadelphia yellow fever epidemic of 1793.

According to Dunlap, Wright taught William Rush to model. Thus it is thought that as a kind of homage to his deceased mentor Rush modeled this portrait from memory years after Wright's death. This likeness relates closely to Wright's self-portrait in his painting of his family (Pennsylvania Academy of the Fine Arts), which he did shortly before his death at the age of thirty-seven.

Since Rush's bust was exhibited in the Academy's First Annual Exhibition of 1811, Marceau dated it "before 1811." He observed that there was "a vague look in the eyes which suggests the absence of a living model," and that the hair was not as crisply delineated as in Rush's other life portraits. Marceau did not, however, rule out the possibility that the bust could have been modeled from life, before 1793, and that its weaknesses related to Rush's immaturity in a new medium.

Without further documentary evidence, it is impossible to resolve this date problem. The generalization of Wright's facial features because of the lack of modeling and indication of underlying bone structure is uncharacteristic of Rush's more vigorous portrayals of the teens. In fact, the curiously shaped elfin lips, and the vague hair treatment make this closer stylistically to Rush's likeness of his daughter Mary [40], one of his earliest known and roughly datable terracottas. Thus this terracotta of Wright is dated about 1810.

Exhibitions: PAFA, 1811, 1817, 1818, SE 1818, 1819, 1820. PMA, *Rush*, 1937 (cat.: Marceau, no. 10 [ill.], pp. 31-32). PAFA, *Star Presentation*, 1944–45 (cat.: no. 35, pl. 18). The Art Institute of Chicago, *From Colony to Nation: An Exhibition of American Painting, Silver and Architecture from 1650 to the War of 1812*, 1949 (cat.: no. 99, pp. 65-66). PAFA, *The One Hundred and Fiftieth Exhibition*, 1955 (cat.: no. 18). PAFA, *Held in Trust*, 1973 (checklist: no. 197, p. 40).

References: Dunlap, I, p. 315. Fiske Kimball, "Joseph Wright and His Portraits of Washington: Sculpture," *Antiques*, vol. 18 (January 1930), pp. 35-39, fig. 1 (plaster of Samuel Morris misidentified as Joseph Wright). Charles Coleman Sellers, "Charles Willson Peale as Sculptor," *The American Art Journal*, vol. 2 (Fall 1970), pp. 7, 9-10.

39 Elizabeth Rush

c. 1810. Terracotta. 12½ × 8¾ × 6½ in. (31.8 × 22.2 × 16.5 cm.). Philadelphia Museum of Art; Given by Dr. William Rush Dunton, Jr. (44-39-2). M 36.

Relying on Dunton family tradition, Marceau wrote that Rush modeled this bust of his daughter Elizabeth (1801–1878) when she was about fifteen, in celebration of her doing "up her hair." Indeed her long hair is gathered in an elegant twist and attached to the top of her head with a comb. Her appearance suggests, however, that she is more likely about ten and the portrait therefore done about 1810.

The bust is made of a coarse red clay to which was added crushed brick and sand. This material is similar to a common brick clay and is unusually soft and porous. During firing, several large sections flaked away from the main body of the sculpture and had to be reaffixed, presumably by Rush himself. Rush's lack of technical success with this piece suggests that it was a unique experiment with a new material.

Provenance: Dr. William Rush Dunton, Jr., Towson, Maryland, to 1939.
Exhibitions: PMA, *Rush*, 1937 (cat.: Marceau, no. 36 [ill.], pp. 49-50). PMA, *Children in Art*, 1965.

40 Mary Simpson Rush

c. 1810. Terracotta. 13 × 9 × 7 in. (33 × 22.9 × 17.8 cm.). Philadelphia Museum of Art; Given by Dr. William Rush Dunton, Jr. (44-39-1). M 37.

Marceau suggested that Rush modeled this bust of his fourth and youngest daughter, Mary Simpson (1803–1887), about the same time he did Eliza-

[38]

[39]

[40]

beth's, that is, about 1816 when Mary would have been thirteen. Physically Mary looks much too young for thirteen, so the bust has been redated to about 1810. This earlier date also has stylistic support: like Rush's portrait bust of Joseph Wright [38], the facial features in *Mary Simpson Rush* are generalized and meekly described. The attempts Rush made at defining the underlying anatomical structure of the face lack the comprehension of anatomy and the finesse of his work later in the decade. Neck muscles, for example, are suggested but are incomplete and misplaced. The gaps between the upper eyelids and the eyebrows are unnaturally large. The eyes themselves are tentatively incised and described.

On May 5, 1825, Mary Simpson Rush married Isaac Dunton, listed as a merchant in the Philadelphia Directories of 1837 and 1839. They had eight children, one of whom, William Rush Dunton, was

the father of the donor to the Philadelphia Museum of Art of this portrait bust and the one of Elizabeth.

Provenance: Dr. William Rush Dunton, Jr., Towson, Maryland, to 1939.
Exhibitions: PMA, *Rush*, 1937 (cat.: Marceau, no. 37, p. 50). PMA, *Children in Art*, 1965.

41 Crucifixion

c. 1810. Wood. St. Augustine's Church, Philadelphia; destroyed by fire in 1844. M 7.

Rush's *Crucifixion*, carved for St. Augustine's Church at Fourth and Vine Streets, was lost when St. Augustine's was totally destroyed by fire on May 8, 1844, during the anti-Catholic riots in Philadelphia. In 1860, Abraham Ritter recalled:

The representation of the Crucifixion, in St. Augustine's Church, was the boast of the city, for the accuracy of its delineations at the hands of William Rush.

Time, in due course, scathed the features, and the fragments of the former; after they had served their purpose—but, alas for a reckless mob—the torch of the incendiary of 1844, fired by an unholy, unrighteous, and inhuman spirit of persecution, destroyed the temple, the altar, and its adornments at one fell swoop.

This piece of sculpture was of life size, and generally considered his *chef d'oeuvre*.

References: Dunlap, I, p. 374. Watson, *Annals*, III, p. 322. Abraham Ritter, *Philadelphia and Her Merchants as Constituted Fifty or Seventy Years Ago* (Philadelphia, 1860), p. 104. Scharf and Westcott, II, p. 1066; III, p. 2337. Marceau, no. 7, pp. 29-30.

42 Virtue

c. 1810–20. Wood, painted white. 70 × 24 × 24 in. (177.8 × 61 × 61 cm.). The Grand Lodge of Free and Accepted Masons of Pennsylvania, Philadelphia. M 82.

The history of *Virtue* is baffling and its date is unresolved. It is one of seven full-length figures in the collection of the Grand Lodge at Broad Street, where ·it is now displayed in the library. The others are the *Cherubim* [82, 83], *Faith* [84], *Hope* [85], *Charity* [86], and *Silence* [87].

Marceau and subsequent historians have perpetuated the tradition that all seven works were carved about 1810 during the building of the Masonic Hall, then located on Chestnut Street between Seventh and Eighth. The hall, which may have been designed by William Strickland, was dedicated on June 24, 1811. By around 1813 there were three standing figures representing Faith, Hope, and Charity in the niches of the facade, but the name of the sculptor was not recorded (Minutes of the Grand Lodge, April 19, 1813). *Virtue* bears no apparent resemblance to any of the cursorily delineated figures in Strickland's view of the facade (fig. 104), which was drawn by 1812, before their installation, but one cannot help wondering whether it might have been one of them.

All seven statues were supposedly saved when the hall was gutted by fire on March 9, 1819. Enough was left of the stone walls to serve as the shell of the rebuilt hall, which was dedicated on November 1, 1820. While the dates of the six other statues have now been firmly documented to this period of

[42]

Fig. 104. William Kneass (1780–1840). *Masonic Hall Philadelphia*, 1813, after drawing by William Strickland (1788–1854). Engraving, 19½ × 18¼ in. (49.5 × 46.5 cm.). Historical Society of Pennsylvania, Philadelphia.

reconstruction, no similar mention of *Virtue* has been discovered in extant minutes, bills, or receipts concerning either the first or the second hall.

Dating *Virtue* by stylistic comparison of drapery patterns with Rush's work has met with contradictory results because some of the folds over the right leg seem to have been lost through sanding or repairs. In general, the simplified patterns and lack of movement is analogous to the Masonic Temple pieces of 1820–21, but the long vertical folds broken by tightly spaced horizontal folds which gather between the upper thighs to emphasize the underlying form of the legs is not unlike Rush's *Allegory of the Schuylkill River* of 1809 [35].

To further confuse the issue, the striding pose with the left foot on an acanthus scroll, which is in the form of a billethead of a ship, is related to Rush's figurehead *Peace* [29], dated 1805–10. In fact Marceau listed *Virtue* in the "Ship Carvings" section of his catalogue, and since 1937 *Virtue* has been included in ship-carving literature. Unlike *Peace*, however, *Virtue* is carved completely in the round and has no apparent functional elements with which it could have been attached to a ship: it lacks metal fittings or a bracket at the back. That the base of *Virtue* is of a similar height and shape to that of *Silence* [87] suggests the two statues were carved at the same time and intended to be paired. However, whereas *Silence*'s figure and base are carved from one piece of wood, *Virtue*'s are carved from two. It therefore seems unlikely that the two statues were conceived initially as companions.

Iconographically *Virtue* is also curious. Masonic emblems emphasize moral principles, among which the importance of personal and collective virtue is paramount. But Rush's *Virtue* has none of the traditional attributes, such as wings at her shoulders or a sun at her breast, and therefore one concludes she may be so-called by tradition.

Exhibition: PMA, *Rush*, 1937 (cat.: Marceau, no. 82 [ill.], p. 75).
References: Pinckney, pl. IX, pp. 61-62. Brewington, fig. 33, pp. 36-38. " 'Father of American Sculpture': Grand Lodge Features William Rush Carvings," *The Pennsylvania Freemason*, vol. 24 (February 1977), p. 7.

Fig. 105. Reuben S. Gilbert (active 1829–1849). *Interior of St. John's Church*, 1829. Watercolor on paper, 7⅛ × 11⅝ in. (18.1 × 29.5 cm.). St. John's Lutheran Church, Philadelphia.

[43]

43 Eagle

1811. Wood, painted. 63 × 65 in. (160 × 165.1 cm.).
St. John's Lutheran Church, Philadelphia. M 9.

Built in 1808, St. John's Evangelical Lutheran
Church was originally located on Race Street between Fifth and Sixth. Church minutes for April 6,
1811, record: "Mr. William Rush done the carving
of the eagle. Cost $70" (quoted in Marceau, p. 31).
The eagle, attribute of St. John the Evangelist for
whom the church was named, is shown in an 1829
watercolor (fig. 105), in its original position above
the curved cornice, holding the sounding board of
the pulpit by a chain in its beak.

In 1847 the eagle was presented to the City of
Philadelphia and was exhibited in Independence Hall.

The orb was probably added for its new installation.
An 1856 lithograph of the Assembly Room of Independence Hall (fig. 110) illustrates the eagle
perched on a globe with a ribbon through its beak,
above Rush's statue of *George Washington* [68].

In 1914 the eagle was returned to the congregation of St. John's. Ten years later the church was
razed, and between 1928 and 1929 a new one was
erected at Columbia Avenue and Sixty-first Street,
and the eagle was placed over the right gallery to
allude to its original position in the old building.
The ribbon is no longer there, and sometime within
the last fifteen years the eagle was painted its present
gold color.

Exhibition: PMA, *Rush*, 1937 (cat.: Marceau, no. 9, pp.
30-31).

44 Indian

Figurehead for the *North America*. 1811. Wood. Whereabouts unknown.

This ship was built for Stephen Girard in Philadelphia in 1811 by shipwrights Joseph and Francis Grice. The following bill is the only evidence that Rush worked on it:

Philad^a	Stephen Gerrard
Octo^r 10th, 1811	Wm Rush
to Carving Large Indian Figure for Ship	
North America	$100.00

According to a May 1823 bill, the painter John Heppard supplied "small colours for head," and an October 1826 bill is for George Swope's painting and ornamenting the Indian figure.

References: Girard Papers, series II, reels 154, bill dated October 10, 1811; 158, bill dated May 31, 1823; 159, bill dated October 16, 1826.

45 Winter

c. 1811. Pine (originally painted gray-white). Height 28 1/16 in. (71.3 cm.). The Brooklyn Museum; Dick S. Ramsay Fund. M 11.

Only once, in the Pennsylvania Academy's First Annual Exhibition of 1811, did William Rush exhibit "Winter, represented by a child shrinking from the cold, in wood." According to Marceau (p. 32), *Winter* was "through the middle years of the nineteenth century" at the Germantown estate of George W. Carpenter, and purchased at his 1893 estate sale by Mrs. Thomas Meehan.

Indeed an untitled figure conforming to *Winter*'s description was at that estate: it was "a beautiful carved figure . . . by Rush, representing a youth in a shivering position seated on blocks of ice, with his mantle drawn around him" (quoted in *A Brief Description of Phil-Ellena, the Country Seat of George W. Carpenter* [Philadelphia, 1844], p. 25). Appropriately, this statue embellished the Summer House, under which was the Ice House. However it was William Rush's son John whom Carpenter praised as one of the three carvers who executed the numerous wood figures that dotted his estate, the building of which was begun in 1844, eight years after the death of William Rush. Moreover, no figure

of *Winter* was listed in the 1893 Carpenter estate sale at Thomas Birch's Sons, although in an annotated copy in the collection of the Library Company of Philadelphia there is inscribed in ink at the bottom of page 38, "Winter (wood)," without an artist's name. If the history of the Brooklyn Museum's *Winter* is correct, this raises the provocative question of whether it might have been carved by John, but there is not enough known sculpture by John Rush to resolve this issue.

Winter is carved from a solid piece of pine. In 1937 its many layers of paint were removed, and its surface was refinished with its present stain (letter from Henri Marceau to Mrs. Emma Middleton, February 18, 1937, PMA Archives).

A second statue of *Winter*, remarkably similar in design and size to the Brooklyn Museum's *Winter*, was acquired in 1981 by the M. H. de Young Museum in San Francisco and attributed to the "School of William Rush" (fig. 106). This polychromed figure is made of several pieces of pine, with the most obvious joins at the front of face and the left forearm,

Fig. 106. Artist unknown. *Winter*, n.d. Pine, polychrome, 27 × 16 1/2 × 13 in. (68.6 × 41.9 × 33 cm.). Fine Arts Museums of San Francisco, M. H. de Young Memorial Museum; Art Trust Fund.

[45]

a method technically inconsistent with Rush's other works. The figure is also dissimilar stylistically to the Brooklyn Museum's *Winter*: it is fleshier and pudgier, particularly at the thighs and belly. More unusual is the inclusion of his sex, something William Rush would prudishly have avoided by arrangement of drapery. The sensuality of the de Young Museum's *Winter* raises the question of whether it is even carved by an American, but its existence suggests that both derived from a common graphic or other source.

Provenance: George W. Carpenter, by 1844 to 1893; George W. Carpenter Estate sale, "Paintings and Statuary," Thomas Birch's Sons, Philadelphia, June 6, 1893, p. 38; Mrs. Thomas Meehan, 1893; her daughter, Mrs. Emma Middleton, Philadelphia, by 1937; Carl Lindborg, to 1942.
Exhibitions: PAFA, 1811. PMA, *Rush*, 1937 (cat.: Marceau, no. 11 [ill.], p. 32).

46 A Citizen

c. 1811. Wood. Life-size? Whereabouts unknown. M 16.

This portrait was exhibited at the Pennsylvania Academy's First Annual Exhibition.

Exhibition: PAFA, 1811.
Reference: Marceau, no. 16, p. 33.

47 Crucifix

1811–12. Wood. Carved for St. Mary's Church, Philadelphia; present whereabouts unknown. M 6.

In 1809 the congregation of St. Mary's Church resolved to enlarge and improve, by subscription, their

South Fourth Street building according to plans drawn up by Charles Johnson, a master carpenter and trustee of the church. With its prestigious congregation, and as the cathedral of a diocese overseeing Pennsylvania, Delaware, and New Jersey, St. Mary's was destined during the next twenty years to be one of Philadelphia's most important churches.

The enlarged building was formally opened on January 6, 1811, although the improvements had not been completed (Joseph L. J. Kirlin, *Catholicity in Philadelphia* [Philadelphia, 1909], p. 196). It was then decided that the old crucifix should be replaced. Minutes from a meeting of February 4, 1811, record the decision to hire Rush to execute the new crucifix: "Resolved that a committee be appointed to have a crucifix carved for St. Mary's church, and that Charles Johnson be appointed to apply to Mr. Wm. Rush for the same." The church disbursements indicate that on February 14, 1812, Rush was paid $250 "for carving Crucifix."

References: "Minute Book of St. Mary's Church, 1788–1811," *Records of the American Catholic History Society of Philadelphia*, vol. 4 (December 1893), p. 434. Treasurer Reports, 1811–12, St. Mary's Roman Catholic Church, SC27, box 1, Ryan Memorial Library, Archives and Historical Collections, Philadelphia. Dunlap, I, p. 315. Marceau, no. 6, pp. 29-30. Dennis C. Kurjack, "St. Joseph's and St. Mary's Churches," *Historic Philadelphia: From the Founding until the Early Nineteenth Century*, Transactions of the American Philosophical Society, vol. 43, part 1 (1953; reprint, Philadelphia, 1980), pp. 207-08.

[48] Back view, showing signature.

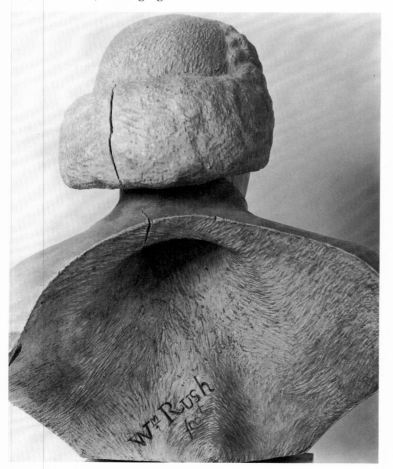

48 Samuel Morris

1812. Pine, painted white. 20½ × 19 × 12 in. (52.1 × 48.3 × 30.5 cm.). Incised at center back: W^m. Rush/Fec^t. The Schuylkill Fishing Company of the State in Schuylkill, Cornwells Heights, Pennsylvania. M 20.

The portrait of Samuel Morris (1734–1812) has been in the same collection since it was carved in 1812. It is the only known bust signed by Rush, and it retains its original paint surface.

Born in Philadelphia, Samuel Morris joined the Schuylkill Fishing Company in 1748, when he was fourteen or fifteen, and served as its governor from 1766 until his death. That society was founded in 1732 for the purpose of fishing and feasting, and it is still in existence.

During the early days of the Revolution, Morris was politically active as a signer of the Non-Importation Resolutions in 1765 and as a member of the Committee of Safety in 1775. As captain of the Philadelphia Troop of Light Horse, he received special commendation from George Washington for his active service to the American cause. From 1776 to 1777 he served on the Provincial Assembly and from 1781 to 1783 on the General Assembly.

After Morris's death on July 7, 1812, the members of the Fishing Company commissioned Rush to carve this likeness of their beloved governor. As Fishing Company member William Milnor, Jr., noted in 1830, Morris "uniformly declined in his latter years to sit for his portrait. . . . The bust was executed by our unrivalled artist, William Rush, Esquire, from occasional views of the original unknown to him."

Fishing Company minutes record that on July 23, the bust was installed at the north end of the new building, called the Castle, above and behind the Governor's seat. Its pedestal was presented by Daniel Knight, master builder of the 1812 Castle

[48]

Fig. 107. *Interior of the Castle, State in Schuylkill*, 1883, showing Rush's bust of Samuel Morris. Photograph from Joseph Jackson, *Encyclopedia of Philadelphia* (Harrisburg, 1931), II, p. 478.

and later its house carpenter. For the installation, a memorial ceremony was held at the Castle in honor of Morris and, as recorded in the minutes, member Curtis Clay spoke of

the recollection of the many happy scenes which we have enjoyed in his company, on this attractive spot will mingle with, and infuse a melancholy pleasure in, all our future meetings. Let us . . . always Imagine, that that escquisitely Sculptured representative of our departed Governor, is the silent medium of his benignant looks upon us, from an abode of bliss. Let this idea chasten our pleasure and controul our passions.—Then, indeed, we may justly exclaim, that although his revered form is withdrawn from our mortal view, yet we inherit and feel the influence of his dignified principles and of his unadulterated benevolence.

An 1883 photograph of the interior of the Castle shows the Morris portrait in situ, much as it is today (fig. 107).

Three plaster reproductions were cast from a mold made from wood in 1905 by P. G. Tognarelli of Philadelphia. The State in Schuylkill presented one to the First Troop Philadelphia City Cavalry and one to the Pennsylvania Academy (1905.8). The location of the third is unknown. Tognarelli cast three more in 1928, and in 1943 Peter C. Suffredini of Philadelphia cast two, all for Morris descendants.

Exhibition: PMA, *Rush*, 1937 (cat.: Marceau, no. 20 [ill.], pp. 35-36).
References: [William Milnor, Jr.], *An Authentic Historical Memoir of the Schuylkill Fishing Company of the State in Schuylkill . . . by a Member* (Philadelphia, 1830), pp. 62-63. Watson, *Annals*, III, pp. 294-95. Fiske Kimball, "Joseph Wright and His Portraits of Washington," *Antiques*, vol. 17 (January 1930), p. 34, fig. 1 (plaster misidentified as Joseph Wright).

49 Benjamin Rush

1812. Terracotta. 18¾ × 15½ × 12½ in. (47.6 × 39.4 × 31.8 cm.). Pennsylvania Academy of the Fine Arts, Philadelphia (1864.4). M 28.

The portrait of Dr. Benjamin Rush (1745–1813), a second cousin of the sculptor, is listed in the catalogue for the Academy's Third Annual Exhibition (1813). However, a letter of June 1, 1813, from William Rush to the doctor's son James indicates that, at the family's request following the death of Benjamin Rush on April 19, 1813, the portrait was withheld from the exhibition (quoted in Marceau, p. 41).

While Marceau dated the bust 1812–13, Rush's March 12, 1815, letter to the painter Benjamin West in London (New-York Historical Society) documents the 1812 date. In it, Rush, while notifying West he was sending him a plaster cast of his clay portrait bust of Benjamin Rush for the Royal Academy, explained how he modeled the likeness of the doctor, eight months before his death, based on actual head measurements.

William Rush portrayed the influential doctor as a vigorous, determined septuagenarian. This conception coincides with a verbal description by one of his students, Samuel Jackson (1787–1872), who characterized Rush as having a rather long head which was nearly bald from the crown forward, sunken cheeks, and a careworn, wrinkled face (Carl Binger, *Revolutionary Doctor, Benjamin Rush, 1746–1813* [New York, 1966], pp. 292-93).

Benjamin Rush received a medical degree from the University of Edinburgh, returned to Philadelphia in 1769, and began teaching at the College of Philadelphia. During the Revolution, he was elected to the Provincial Conference, signed the Declaration of Independence, and served as a member of the Pennsylvania Ratifying Convention for the Constitution. After 1789, he was primarily involved with medicine; indeed this period of medical history has been called the "age of Rush." From 1783 to 1813, he was a member of the staff of the Pennsylvania Hospital. His controversial theories of bleeding and purging for treating diseases were delineated in the first volume of *Medical Inquiries and Observations* (1789) and utilized during Philadelphia's yellow fever epidemics of the 1790s.

Rush was also an ardent social reformer; he advocated abolition of slavery and capital punishment, and he supported temperance, prison reform, and education for women. Known as the "Father of American Psychiatry," he championed more humane treatment for the emotionally disturbed. His *Medical Inquiries and Observations Upon the Diseases of the Mind* (1812) was the first American medical text treating mental illness.

Exhibitions: PAFA, 1814–15, SE May & October 1816, 1817–18, SE 1818, SE 1821, 1819–32, 1834, SE 1836–38, SE 1840, SE 1843, 1865–66, 1868–69, 1876, SE 1877. PAFA, *A Gallery of National Portraiture and Historic Scenes*, 1926 (checklist: no. 440). PAFA, *Star Presentation*, 1944–45 (cat.: no. 32, pl. 8). PAFA, *One Hundred and Fiftieth Anniversary Exhibition*, 1955 (cat.: no. 16, pp. 20 [ill.], 23).
References: PAFA, Catalogues of the Permanent Collection, 1864–66, 1869–70, 1877–91, 1969. Marceau, no. 28, pp. 40-42. Robert Erwin Jones, M.D., "Portrait Busts of Benjamin Rush, M.D., by his contemporaries," *Antiques*, vol. 108 (July 1975), fig. 22, pp. 109, 111-12. William H. Gerdts, *The Art of Healing: Medicine and Science in American Art* (Birmingham Museum of Art, 1981), p. 12 (ill.).

PLASTER CASTS

The Library Company of Philadelphia (fig. 81). Painted black.

The College of Physicians of Philadelphia (fig. 82). Inscribed in pencil on pedestal: Do^r John C Otto. Otto (1774–1844) was a pupil of Benjamin Rush.

Collection of the late Andrew Oliver, Boston (fig. 84). Painted white.

Pennsylvania Hospital, Philadelphia; gift of Joseph S. Coates, October 15, 1813 (fig. 83). Painted black. *Exhibitions*: PMA, *Rush*, 1937 (cat.: Marceau, no. 28 [ill.], pp. 40-42). PMA, *The Art of Philadelphia Medicine*, 1965 (cat.: no. 24 [ill], p. 35). *References*: Thomas George Morton, *The History of the Pennsylvania Hospital 1751–1895* (1895; reprint, New York, 1973), p. 343. Francis Randolph Packard, M.D., *Some Account of the Pennsylvania Hospital From Its First Use to the Beginning of the Year 1938* (Philadelphia, 1938), pp. 89, 90 (ill.).

Stephen Girard (1750–1831), Philadelphia, acquired by 1813; transferred to Girard College, May 25, 1833; whereabouts now unknown. *References: Girard Papers*, series III, reel 63, "Inventory and Appraisement of Goods and Chattels

... of Stephen Girard at the time of his Decease, . . ." January 26, 1832; indicates a value of $1.00 for the bust which was located in "Front Parlor upstairs" along with that of Dr. Physick and "4 marble statues—the seasons." Robert D. Schwarz, *The Stephen Girard Collection: A Selective Catalog* (Philadelphia, 1980), introduction by Wendy Wick, p. vii.

Royal Academy, London; whereabouts now unknown. *References*: Letter from William Rush to Benjamin West, March 12, 1815, The New-York Historical Society: "By the ship Electra . . . you will receive for the Royal Academy, a plaster taken from a clay model, of Dº. Rush. . . ." PAFA, Accounts 1813–16, I, April 17, 1815, check no. 34: for $11.93 for incidental expenses "To Philadelphia Bank for Bust of Dr. Rush sent to the Royal Academy."

50 Agriculture
51 Commerce

Permanent Bridge, Philadelphia. 1812. Wood. Probably over life-size. Whereabouts unknown. M 24, M 25.

Rush's recumbent figures embodying Agriculture and Commerce were designed as pedimental ornaments for the Schuylkill Permanent Bridge, also called the Market Street Bridge, which was erected between 1801 and 1805. The covered wood bridge, painted, dusted with sand and stone dust, and scored to resemble stone, was a major attraction. As one of the chief arteries by which Chester County farm goods reached Philadelphia, it was appropriate that *Agriculture*, "with the implements of husbandry" (PAFA, 1812, no. 1, p. 3) faced Chester County to the west, and *Commerce* overlooked the city to the east. Because Rush's sculptures are not visible in any views of the bridge, one may assume that they were carved in low relief and contained within the pediments.

Richard Peters (1744–1828), chairman of the building committee, superintended the construction of the bridge. Timothy Palmer, a self-taught architect of Newburyport, Massachusetts, designed the bridge and apparently included the symbolic figures in his original design. Evidently because of insufficient funds, their execution was curtailed, but in 1807, Peters argued on their behalf:

The Pediments of the entrances were intended to be finished with Emblems of Commerce, on the east; and of Agriculture, on the west. They were designed, and were to be executed, by the eminent American naval sculptor, William Rush of Philadelphia. . . . It is desirable that this finish, the expence

whereof will be small, should yet be added. The Pediments require it; to complete the design.

By December 1812, Peters could finally report that the figures were in place:

The masterly chisel of Mr. William Rush, has, at length, embellished the entrances of our bridge. . . . These ornaments were contemplated in the original design; and it was deemed obligatory on us to fulfil the engagements of our predecessors.

The bridge was destroyed by fire in 1875, but it is unknown whether *Agriculture* and *Commerce* were in place at that time.

Exhibition: PAFA, 1812 (*Agriculture* only).
References: [Richard Peters], *A Statistical Account of the Schuylkill Permanent Bridge Communicated to the Philadelphia Society of Agriculture* (Philadelphia, 1807), p. 33, copy in the Historical Society of Pennsylvania. Richard Peters et al., "A Report of the Schuylkill Permanent Bridge Committee, on the present state of the Bridge," December 22, 1812, in *Memoirs of the Philadelphia Society for Promoting Agriculture . . .* (Philadelphia, 1815), I, pp. 83-88. Scharf and Westcott, II, p. 1066; III, p. 2142. Marceau, nos. 24, 25, pp. 38-39.

52 Exhortation
53 Praise
54 Cherubim Encircled by a Glory

1812. Pine, painted. *Exhortation*, 56 × 19 × 18 in. (142.2 × 48.3 × 45.7 cm.); *Praise*, 57½ × 24½ × 18 in. (146.1 × 62.2 × 45.7 cm.); *Cherubim*, 20½ × 43 in. (52.1 × 109.2 cm.). St. Peter's Church, Philadelphia. M 21, M 22, M 23.

These three pieces, shown in 1812 in the Pennsylvania Academy's Second Annual Exhibition, were originally designed to ornament the new organ of St. Paul's Church which was completed in 1813. In 1760, a group of Anglican dissenters of Christ Church had formed St. Paul's and began to build their first church on Third Street in Philadelphia. By the late eighteenth- and early nineteenth-century, under the leadership of Samuel Magaw and Joseph Pilmore, St. Paul's had a major role in establishing the Protestant Episcopal Church in the United States. So successful was St. Paul's that around 1812 major alterations were made to provide more space for the congregation and for an organist and a choir. The first subscription to pay for the organ was offered

[52]

[53]

[54]

as early as 1806. The "splendid new organ," built by John Lowe at a cost of $3600, was installed at the rear gallery space six years later. It was recorded in St. Paul's daybook for July 29, 1812, that Rush was paid $150 "for Figures on top of the new organ."

In 1816, St. Paul's established one of the first Episcopal Sunday schools in the United States. By around 1830 when more space was required for the Sunday school, William Strickland was hired to transform the two-level church structure into three. As a result of these changes, there must no longer have been room for Rush's figures, and they were transferred to St. Peter's Episcopal Church, a few blocks away on Pine Street. There a new organ, built by Henry Carrie, was "opened" on November 29, 1829. One of St. Peter's vestrymen, Francis Gurney Smith, recorded in his diary (now in the Historical Society of St. Peter's Church): "The two female figures presented by St. Pauls to St. Peters Church were placed on the pillars each side of the organ on Monday 7th day of March 1831 at 4 p.m.

by Henry Flickwin." He added that the *Cherubim* were installed on March 11.

The figure of *Praise*, on the right as the viewer faces the organ (fig. 10), is portrayed playing a harp, a traditional angelic attribute. *Exhortation*, to the left, leans on two books, presumably the Old and the New Testaments, which are placed on a pedestal under her left arm: she gestures toward heaven with her right hand, proclaiming the truth contained within the scriptures. *Cherubim Encircled by a Glory* is on top of the organ at the center. Composed of four small winged heads grouped in an aureole, it evokes the presence of God in the sanctuary.

Exhibitions: PAFA, 1812. PMA, *Rush*, 1937 (cat.: Marceau, nos. 21-23, p. 37).

References: Daybook, Journal of Saint Paul's Church, July 29, 1812, p. 54, Diocese of Pennsylvania, Philadelphia. Scharf and Westcott, II, p. 1066. Norris Stanley Barratt, *Outline of the History of Old St. Paul's Church* (Philadelphia, 1917), p. 136. John Milner Associates, *A Preliminary Historic Structure Report for Old Saint Paul's Church and the Bishop Stevens House* (West Chester, Pa., February 1981), pp. 12, 27, 35.

55 Henry Ernest Muhlenberg

c. 1812. Wood. Life-size? Whereabouts unknown. M 17.

This work was shown in the Pennsylvania Academy's Second Annual Exhibition in 1812 as a "Bust of the Rev. Henry Muhlenburgh [*sic*]."

Marceau speculated that the bust might have been a life portrait of Reverend Henry Melchior Muhlenberg (1711–1787), founder of the Lutheran Church in America after whom Muhlenberg College, formerly, the Allentown Seminary, in Allentown, Pennsylvania, was named.

It seems more likely it is a life portrait of the Lutheran patriarch's son Gotthilf Heinrich Ernst Muhlenberg (1753–1815), also referred to as Henry Ernest, a prominent botanist and Lutheran pastor in Philadelphia and Lancaster. In 1810 Charles Willson Peale painted an oil portrait of Henry Ernest (Independence National Historical Park Collection, Philadelphia) for his museum gallery of "distinguished characters." In 1812, the same year Rush's bust was exhibited at the Academy, Henry Ernest published an English-German, German-English dictionary. In the Academy exhibition catalogue, the bust of Muhlenberg was listed immediately following Rush's figure of *Agriculture* for the Schuylkill Permanent Bridge [50], and with portraits of the botanists Linnaeus and William Bartram [56, 57], clearly a series on botany and botanists analogous to Rush's later series on physicians. Muhlenberg, elected a member of Philadelphia's Linnaean Society in 1809, was called "the Linnaeus of our Country" by physician and botanist William Baldwin (1779–1819) (quoted in Paul A. W. Wallace, *The Muhlenbergs of Pennsylvania* [Philadelphia, 1950], p. 319). Muhlenberg corresponded and exchanged specimens with European scientists, published works on North American plants, and in 1814 received commendation on his scientific pursuits from Thomas Jefferson (Wallace, p. 317).

The collections of Muhlenberg College and of the Lutheran Theological Seminary in Philadelphia do not own a wooden bust by Rush of either of the Muhlenbergs.

Exhibition: PAFA, 1812.
Reference: Marceau, no. 17, p. 34.

56 Linnaeus

c. 1812. Pine, painted white. 24¼ × 18½ × 12 in. (61.6 × 47 × 30.5 cm.), with base. The Corcoran Gallery of Art, Washington, D.C. (51.20). M 18, 56.

Rush exhibited a wood portrait of the Swedish botanist Carl von Linné (1707–1778) in the Pennsylvania Academy's Second Annual Exhibition in 1812. Linnaeus, as he was called, was one of the most influential botanists of the period, and he had many American followers although he never set foot on American soil.

In 1937 Marceau included this bust, described as an unidentified head, in the *Rush* exhibition and in the catalogue under "Attributed Works." In the section of the catalogue headed "Wood Sculpture, Portraits, Etc.," he listed a wood bust of Linnaeus with whereabouts unknown. In fact, a comparison of the bust that was exhibited in 1937 with a Dutch engraving of Linnaeus (fig. 108) makes it seem cer-

Fig. 108. Pierre Tanjé (1706–1761). *Carolus Linnaeus*, 1730–40. Engraving, 10½ × 7 in. (26.7 × 17.8 cm.). Simon Gratz Collection, Historical Society of Pennsylvania, Philadelphia.

tain that the unidentified head (Marceau, no. 56) and Rush's portrait of Linnaeus (Marceau, no. 18) are one and the same work.

Rush carved the bust and its pedestal from a solid piece of pine, but neither the commission nor the source for the portrait is known. In Philadelphia, Linnaeus's system of botanical classification and criteria for defining the genera and species of plants was greatly admired and utilized. There was a Philadelphia Linnaean Society (also known as the American Botanical Society), founded for the purpose of investigating natural history based on Linnaeus's system (Joseph Jackson, *Encyclopedia of Philadelphia* [Harrisburg, 1932], III, p. 842). Charles Willson Peale named a son Linnaeus and organized his museum according to the Linnaean system. In 1802, Peale requested his sons Rembrandt and Rubens, then in London, to bring home a bust of Linnaeus (Charles Coleman Sellers, "Charles Willson Peale as Sculptor," *The American Art Journal*, vol. 2 [Fall

[56]

1970], p. 10). Whether they did or not is unknown, and so it is interesting to speculate whether Peale commissioned Rush to execute this one.

As to the source of the image, an engraving such as the one in figure 108 could have been brought from Europe by the young Peales or by any of the Philadelphians who traveled to Europe to study during the second half of the eighteenth century. For instance, Dr. Adam Kuhn (professor at the University of Pennsylvania whose students included Philip Syng Physick [60]) studied botany with Linnaeus at Upsala during 1761–64.

Provenance: unknown New Jersey estate; Kendrick Scofield, Doylestown, Pennsylvania, by 1937 to 1951; Leon F. Stark, Philadelphia, 1951.

Exhibitions: PAFA, 1812. PMA, *Rush*, 1937 (cat.: Marceau, no. 56 [listed as unidentified head, c. 1811], pp. 60-61). National Gallery of Art, Washington, D.C., *The Eye of Thomas Jefferson*, 1976 (cat.: William Howard Adams, ed.; no. 581 [ill.], p. 337).

Reference: Marceau, no. 18, pp. 34-35.

[56] Back view.

57 William Bartram

c. 1812. Wood. Whereabouts unknown. M 19.

Rush exhibited a portrait in wood of William Bartram (1739–1823) in the Pennsylvania Academy's Second Annual Exhibition (1812). There is no information about its subsequent history.

Bartram was a son of the noted Pennsylvania botanist John Bartram (1699–1777). Under the patronage of an English botanist, William Bartram explored the southeastern United States between 1773 and 1777, collecting seeds and plant specimens and making botanical drawings to be sent back to England, a journey he recounted in *Travels through North and South Carolina, Georgia, East and West Florida, the Cherokee Country, the Extensive Territories of the Muscogulges, or the Creek Confederacy, and the Country of the Choctaws* (1791). In 1792 he was elected professor of botany at the University of Pennsylvania, although he chose not to occupy the chair because of poor health, and from 1786 until his death he was a member of the American Philosophical Society.

Exhibition: PAFA, 1812.
References: Scharf and Westcott, II, p. 1066. Marceau, no. 19, p. 35.

58 Columbia

Possibly by William Rush. c. 1812. Drawing, red chalk on paper. 9¼ × 6¾ in. (23.5 × 17.1 cm.). Inscribed on scroll at left with motto: *God . . .* [God Armeth the Patriot]; lower right in red chalk: *Go . . .* ; lower left in pencil: T. Badger. Museum of Fine Arts, Boston; M. and M. Karolik Collection (61.250).

On the basis of style and subject, Colin Eisler has attributed this drawing to Rush. He relates the pose, a conventional one dating back to the antique, to Rush's *Water Nymph and Bittern* of 1809 [35]. A flag billows around *Columbia* as she holds a dragon beneath her feet.

Although the sketch is inscribed with the name T. Badger, possibly the American portrait painter and lithographer Thomas Badger (1792–1868), Eisler believes that the inscription was added later and does not belong to that artist. This sketch does not relate stylistically to the only known sketch by Rush [93a], a Hercules figurehead dated 1824, whose present whereabouts is unknown.

There was a frigate *Columbia* under construction at Washington Navy Yard in 1814, which was burned to prevent its falling into enemy hands. If this sketch is of a figurehead called *Columbia*, it might have been for that ship, but so far no evidence has been discovered that Rush did any of the ship's carvings.

References: DANFS, II, 1963, p. 146. Colin Eisler, *Sculptors' Drawings Over Six Centuries 1400–1950* (New York, 1981), no. 54.

59 Caspar Wistar

1812–13. Terracotta. 20 × 17 × 13½ in. (50.8 × 43.2 × 34.3 cm.). Pennsylvania Academy of the Fine Arts, Philadelphia (1864.7). M 26.

This life-size terracotta bust of Dr. Caspar Wistar (1761–1818) was first exhibited in the Academy's Third Annual Exhibition in 1813, although the catalogue does not identify the material. In subsequent

[59]

Academy exhibition catalogues, however, it is listed as "clay burnt."

Wistar received medical degrees from the University of the State of Pennsylvania and the University of Edinburgh. In 1787, he was elected a junior fellow of the newly organized College of Physicians in Philadelphia, and two years later, succeeded Benjamin Rush [49] as professor of chemistry in the medical school. After several years of distinguished teaching, Wistar was offered a full professorship at the University of Pennsylvania. In 1810, a chair of anatomy was created for him which he held until his death. His first volume of *A System of Anatomy for the Use of Students of Medicine* was published in 1811, an early American textbook on that subject. A member of the American Philosophical Society (Vice President, 1795–1815; President, 1815-18), Wistar held a weekly gathering comprised mostly of members of this organization. It became a regular feature of Philadelphia social and intellectual life, and after Wistar's death, the group formed a Wistar society to insure the continuation of these Saturday evening gatherings.

Rush surely modeled his portrait of Wistar from life, since at this time he was also working with Wistar on anatomical models [33]. The two had other interests in common, for Wistar's name shows up in the 1810 list of subscribers to the Pennsylvania Academy (PAFA, Archives), of which Rush was a founding member.

Exhibitions: PAFA, 1813, 1815, 1817–18, SE 1818, SE 1821, 1821–32, 1834, SE 1836–38, SE 1840. PMA, *Rush*, 1937 (cat.: Marceau, no. 26 [ill.], pp. 39-40). PAFA, *Star Presentation*, 1944–45 (cat.: no. 34, pl. 18). PAFA, *Pennsylvania Academicians*, 1973 (checklist: no. 56). The Art Institute of Chicago, *From Colony to Nation: An Exhibition of American Painting, Silver and Architecture from 1650 to the War of 1812*, 1949 (cat.: p. 65, no. 98). PMA, *The Art of Philadelphia Medicine*, 1965 (cat.: pp. 42-43, no. 32 [ill.]).

References: PAFA, Catalogues of the Permanent Collection, 1864–66, 1869–70, 1878–91, 1969.

PLASTER CASTS

The American Philosophical Society, Philadelphia (58.S.9); probably gift of John Vaughan (1756–1841), 1818 (fig. 86). Painted white. *Reference: Catalogue of Portraits and Other Works of Art in the Possession of the American Philosophical Society* (Philadelphia, 1961), p. 105, fig. 24, p. 138.

The College of Physicians of Philadelphia; donated by the Wistar Institute of Anatomy and Biology, Philadelphia, 1958 (fig. 87). Painted white.

Pennsylvania Hospital, Philadelphia; presented by Zaccheus Collins, 1818 (fig. 85). Painted black. *Exhibition*: PMA, *Rush*, 1937 (cat.: Marceau, no. 26, pp. 39–40). *References*: Thomas George Morton, *The History of the Pennsylvania Hospital 1751–1895* (1895; reprint, New York, 1973), p. 343. Francis Randolph Packard, *Some Account of The Pennsylvania Hospital from its First Use to the Beginning of the Year 1938* (Philadelphia, 1938), p. 90.

Wistar Institute of Anatomy and Biology, Philadelphia. In 1937 Marceau listed two plasters belonging to the Wistar Institute. In 1958 one was given to The College of Physicians, and the location of the second is now unknown.

60 Philip Syng Physick

1812–13. Terracotta. 19 × 14¾ × 11¼ in. (48.2 × 37.5 × 28.5 cm.). Pennsylvania Academy of the Fine Arts, Philadelphia (1944.28). M 27.

Because this bust was first exhibited in the Pennsylvania Academy's Third Annual Exhibition (1813), it is dated 1812–13. Rush portrayed Dr. Philip Syng Physick (1768–1837) as a man of great composure and with a forceful presence. According to a fellow physician, Physick's "personal appearance was commanding in the extreme. . . . His head and face were excellently well shaped; his eyes hazel, bright and penetrating, heightened in effect by the habitual pensiveness and statue-like composure of his countenance" (William Elder, M.D., "Dr. Philip Syng Physick," in *Lives of Eminent Philadelphians, Now Deceased* [Philadelphia, 1859], p. 797).

Physick, often called the father of American surgery, graduated from the University of Pennsylvania in 1785 and then studied with John Hunter, the renowned British surgeon, in London, where he became the first American to act as house surgeon at St. George's Hospital. He received a medical degree from the University of Edinburgh in 1792.

Returning to Philadelphia in 1793, during the yellow-fever epidemic, he worked closely with his friends Stephen Girard, who contributed financial assistance to the fever victims, and Dr. Benjamin Rush. Physick was a member of the staff of the Pennsylvania Hospital from 1794 to 1816. He was also Girard's physician, and according to a household inventory, Girard owned a now lost plaster of Rush's portrait bust of Physick. In 1805 Physick was appointed to the newly created chair of surgery at the University of Pennsylvania, a position he held until 1819 when he replaced Caspar Wistar as professor of anatomy. Physick was extremely influential as a teacher, and his lectures and surgical procedures were compiled by John Syng Dorsey in 1813 and published as *Elements of Surgery*.

Exhibitions: PAFA, 1813–15, SE May & October 1816, 1817–18, SE 1818, 1819–21, SE 1821, 1822–30, 1834, SE 1836–38, 1840, 1843, 1866 and 1868 (unattributed). PAFA, *A Gallery of National Portraiture and Historic Scenes*, 1926 (checklist: no. 434). PMA, *Rush*, 1937 (cat.: Marceau, no. 27 [ill.], p. 40; also under no. 28, pp. 40–42). PAFA, *Star Presentation*, 1944–45 (cat.: no. 31, pl. 9). PAFA, *The One Hundred and Fiftieth Anniversary Exhibition*, 1955 (cat.: no. 21, p. 23). PMA, *The Art of Philadelphia Medicine*, 1965 (cat.: no. 40, p. 47).

References: PAFA, Catalogues of the Permanent Collection, 1879–91, 1969. The 1865, 1866, 1869, 1870, and 1878 Catalogues of the Permanent Collection list an unattributed bust of Dr. Physick, probably Rush's terracotta. William H. Gerdts, *The Art of Healing: Medicine and Science in American Art* (Birmingham Museum of Art, 1981), p. 12 (ill.).

PLASTER CASTS

The American Philosophical Society, Philadelphia (58.S.6) (fig. 89). Painted white. *Reference: Catalogue of Portraits and Other Works of Art in the Possession of the American Philosophical Society* (Philadelphia, 1961), fig. 28, pp. 78, 142.

The Library Company of Philadelphia (fig. 91). Painted black.

Robert Erwin Jones, M.D., Philadelphia (fig. 88). Traces of white paint.

The College of Physicians of Philadelphia (fig. 90). Painted white.

Pennsylvania Hospital, Philadelphia; presented by Joseph Coates, October 15, 1813; whereabouts now unknown. *References*: Thomas G. Morton, *The History of the Pennsylvania Hospital 1751–1895* (1897; reprint, New York, 1973), p. 343. Board of Manager Minutes, Pennsylvania Hospital, 1804–33, VIII, p. 219.

Stephen Girard (1750–1831), Philadelphia, acquired by 1813; transferred to Girard College, May 25, 1833; whereabouts now unknown. *References: Girard Papers*, series III, reel 63, "Inventory and Appraisement of Goods and Chattels . . . of Stephen Girard at the time of his Decease, . . ." January 26, 1832; indicates a value of $1.00 for the bust which was located in the "Front Parlor upstairs," along with that of Dr. Rush and "4 marble statues—the seasons." Robert D. Schwarz, *The Stephen Girard Collection: A Selective Catalog* (Philadelphia, 1980), introduction by Wendy Wick, p. vii.

[60]

61 Wisdom
62 Justice

After 1812–by 1824. Pine (originally painted). *Wisdom* 92¾ × 37 × 26 in. (235.6 × 94 × 66 cm.); *Justice* 93¼ × 38½ × 19¼ in. (236.9 × 97.8 × 48.9 cm.); height of each includes base, 13½ in. (34.3 cm.). The Fairmount Park Commission, Philadelphia. M 44, M 45.

Lafayette's arrival in Philadelphia in September 1824 precipitated great pomp and ceremony, the planning of which Rush, as a city council member, was intimately involved [94]. Accompanied by 10,000 troops, Lafayette and Governor Schulze of Pennsylvania and other civic leaders were escorted from the Delaware River near Trenton to the State House (Independence Hall). On their route they passed through thirteen triumphal arches, alluding to the original thirteen states. The final and most elaborate was the Grand Civic Arch, designed by the architect William Strickland (1788–1854) with the assistance of his young pupil, Samuel Kneass (1800–1858). It spanned Chestnut Street in front of the State House. Forty-five feet tall and twelve feet deep, it was of a frame construction and covered with canvas painted by scene painters of the Chestnut Street Theatre, to simulate stone niches containing allegorical figures such as liberty, victory, and independence, each with their respective mottoes. Over the arch were painted flying figures of Fame (see fig. 109). The whole was surmounted by a stepped entablature on top of which was an eight-foot-high canvas representing the arms of the City of Philadelphia, painted by Thomas Sully (see fig. 24). That was flanked by Rush's almost seven-foot-high statues of *Justice* and *Wisdom*. *Justice* has her traditional attributes, the scales and sword; *Wisdom*, the books, snake, and mirror. According to the 1824 account in *The Port Folio*, Rush's figures "had all the beauty and lightness of drapery, of the Grecian School; and so excellent was the workmanship, that it was not until after positive assurances, that a spectator would give up the belief that they were executed in marble."

In 1976, D. Dodge Thompson suggested that *Wisdom* and *Justice* were part of an iconographic scheme which alluded to the State of Pennsylvania, because their symbols are also similar to the emblems of William Penn, Pennsylvania's first proprietor: on Penn's 1773 arms engraved by John Hall after a drawing by Pierre Eugène du Simitière (see fig. 25) there appear a mirror and snake for Mercy, and scales for Justice. Thompson also observed that the general iconographic types of Wisdom and Justice were established by the early eighteenth century in such publications as James Gibbs's *Book of Architecture*, plates 116 and 118, first published in London in 1728 (PMA, *Philadelphia: Three Centuries of American Art*, 1976, p. 262).

Rush's statues are not executed fully in the round but rather hollowed out at the backs like *Comedy* and *Tragedy* [31, 32]. During the Lafayette ceremonies, pieces of skillfully draped and painted linen were tacked to the backs to conceal these excavations. (Some tacks are extant.) Because of this unusual camouflage, Thompson suggested that *Wisdom* and *Justice* were intended to be placed in niches for another unrealized project where such cavities would not have been visible.

The most likely was that of Robert Mills for the redesign of the main building of the State House. According to a description of the plan, which was exhibited at the Pennsylvania Academy in 1812, Mills proposed restoring the steeple and moving the clock. At the front entrance, he projected a balustrade-crowned portico to enclose a rostrum for public speaking, and "the removal of two blank windows under the portico, and putting in their place

niches for the reception of statues of Wisdom and Justice" (PAFA, 1812, no. 15, pp. 5-6). While Mills's other plans for building new fireproof office wings were carried out, the improvements to the main building apparently never got off the drawing boards. Speculation that Rush's figures of *Wisdom* and *Justice* were somehow connected to this project is unavoidable. Moreover, each statue averages about 93 inches tall with its pedestal, just the right height to slip into Mills's proposed niches which, assuming they were designated the same size as the present window openings, would have been 10 feet, 5 inches high and 5 feet, 10 inches wide and elevated about 5½ feet from the ground. There were niches on the new wings, but they were only about 6 feet high, too small to accommodate Rush's statues. Unfortunately, none of Mills's plans and papers concerning this project have been found.

Conceptually and stylistically, *Wisdom* and *Justice* also relate to Rush's works of the period of Mills's design, works such as *Exhortation* and *Praise* of 1812 [52, 53] and the full-length statue of *George Washington* of 1815 [68]. All have in common the column on which rests books or other attributes. The drapery treatment of *Wisdom* and *Justice* has more in common with Rush's work of the teens than of the 1820s. Like *Washington*, there is an extra piece of cloth draped diagonally across the underlying garment, an allusion to a Roman toga that is particularly appropriate for sculptures destined for governmental use. Like *Praise* and *Exhortation*, the abundant drapery flares and curls at the feet, clinging to the legs and articulating each in a series of short parallel folds carved perpendicularly to them. By 1820, the folds below the knees became simpler and more diagonal in design, and less descriptive of the contour of each leg (see *Silence* [87]). If *Wisdom* and *Justice* were done after 1812, however, and were not utilized, it is curious that Rush never exhibited them at the Pennsylvania Academy.

For a few years after Lafayette's 1824 tour, Rush's statues were unexhibited. Then, according to *Hazard's Register* of August 19, 1829, *Justice* was placed on the west side of the State House yard, corresponding to public buildings occupied by the courts, and *Wisdom* was placed on the east, corresponding to buildings occupied by City Council. A writer in the September 5, 1829, issue of the *Saturday Evening Post* claimed that "these figures were carved some years ago, we believe, by Mr. Rush, and were originally destined to fill niches at a considerable

[61]

[62]

elevation." In the State House yard, they were elevated on three- or four-foot-high pedestals, and apparently their linen backings were now tattered enough to elicit the press's wry comments (see D. Dodge Thompson, "The Public Work of William Rush"). Their location thereafter is unknown, although they must have been stored indoors or, with their excavated backs, they would not today be in such good condition. Scharf and Westcott wrote that the statues were placed in niches of the Assembly Room at the Fairmount Waterworks in 1835, (III, p. 1853); Marceau said 1848. They were there until the Rush exhibition in 1937, and they are now on deposit at the Pennsylvania Academy of the Fine Arts.

In 1941 the paint was removed from both *Wisdom* and *Justice*, and the wood was waxed. *Wisdom*, at some earlier time, seems also to have undergone other, more extensive restoration. X-radiographs taken at the Pennsylvania Academy in 1981 indicate pegged joins at the shoulders, a technique Rush is not known to have used. The column, a later replacement, is carved of juniper, not pine like the rest of the statue, and its regularity indicates that it is machine-turned; *Justice*'s column is hand carved. A photograph of *Wisdom* in the Assembly Room at the Waterworks, probably taken in the late nineteenth century, indicates a totally different number and configuration of books, which are arranged randomly and stacked on the column (figs. 11, 12). When the present alteration took place is unknown, but the spatial gap under the arm is closer now, but

Fig. 109. Attributed to George Gilbert (active 1824–1831). *Civic Arch for Lafayette*, c. 1824. Illustration in John Fanning Watson, *Annals of Philadelphia*, in manuscript, II, p. 460. Courtesy of the Historical Society of Pennsylvania, Philadelphia.

not identical, to what appears in the illustration of the Grand Civic Arch (fig. 109).

Exhibitions: PMA, *American Folk Art*, 1933. PMA, *Rush*, 1937 (cat.: Marceau, nos. 44, 45 [ill.], p. 56). PAFA, *The One Hundred and Fiftieth Anniversary Exhibition*, 1955 (cat.: *Justice*, no. 14, p. 23; *Wisdom*, no. 15, p. 23 [ill. p. 22]). PAFA, *Acres of Art*, 1972 (checklist: nos. 90-91). PAFA, *Pennsylvania Academicians*, 1973 (checklist: nos. 53-54). PMA, *Philadelphia: Three Centuries of American Art*, 1976 (cat.: no. 218 [ill., *Justice* (reversed)], pp. 260-62, by D. Dodge Thompson).

References: *Poulson's American Daily Advertiser*, Philadelphia, September 30, 1824, p. 2. "The Visit of General Lafayette," *The Port Folio*, vol. 18 (October 1824), pp. 335-36. *Hazard's Register*, vol. 4 (August 29, 1829), p. 144. *Saturday Evening Post*, vol. 8 (September 5, 1829), p. 3. Watson, *Annals*, III, p. 444 (*Wisdom* misidentified as *Faith*). Scharf and Westcott, III, pp. 1853, 1868. Edward M. Riley, "The Independence Hall Group," in *Historic Philadelphia: From the Founding Until the Early Nineteenth Century*, Transactions of the American Philosophical Society, vol. 43, part 1 (1953; reprint, Philadelphia: 1980), p. 33.

63 Figurehead

For the *Guerriere*. 1814. Wood. Whereabouts unknown.

On July 30, 1814, Rush charged $286.00 for carving for the *Guerriere*, presumably a figurehead but unspecified in the bill. This 1508-ton, 44-gun Navy frigate was named after the 49-gun British ship *Guerriere* which was seized by the *Constitution* and burned during the War of 1812 in a major naval victory near the Gulf of St. Lawrence. The American *Guerriere* was launched in Philadelphia on June 20, 1814. Commanded by John Rodgers, she sailed from New York on May 20, 1815, as the flagship of a squadron led by Stephen Decatur, Jr., against Algeria. In 1841 she was broken up at the Norfolk Navy Yard.

References: Navy Records, "An estimate of the cost of building, equipping, arming . . . the United States frigate Guerriere," U.S. Navy, 1775–1900, AC—Construction of U.S. Ships. DANFS, III, 1968, pp. 181-82.

64 Oliver Hazard Perry

c. 1814. Terracotta. Whereabouts unknown. M 30.

Commodore Oliver H. Perry (1785–1819) served

Winfield Scott, plaster.

on board the frigates *Adams* in 1802–03 and *Constellation* [20] in 1804–06 during the war with Tripoli. During the War of 1812 he was instrumental in securing an important American victory in the Battle of Lake Erie, as well as helping defeat the British at the Battle of the Thames which established American supremacy in the northwest.

On January 6, 1814, Congress adopted a resolution thanking this heroic naval officer and requesting that the President present him with a gold medal. Rush's work was first exhibited that same year as the "Bust of Commodore Perry." In subsequent catalogues it was described as "modelled in clay burnt." Perry died of yellow fever while in command of a fleet on a South American mission.

Exhibitions: PAFA, 1814, 1815, SE May & October 1816, 1817, 1818, SE 1818, 1821, SE 1821, 1822–25, SE 1838, SE 1843.
Reference: Marceau, no. 30, pp. 46-47.

65 Winfield Scott

c. 1814–17. Terracotta. Life-size? Whereabouts unknown. M 39.

In 1817, Rush's now lost terracotta portrait of Major General Winfield Scott (1786–1866) was first shown at the Pennsylvania Academy in its Sixth Annual Exhibition. Margaret Christman, in the 1978 National Portrait Gallery exhibition catalogue *Fifty American Faces*, suggested that it was more likely executed three years earlier. It was in the summer of 1814 that Scott, already the hero of Chippewa, was triumphant in the battle of Lundy's Lane in upper New York State, a key contest during the close of the War of 1812. Shortly thereafter, he was promoted to major general and became a national hero. Having sustained severe wounds, he spent the next several months convalescing in Philadelphia under the care of **Dr. Philip Syng Physick**, whose bust Rush had modeled in 1812–13 [60]. Christman speculated that it was probably during this convalescent period that Scott "sat to Rush."

Scott was the author of *General Regulations for the Army* (1825) and *Infantry Tactics* (1835). In his sixties he commanded the victorious American army during the close of the Mexican War in 1847. In 1852, he was the Whig nominee for president, but was overwhelmingly defeated by Democrat Franklin Pierce.

Scott was a robust and dashing soldier, weighing over two hundred pounds and standing almost six and a half feet tall. His passion for uniforms elaborately embellished with gold braid and silk sashes earned him the nickname "Old Fuss and Feathers."

Exhibitions: PAFA, 1817, 1818, SE 1818, 1819, 1821, SE 1821, 1822–32, 1834, SE 1836–38, SE 1840, SE 1843.
Reference: Marceau, no. 39, pp. 51-52.

Winfield Scott. *Attributed to Rush.*

Plaster, painted white. 19⅞ × 21¾ × 14⅛ in. (50.5 × 55.2 × 35.9 cm.). National Portrait Gallery, Smithsonian Institution, Washington, D.C. (73.19).

The life-size plaster illustrated here was found in Philadelphia in the early 1950s and identified by Charles Coleman Sellers as the lost Rush bust of Winfield Scott. Scott is depicted dressed in a non-regulation army uniform of the period which is unusually ornamented with painted wood buttons not original to the bust. In 1960, Jessie J. Poesch wrote that this bust appears as the last in the row of busts, some by Rush, which are illustrated in Titian Ramsay Peale's *Interior of Peale's Museum*, 1822 (fig. 55).

Unlike Rush's known plasters, however, the upper arm of General Scott is included, the form is modeled fully in the round, and the cast is closed or solid-backed, not Rush's characteristic open-back. A 1981 technical examination indicated that several layers of paint conceal details and numerous repairs.

Provenance: Joseph T. Fraser, Jr., Philadelphia, c. 1952 to 1973.
References: Jessie J. Poesch, "A Precise View of Peale's Museum," *Antiques*, vol. 78 (October 1960), fig. 6, p. 345. Margaret C. S. Christman, *Fifty American Faces: From the Collection of the National Portrait Gallery* (Washington, D.C., 1978), pp. 71-75.

66 Joseph Stansbury

By 1815. Clay and/or terracotta. Whereabouts unknown. M 32.

Rush's portrait of Joseph Stansbury (1742?–1809) was exhibited in the Pennsylvania Academy's Fifth Annual Exhibition, 1815, and in the catalogue it is described as "modelled in clay." However, in catalogues for subsequent annual exhibitions, the material is listed as "clay burnt."

Stansbury was born in London and emigrated to Philadelphia in 1767. During the Revolution he was imprisoned briefly for his loyalist actions, including political song-writing and transmitting communications between Benedict Arnold and the British. After the war he was again imprisoned, and he subsequently moved to Nova Scotia and then to England. He returned to Philadelphia in 1786, but seven years later he was forced to leave because of his loyalist background. He next moved to New York where he became involved in the insurance business, and for many years he was secretary of the now-defunct United Insurance Company.

If this bust was modeled in 1815, six years after Stansbury's death, it would have to have been done from memory. It is unclear why Rush chose such a controversial subject, although he certainly could have known him when Stansbury was living in Philadelphia. The only other possible link between Stansbury and Rush is indirect: Stansbury was a friend of Charles Willson Peale (Charles Coleman Sellers, *Charles Willson Peale* [New York, 1969], p. 429).

Exhibitions: PAFA, 1815, SE October 1816, 1817, 1818.
Reference: Marceau, no. 32, pp. 47-48.

67 Samuel M. Fox

By 1815. Terracotta. Whereabouts unknown. M 31.

Rush first entered this portrait of Samuel M. Fox (1763–1808) in the Pennsylvania Academy's Fifth Annual Exhibition (1815). Since Rush seems usually to have shown his works shortly after completion, it is a mystery why he exhibited this bust seven years after Fox's death if it was modeled from life, or whether it was instead a posthumous portrait.

Rush probably knew Fox, who was a member of the Select Council of Philadelphia (1796), served on one or more of the city's Watering Committees (John W. Jordan, ed., *Colonial Families of Philadelphia* [New York, 1911], I, pp. 329-31), and was among the first group of subscribers to the Pennsylvania Academy.

Fox was a leader in the incorporation of the Bank of Pennsylvania (1793), serving as its president from 1796 until his death. He was the primary sponsor of the execution of Benjamin Henry Latrobe's architectural design for the bank, built 1799–1801, and demolished about 1871.

Exhibitions: PAFA, 1815, SE May & October 1816, 1817, SE 1818, 1819, 1820.
Reference: Marceau, no. 31, p. 47.

68 George Washington

1815. Pine, painted white. Height, 73 in. (185.4 cm.). Independence National Historical Park Collection, Philadelphia (11859). M 29.

Rush's standing, full-length figure of George Washington is a dramatic and spirited interpretation of the first American president as a statesman. Rush endowed Washington with all the dignity of his office by specifying that the statue be elevated on a three and a half-foot pedestal and surrounding him with paraphernalia, replete with regal and classical associations. Posed in an accentuated contraposto, Washington wears the costume of the period, over which is draped a "flowing Grecian mantle" (to use Rush's words from his broadside), which cascades over the edge of the pedestal. In his right hand, Washington holds an unfurling scroll while leaning on a book (a common symbol for wisdom), on top of a Doric column (for fortitude); his right foot is thrust forward, catching the edge of a second scroll as it too unfurls.

Although Marceau dated *George Washington* 1814, it was more likely carved in 1815, the year it was shown in the Pennsylvania Academy's Fifth Annual Exhibition. That year the Academy paid Rush $100 "in consideration of the aid afforded to the late exhibition by the statue of Washington, and as an acknowledgement of the distinguished merit of the artist" (PAFA, Board of Directors Minutes, July 1815).

[68]

On June 2, 1815, a notice appeared in the *American Daily Advertiser* praising the statue as "preeminent amidst the objects which surround it" and urging the sculptor "to multiply copies of it, by casts in brass, or some other suitable substance." Rush, heeding this advice, circulated a broadside dated July 4, 1815:

I take the freedom to address you on the subject of the immortal Washington; a figure of whom, after much labour and study, I have executed, which gives general satisfaction, more particularly so to those who were intimately acquainted with him . . . . It is my intention, if liberally encouraged, to furnish Plaister Casts from the original Statue. . . .

Rush required twenty orders at $200 each. A letter the following November 30 to President James Madison expressed his disillusionment at having received only two orders:

I regret very much, that my design for delivering plaster paris cast of Genl Washington, to the public, by way of Subscription is vanished, it necessarily deprives me of the happiness of complying with the order, your Excellency so highly honored me with, it is the only positive order I have received, Except one from Governor Tompkins [presumably Daniel E. Tompkins (1775–1825), governor of New York from 1807 to 1817]. . . .
  After such high boasting professions, and wonderful attachments, to the Character & memory of Genl Washington, especially by a particular class of citizens, who would believe it, that only two subscriptions could be obtained throughout the United States, for his statue. . . .

Having abandoned the idea of the full-length plaster casts, Rush instead suggested in the same letter that he would be honored to have the wood original placed in the nation's Capitol. This proposal must have been ignored since the statue remained in Rush's possession.

In 1816, *Washington* was exhibited in Rembrandt Peale's recently established museum in Baltimore. Rush sent the statue with the understanding that Peale would have it painted. Peale, absorbed with his new interest in gas illumination, did not fulfill his agreement. In a letter to John Rogers of Baltimore, written May 23, 1816, Rush expressed his annoyance: "I think he has treated me very unfriendly, in not having the figure painted; he above all men must see the necessity of it, but I suppose his eyes are so dazzled with the gas lights that he cannot see that he is doing me an injury every time the figure is seen in its present condition—." Rush urged Rogers to see that Peale fulfill his promise, suggesting that "perhaps Mr. Findly the coach painter [could] get it done." As a last resort he threatened, "if Mr. Peal [*sic*] refuses, I wish you to request him to cover the figure up. . . ."

Wayne Craven suggests that the next location for *Washington* was the niche above the entrance of Robert Mills's Washington Hall in Philadelphia (completed 1816, destroyed by fire 1823). He bases this proposal on a lithograph of the building by George Strickland (1818), which shows a standing figure in a pose similar to Rush's statue above the entrance (Craven, "The Origins of Sculpture in America," fig. 23, pp. 27, 29). However, no primary evidence has been found to document this suggestion. Scharf and Westcott mention that Rush's sculpture was placed in the interior of Washington Hall in 1819 or 1820 (I, p. 590).

In honor of Lafayette's visit to Philadelphia in

Fig. 110. Max Rosenthal (1833–1918). *Interior View of Independence Hall, Philadelphia*, 1856. Chromolithograph, 14½ × 18¾ in. (36.8 × 47.6 cm.). Independence National Historical Park Collection, Philadelphia.

1824, *George Washington* was placed in Independence Hall. Lafayette declared that the statue revived in his memory Washington's "majesty of countenance, the affability of his manner, and the dignity with which he addressed those about him" (quoted in Whittemore, p. 9). The sculpture stayed on view there, although it still belonged to Rush until 1831, when it was offered for sale to the City of Philadelphia. At that time, he recommended that it remain in Independence Hall, which was being restored to the architectural style of the Revolution. To Thomas Kittera, chairman of the Committee of Independence Hall and Independence Square, Rush wrote (quoted in Marceau, p. 43):

I wish a perpetual place in the Hall, that it may be said that a prophet may obtain some honor in his native place.

I think that you need not have any doubts as to its being a good likeness—I have modeled Gen Washington in his life frequently, in miniature and as large as life.

In the same letter, Rush mentioned he had refused an earlier offer of $500 from a Dennis Smith because it would scarcely have paid for his four months' labor, lamenting: "I have been above sixty years at my business . . . that would entitle me to some consideration more than a mere laborer." That disclosure proved to be costly and naive. On September 8, 1831, Philadelphia's unsympathetic Select Council, of which Rush was no longer a member, took the hint and voted exactly $500 to purchase the statue. The statue was placed on view in Independence Hall (see fig. 110) where it remained until 1970 when it was transferred to the Independence Hall Portrait Gallery at the Second Bank of the United States.

In 1916, a bronze cast of *George Washington* was made by Roman Bronze Works of Brooklyn, New York. At that time, the sculptor Charles Grafly (1862–1928), then an instructor at the Pennsylvania Academy of the Fine Arts, made a mold from the original painted wood statue and a plaster cast. The bronze and a plaster cast were presented to the Academy by Edward H. Coates, its president from 1890 to 1906.

Exhibitions: PAFA, 1815, SE 1821, 1821–24. PMA, *Rush*, 1937 (cat.: Marceau, no. 29 [ill.], pp. 42-46). Ackland Art Center, Chapel Hill, North Carolina, *Arts of the Young Republic: The Age of William Dunlap*, 1968 (cat.: essay by Harold Dickinson; no. 189, p. 90).

References: "Statue of Washington, by Rush," *Poulson's American Daily Advertiser*, June 2, 1815, p. 3. PAFA, Board of Directors Minutes, July 1815. Broadside, July 4, 1815, Stauffer Collection, Historical Society of Pennsylvania. PAFA Accounts, vol. 1, July 31, 1815. Autograph Collection of Simon Gratz, letter from William Rush to James Madison, November 30, 1815, Historical Society of Pennsylvania. Letters from William Rush to John Rogers, May 23 and 31, 1816, The Library Company of Philadelphia. *Minutes of the Select Council, 1830–32*, September 8, 1831, p. 106, City Hall Archives, Philadelphia. Watson, *Annals*, I, p. 576; III, p. 444. D. W. Belisle, *History of Independence Hall From the Earliest Period to the Present Time* (Philadelphia, 1859), pp. 89-90. Elizabeth Bryant Johnston, *Original Portraits of Washington, including Statues, Monuments, and Medals* (Boston, 1882), p. 172, pl. XXVIII. Scharf and Westcott, I, p. 590; II, p. 1066; III, pp. 1873, 2337. Francis Davis Whittemore, *George Washington in Sculpture* (Boston, 1933), pp. 8-9, pl. 3. Wayne Craven, "The Origins of Sculpture in America: Philadelphia," *The American Art Journal*, vol. 9 (November 1977), fig. 22, p. 26.

69 Alexander Contee Hanson

c. 1815. Clay and/or terracotta. Whereabouts unknown. M 33.

This portrait bust was exhibited at the Academy in 1815 as "Hanson, Esq. modelled in clay" and in subsequent years as "Alex'r C. Hanson esq. (Modelled in clay-burnt)." While the Annual Exhibition catalogues do not specify whether the elder or the younger Alexander Hanson was depicted, Marceau speculated that Rush executed a life portrait of Alexander Contee Hanson, Jr. (1786–1819), who in 1808 founded the Baltimore newspaper *The Federal Republican*. At the onset of the War of 1812, this paper was the object of mob violence for taking a position in opposition to the war and to President Madison. Hanson responded by advocating freedom of opinion and of the press. From 1813 to 1816 he was a representative in Congress for the state of Maryland, and from 1817 to 1819 he served as a United States Senator.

Although the bust is more likely a portrait of the younger Hanson, there is a remote possibility that it shows the elder Alexander Contee Hanson (1749–1806). It would, in that case, have been executed posthumously, as may have been the busts of Joseph Stansbury [66] and Samuel Fox [67]. The elder Hanson served as assistant private secretary to General George Washington in 1776, was an associate judge of the general court of Maryland from 1778 to 1781, and was appointed chancellor of Maryland in 1789.

Exhibitions: PAFA, 1815, SE October 1816, 1817, 1818, SE 1818, 1819, 1820.
Reference: Marceau, no. 33, p. 48.

70 Piety

c. 1815. Clay. Whereabouts unknown. M 34.

Described as a "Basso Relievo" in the catalogue of the Pennsylvania Academy's Fifth Annual Exhibition (1815), *Piety* is the only clay relief known to have been executed by Rush. Marceau proposed that Rush's knowledge of this form of sculptural expression was related to his decorative carving for trail boards and stern ornaments of ships. The Academy's exhibition catalogue states that *Piety* was "modelled in clay," not terracotta as Marceau suggested.

Exhibition: PAFA, 1815.
Reference: Marceau, no. 34, p. 48.

71 Charles Thomson

c. 1815. Terracotta. Whereabouts unknown. M 35.

In 1740, Charles Thomson (1729–1824) emigrated from Ireland to America. When he was about twenty years old, he met Benjamin Franklin who was influential in obtaining a teaching appointment for him. Over the years, Thomson successfully turned from teaching to the mercantile trade, and finally to politics. Along the way, he earned a solid reputation for personal integrity and honesty. During the Revolution he early took up the colonial cause and served as the Secretary of the Continental Congress from 1774 until 1789. He then retired to his estate at "Harritan" near Philadelphia to begin a fourth career as a biblical scholar, translating the Septuagint and the New Testament. In 1815, the year Rush exhibited Thomson's portrait bust at the Academy, Thomson published *A Synopsis of the Four Evangelists*.

Presumably Rush sculpted Thomson from life. He might have met him several years earlier through the artist Joseph Wright, who had instructed Rush in modeling. In 1783 Secretary Thomson had recommended Wright to Washington "as an Artist skilled in taking Busts" (Fiske Kimball "Joseph

Fig. 111. Artist unknown. *Charles Thomson* (or *Benjamin Rush*?), c. 1815. Clay, height 19¾ in. (50.2 cm.). The American Philosophical Society, Philadelphia.

Wright and His Portraits of Washington," *Antiques*, vol. 17 [January 1930], p. 35).

Rush's bust of Thomson was exhibited at the Pennsylvania Academy only in the 1815 exhibition. It was listed in the catalogue as "clay burnt" (no. 4, p. 5), or terracotta, and Thomson was described as "formerly Secretary to Congress."

In 1961, a bust of Benjamin Rush by an unknown artist, in the collection of the American Philosophical Society since at least the end of the nineteenth century, was mistakenly reidentified as William Rush's lost bust of Thomson (see fig. 111; *A Catalogue of Portraits and Other Works of Art in the Possession of the American Philosophical Society* [Philadelphia, 1961], fig. 6, pp. 91, 120). However, that bust is unfired clay, not terracotta, and while it is incised "Rush" at the center back, the inscription bears no similarity to Rush's signatures. In fact the fractured edges around the letters of the inscription, a result of tool pressures on dry clay, indicate that it could have been added at any time by anyone.

More than likely this inscription identifies the sitter, not the artist. From at least 1898 until 1960, the bust was labeled Benjamin Rush (see *Portraits and Busts in the Collection of the American Philosophical Society* [Philadelphia, 1898], pl. 58). Indeed, the facial structure and hairline compare more with the contemporary portraits of the physician (see Robert Erwin Jones, M.D., "Portraits of Benjamin Rush, M.D., by his contemporaries," *Antiques*, vol. 108 [July 1975], pp. 94-111, pl. VII, fig. 18) than with likenesses of Charles Thomson such as the 1781–82 or 1819 portraits by Charles Willson Peale (Independence Hall Historical Collection).

In addition, the Philosophical Society's bust does not relate stylistically to Rush's other work. Its contour, with the upper arm clearly suggested, is unique. The jabot is too detailed in description and execu-

tion. Finally, the modeling of the face is overly expressive in its definition of sagging facial muscles, and the incised tooling of individual features such as wrinkles, eyes, and mouth are tentative in execution and lack the characteristic crispness of Rush's hand.

Exhibition: PAFA, 1815.
Reference: Marceau, no. 35, p. 49.

72 Benjamin Rush

Figurehead for the *Benjamin Rush*. c. 1815. Pine. 21½ × 18 × 14 in. (54.6 × 45.7 × 35.6 cm.). The Mariners Museum, Newport News, Virginia (OF 88).

[72]

In late February and early March of 1815, an advertisement in the *American Daily Advertiser* reported that two new ships named after prominent Philadelphians who had recently died, *Benjamin Rush* and *Thomas Scattergood*, should be finished within ten days and then proceed to Liverpool, England. The *Benjamin Rush*, owned by Edward Thomson, left Philadelphia for Norfolk under the command of Captain Ansley on March 20.

It is probable that the bust shown here was its figurehead. An X-radiograph reveals a hollow area inside, which may be internal rot as a result of a hollowing out in order to fit over the knee of the ship. The modern base appears to have been set into this original mortise.

The attribution of this work to William Rush is based on the figurehead's striking resemblance to Rush's terracotta portrait bust of the doctor of 1812 [49]. The figurehead is slightly larger than the terracotta and more simply conceived, and it differs in several other details: most noticeably, the head is turned only slightly to the right, the hair is more broadly carved, the eyebrows and buttons are incised instead of raised, the buttons and buttonholes are reversed, and the S-shaped cravat is fussier in its pleating details.

Provenance: A. P. Grice III, Norfolk, Virginia, to 1959.
References: *Poulson's American Daily Advertiser*, Philadelphia, March 4, 1815, p. 1; March 20, 1815, p. 3.

73 Benjamin Franklin

Figurehead for the *Franklin*. c. 1815. Pine, painted white. 55½ × 27 × 22 in. (141 × 68.6 × 55.9 cm.). U.S. Naval Academy Museum, Annapolis, Maryland (70.3).

Rush was the chief carver of this ship *Franklin*, according to Pinckney, and executed her first figurehead (pp. 85, 86). An undated ink sketch by Thomas Birch (1779–1851) shows what appears to be Rush's bust of Franklin on a scroll base at the ship's prow (fig. 112). Sellers described this bust as the Caffieri type—the most popular early nineteenth-century likeness of Franklin—because it was derived from the 1777 life portrait by the French sculptor Jean-Jacques Caffieri (1725–1792).

The 74-gun ship of the line *Franklin*, constructed in 1815 under the supervision of Samuel Humphreys, was the first ship built at the Philadelphia Navy Yard. She was launched on August

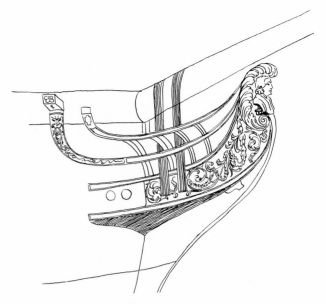

Fig. 112. Thomas Birch (1779–1851). Sketch of the *Franklin* figurehead, c. 1815. Pen and ink on paper, 6¼ × 7⅛ in. (15.9 × 18.1 cm.). Historical Society of Pennsylvania, Philadelphia.

21, 1815, according to the *United States' Gazette*. The ship first sailed in October 1817 under the command of H. E. Ballard. She was broken up at Portsmouth in 1852, and the figurehead was probably removed then. In 1870 it was sent to the U.S. Naval Academy Museum.

Remnants of the ship of the line *Franklin* were used in constructing the frigate *Franklin* in 1854, and a new figurehead was carved by Woodbury Gerrish (died 1868). This reproduction of Rush's bust of Franklin is also now in the collection of the U.S. Naval Academy Museum, Annapolis.

References: *United States' Gazette*, Philadelphia, August 22, 1815, p. 3. Pinckney, pl. xv, pp. 85-87. Charles Coleman Sellers, *Benjamin Franklin in Portraiture* (New Haven, 1962), p. 359. DANFS, II, 1963, p. 443.

74 Agriculture
75 Commerce

Penn Street Bridge, Reading, Pennsylvania. c. 1816. Wood. Over life-size? Whereabouts unknown.

Construction of this Berks County bridge, later referred to as the Reading and Harrisburg Bridge, was begun by Lewis Wernwag and Joseph Johnson

[73]

in 1814 (Montgomery, p. 41). It was opened to traffic across the Schuylkill River in December 1815 although it was not fully completed until late 1818. The wooden covered toll bridge spanned three arches for a total of six hundred feet.

Mrs. Anne Royall, as cited in J. Bennett Nolan's *Early Narratives of Berks County* (pp. 177-78), traveled through Reading in the late 1820s and remarked that the city had

one of the finest bridges in the United States. . . . It unites beauty and strength in an uncommon proportion—it is built on piers of great strength, handsomely cornered, . . . the ornamental figures on the pediments, at each end, . . . (I presume) are designed to represent commerce and agriculture—a female is represented, reclining upon a wagon laden with yellow wheat just reaped; the wagon, or cart, is drawn by oxen, and the wheat is hanging down upon the heads of the oxen . . . and the whole displays the hand of a master.

The figures had been completed by 1817 according to the following entries in the County Commissioner's orders (quoted in Richards, p. 72): "January 14. To Benneville Keim, for William Rush, for the images for the Reading Bridge, $243." "To John Sell, for hauling the images from Philadelphia, $16."

In 1812, for the Market Street Bridge in Philadelphia, Rush had carved figures of *Agriculture* and *Commerce* [50, 51] from which, Richards speculated, replicas were made for the Reading Bridge (p. 72).

None of the known illustrations of the Reading Bridge show the figures in place. The bridge and figures were washed away during a flood in September 1850.

References: Major William Stahle, *The Description of the Borough of Reading* (Reading, 1841), p. 36, copy in the Map Collection, Free Library, Philadelphia. Morton L. Montgomery, compiler, *History of Reading, Pennsylvania (1748–1898) and the Anniversary Proceedings of the Sesquicentennial* (Reading, 1898), p. 41. Louis Richards, "A Goddess in Retirement: An Historic Court House Ornament" (paper read September 13, 1910), *Transactions of the Historical Society of Berks County*, vol. 3 (1923), p. 72. J. Bennett Nolan, *Early Narratives of Berks County* (Reading: Historical Society of Berks County, 1927), pp. 176-78. Raymond W. Albright, *Two Centuries of Reading, Pennsylvania 1748–1948* (Reading: Historical Society of Berks County, 1948), p. 104.

Fig. 113. Rembrandt Peale (1778–1860). *George Washington*, 1795. Oil on canvas, 15¼ × 11⅜ in. (38.7 × 28.9 cm.). Historical Society of Pennsylvania, Philadelphia.

76 George Washington

c. 1817. Terracotta. 22½ × 20¼ × 14 in. (57.2 × 51.4 × 35.6 cm.). The Valley Forge Historical Society, Valley Forge, Pennsylvania. M 38.

When Rush obtained only two of the twenty subscriptions he required to begin making plaster casts of the full-length statue of *George Washington* [68], he modeled this terracotta bust of the first United States President, and included it in the Pennsylvania Academy's Sixth Annual Exhibition (1817). Presumably he felt that plaster casts from the smaller bust-length terracotta would be more marketable.

The bust differs both in concept and in details from the wood portrait. For the bust, Rush changed the turn of the head from left to right. Since it would be viewed more intimately than the full-size statue, which was elevated on a three and a half-foot pedestal, in the terracotta Rush also reduced the scale of the buttons and the length and complexity of the jabot, and gave Washington a fuller head of hair. The facial details are more finely articulated and naturalistic, particularly around the eyes and brows where the sculptor used smaller tools on the more

[76]

pliant wet clay than on the resistant wood block. The "dismal countenance" of Rush's *Washington* echoes Rembrandt Peale's 1795 oil portrait (fig. 113) in the sagging skin under the chin, the unusually square jaw, the lines around the eyes, and the peculiar bulging ridges across the upper bridge of the nose. Rush claimed to have sketched Washington from life and so would surely have relied as much on his own memory as on a secondary source. In 1937 in the *Rush* catalogue, Marceau transcribed a now lost label which was attached to the terracotta. He felt it was "unquestionably" the label printed for the 1817 exhibition:

This Bust of George Washington was modelled by Rush. From the familiarity of the artist with Washington, his opportunities of comparing his work with the original and his acknowledged talent, it is claimed that this bust is the most perfect likeness existing.

In 1856 J. Augustus Beck (1831–by 1912) made a marble copy (Historical Society of Pennsylvania) of Rush's terracotta, which was then "in the possession of Mr. J. E. Trautwine" (quoted in Marceau, p. 51). (Was there possibly a transcription error in the terracotta's history, and this Trautwine was John Cresson Trautwine [1810–1883], a student of William Strickland and an engineer?) From the marble, a plaster was cast which was, in 1937, owned by the Grand Lodge of Free and Accepted Masons of Pennsylvania. Its present whereabouts is unknown.

A plaster cast owned by the Art Museum at Princeton University is the only one thought to be by Rush's hand. During the second half of the nineteenth century, plaster reproductions were also cast, probably by Shaw and Co.; these are now at the New-York Historical Society and in a private Philadelphia collection. Bronze reproductions, of various sizes, were cast in the twentieth century.

Provenance: J. E. Trautwine, by 1856; PAFA, 1864 to 70; Alfred D. Young, by 1876; deposited at Valley Forge, Pennsylvania, by Mrs. Mina Young, loaned by Mrs. E. W. Craven.
Exhibitions: PAFA, 1817, 1818, 1865, 1866, 1868. *U.S. International Exhibition of 1876*, Philadelphia, 1876 (cat.: *Official Catalogue of the U.S. International Exhibition*, no. 1183a, p. 50). PMA, *Rush*, 1937 (cat.: Marceau, no. 38 [ill.], pp. 50-51).
References: PAFA, Catalogues of the Permanent Collection, 1864–65, 1869–70. Elizabeth Bryant Johnston, *Original Portraits of Washington, Including Statues, Monuments and Medals* (Boston, 1882), p. 172. Francis Davis Whitte-

more, *George Washington in Sculpture* (Boston, 1933), pp. 9-10.

PLASTER CAST
The Art Museum, Princeton University, Princeton, New Jersey; purchased through the John MacLean Magie and Gertrude Magie Fund (46.78) (fig. 80). Painted black. *Provenance*: Thomas Jefferson, "Poplar Forest" estate sale, January 15, 1827; Mr. Gaddess, Lynchburg, Virginia, 1827 to 1840; his son, John Gaddess, c. 1840 to 1867; J. I. Van Ness, 1867 to ?; Clarence Loving, to 1924; Mrs. George Vaughan Curtis, 1924 to 1946. *References*: John Hill Morgan and Mantle Fielding, *The Life Portraits of Washington and Their Replicas* (Philadelphia, 1931), p. 107, no. 7 (listed under "Houdon"; authors say it does not resemble any of Houdon's busts of Washington, and they question provenance). Donald Drew Egbert, *Princeton Portraits* (Princeton, 1947), fig. 219, pp. 328-29.

77 Columbus

Figurehead, and trail boards and stern carvings, for the *Columbus*. 1819. Wood. Whereabouts unknown. M 83.

The 74-gun ship of the line was authorized by an act of Congress on January 2, 1813, but built along with nine first-class warships as part of the April 29, 1816, "Act for the Gradual Increase of the Navy of the United States." It was launched in Washington on March 1, 1819.

Pinckney wrote that in April 1819, at the request of the Navy Board, Rush submitted sketches for the decoration of the head and stern of the *Columbus*. These were accepted by the Board on May 24, except for Rush's choice of a costume. The figure, the Navy Board proposed, could be depicted "with or without the hat and plume as may best suit the sculptor," but it should appear in a ruff and short cloak (fig. 115), and "no doubt Mr. Rush will be able to lay his hands on some print or painting which will afford a correct representation of the Old Spanish dress" (quoted in Pinckney, p. 89).

The final sketch was submitted June 1, 1819, and when the bust was completed it was sent in pieces, "to be tacked together according to pencil marks . . ." along with specifications as to the way it was to be colored (Pinckney, p. 90). Rush was reportedly requested to superintend the assembling of the pieces; he replied on September 9, 1819 (quoted in Marceau, pp. 75-76):

Fig. 114. Possibly by William Rush. *Columbus*, 1819. Figurehead for the *Columbus*. Wood. Photograph from Pauline Pinckney, *American Figureheads and Their Carvers* (New York, 1940), pl. XVI.

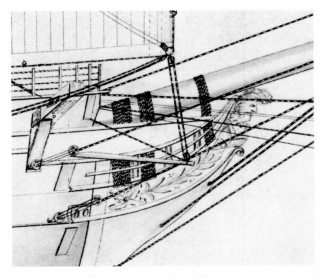

Fig. 115. Charles Cassell. Detail of *Columbus* (sail plan of battleship), c. 1822. Pen and ink on paper, mounted on linen, 22¾ × 32¾ in. (57.8 × 83.2 cm.). The Lenthall Collection, The Franklin Institute Science Museum, Philadelphia.

I am at present just making a finish of all the sternwork that was sent on, I think in the course of five or six days I shall have it cased up—I shall then have the top and bottom finishings of the quarter gallery, the droops for the windows and stars to do which will compleat all that I have hear to do—

He stated that he couldn't spare his son, his equal partner, or the journeyman in his shop, but as soon as his work was completed he would try to accompany them to Washington if his health permitted (Marceau, p. 76).

On April 28, 1820, the ship left Norfolk under the command of J. H. Elton, and on April 20, 1861, she was sunk there, although the figurehead was salvaged and sometime thereafter given to the Naval Academy at Annapolis (Denig, p. 693).

There are two extant images of the figurehead, neither of which seem to relate stylistically to Rush's work. Pinckney's illustration is dated about 1874 (fig. 114). The later image of about 1893 in Denig, shows it with a restored head.

References: Robert G. Denig, "Historic Figure-Heads," *The Cosmopolitan*, vol. 14 (April 1893), pp. 692 (ill.), 693. Marceau, no. 83, pp. 75-76. Pinckney, pl. XVI, pp. 89-90. DANFS, II, 1963, p. 150.

78 Commerce

1819. Wood. Over life-size? Whereabouts unknown. M 40.

This personification of Commerce was designed and carved by Rush to decorate the facade of William Strickland's Custom House in Philadelphia, located on the west side of Second Street below Dock. On July 12, 1819, the building was opened to the public. The following notice with the dateline Philadelphia, November 22, 1819, appeared in the *American Beacon*:

The New Custom House that has just been completed forms one of the most striking ornaments of our city, attracting the attention of strangers. It is of the chastest class of architecture. The front is embellished with an elegant figure of Commerce, executed in his best style, by that admirable sculptor RUSH.

A copy of an 1834 sketch showing the Strickland building depicts the figure in a niche beneath the gabled roof above the third floor (fig. 116).

About 1845 the Custom House moved into the recently vacated Second Bank of the United States,

Fig. 116. D. J. Kennedy (active 1841–1871). *Old Custom House*, 1871, after an 1834 sketch by W. T. Small. Watercolor on paper, 9⅞ × 13⅜ in. (25.1 × 34 cm.). Monogrammed, lower right: D.J.K.; dated, lower left: 1871. Historical Society of Pennsylvania, Philadelphia.

built during 1818–24 by Strickland, on Chestnut Street where it remained until 1935. The first Custom House no longer stands.

References: "The New Custom House," *American Beacon and Norfolk & Portsmouth Daily Advertiser*, November 30, 1819, p. 3. Scharf and Westcott, III, p. 1803. Marceau, no. 40, p. 52.

79 Andrew Jackson

1819. Plaster cast. Life-size. Whereabouts unknown. M 41.

In 1819 when Rush created his portrait of Andrew Jackson (1767–1845), Old Hickory was already a national figure emerging as a viable presidential candidate. During the teens, he was the victor of three battles: he defeated the Creek Indians at the Battle of Horseshoe Bend in 1814; he successfully defended New Orleans against the British in 1815 (and was thus a major hero of the War of 1812); and he overwhelmed the Seminole Indians in Spanish-Florida in 1818. This last contest, however, which included Jackson's capturing two Spanish forts and

executing two British subjects accused of inciting the Indians, threatened to involve the United States in conflicts with Spain and Great Britain. Because of the international repercussions of his actions, Jackson's detractors accused him of being over-zealous and of having exceeded his authority by acting without executive or congressional approval. He was censured by Congress, and there ensued almost a month of investigations into and debates about his conduct, which, to the relief of many Americans, culminated in his exoneration.

After the hearings ended in early February 1819, Jackson, whose popularity had in the meantime soared, left Washington, D.C., to visit a godson in West Point, New York, and to his surprise he was greeted along the route by throngs of well-wishers. There was a four-day ovation in Philadelphia where he was honored with public dinners, speeches, and cheers.

Rush, who surely saw Jackson at this time, seized this moment of triumph to portray the fifty-two-year-old major general. Within a few months plaster casts were available outside Philadelphia, according to the following notice with the Philadelphia dateline of May 25, which appeared in the Charles Town,

West Virginia, *Farmer's Repository* of June 2, 1819, and elsewhere:

Several gentlemen intimate with the general . . . unhesitatingly declare [the Bust of Gen. Jackson] to be an admirable portraiture of this distinguished hero. It is the intention of Mr. Rush, if the public patronage should be adequate, to furnish any number of casts, at a reasonable price; and we cannot but hope, that patriotism and a love of the arts combined, will insure him success in the undertaking.

By December 14, the *Daily National Intelligencer* of Washington, D.C., indicated that busts were for sale through W. Cooper's Music and Book Store on Pennsylvania Avenue and that "the likeness is perfect, and the work another proof that the nation progresses not less in arts than in arms. This probably will rank as Rush's masterpiece."

One of Rush's patrons for the busts prior to Jackson's first, and unsuccessful, campaign for the Presidency in 1824 was James Ronaldson (died 1841). This native of Scotland, who came to Philadelphia in his youth and became a prominent typefounder, distributed at least four plaster casts of Jackson by Rush to various American institutions from Boston to South Carolina; all these casts have disappeared (see plaster casts below). Ronaldson was a friend and admirer of Jackson, and according to William Cobbett, an early biographer of Jackson, he "was the first man in America to propose Jackson for president: that he called a meeting for the purpose in Philadelphia, and from that meeting the proposition spread itself over the union . . ." (*Life of Andrew Jackson* [New York, 1834], p. 161).

Fig. 117. Possibly after William Rush's bust of 1819. *Andrew Jackson*, n.d. Plaster, 28½ × 21 × 10 in. (72.4 × 53.3 × 25.4 cm.). Louisiana State Museum, New Orleans.

The bust of Jackson, which Ronaldson presented to Peale's Museum on January 26, 1822, appears in Titian Ramsey Peale's *Interior of Peale's Museum*, painted that same year (fig. 55) and portrays the general with his gaunt features and in uniform. It is the one on the wall bracket, at the end of the middle tall display cabinet, on top of which sits a bust of Washington.

There are surviving busts of Jackson which closely conform to the image in Peale's watercolor: for example, an unsigned marble at the Ladies Hermitage Association in Tennessee and a plaster in the Maryland Historical Society, incised on back "Gen. Jackson/C. Hennecke & Co./Milwaukee" (a company established by Caspar Hennecke in 1865, which made statuary from 1868 to 1896). The plaster version that seems closest in design to Peale's representation is in the Louisiana State Museum (fig. 117). With its closed back, however, it is inconsistent technically with Rush's casts such as those of Physick or Wistar, probably because it was cast from a solid plaster or unfired clay model. All these busts of Jackson differ from one another in minor ways, but their basic concept is so similar that there must be a common source. The advertisements were widespread enough to suggest that Rush's bust of Jackson was often multiplied, and one therefore cannot avoid speculating that these later offspring are derived from that 1819 prototype.

Rush first exhibited a bust of Jackson at the Pennsylvania Academy in 1820, and there was no medium listed in the catalogue. Marceau, in his catalogue of 1937, therefore dated the portrait about 1820 and described it as "terra-cotta, life-size?" There is no evidence that Rush exhibited a terracotta of this work, however, and subsequent Academy catalogues listed it as a "cast."

Exhibitions: PAFA, 1820, SE 1821, 1822–2f, 1831, 1832, 1834, SE 1836–38, SE 1840, SE 1843. Franklin Institute, Philadelphia, October 6-8, 1825 (cat.: *Catalogue Notebook*, no. 434, bronzed cast deposited by James Ronaldson).
References: *Farmer's Repository*, Charles Town, West Virginia, June 2, 1819, p. 3. *Lynchburg Press*, Virginia, June 7, 1819, p. 2. *Daily National Intelligencer*, Washington, D.C., December 14, 1819, p. 3. Marceau, no. 41, pp. 52-53. Jessie J. Poesch, "A precise view of Peale's Museum," *Antiques* , vol. 78 (October 1960), p. 345.

OTHER PLASTER CASTS
American Academy of Fine Arts, New York; gift of James Ronaldson; whereabouts now unknown. *Reference:* Minute Book, October 2, 1819, p. 86, New-York Historical Society.

Boston Athenaeum; gift of James Ronaldson; whereabouts now unknown. *Reference:* Donations Record, March 10, 1820, Boston Athenaeum. In a letter of December 4, 1981, Jonathan Harding of the Library of the Boston Athenaeum stated that there was no other mention of this bust in the Athenaeum's records, and that presumably it disappeared "sometime between 1820 and 1839 [the date of the first sculpture exhibition at the Athenaeum Gallery]."

State Library of South Carolina, Columbia; gift of James Ronaldson; whereabouts now unknown. *Reference*: South Carolina House of Representatives' *Journal*, December 11, 1820, South Carolina Department of Archives and History, Columbia. It is believed this cast was destroyed when the Old State House containing the library was burned by General Sherman's troops during the Civil War.

Philadelphia Museum (Peale's Museum); gift of James Ronaldson; whereabouts now unknown. *Reference:* Records, Philadelphia Museum, January 26, 1822, p. 118, Peale Collection, Historical Society of Pennsylvania, Philadelphia. By 1849 or 1850 Peale's Museum was bankrupt, and the collections became widely dispersed (Charles Coleman Sellers, *Mr. Peale's Museum: Charles Willson Peale and the First Popular Museum of Natural Science and Art* [New York, 1980], pp. 307-35).

80 Benjamin Franklin

Figurehead for the *Benjamin Franklin*. 1819. Wood. Whereabouts unknown. M 58.

On May 12, 1819, *The Union* recorded that Rush, "in his masterly and superior style," executed a full-length figurehead of Benjamin Franklin. Ritter described it as one of several such figures carved for a merchant ship and depicted "in plain garb." Marceau, citing Scharf and Westcott, listed a full-length Franklin figurehead as "possibly by Rush."

Prior to 1819 Rush executed two portrait busts of Franklin, one of which was a figurehead [2, 73]. This 1819 figurehead was executed for a 400-ton merchant vessel owned by Philadelphia merchants Chandler Price and Thomas A. Morgan, trading as the firm of C. Price & Morgan. The ship was built by local shipbuilders Joseph Ogilby and William Vinyard and was launched in Philadelphia on May 13, 1819.

References: The Union-United States' Gazette and True American, Philadelphia, May 12, 1819, p. 2. Abraham Ritter, *Philadelphia and Her Merchants as Constituted Fifty or Seventy Years Ago* (Philadelphia, 1860), p. 104. Scharf and Westcott, II, p. 1066. Marceau, no. 58, p. 62. Charles Coleman Sellers, *Benjamin Franklin in Portraiture* (New Haven, 1962), no. 2, pp. 358-59.

81 Sir Walter Raleigh

Figurehead for the *North Carolina*. 1820. Wood. Where-abouts unknown.

Work on the 74-gun ship of the line, designed by naval constructor William Doughty, was begun in 1818 at the Philadelphia Navy Yard under the supervision of Samuel Humphreys. The ship's name was assigned by lot for the name of a state, as specified in an act of Congress on March 3, 1819. Prior to that time it was designated the "74" (Pinckney, p. 87).

The 2633-ton ship was launched on September 7, 1820, after which it was sent to Norfolk for completion and preparation for service under the command of Charles W. Morgan.

A report from *Relf's Philadelphia Gazette* which appeared in the *American Beacon* on November 22, 1820, cites Rush as the ship's carver:

We yesterday had the satisfaction of viewing the head intended for this superb ship of war. It is the figure of Sir Walter Raleigh, the first founder of the State of North Carolina, executed by Mr. Rush, of this city, whose skill and judgment in the science of sculpture, is known and admired in every part of the world where Philadelphia vessels are known. It must be an additional satisfaction to our fellow citizens of North Carolina, after having the fortunate lot of giving a name to one of the finest vessels in the world, to have her prow ornamented with a masterly likeness of their original founder, by one of the ablest artists of Pennsylvania. The bust of Sir Walter is acknowledged, by the ablest judges, to be an admirable portraiture from the first prints extant. The Commissioners of the Navy, in ordering this significant head for this noble ship, have evinced a judgment that reflects credit upon their understanding and national feeling.

According to Pinckney when the ship was repaired in Norfolk in 1836, the rotted figurehead was replaced by a billethead (p. 88). The vessel itself was sold in New York on October 1, 1867. The *Dictionary of American Naval Fighting Ships* recorded that the figurehead was presented to the State of North Carolina in July 1909 (IV, p. 596). However, the North Carolina Museum of History, the most likely recipient of such a gift, has no record of ever owning a figurehead of Sir Walter Raleigh.

References: "The North Carolina Seventy Four," *American Beacon and Norfolk & Portsmouth Daily Advertiser*, November 22, 1820, p. 3. Pinckney, pp. 87-88. DANFS, IV, 1969, Appendix IV, p. 596; V, 1970, p. 107.

82 Cherubim
83 Cherubim

1820–21. Wood, painted white. 48 × 56 in. (121.9 × 142.2 cm.). The Grand Lodge of Free and Accepted Masons of Pennsylvania, Philadelphia.

These *Cherubim* were unknown to Marceau in 1937 and have never been published. That they were carved by Rush is substantiated by the recent discovery of the Building Committee minute book related to the 1819–20 reconstruction of the Grand Lodge.

On March 1, 1820, the Building Committee resolved "to employ William Rush to carve the Cherubims for the Grand Lodge," and an accounting of May 25, 1821, indicates he was paid $90 for "carving two cherubims." These unusual armless *Cher-*

Fig. 118. Amos L. Doolittle (1754–1832). *Royal Arch Masonry*. Pl. 39 in *The True Masonic Chart, or Hieroglyphic Monitor* (New Haven, 1820). Engraving. The Grand Lodge of Free and Accepted Masons of Pennsylvania, Philadelphia.

[82]

ubim, each with one wing outstretched, were probably originally intended for the newly situated and furnished Royal Arch room on the second floor of the lodge. They relate to the symbols of Royal Arch Masonry, such as illustrated in Amos Doolittle's engraving *Royal Arch Masonry*, an image dating back at least to the last quarter of the eighteenth century and published in America in 1819 by Jeremy L. Cross in his popular reference work *True Masonic Chart, or Hierglyphic Monitor* (fig. 118).

Today in Pennsylvania, Royal Arch Masonry is a separate and independent degree of Masonry. The arch in Royal Arch Masonry generally symbolizes the "arch of Heaven," and it is flanked by Cherubims, high ranking angels who in the Old Testament attend the enthroned God. During ceremonies, such as conferring of degrees, which are heavily inspired by religious texts, there is placed beneath the arch a Substitute Ark, symbolic of the Ark of the Covenant, which contains Moses' two stone tablets, inscribed with the Ten Commandments and surrounded by a glow synonymous with God's spiritual presence. Crucial to the rituals of Royal Arch Masonry is the understanding of the Lost Word in order to gain knowledge of God in the pursuit of the ultimate goal, Truth.

References: Building Committee 1819–20, Minutes, March 1, 1820, pp. 48, 78; Correspondence, Handwritten, 1821–23, Accounts of the Building, Gas and Furnishing Committees, May 25, 1821, The Grand Lodge of Free and Accepted Masons of Pennsylvania, Philadelphia.

84 Faith
85 Hope
86 Charity

1820–21. Wood, painted white. *Faith*, 26¾ × 58¾ × 12 in. (67.9 × 149.2 × 30.5 cm.); *Hope*, 32 × 64 × 14 in. (81.3 × 162.6 × 35.6 cm.); *Charity*, 37 × 69½ × 21 in. (94 × 176.5 × 53.3 cm.). The Grand Lodge of Free and Accepted Masons of Pennsylvania, Philadelphia. M 12, M 13, M 14.

Faith, Hope, and Charity are three cardinal principals of the Ancient York Masons, the order of the Grand Lodge of Pennsylvania. Charity, considered the greatest Masonic virtue, is traditionally personified as a mother surrounded by her children, one of whom she suckles. The woman resting her right arm on a book, presumably the Bible, is the traditional emblem of Faith. Hope supports an anchor. In Masonic iconography, the anchor symbolizes hope and the prospect of refuge for the weary (*Masonic Symbols in American Decorative Arts*, Scottish Rite Masonic Museum of Our National Heritage [Lexington, Mass., 1976], pp. 47-52).

Marceau dated *Faith*, *Hope*, and *Charity* about 1811 to coincide with the newly built Masonic Hall which was dedicated on June 24, 1811. That hall burned in 1819, and the following receipt documents that it was for the reconstructed hall, dedicated November 1, 1820, that Rush carved *Faith* and *Hope*, as well as *Silence* [87]:

[83]

[84]

[86]

[85]

Masonick Hall   William Rush & Son
1821 Feb 12 to Carving 3 Figures—one of Silence—
      2 of Faith & Hope $180

This statement also lists a charge of $30 for two
cornucopias.

Charity was commissioned approximately the same
time. According to an account of the Building, Gas
and Furnishing Committees for May 25, 1821, William Rush & Son were paid $150 for *Charity*. The
cost difference between *Charity*, and *Faith* and *Hope*
is probably because *Charity* was larger, more complex in design, and carved in the round. Rush's three
statues were intended to be placed in the Grand
Lodge Room ("Communication from the Building
Committee respecting balance of Account for Carving the Figures of Hope & Charity by Mr. Rush,"
September 20, 1822). The shallowness of *Faith* and
Hope, their downward turned heads, and the fact
that they are not carved in the round suggests that
they were probably originally against a wall, perhaps elevated in niches. The original arrangement
of the three statues may well have been similar to
that which appears on the Masonic membership
certificate of the period, with Faith at the left, Hope
at the right, and Charity in the center below (fig.
119).

Exhibition: PMA, *Rush*, 1937 (cat.: Marceau, nos. 12,
14 [ill.], pp. 32-33).

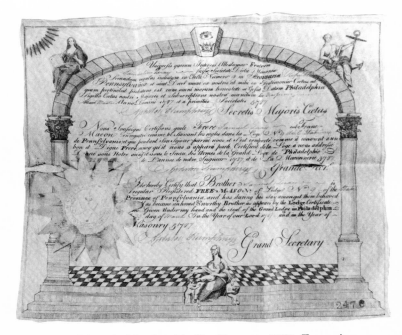

Fig. 119. Masonic Membership Certificate, c. 1780. Engraving.
The Grand Lodge of Free and Accepted Masons of Pennsylvania, Philadelphia.

[87]

References: Correspondence, Handwritten, 1821–23, receipt, February 12, 1821, The Grand Lodge of Free and Accepted Masons of Pennsylvania. " 'Father of American Sculpture': Grand Lodge Features William Rush Carvings," *The Pennsylvania Freemason*, vol. 24 (February 1977), p. 7.

87 Silence

1820–21. Wood, painted white. 66 × 32 × 29 in. (167.6 × 81.3 × 73.7 cm.). The Grand Lodge of Free and Accepted Masons of Pennsylvania, Philadelphia. M 15.

Silence is one of the most important elements in Masonic philosophy: enlightenment attained through a willingness to listen. It also relates to Masonic ritual by serving as a reminder of the vows of secrecy taken upon initiation.

Charles Coleman Sellers has suggested that Rush's design of a woman with her finger to her lips is related to Charles Willson Peale's 1808 transparency of *Silence* (unlocated) conceived to be illuminated during concerts at his museum ("Charles Willson Peale as Sculptor," *The American Art Journal*, 2 [Fall 1970], pp. 10-11).

Rush's *Silence*, previously dated about 1811, was in fact commissioned during the rebuilding program of the Masonic Temple after the 1819 fire. On September 20, 1820, the Building Committee resolved "that a figure of Silence be placed in the niche on the Stairs and the architect be requested to employ Mr. Rush to proceed therewith as speedily as possible." On April 25, 1821, the Committee noted that "an order was drawn . . . for the sum of Sixty dollars . . . to William Rush & Son for carving a figure of Silence as per account & receipt exhibited to the committee."

Silence holds in her left hand a flame-shaped light which is fitted at the back with pipes for gas. The Masons were one of the earliest organizations in Philadelphia to introduce the new technology of gas illumination.

Exhibition: PMA, *Rush*, 1937 (cat.: Marceau, no. 15, p. 33).

References: Building Committee, 1819–20, Minutes, September 20, 1820, p. 100; April 25, 1821, p. 120, The Grand Lodge of Free and Accepted Masons of Pennsylvania, Philadelphia. " 'Father of American Sculpture': Grand Lodge Features William Rush Carvings," *The Pennsylvania Freemason*, vol. 24 (February 1977), p. 7.

88 Figurehead

For the *Ellen*. 1821. Wood. Whereabouts unknown. M 84.

The following bill is the only evidence that Rush worked on a ship named *Ellen*:

Philadᵃ
July 26—1821   Messʳˢ Bevin & Porter
    to Bust head & trailboards   to Wᵐ Rush & Son
    for Ship Ellen $38.00
Paid Oct 15 1821

References: Etting Collection, Miscellaneous Manuscripts II, p. 121, Historical Society of Pennsylvania. Marceau, no. 84, p. 76.

89 Captain John Smith

Figurehead for the *Potomac*. 1822. Wood. Whereabouts unknown.

The estimate of expenses for building the *Potomac* includes a total of $970.08 for carved work but does not specify the carver. Pinckney credited Rush as being the *Potomac*'s chief carver, and she quoted a letter from John Rodgers of the Navy Board to a Mr. Harrison in Philadelphia (p. 87): "You will receive herewith Messrs. William Rush and Sons' bill for carved work for the frigate Potomac, amounting to $948.13. . . ." She cited other Navy letters which indicated that the head of Captain John Smith was begun by Rush in May 1822, and by August the carved work was complete and had been painted twice.

Work on the 1726-ton U.S. Navy frigate was begun in Washington, D.C., on August 9, 1819, and according to the Philadelphia *National Gazette* she was launched March 23, 1822. Under the command of Captain John Downes she left on her first cruise August 19, 1831, and on May 24, 1877, she was sold to E. Stannard and Company.

References: Navy Records, "Estimate of the Expenses attending the Building of the U. States Frigate Potomac," U.S. Navy, 1775–1900, AC—Construction of U.S. Ships. *The National Gazette and Literary Register*, Philadelphia, March 25, 1822, p. 2. Pinckney, p. 87. DANFS, v, 1970, pp. 362-63.

90 Self-Portrait

c. 1822. Terracotta. 15½ × 18 × 11 in. (39.4 × 45.7 × 27.9 cm.). Pennsylvania Academy of the Fine Arts, Philadelphia (1849.1). M 42.

The self-portrait of William Rush, also called the *Pine Knot*, was first shown in the Pennsylvania Academy's Eleventh Annual Exhibition (1822). The catalogue lists the portrait as "Wm. Rush, Carver, modelled in Clay burnt." This portrait has often been considered something of an anomaly, as indicated by Lorado Taft's description of it (*The History of American Sculpture* [New York, 1903], p. 23):

The bust is a unique and curious work. The shaggy shoulders are in appearance but a rough, knotty log over which a pine sprig has fallen, its needles mingling with the artist's long, thin locks. . . . There is no question of its veracity; it shows us exactly what manner of man was William Rush. . . . The pose is strong but contained, and despite the unconventionality, not to say grotesqueness, of the wood-carver's fancy, the whole effect is one of power.

In concept Rush's self-portrait relates to the trompe l'oeil tradition in paintings by such as Charles Willson Peale's *Staircase Group*, 1795 (Philadelphia Museum of Art), or Raphaelle Peale's *After the Bath*, 1823 (Nelson Gallery—Atkins Museum, Kansas City). The carefully modeled pine branch, complete with needles, from which the sculptor's head emerges, is as clever a sculptural deception as the Peales'. Rush incorporated a pine knot into his self-portrait to allude to his craft of wood carving and used the illusion of terracotta modeled to look like wood to advertise his technical virtuosity.

Rush's success in this deception is suggested by the fact that later nineteenth- and early twentieth-century sources often described the terracotta as a cast from the wood original. During Rush's lifetime, and in subsequent Academy Annual Exhibition catalogues, the bust was described as "clay burnt." However, in 1864, the Pennsylvania Academy's Catalogue of the Permanent Collection first listed it as "Bust of William Rush (cast from a bust carved out of a pine tree knot)." This inaccuracy was perpetuated in most subsequent writings on American sculpture until 1937 when Marceau refuted it. He noted that Watson's *Annals*, William Dunlap, and Scharf and Westcott did not mention any self-portrait in wood, which "would have been in the nature of a *tour de force* and almost certainly would have been reported" (p. 54).

[90]

[90] Back view.

There are no known plaster reproductions of this terracotta. In 1905, a bronze cast of it was made by Bureau Brothers, Bronze Statuary and Founders. Edward H. Coates, then president of the Academy, initiated the project and presented the bronze to the Academy (1905.6). In 1970 a plaster mold was made from the terracotta for another bronze casting in a limited edition sponsored by Kennedy Galleries, New York.

Exhibitions: PAFA, 1822–32, 1834, SE 1836–38, SE 1840, 1843, 1849, SE 1856, 1858, 1860, 1865, 1866, 1868–69, 1878. PAFA, *A Gallery of National Portraiture and Historic Scenes,* 1926 (cat.: no 42, pp. 53-55). PMA, *Rush,* 1937 (cat.: Marceau, no. 42 [ill.], pp. 53–55). PAFA, *Star Presentation,* 1944–45 (cat.: no. 33, pl. 27). PAFA, *Pennsylvania Academicians,* 1973 (checklist: no. 55). PAFA, *In This Academy,* 1976 (cat.: p. 15 [ill.], no. 34, p. 276).

References: PAFA, Catalogues of the Permanent Collection, 1855, 1864, 1865, 1869, 1870, 1879–97, 1900, 1903, 1969.

91 Hercules

Figurehead for the *Superb.* 1823. Wood. Whereabouts unknown.

In a letter of March 18, 1823, Girard invited Rush to discuss the subject of a figurehead for the ship *Superb.* According to a bill of April 20, 1823, William Rush and Son carved a large bust of Hercules for the ship, and an entry under *Superb* disbursements for June 24, 1823, indicates they were paid $50.00. In September 1823 George Swope billed $5.00 for "Painting head four Coats & finding Paint," in December 1825 he submitted another bill, for $2.00 for repainting the figurehead, and in 1830 he charged $2.50 for ornamenting the head and lettering the stern.

References: Girard Papers, series II, reels 168, bills dated April 20, 1823, and September/October 1823; 169, bill dated December 1825; 170, bill dated June/July 1830; series III, reels 63, disbursement dated June 24, 1823; 127, letter book no. 18, letter no. 620, dated March 18, 1823.

92 Plan for North East or Franklin Public Square, Philadelphia

1824. Watercolor and pen and ink on paper. 14⅝ × 17¾ in. (37.1 × 45.1 cm.). Inscribed lower left: Coloured by Thos Birch; signed lower right: Design'd & Drawn by Wm Rush 1824. The Library Company of Philadelphia.

This is Rush's only extant plan for a public square, although about 1827 he drew up a plan for Penn Square [98] which has not been located. According to Watson's *Annals* (III, p. 230), between 1821 and 1822 Rush made a survey of North East or Franklin square located between Sixth and Franklin Streets and Vine and Sassafras (now Race) Streets. This was one of four plots designated by William Penn as public spaces.

Rush drew up this plan in 1824, and it was colored by the marine and landscape painter Thomas Birch (1779–1851). In presentation technique and design, it shows that Rush had some knowledge of contemporary trends in western landscape design. It is drawn both in plan and in elevation. The elevations are rendered by the shadows of the trees, a conventional drawing technique of the period. The plan combines axial symmetry which reminds one of French formal gardens with the curving pathways which recall English gardens. The pile of rocks ornamenting the center of the fountain is similar to the original base of *Water Nymph and Bittern* (see pl. IV). The trees are precisely enough described to be generally recognizable. Around the fountain, the curved walkways isolate circular plots each highlighted by a tree, perhaps to show off a new species. Each entrance to the square and to the fountain area is flanked by willows, and two copses of evergreens are symmetrically located along the east and west sides of the park.

In 1825, a year after Rush drew his plan, the North East public square became officially known as Franklin Square (Joseph Jackson, *Encyclopedia of Philadelphia* [Harrisburg: National Historical Association, 1932], III, p. 695), and Rush was appointed by Select Council to serve on the committee, which proposed $250 for the square's improvement and maintenance (*Minutes*, pp. 276, 314). He was also a member of the committee to try to persuade the German Reformed Church to relocate their burial ground which was then on Franklin Square (*Minutes*, pp. 276-77). In 1836, three years after Rush's death, the Supreme Court evicted the church from the property (Jackson, p. 693), and Rush's plan could finally be implemented.

[92]

Improvements to the square were begun the following year. Gas lights and a marble fountain, not of Rush's design, were installed. By 1838, as a print of the square indicates, willow trees had been planted near the fountain (Jackson, p. 694 [ill.]).

In 1883, several changes were made to the square: the curved gravel walkways were replaced by straighter concrete paths (Sachse, p. preceding pl. 51), the iron railing was removed, and electricity was installed (Sachse, p. 695). The square with a central fountain exists today, but there are now no willows.

According to Kenneth Finkel of the Library Company, Rush's plan was probably given to the institution as part of the bequest of Charles A. Poulson (1790–1866), a major nineteenth-century collector of Philadelphia views.

Exhibition: Philadelphia Maritime Museum, *Thomas Birch 1779–1851: Paintings and Drawings*, 1966 (cat.: essay by William H. Gerdts; no. 91 [ill.], p. 64).

References: Minutes of the Select Council, June 16, 1821–September 30, 1830, R.S. 120.3, pp. 276-77, 314, City Hall Archives, Philadelphia. Watson, *Annals*, III, p. 230. *Ward Atlases*, maps of the City of Philadelphia surveyed by Ernest Hexamer and William Locher, 1857, R.S. 227.1. pl. 13. Julius Friedrich Sachse, *Pictures of Old Philadelphia from the originals in the collection of The Library Company of Philadelphia* (Philadelphia, 1901), II, pl. LI.

93 Designs for ship carvings

For the *Pennsylvania*. 1824. M 85.

a. *Hercules figurehead*

Drawing. Inscribed center bottom: D[rawn?] & [illegible] by Wm Rush Philad^a Septr 14 1824. Whereabouts unknown.

b. *Stern plan*

Probably after William Rush. Pen and ink on paper. 25 × 48 in. (63.5 × 121.9 cm.). Inscribed lower left: Ship of the Line Pennsylvania building at Philadelphia/ ornamental part of the Stern designed & executed by William Rush Esqr of Phila in August 1824. National Archives, Washington, D.C. (41-10-2-C).

In a letter of about 1822, Commodore William Bainbridge (1774–1833) of the Philadelphia Navy Yard wrote that Rush was "desirous of carving the head of the ship *Pennsylvania*" and highly recommended him to the Navy Commissioners in Washington (quoted in Pinckney, p. 91). Rush suggested a figurehead of Hercules, the personification of physical strength and courage, as the most appropriate image for the *Pennsylvania*, a vessel he called the "Hercules of old Neptune's Domain." He noted that he had previously drawn a Hercules "as tho'

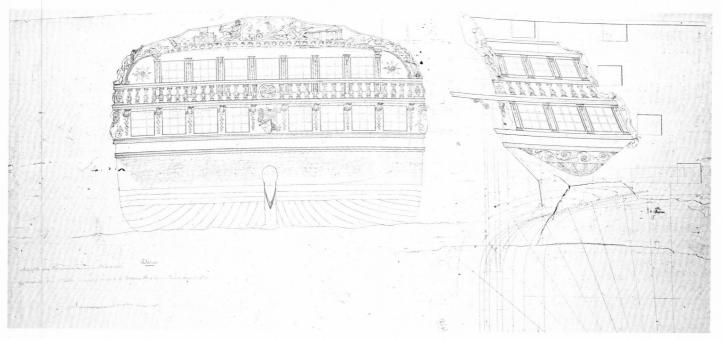

[93b]

In August 1824, a month before he did the figurehead sketch, Rush drew designs for the *Pennsylvania*'s stern. A plan of the front and side elevations is illustrated here. Rush probably did not write the inscription of this plan because he would not have referred to himself as esquire and the signature does not match other known examples of his writing. Pinckney suggested that it was a draftsman's copy of Rush's sketches (p. 92).

It is not known whether Rush executed any of these carvings. Although the 136-gun ship of the line designed by Samuel Humphreys was authorized by Congress on April 29, 1816, and her keel

Fig. 120. Artist unknown. *Design for Figurehead of Hercules*, c. 1837. Pen and ink drawing on paper, 28 × 38 in. (71.1 × 96.5 cm.). Inscribed, lower right: "Pennsylvania"/Launched July 18th 1837. National Archives, Washington, D.C.

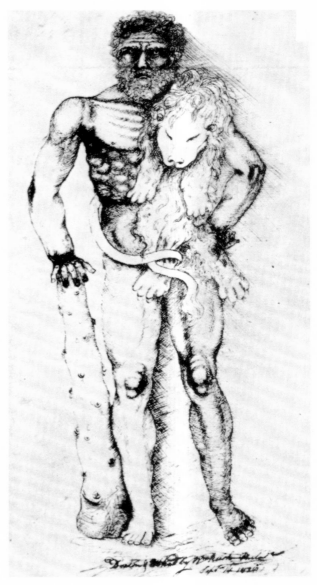

[93a]

he was in violent action, but would prefer placing him in an attitude of expressive rest, as it would look more dignified" (quoted in Pinckney, p. 91). Prior to 1824 Rush had designed other Hercules figureheads [14, 24, 91].

According to Pinckney, Rush's September 1824 sketch of a full-length Hercules with his attributes—a club and a lion's skin—was enclosed with a letter to Bainbridge; neither have been located. The sketch is Rush's only known figural drawing, and, as a unique example of his draftsmanship, is an important document for future attributions. This image, wrote Pinckney, was the source for an 1837 sail plan of the *Pennsylvania* by an unknown artist (fig. 120).

laid in Philadelphia in September 1821, due to limited funds the vessel was not launched until July 18, 1837, over four years after Rush's death. According to a *United States' Gazette* account of the launching, a figurehead of Hercules was in place. There is some evidence that John Rush may have been commissioned to execute his father's designs.

In a letter of December 14, 1836, to the Secretary of the Navy, John enclosed copies of letters of recommendations, noted that his father was long a recipient of Navy patronage, and stated that he, the son, was familiar with his father's designs for the *Pennsylvania* and was equally qualified to carve them. Whether John did obtain the commission is unclear. An 1837 letter "Relative to Head for ship Pennsylvania" is listed in the index booklet to the 1836–41 Navy Commissioner's letter book (p. 113) and may mention who was finally chosen as carver, but that letter book is missing from the Federal Archives in Philadelphia and from the National Archives in Washington.

The 3105-ton *Pennsylvania*, the largest sailing warship ever built for the U.S. Navy, remained uncommissioned until 1842 when she became a receiving ship for the Norfolk Navy Yard. In 1861 the vessel was burned to prevent her falling into Confederate hands, and it is not known whether any carvings were saved.

References: Autograph Collection, letter from John Rush to Mahlon Dickerson, Secretary of the Navy, December 14, 1836; letter from Mahlon Dickerson to John Rodgers, President of the Board of Navy Commissioners, December 20, 1836, Historical Society of Pennsylvania. *United States' Gazette*, Philadelphia, July 19, 1837, p. 2. Marceau, no. 85 (ill.), p. 77. Pinckney, pl. III, pp. 91-92. DANFS, V, 1970, p. 250.

94 Marquis de Lafayette

1824. Terracotta. 21¹⁵⁄₁₆ × 18¾ × 11⅛ in. (55.7 × 47.6 × 28.3 cm.). Pennsylvania Academy of the Fine Arts, Philadelphia; Gift of Dr. William Rush Dunton, Jr. (1911.3). M 43.

In 1824, at the invitation of President Monroe, Lafayette (1757–1834), the celebrated French statesman who in his youth achieved glory as a general during America's Revolution and was a friend and confidant of George Washington, returned to America for a year-long triumphal tour. As a symbol of a bygone heroic era, Lafayette was everywhere extravagantly feted, and in no city was he more honored than in Philadelphia. On July 8, 1824, over two months before Layfayette's scheduled arrival, Rush was appointed one of six members of a Joint Committee of Councils to begin planning the reception and entertainments (*Minutes of the Select Council*, City Hall Archives, Philadelphia).

On September 28, 1824, Lafayette was formally received at the newly redecorated Hall of Independence (today the Assembly Room) where Rush's statue of George Washington [68] was installed especially for the occasion. Rush attended the reception (his admission ticket is in the Independence National Historical Park Collection), and because of his role in all the festivities, he undoubtedly had several opportunities to sketch Lafayette from life. The only artist for whom Lafayette had officially agreed to sit during the tour, however, was Thomas Sully, who was commissioned on October 2, 1821, by the Joint Committee of Councils to paint a full-length portrait (see Edward Biddle and Mantle Fielding, *The Life and Works of Thomas Sully* [Philadelphia, 1921], pp. 34-37). Lafayette left for Washington on October 5.

According to Marceau, Rush family tradition held that Rush studied Lafayette's face at one of the city dinners. At another dinner, Rush unveiled his bust for Lafayette, who proclaimed it an excellent likeness and, as a token of esteem, gave Rush an engraving of himself after the painting (now in the museum at Rouen) by the Dutch-born artist Ary Scheffer (1795–1858).

The bust was certainly finished in 1824 because Rush exhibited it at the Franklin Institute that October. Luigi Persico, the Italian sculptor who had done work on the U.S. Capitol, also exhibited a likeness of Lafayette. In the *First Annual Report* of the Franklin Institute, both sculptures were pronounced "Excellent of their kind [but] as neither of these gentlemen desired to compete for a premium, it would be improper to institute a comparison between them" (p. 89).

The following summer, 1825, Lafayette made a second stop in Philadelphia on his way back to France. Again Rush was on the Joint Committee of Councils to make special arrangements (*Minutes of the Select Council*, May 19, 1825, p. 286, City Hall Archives, Philadelphia). In this capacity, Rush was a guest on July 21 at a dinner at the State in Schuylkill Fishing Company, during which time Lafayette

[94]

was made an honorary member of the company. One wonders whether it was not at this special event that Rush took the opportunity to unveil his bust (*A History of the Schuylkill Fishing Company off the State in Schuylkill, 1732–1888* [Philadelphia, 1889], p. 93).

Rush never exhibited this portrait at the Pennsylvania Academy but seems to have retained it in his possession until his death. It was presented to the Pennsylvania Academy in 1911 by his great-grandson William Rush Dunton, Jr., who according to Marceau had inherited it. While no plasters were cast in Rush's lifetime, the Academy had one made in 1912 and presented it to the State in Schuylkill Fishing Company in exchange for a plas-

ter cast of Rush's *Samuel Morris* [48]. A limited edition of bronze reproductions was authorized by the Academy in 1970.

Provenance: William Rush Dunton, Jr., Towson, Maryland.

Exhibitions: The Franklin Institute, Philadelphia, October 18-20, 1824. PMA, *Rush*, 1937 (cat.: Marceau, no. 43 [ill.], p. 55; medium inaccurately listed as plaster). PAFA, *Star Presentation*, 1944–45 (cat.: no. 30, pl. 26). PAFA, *The One Hundred and Fiftieth Anniversary Exhibition*, 1955 (cat.: no. 13 [ill.], pp. 20, 23). PAFA, *Held in Trust*, 1973 (cat.: no. 194, p. 40). PAFA, *In This Academy*, 1976 (cat.: no. 35, pp. 276-77).

References: *First Annual Report of the Proceedings of the Franklin Institute* (Philadelphia, 1825), p. 89, no. 3. Scharf and Westcott, II, p. 1066.

95 Indian Chief

Figurehead for the *Algonquin*. c. 1824. Wood. Whereabouts unknown.

In 1828 an article in the *American Daily Advertiser* reported that William Rush had executed several figureheads of Indians since the 1790s [see 3]. Brewington has credited Rush with carving "an Indian Chief in a beaver robe in the attitude of declaiming," in 1824 for Thomas Pym Cope. Cope (1768–1854), a shipowner and merchant, established in 1821 the first regular line of packet ships between Philadelphia and Liverpool, England (Scharf and Westcott, III, p. 2337).

References: "Dry Goods," *Poulson's American Daily Advertiser*, Philadelphia, December 16, 1828, p. 2. Brewington, p. 53.

96 Allegory of the Schuylkill River in Its Improved State

97 Allegory of the Waterworks

1825. Spanish cedar, painted. *Allegory of the Schuylkill River*, $39\frac{3}{8} \times 87\frac{1}{4} \times 26\frac{7}{16}$ in. (100 × 221.6 × 67.2 cm.); *Allegory of the Waterworks*, $41\frac{3}{16} \times 87\frac{1}{16} \times 30\frac{7}{16}$ in. (104.6 × 221.1 × 77.3 cm.). The Fairmount Park Commission, Philadelphia. M 49, M 50.

Frederick Graff (1774–1847) was from 1805 until his death superintendent of Philadelphia's waterworks. In this capacity, he was responsible for its construction, expansion, and technological innovations. In 1819 the waterworks, which four years earlier had been moved to Fairmount from Centre Square, were converted from expensive and inefficient steam power to water power. A dam was added, and a neoclassical millhouse was designed by Graff to accommodate the breast wheels which would drive the pumps to raise the water through pipes from the forebay up Fairmount hill to the city's reservoir, located on the bluff now occupied by the Philadelphia Museum of Art. Upon completion of the millhouse in about 1822, the Fairmount Waterworks became one of Philadelphia's most popular scenic attractions.

In 1825 William Rush and his son John finished these sculptures designed to ornament each of the two entrances to the millhouse (see pl. v). The male, symbolic of the river's "improved state" was appropriately placed over the north entrance, nearest the dam. As writers have often pointed out, the form of the recumbent, bearded male figure is a common one for river gods. It is derived from antique sources, the images of which Rush would have known well

[96]

through a variety of printed books and engravings (see D. Dodge Thompson, "The Public Work of William Rush").

While Scharf and Westcott accurately dated the sculptures 1825, Marceau redated them about 1828 because they were not shown in a view of the new waterworks buildings, lithographed by Arnout after a drawing "made from nature by J. Milbert in *L'Amerique Septentrionale*, *Etat de Pennsylvania*, published by H. Gaugain, c. 1826" (Marceau, pp. 57-58, fn. 5, and p. 28, fn. 1), but all the sculptures appeared in the views by George Lehman, published early in 1829. The bill from Rush and his son to the City of Philadelphia, March 1825, for $450, however, documents Scharf and Westcott's earlier date.

Only since the 1937 Rush exhibition have these sculptures been titled *Schuylkill Chained* for the male, and *Schuylkill Freed* for the female. The text of Rush's 1825 bill specifically describes the iconography of the figures as follows:

One male figure Emblematic river schuylkill in its improved
    state
One female Ditto Emblematic of the water works. . . .

Throughout the nineteenth century, these general titles were used, and a contemporary undated account cited by Scharf and Westcott (III, p. 1853) interprets their symbolism:

Fig. 121. *The Plaza at Fairmount Waterworks*, c. 1880. Photograph courtesy of the Philadelphia Museum of Art.

[97]

The male figure represents the Schuylkill in its present improved state, no longer running uncontrolled. . . . The female personifies the water. . . .

The male figure is recumbent on a bed of rocks, the water flowing in several directions from him. It represents Old Age, the head covered with flags, a long flowing beard, the body covered with water-grass, etc., and a chain attached to the wrist, intended to emblemize the neutralized state of the Schuylkill by locks and dams. A bald eagle at his feet with wings opening is about to abandon the banks of the Schuylkill in consequence of the busy scene which art is introducing.

The female figure is represented as seated near the pump which pours water into the reservoir. On the left side is represented a water-wheel; her left arm gently waved over it is indicative of the waterpower; her right arm or elbow rests on the edge of a large vase, representing the reservoir at Fairmount. On the side of the vase a pipe represents the ascending main. . . .

A bill of May 7, 1825, preserved in the City Archives indicates that George Swope charged $10 for applying five coats of paint to each figure. This surface was presumably white to simulate marble. In 1939, the paint was removed from both sculptures. In 1982 their white surfaces were recreated at the Philadelphia Museum of Art, where they have been on deposit since the 1937 Rush exhibition.

Exhibitions: PMA, *Rush*, 1937 (cat.: Marceau, nos. 49-50, pp. 57-58 [ill.]). PMA, *19th-Century America: Paintings and Sculpture*, 1970 (cat.: intro. by John K. Howat and John Wilmerding; no. 34 [ill.]; *Allegory of the Waterworks* listed as *The Schuylkill Freed*). PMA, *La Première Pose: The Nude in Philadelphia*, 1975. PMA, *Philadelphia: Three Centuries of American Art*, 1976 (cat.: nos. 219a and 219b [ill.], pp. 262-64, by Dorinda Evans).

References: Committee on Water, Bills Received, 1804–54, R. S. 120.43, March 1825 bill, May 7, 1825, City Hall Archives, Philadelphia. *Report of the Watering Committee to the Select and Common Councils*, Philadelphia, 1826, payments May 2, June 1, 1825, p. 10. Scharf and Westcott, II, p. 1066; III, pp. 1853, 1868. "Sculpture Checklist of the 19th & 20th Centuries at the Philadelphia Museum of Art," *Bulletin: Philadelphia Museum of Art*, vol. 56 (Spring 1961), nos. 218-19, p. 82. Gordon Hendricks, "Eakins' William Rush Carving His Allegorical Statue of the Schuylkill," *The Art Quarterly*, vol. 31 (1968), pp. 382-404, figs. 4, 5. Charles Coleman Sellers, "William Rush at Fairmount," in *Sculpture of a City: Philadelphia's Treasures in Bronze and Stone* (New York, 1974), pp. 8-15 (ill.). Richard Webster, "Fairmount Waterworks," *Philadelphia: Three Centuries of American Art* (PMA, 1976), no. 183, pp. 223-24.

98 Plan for Penn Square

c. 1827. Whereabouts unknown.

In a Philadelphia City Council meeting on November 10, 1825, Rush, who had suggested that committees be formed to maintain several public squares, was appointed to serve on the Penn and Logan Squares committee (*Minutes of the Select Council*, p. 314). The year before he had drawn up a plan for Franklin Square [92].

The following year Rush was selected for a committee "to enquire into the expediency of taking down the building [Latrobe's Pump House?] in the middle of Centre (Penn) Square and of improving and ornamenting [the square]" (*Minutes*, p. 340). At a council meeting on March 8, 1827, petitions were received for improving Penn Square based on a plan submitted by Rush (*Minutes*, p. 409). Whether he ever made a proposal for Logan Square is unknown.

Reference: Minutes of the Select Council, June 16, 1821–September 30, 1830, pp. 314, 340, 409, City Hall Archives, Philadelphia.

99 Mercury

1828–29. Spanish cedar (originally painted). 44½ × 13 × 20 in. (113 × 33 × 50.8 cm.). The Fairmount Park Commission, Philadelphia. M 47.

On February 3, 1829, Philadelphia's Watering Committee paid William Rush & Son $60 for "carving figure of Mercury for fair mount." This almost four-foot-high figure of the messenger of the gods is shown in a striding pose, with forward movement indicated by the short cape (some now missing), which would have appeared to flutter outward in the wind. *Mercury* wears an antique-style cuirass and a winged helmet; the winged parts of the sandals and the feet are now missing (the left heel is a restoration). *Mercury* carries in his outstretched right hand a purse, or packet of good news, one of his attributes as a god of commerce. In his left hand there is an opening to accept a pole of some sort (a fragment still exists), which may have been a caduceus, a herald's symbolic winged staff entwined with two snakes.

An 1835 lithograph (fig. 38) shows *Mercury* in

its original function as the ornament crowning an octagonally shaped gazebo situated halfway up Fairmount. The gazebo provided a convenient and scenic spot for viewing the activity below on the Schuylkill River and to admire the waterworks.

Mercury was affixed to the roof by an iron rod. The statue was originally painted, but in 1937 Marceau noted that "it has [recently] been cleaned of its many coats of paint to reveal intricate carved surface decoration."

Exhibitions: PMA, *Rush*, 1937 (cat.: Marceau, no. 47 [ill.], p. 57). The University Museum, University of Pennsylvania, Philadelphia, *Cigar Store Indians*, 1966. Atwater Kent Museum, Philadelphia, 1979.

References: Committee on Water, Bills Received 1804–54, R.S. 120.43, voucher, February 3, 1829, City Hall Archives, Philadelphia. Charles Coleman Sellers, "William Rush at Fairmount," in *Sculpture of a City: Philadelphia's Treasures in Bronze and Stone* (New York, 1974), pp. 12-15 (ills.).

100 Mercury

c. 1830. Pine, polychromed. Height with base, 49⅞ in. (126.7 cm.). Museum and Library of Maryland History, The Maryland Historical Society, Baltimore; Gift of the Honorable A. J. Foble (26.11.1).

In 1970 Frederick Fried (pp. 18, 121) attributed this tobacco store figure, formerly thought to have been made in Italy, to William Rush. Indeed, it resembles Rush's Fairmount Park *Mercury* [99] in stance, costume, and the incised decoration of the cuirass. X-radiographs taken in 1982 at the Pennsylvania Academy reveal that under ten to eleven layers of polychrome paint the quality of the carving, the delineation of details of face and hands, and the joinery are all characteristic of Rush's work.

According to the Honorable A. J. Foble, who in 1926 donated the piece to the Maryland Historical Society, it stood in front of John Foble's Tobacco Store in Cambridge, Dorchester County, Maryland from 1830 to 1926. No additional history of the work or documentation of its connection with Rush has been discovered.

Rush may have executed a similar figure about 1830 for a Philadelphia tobacconist [101].

Exhibition: Museum and Library of Maryland History, The Maryland Historical Society, Baltimore, *Weathervanes, Carvings and Quilts*, 1978 (cat.: no. 6).

[99]

Reference: Frederick Fried, *Artists in Wood: American Carvers of Cigar-Store Indians, Show Figures, and Circus Wagons* (New York, 1970), pp. 18, 121.

[100]

101 Mercury

c. 1830. Wood. Wherabouts unknown. M 48.

Marceau cited this as a figure known to William Rush Dunton, Jr., in the 1890s. Dr. Dunton's Scrapbook contains an undated article from the Philadelphia *Evening Telegraph* (first published in 1864), that credits Rush with carving a *Mercury* for a Philadelphia tobacconist at Second and Dock Streets (quoted in Fried, p. 18). According to the same account, the figure later stood in front of a store on Market Street near Twenty-first. The article describes the *Mercury* as "a soldier in his red and yellow instead of being in pure white as the sculptor meant him to be" (quoted in Fried, p. 121).

References: Marceau, no. 48, p. 57. Frederick Fried, *Artists in Wood: American Carvers of Cigar-Store Indians, Show Figures, and Circus Wagons* (New York, 1970), pp. 18, 121.

102 James Madison
103 Thomas Jefferson

c. 1830. Plaster or terracotta? Whereabouts unknown.

The only documentation for Rush's portrait busts of Thomas Jefferson (1743–1826) and James Madison (1751–1837) is a notice in the *United States' Gazette*, October 27, 1830:

Mr. William Rush has recently sculptured busts of Jefferson, Madison, Washington, and La Fayette, for a gentleman in Covington, opposite Cincinnati, and a bust of Dr. Benjamin Rush, for a gentleman in New York. They may be seen for a few days, at his shop on Front St. near the Lehigh Coal Yard; and are well deserving the attention of lovers of the arts. . . .

Whether Rush modeled these busts from life is unknown, but both Madison and Jefferson were familiar with Rush's work. Madison was one of two subscribers for the never-executed plaster cast of the full-length statue of George Washington [68], and Jefferson owned a plaster cast of the terracotta bust of George Washington [76].

Reference: United States' Gazette, October 27, 1830, p. 2.

104 Bust of a Gentleman

c. 1831. Terracotta. Life-size? Whereabouts unknown.

Marceau speculated that this bust might be "identical with" *A Citizen* [46] which was exhibited in 1811 at the Academy's First Annual Exhibition, but he seems not to have taken into account the different mediums. Annual Exhibition catalogues listed *A Citizen* as carved in wood and this *Gentleman* as "clay burnt."

Exhibitions: PAFA, 1831, 1832, 1834, SE 1836–38, SE 1840, SE 1843.
Reference: Marceau, no. 51, p. 58.

105 Bust of a Gentleman

c. 1831. Clay. Life-size? Whereabouts unknown.

The bust was shown at the same Pennsylvania Academy exhibitions as the previous bust [104]. The material was described as "clay model." This is the fourth instance in which Rush exhibited a work in its unfired state [66, 69, 70].

Exhibitions: PAFA, 1831, 1832, 1834, SE 1836–38, SE 1840, SE 1843.

106 General Wade Hampton
107 Montezuma
108 An Indian Orator
109 William Penn

Figureheads for unknown vessels. Whereabouts unknown. M 59, M 60, M 61, M 62.

According to Ritter, Rush executed the full-length figureheads *General Wade Hampton* and *William Penn*; the General was depicted "in regimentals," and Penn and others "in plain garb." Scharf and Westcott added to this list *An Indian Orator* and *Montezuma*, presumably figureheads. Both of these sources also mentioned a full-length *Benjamin Franklin* which is now firmly documented as a figurehead and dated 1819 [80]. Marceau categorized all these works as "possibly by Rush," but except for *Franklin* no other new information has been discovered.

References: Abraham Ritter, *Philadelphia and Her Merchants as Constituted Fifty or Seventy Years Ago* (Philadelphia, 1860), p. 104. Scharf and Westcott, II, p. 1066; III, p. 2337. Marceau, nos. 59-62, p. 62.

WORKS MISATTRIBUTED TO WILLIAM RUSH

ARTIST UNKNOWN

Benjamin Franklin

c. 1785–90. Pine, painted. 34 × 21 × 12½ in. (86.4 × 53.3 × 31.8 cm.). The Historical Society of Delaware, Wilmington.

The Historical Society of Delaware records indicate this bust (fig. 122) was purchased in Philadelphia between 1930 and 1940. That institution attributed it to Rush, and it was first published as such in 1976 in the Whitney Museum's *200 Years of American Sculpture* (fig. 37, pp. 32-33). It relates to Rush's bust of Franklin at the U.S. Naval Academy [73]. Both are clearly derived from Jean-Jacques Caffieri's 1777 portrait of the venerable statesman, taken from life in Paris and widely copied in a variety of mediums. The artist who carved the Delaware bust closely followed his model, but Rush, always original, transformed the image into a more personal statement by simplifying, carving broadly, and redescribing the tie.

Stylistically, the Delaware bust is unrelated to Rush's work in several ways. In none of Rush's busts

Fig. 122. Artist unknown. *Benjamin Franklin*, c. 1785–90. The Historical Society of Wilmington, Delaware.

Fig. 123. Artist unknown. Figurehead for the *John*, before 1797. The Cumberland County Historical Society, Greenwich, New Jersey.

does the bottom edge appear as a simple unarticulated semicircular shape. Here, unlike Rush's *Franklin*, there are no shoulders or other body structure suggested underneath the cloak; the front is flat and unarticulated. Also the eyes are awkwardly delineated, unnaturally large, and out of scale with the face, with the eyelids partially covering the convex pupils (Rush's are always uncovered and concave). Finally, there is no personality projected. Rush cap-

tured a likeness by skillfully describing subtleties of facial features and slightly turning the head to give it a more lively quality.

Reference: Wayne Craven, "Images of a Nation in Wood, Marble and Bronze: American Sculpture from 1776 to 1900," in *200 Years of American Sculpture* (New York, 1976), fig. 37, pp. 32-33.

ARTIST UNKNOWN

Young Girl

Figurehead for the *John*. Before 1797. Wood. Height with base, 42 in. (106.7 cm.). The Cumberland County Historical Society, Greenwich, New Jersey.

The figurehead of the packet ship *John* from Newburyport, Massachusetts, was attributed to William Rush by Pauline Pinckney. However, the drapery treatment, the configuration of the face, and the execution of the hair lack the imagination and quality of Rush's known works (fig. 123). The *John*, under the command of Captain Folger, was wrecked in 1797 off the New Jersey coast on its way to Philadelphia from Hamburg, Germany. It is said that the head was rescued at that time, and by the 1850s it was housed near Bridgeton, New Jersey, in the Ship John Lighthouse named for the wreck that happened nearby (Pinckney, pp. 63-64).

The figurehead was shown in a 1939 Maritime Exhibition in conjunction with the Triennial Exhibition of the Ship Model Society at the Atwater Kent Museum in Philadelphia.

Reference: Pinckney, pl. vii, pp. 63-64.

ARTIST UNKNOWN

Eagle

c. 1810–20. Pine, painted. 24¾ × 29¾ × 28 in. (62.8 × 75.5 × 71.1 cm.). Philadelphia Museum of Art (89-35). M 8.

Marceau assigned this eagle to Rush (figs. 124, 125), but there is no documentary or stylistic evidence to support the attribution. It was formerly thought that Rush carved this eagle for the volunteer Hibernia Fire Company, often referred to as Hibernia Engine House, in Philadelphia. Although the eagle was their symbol, the Hibernia Fire Company minutes between 1800 and 1822 do not mention a Rush carving (see Lynne A. Leopold, pp. 241-42, in *Philadelphia: Three Centuries*). The establishment in 1823 of the Hibernia Hose Company, for which there are no extant records, further complicates the question of the source for the commission. In 1889 Thomas A. Andrews, a superintendent of Horticultural Hall at Fairmount Park, gave this eagle to the Pennsylvania (now Philadelphia) Museum. Leopold was unable to find any tangible connection between Andrews and either of the Hibernia companies.

Typically in Rush's documented eagles, such as the one at St. John's Church [43], there is a distinct textural differentation between the short leaf-shaped feathers of the upper part of the wing and the long quill-shaped feathers of the lower half of the wing. The outline of the wing is simple and self-contained. On the Philadelphia Museum's eagle, however, the carving is shallow, the feathers uniformly delineated, and the silhouette, defined by the pointed tips of the feathers, forms a zigzag pattern.

References: Marceau, no. 8 (ill.), p. 30. *Philadelphia: Three Centuries of American Art* (PMA, 1976), no. 199 (ill.), pp. 241-42.

The following *Eagles* cannot be attributed to Rush either on the basis of style or historical documentation.

Formerly Independence National Historical Park Collec-

Fig. 126. Artist unknown. *Eagle*, before 1808. Whereabouts unknown.

Fig. 127. Artist unknown. *Eagle*. Pennsylvania Academy of the Fine Arts, Philadelphia.

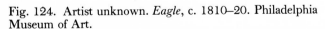

Fig. 124. Artist unknown. *Eagle*, c. 1810–20. Philadelphia Museum of Art.

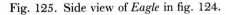

Fig. 125. Side view of *Eagle* in fig. 124.

tion, Philadelphia; whereabouts now unknown (fig. 126). Before 1808. Wood. *Reference*: Marceau, no. 55, p. 60.

Pennsylvania Academy of the Fine Arts, Philadelphia (1947.12) (fig. 127). Undated. Wood, painted. Width 36 in. (91.4 cm.). *Reference*: Marceau, no. 53, p. 60.

Walnut Street Theatre, Philadelphia. c. 1810. Pine, gilded and painted. Width 46 in. (116.8 cm.). *Reference*: Philip M. Isaacson, *The American Eagle* (Boston, 1975), figs. 78 A and B, pp. 73-74.

ARTIST UNKNOWN

Pocahontas

Figurehead for an unknown vessel. c. 1820–30. Pine, polychrome. 33½ × 23 × 33 in. (85.1 × 58.4 × 83.8 cm.). The Kendall Whaling Museum, Sharon, Massachusetts.

In 1962 M. V. Brewington attributed *Pocahontas* to William Rush because "every element in the extraordinarily fine figurehead of the Indian girl, called Pocahontas . . . proclaims it to be Rush's work" (p. 38). While stylistic, documentary, and technical evidence is conflicting and problematic, this work was probably not by Rush, but rather a German carver (fig. 128).

The only extant history of *Pocahontas* is based on hearsay which dates to 1928. Around that time, the statue was part of the estate of William H. Dentzel, a Philadelphia manufacturer of carousels and organs. A letter written by his executor contains the information that the figurehead was carved in "southern Germany by one of Dentzel's ancestors" and used as a decoration on a merchant vessel belonging to Stephen Girard, whose profile portrait purportedly appears on the medallion Pocahontas holds at her chest. Girard did have mercantile connections in Germany, but the figurehead is carved in pine, a material often used in America but less commonly in Germany. Girard's household accounts indicate that he employed many Germans, and though no carver by the name of Dentzel is listed in the Philadelphia directories between 1795 and 1870, it is possible that the Dentzel ancestor immigrated from Germany to America between 1820 and 1830 and either copied Rush's popular style or worked in his shop, particularly after 1800 when Girard hired William and John Rush almost exclusively as his ship carvers.

Fig. 129. Artist unknown. Stern carvings for an unknown vessel. State Street Bank and Trust Company of Boston.

Stylistically, the striding pose, the position of the arms, the style of dress and the fringed shawl, the way the body is articulated underneath, all are characteristics found in such works by Rush as *Peace* [29] and *Virtue* [42], but several other details are totally dissimilar. The carving of the drapery, for instance, is less crisp and assured than that of Rush, and the patterns of the folds are too large, sparse, and regular; they lack the verve and variety of Rush's hand. The ears are unusually large in relation to the head and strangely misshapen. In profile, the nose is large and somewhat hooked, giving the face more the appearance of a specific portrait than the generalized likenesses characteristic of Rush. The chest area, normally unarticulated and revealed under modest clothing in Rush's works, is sensually described with an unusual plunging neckline.

The figurehead has undergone major modifications, which makes it impossible to decipher its original appearance and form. The letter written by Dentzel's executor again provides the existing information: Dentzel claimed to have salvaged the figurehead after the Girard ship was junked, and altered it into "a cigar store Indian by adding a crown and a hand of tobacco." This seems plausible based on close visual examination. Brewington records that when the figurehead was acquired by the Kendall Whaling Museum in the early 1960s, it was covered with so many layers of paint that details of the carving were lost. All paint was removed to the bare wood, and "the color above the priming coat was replaced by Mrs. Kendall," so that its present appearance approximates that of the original (Brewington, p. 38). There are no conservation records to document this metamorphosis, but compensation was obviously made for surface irregularities; carving techniques seem to be obscured, and methods of joinery and later additions are not discernible.

Brewington also attributed to Rush and to the same unknown vessel two quarter figures owned by the State Street Bank and Trust Company of Boston (fig. 129), apparently because of the similar Indian theme and incised decorative details. Without documentary evidence, I find that these awkwardly formed and carved stern ornaments lack the mastery of William Rush's chisel.

References: Letter from executor of estate of William H. Dentzel to William F. Mangels, Coney Island, November 22, 1928, p. 3, Frederick Fried Archives. Brewington, cover and frontispiece, pp. 38-39, fig. 35.

Fig. 128. Artist unknown. *Pocahontas*, c. 1820–30. The Kendall Whaling Museum, Sharon, Massachusetts.

FREDERICK GRAFF (1774–1847)

Design for Boy and Dolphin fountain

1829. Watercolor and pen and ink on paper. $17^{11}/_{16}$ × $13^3/_{16}$ in. (44.9 × 33.5 cm.). Philadelphia Museum of Art Library. M 46.

Marceau attributed this fountain to Rush because Scharf and Westcott listed it among the works at the Fairmount Park Waterworks. They did not, however, mention a sculptor's name, and there is no documentary evidence that Rush was the carver. The fountain was designed by the architect and engineer of the Fairmount Waterworks, Frederick Graff, since an undated sketch of the *Boy and Dolphin* (fig. 130) is in his scrapbook (p. 18). It is most likely of about the same date as a pipe plan for the fountain, dated September 21, 1829, also found in the scrapbook (p. 28).

Bills for the only Fairmount Park fountain built about this time (thus, presumably the *Boy and Dolphin*) show that in July 1832 Jesse Williamson charged $250 for a marble figure, and in August 1833 Peter Fritz charged $1050, as per an 1832 contract (whose present whereabouts is unknown), for a marble fountain basin.

Boy and Dolphin, an ancient symbol of navigation safety, stood near the Callowhill entrance to Fairmount Park (fig. 131) until the bronze cast of *Allegory of the Schuylkill River* or *Water Nymph and Bittern* [35] was placed there about 1872. It was then moved to the north side of the entrance at Green and Twenty-fifth Streets near the Graff memorial.

References: "Gleanings of Frederick Graff," Philadelphia Museum of Art Library, Scrapbook I, pp. 18, 28 (ills.). Committee on Water, Bills Received 1804–54, bills dated July 26, 1832, August 1, 1833, R.S. 120.43, City Hall Archives, Philadelphia. Scharf and Westcott, III, p. 1868. Marceau, no. 46, p. 57.

Fig. 130. Frederick Graff. Design for *Boy and Dolphin* fountain, 1829. Philadelphia Museum of Art Library.

Fig. 131. *Boy and Dolphin Fountain at Fairmount Waterworks*, c. 1850–76. Photograph courtesy of The Frederick Graff Collection, The Franklin Institute Science Museum, Philadelphia.

Fig. 132. Artist unknown. *Music*, c. 1830. Historical Society of Pennsylvania, Philadelphia.

ARTIST UNKNOWN

Music

c. 1830. Pine. 37½ × 17¾ × 10½ in. (95.3 × 45.1 × 26.7 cm.). Historical Society of Pennsylvania, Philadelphia. M 57.

In his catalogue on Rush, Marceau included *Music* in the section of "Attributed Works" because of its flowing drapery which "follows the movement of the form underneath," the detailed treatment of the finger- and toenails, and the typical Rush eye treatment (fig. 132).

On the basis of costume it is dated about 1830. The drapery does have a movement often associated with Rush, but it does not closely correspond to any of Rush's documented pieces of a similar date. The carving is tentative, the drapery folds are bulky and unconvincingly described, and the body underneath is only partially revealed—the left leg is barely suggested. The feet and the right hand no longer exist. The left arm disappears behind the lyre and culminates in a kind of stump, an unfinished quality not seen in any of Rush's other works. The general configuration of the eyes does somewhat relate to Rush's style but they are uncharacteristically out of scale with the face. According to X-radiographs taken in 1981, the joinery and use of nails have little in common with Rush's other wooden sculptures.

Exhibition: PMA, *Rush*, 1937 (cat.: Marceau, no. 57, p. 61).

WILLIAM LUKE (1790–1839)

Tamanend

Figurehead for the *Delaware*. 1836. Wood. 96 × 58 × 46 in. (243.8 × 147.3 × 116.8 cm.). U.S. Naval Academy Museum, Annapolis, Maryland (68.1). M 86.

Fig. 133. William Luke. *Tamanend*, 1836. U.S. Naval Academy Museum, Annapolis, Maryland.

Since 1937 it has been established that Rush did not carve this head; instead it is the work of the Portsmouth carver William Luke (fig. 133).

Work on the 74-gun ship of the line was begun in Norfolk in August 1817 to the design of William Doughty, and she was launched October 21, 1820. By February 10, 1828, she bore a nine-foot full-length figure of Tamanend carved by Luke. Chief of the Delaware Indians of the area now comprising Bucks County, Pennsylvania, Tamanend (c. 1628–1698) was considered a "patron saint" in colonial times (Cheevers, p. 4).

When the 2633-ton ship was repaired in 1837, the figure was presumably replaced by this bust of

Tamanend, also by William Luke. The carver's obituary in an 1839 Norfolk newspaper mentions "the splendid and appropriate head of St. Tammany which adorns the fine model of naval architecture, the Delaware 74" (quoted in Cheevers, p. 2). The ship was set afire and sunk in Norfolk in April 1861, and when salvaged seven years later the bust of Tamanend was retrieved.

References: Marceau, no. 86 (ill.), pp. 78-79. Pinckney, p. 96. DANFS, II, 1963, p. 255. James W. Cheevers, "The Story of Tecumseh-God of 2.5" (manuscript), after 1971, pp. 1-4, document file, U.S. Naval Academy Museum.

Fig. 134. Artist unknown. *Liberty Crowning the Bust of Washington*, c. 1850–60. The Henry Francis du Pont Winterthur Museum, Delaware.

ARTIST UNKNOWN

Liberty Crowning the Bust of Washington

c. 1850–60. Wood, painted white. Height, 74 in. (188 cm.). The Henry Francis du Pont Winterthur Museum, Delaware (57.599).

In 1921, Wilfred Jordan attributed this allegorical group to Rush. It incorporates several themes important to artists of the late eighteenth and early nineteenth century: the apotheosis of Washington, the American spirit symbolized by the eagle, and the personification of Liberty. Marceau doubted the attribution, however, and concluded it was too poorly conceived and executed to be by Rush, and he dated it possibly 1850–60 (fig. 134).

Provenance: Louis Biddle (1863–1940), Philadelphia; Frelinghuysen collection, sale, Parke-Bernet, New York, February 28, March 2, 1946, no. 610; Henry Francis du Pont, 1946 to 1957.

References: Wilfred Jordan, "William Rush: The Earliest Native-Born American Sculptor," *Art and Archaeology*, vol. 11 (June 1921), p. 245 (ill.). Marceau, note p. 63. Frank H. Sommer, "Sculpture at Winterthur," *Antiques*, vol. 85 (February 1964), fig. 1, p. 182.

POSSIBLY BY JOHN RUSH

David Rittenhouse

n.d. Pine, painted white. 24 × 17 × 10½ in. (61.0 × 43.2 × 26.7 cm.) Pennsylvania Academy of the Fine Arts, Philadelphia (1951.28).

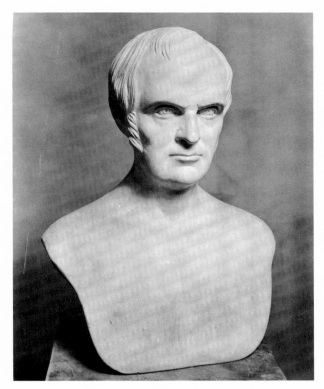

Fig. 135. Possibly by John Rush. *David Rittenhouse.* Pennsylvania Academy of the Fine Arts, Philadelphia.

Fig. 136. Possibly by John Rush. *Archibald Alexander.* Whereabouts unknown.

David Rittenhouse (1732–1796) was born near Germantown, Pennsylvania. In his youth he was a precocious mathematician and instrument maker. He later achieved fame as an astronomer, and in 1790 he moved to Philadelphia, where he is credited with being the first in the British colonies to record an eclipse of the sun. After the Revolution, he was professor of astronomy at the University of Pennsylvania. With his instruments, he also did boundary, canal, and river surveys. He was the first director of the United States Mint, and president of the American Philosophical Society from 1791 until his death.

If John Rush did carve this portrait, it would have been posthumous (fig. 135).

Provenance: George W. Carpenter estate sale, Thomas Birch Sons, Philadelphia, June 6, 1893, *Paintings and Statuary*, no. 664, p. 37; George Staub, Washington, D.C., by 1937 to 1951; Elizabeth K. Sharpe, Conshohocken, Pennsylvania, 1951.

Exhibition: PMA, *Rush*, 1937 (arrived too late to be included in the catalogue, according to letter from George F. Kearney to John F. Lewis, October 1951, PAFA Registrar's file 1951.28).

POSSIBLY BY JOHN RUSH

Archibald Alexander

n.d. Wood, painted white. Life-size. Whereabouts unknown.

Born in Lexington, Virginia, Archibald Alexander (1772–1851) became an influential Presbyterian clergyman. In 1807 he was a minister at Pine Street Church of Philadelphia; in 1812, when its school was relocated to Princeton, he was appointed its first professor of theology. His association with the seminary school lasted the rest of his life, during which time he was an inspired educator and the author of numerous theological essays (fig. 136).

Provenance: George W. Carpenter estate sale, Thomas Birch Sons, Philadelphia, June 6, 1893, *Paintings and Statuary*, no. 666, p. 37; George Staub, Washington D.C., by 1937 to 1951; Elizabeth K. Sharpe, Conshohocken, Pennsylvania, 1951?

Exhibition: PMA, *Rush*, 1937 (arrived too late to be included in the catalogue, according to letter from George F. Kearney to John F. Lewis, October 1951, PAFA Registrar's file 1951.28).

WORKS BY JOHN RUSH

Eagle

1835. Wood. Whereabouts unknown.

In 1835, the Watering Committee erected a second pavilion at the Fairmount Waterworks, an octagonal gazebo which even today overlooks the falls. On November 3, 1835, William Rush's son John billed the committee $30 for carving a cap for the pavilion (fig. 137), $90 for the eagle and its pedestal to ornament the summit, and $10 for sundry blacksmith and painting expenses.

Reference: Bills Received 1804–54, bill November 3, 1835, R.S. 120. 43, City Hall Archives, Philadelphia.

Fig. 137. Pavilion with John Rush *Eagle* at Fairmount Waterworks, c. 1875. Photograph courtesy of the Philadelphia Museum of Art.

Goddess of Liberty

c. 1840. Pine, painted white. Without base, including cap, 120½ × 44½ × 26 in. (306.1 × 113 × 66 cm.). Berks County Historical Society, Reading, Pennsylvania.

The second Reading courthouse, a Greek Revival structure designed by architect Thomas Ustick Walter (1804–1887), was built between 1838 and December 1840 (see fig. 139). Walter used for the spire ornament his *Goddess of Liberty* design that was originally intended for the unexecuted 1837 Philadelphia County Court House (Dunkelberger, p. 6).

An article dated July 14, 1840, in the *Democratic Press* states that the completed wooden figure was done by "the younger Rush [and] . . . is as perfect in execution, as it is graceful and spirited in design. . . . [It exhibits] a degree of taste and skill in the artist of the highest order" (quoted in Stahle, pp. 42-43). John Rush was called the "younger Rush" because his father's figures had ornamented Reading's Penn Street Bridge [74, 75].

The female figure stands with her left arm upraised, holding a staff crowned by a Phrygian or liberty cap (fig. 138). It stood atop the courthouse at a height of 150 feet until 1897 when it was moved inside because of water damage. In 1910 it was given to the Historical Society in Reading. A copper figure of Liberty holding an inverted torch in one hand and a furled American flag surmounted by an eagle in the other replaced Rush's figure on the courthouse until 1931 when the building was razed.

References: Major William Stahle, *The Description of the Borough of Reading* (Reading, 1841), pp. 42-43, copy in the Map Collection, Free Library, Philadelphia. Louis Richards, "A Goddess in Retirement: An Historic Court House Ornament" (paper delivered September 13, 1910), *Transactions of the Historical Society of Berks County*, vol. 3 (1923), pp. 69-72. James E. Dunkelberger, "Berks County Court Houses," *The Historical Review of Berks County*, vol. 17 (October 1951), p. 6. Robert B. Ennis, *Thomas Ustick Walter, Architect: The Early Years* (The Athenaeum of Philadelphia, forthcoming).

Fig. 138. John Rush. *Goddess of Liberty*, c. 1840. Berks County Historical Society, Reading, Pennsylvania.

WORKS FROM THE CARPENTER ESTATE

In the catalogue of the sale of George W. Carpenter's estate (Thomas Birch Sons, Philadelphia, June 6, 1893) the busts of David Rittenhouse and Archibald Alexander were ascribed to William Rush. Both the busts (figs. 135, 136) were in the Pennsylvania Museum's 1937 William Rush exhibition, but their identities were reversed (*Antiques*, vol. 59 [March 1951], p. 227). There is no documentary evidence that William Rush carved either of those busts, and in the bust of Rittenhouse there is no similarity with his usual joinery technique in that he relied on glue instead of nails. The trapezoidal, bare torso is not characteristic of his works, and if the history of the busts is accurate, they may more logically be assigned to John Rush or one of the other sculptors associated with Carpenter's house and grounds.

A pamphlet in the nature of a tribute to the artists and artisans who worked on Carpenter's Germantown estate, called "Phil-Ellena," was published by

Fig. 139. Thomas Ustick Walter. *Berks County Court House*, 1839. Watercolor and pen and ink on paper, 26¼ × 20¹¹⁄₁₆ in. (66.7 × 52.6 cm.). Courtesy of The Athenaeum of Philadelphia.

George Carpenter shortly after its completion in 1844. In it, he wrote that "these and other statues, to be described hereafter, were executed by Rush, in whose work the great genius of his distinguished sire is traced, and by whose pliant hand the inanimate log is suddenly made to start into all the semblance of life and beauty" (*A Brief Description of Phil-Ellena, the Country Seat of George W. Carpenter* [Philadelphia, 1844], p. 14, copy in the Library Company of Philadelphia). It is clear from this quote that John was the sculptor, not his "sire" William, who had died eight years before "Phil-Ellena" was begun. Moreover, only the names John Rush, Bolton & Hamilton, and John Otton appeared as carvers (p. 30). (J. Hare Otton, William Hamilton, and William P. Bolton are listed as carvers in the Philadelphia Directory of 1845.)

The following other works by John Rush are described in the pamphlet, but their whereabouts today is unknown:

Flora
Ceres
Each placed in a niche on the eastern front of the conservatory (p. 14).

Fig. 140. Photograph, c. 1880, of the museum of the George W. Carpenter Estate, showing John Rush's *Minerva* at left, *Eloquence* at right. Courtesy of Mr. and Mrs. Aldbrury Fleitus.

Minerva
Eloquence
"On the south-east [is] the Museum, an oblong building in the Grecian style, with porticos front and back, supported by four columns each, with niches containing statues of Minerva and of Eloquence by Rush [see fig. 140]" (p. 24).

Mercury
This weathervane, "painted by Woodside," was surmounted on the forty-foot spire of the octagonal dome of the Summer House.

Winter (?)
"A youth in a shivering position seated on blocks of ice with his mantle drawn around him," placed on one of the octagonal divisions of the roof of the Summer House. An Ice House was under this structure (p. 25). The description of this object was similar enough to William Rush's *Winter* [45] to assign it the same title, although it was untitled in Carpenter's pamphlet.

Figure of Diana with a Bow, Arrows and Hound
This was a weathervane, "painted by Woodside," which stood one hundred feet off the ground, on the steeple at the center of the barn (p. 27).

Neptune
This weathervane "painted by Woodside," surmounted the spire of the Spring House (p. 27).

Of all these, only *Flora* and *Ceres* (called "Summer") were listed in the catalogue of the 1893 Carpenter estate sale as, respectively, lot numbers 668 and 669 (p. 37), and they were mistakenly ascribed to William Rush. The following works were also credited to him, but whether they are by John Rush or one of the other carvers who did work for Carpenter is unknown: an unidentified bust (no. 667, p. 37); a life-size figure, *Light* (no. 670, p. 37); a life-size figure, *Achilles* (no. 671, p. 38).

Other wood sculptures listed but not assigned to any sculptor were: *Spring* (no. 672, p. 38), a gilt eagle (no. 698, p. 39), a "life-size Figure of Henry Clay, delivering his Celebrated Speech on the Compromise Bill" (no. 699, p. 39), and a "Life-size Figure of Daniel Webster" (no. 700, p. 39).

Appendices

SELECTED BIBLIOGRAPHY

Adams, Adeline. The Spirit of American Sculpture. New York, 1923.
———. "William Rush." *Dictionary of American Biography*. Ed. Allen Johnson and Dumas Malone. New York: Charles Scribner's Sons, 1927–74.
Brewington, M. V. *Shipcarvers of North America*. 1962; corrected republication, New York: Dover Publications, 1972.
The Collected Papers of Charles Willson Peale and His Family. Ed. Lillian B. Miller. Millwood, N.Y.: Kraus Microform, 1980.
Craven, Wayne. *Sculpture in America*. New York: Thomas Y. Crowell Company, 1968.
———. "Images of a Nation in Wood, Marble and Bronze: American Sculpture from 1776 to 1900." In *200 Years of American Sculpture*. Exhibition catalogue. New York: David R. Godine in association with the Whitney Museum of American Art, 1976.
———. "The Origins of Sculpture in America: Philadelphia 1785–1830." *The American Art Journal*, vol. 9, no. 2 (November 1977), pp. 4-33.
Devlin, D. J. "Recalling William Rush." *The Mentor*, vol. 17, no. 6 (July 1929), pp. 48-51.
Dunlap, William. *A History of the Rise and Progress of the Arts of Design in the United States*. 3 vols. 1834; reprint, New York: Dover Publications, 1969.
Fried, Frederick. *Artists in Wood: American Carvers of Cigar-Store Indians, Show Figures, and Circus Wagons*. New York: Clarkson N. Potter, 1970.
Gilliams, E. Leslie. "A Pioneer Sculptor: The Life and Important Works of William Rush, The Philadelphia Wood-Carver." *The Times*, Philadelphia, June 26, 1892, p. 17.
Stephen Girard Papers. Microfilm edition. Philadelphia: American Philosophical Society.
The Grand Lodge of Free and Accepted Masons of Pennsylvania, Philadelphia. *Minutes*. Compiled by Joshua L. Lyte. Reprint, Philadelphia, 1896–1901.
———. Correspondence, 1821–23; Minutes of the Building Committee, 1819.
Hart, Charles Henry. "William Rush Sculptor and William Rush Publicist." *The Pennsylvania Magazine of History and Biography*, vol. 31 (1907), pp. 381-82.
Hendricks, Gordon. "Eakins' William Rush Carving His Allegorical Statue of the Schuylkill." *The Art Quarterly*, vol. 31, no. 4 (Winter 1968), pp. 382-404.
Joshua Humphreys Papers. Historical Society of Pennsylvania, Philadelphia.
Jordan, Wilfred. "William Rush: The Earliest Native-Born American Sculptor." *Art and Archaeology*, vol. 11 (June 1921), pp. 245-47.

Marceau, Henri. *William Rush 1756–1833: The First American Sculptor*. Exhibition catalogue. Philadelphia: Pennsylvania Museum of Art, 1937.
Pennsylvania Academy of the Fine Arts, Philadelphia, Archives. Columbianum: Notes on Its History. The Society of Artists: Minutes of the Board, and Minutes of the Board of Fellows. Pennsylvania Academy: Minutes of the Board of Directors, and Annual Exhibition Catalogues, Permanent Exhibition Catalogues, and Special Exhibition Catalogues (see also, Rutledge, ed., *Cumulative Record of Exhibition Catalogues*).
Philadelphia, City Hall Archives. *Minutes of the Select Council, Minutes of the Common Council*, and Committee on Water, Bills and Papers.
Philadelphia Museum of Art. *Philadelphia: Three Centuries of American Art*. Exhibition catalogue. Philadelphia, 1976.
Pinckney, Pauline A. *American Figureheads and Their Carvers*. New York: W. W. Norton & Company, 1940.
Ritter, Abraham. *Philadelphia and Her Merchants, As Constituted Fifty or Seventy Years Ago*. Philadelphia, 1860.
Rutledge, Anna Wells, ed. *Cumulative Record of Exhibition Catalogues: The Pennsylvania Academy of the Fine Arts, 1807–1870; The Society of Artists, 1800–1814, The Artists Fund Society, 1835–1845*. Memoirs of the American Philosophical Society, vol. 38. Philadelphia, 1955.
Scharf, J. Thomas, and Westcott, Thompson. *History of Philadelphia, 1609–1884*. 3 vols. Philadelphia: L. H. Everts & Co., 1884.
Scrapbook of Dr. William Rush Dunton, Jr. Philadelphia Museum of Art.
Sellers, Charles Coleman. "Charles Willson Peale as Sculptor." *The American Art Journal*, vol. 2, no. 2 (Fall 1970), pp. 5-12.
———. "William Rush at Fairmount." In *Sculpture of a City: Philadelphia's Treasures in Bronze and Stone*. New York: Walker Publishing Co., for Fairmount Park Art Association, 1974.
Sellin, David. *The First Pose, 1876, Turning Point in American Art: Howard Roberts, Thomas Eakins, and a Century of Philadelphia Nudes*. New York: W. W. Norton & Company, 1976.
Taft, Lorado. *The History of American Sculpture*. 1903; new ed. revised and with new matter, 1924; reprint, New York: Arno Press, 1969.
Watson, John F. *Annals of Philadelphia and Pennsylvania, in the Olden Time*. 1830; revised and enlarged to 3 vols. by Willis P. Hazard, 1887; Philadelphia: Edwin S. Stuart, 1905.

NOTES

BANTEL, WILLIAM RUSH, ESQ.

1 *The Philadelphia Gazette, and Daily Advertiser*, Philadelphia, July 20, 1830, p. 2.

2 For further discussion of early forms of sculpture in America see Wayne Craven, *Sculpture in America* (New York, 1968), pp. 1-45.

3 According to Marceau (p. 9), Joseph Rush (1719–1799) was by 1763 an active member of the Carpenters' Company. However, since membership in this organization was limited to house carpenters, a craft unrelated to ship carpentry, it is unlikely this is the same Joseph Rush. In any case, according to a 1786 "List of Names of the Carpenters Company of Philadelphia," Joseph Rush was then deceased. See *The Rules of Work of the Carpenters' Company of the City and County of Philadelphia* (1786; annotated reprint with introduction by Charles E. Peterson, New York, 1971), p. iv.

   Marceau noted that Joseph Rush was a coroner from 1780 to 1785, and was hired by the Council of Safety to give ship appraisals during the Revolution (p. 9). Joseph Rush also seems to have maintained a shop, since in his will he bequeathed all his "Shop Goods Wares and Merchandize" to his second wife, Elizabeth (Will No. 109, 1799, Joseph Rush, City Hall, Register of Wills, Philadelphia). At the time of his death, Joseph Rush resided at 199 North Front Street.

4 Watson, *Annals*, I, p. 575.

5 Watson, *Annals*, I, p. 575.

6 MacPherson's 1785 *Directory for the City of Philadelphia* lists Cutbush's address as 107 Front Street. In his will (No. 206, 1790, City Hall, Register of Wills, Philadelphia), Cutbush numbered among his children a son Edward, a daughter Ann, and two sons, William and James, who were not of age to receive an inheritance. To Edward, he left his house, all the tools, shop furniture, work on hand, and "Benjamin's time on Indenture." To his "Friend Ann Cutbush of London" he gave a mourning ring.

7 William Dunlap, *A History of the Rise and Progress of the Arts of Design in the United States*, 3 vols. (1834; reprint, New York, 1969), I, p. 315.

8 Marceau, p. 11.

9 Marceau, p. 11.

10 *Colonials Records*, Minutes of the Supreme Executive Council of Pennsylvania from its organization to the termination of the Revolution (Harrisburg, 1852), vol. 11, p. 697, February 13, 1779. The following order was drawn on the Treasurer: "One in favor of William Rush for the Sum of One Thousand Five Hundred & fifty Pounds nine Shillings and Eleven Pence half penny, for work done by him (including an order of the late State Navy board, dated March 9th, 1778, for the Sum of One Thousand and One hundred and fifty One Pounds and Six Shillings which appeared to remain unpaid)."

11 Francis Hopkinson, "Account of the grand federal procession in Philadelphia, July 4, 1788," in *American Museum, or Repository of Ancient and Modern Figurative Pieces, Prose and Poetical*, vol. 4 (July 1788), p. 64.

12 The Stephen Girard Papers, comprising over one million items, are preserved at Girard College in Philadelphia. They are also available on 663 reels of microfilm at the American Philosophical Society. It was only possible to research about 20% of these reels, primarily of ship records and only a fraction of the over 100,000 letters. This unusually rich resource warrants further research and should provide more insight into Rush's relationship with Girard. There is a helpful, but very general finding guide, entitled *Papers of Stephen Girard: Listing of Reels*, which was compiled by Murphy Smith. Marvin W. McFarland, former Chief of the Science and Technology Division of the Library of Congress and a Girard College graduate, is most knowledgeable about the organization and contents of this collection and about Girard.

13 Throughout this essay my discussions of maritime history, the United States Navy, and the frigates are derived from Charles Lyon Chandler, Marion V. Brewington, and Edgar P. Richardson, *Philadelphia, Port of History: 1609–1851* (Philadelphia, 1976); Henry E. Gruppe, *The Frigates* (Chicago, 1979; revised 1980).

14 The following letters from the Navy Department document this attitude:

   Letter of July 26, 1798, to Nehemiah & Hubbard, Middletown, Connecticut: "With respect to a head for the Ship it will add to her appearance, but not the value of the Ship, yet a ship of war ought to have a head, which no doubt can be furnished with you.—This ought to be neither tawdry or expensive, you will please to Judge in this case, and determine what you think right."

   Letter of July 28, 1798, to Gibbs & Channing, Newport, Rhode Island: ". . . as to the form of the Head you must consult the carver . . . him with your own judgment & opinions & your determination in this respect will be satisfactory, but there must be nothing tawdry or expensive about it." National Archives, Washington, D.C., Record Group 45, "Naval Records Collection of the Office of Naval Records and Library," Miscellaneous Letters sent by the Navy, vol. 1, M 209.

15 Joshua Humphreys Papers, Correspondence 1775–1831, p. 23, Historical Society of Pennsylvania.

16 Quoted in L. G. Carr Laughton, *Old Ship Figure-Heads & Sterns* (1925; reprint, New York, 1973), p. 81.

17 One wonders whether Rush might have relied on a full-length portrait of Christopher Columbus copied from "a picture in the possession of the Duke of Veraguas" and presented to the Pennsylvania Academy on August 14, 1818. Donations to the Pennsylvania Academy of the Fine Arts, Pennsylvania Academy Archives.

18 Robert D. Schwarz, *The Stephen Girard Collection: A Selective Catalogue* (Philadelphia, 1980), p. 70.

19 Donations to the Pennsylvania Academy of the Fine Arts, April 1809, Pennsylvania Academy Archives.

20 For fuller discussions of subject matter of European figureheads, see Laughton, *Old Ship Figure-Heads*, pp. 63-101, and Peter Norton, *Ships' Figureheads* (New York, 1976), pp. 64-87.

21 John F. Watson, *Annals of Philadelphia and Pennsylvania, in the Olden Time*, 3 vols. (1830; revised and enlarged, Philadelphia, 1905), I, pp. 575-76.

22 Benjamin Henry Latrobe, "Anniversary Oration, Pronounced Before The Society of Artists of the United States, . . . On the Eighth of May, 1811," *The Port Folio*, vol. 5 (1811), p. 24.

23 For carvings attributed to Samuel McIntire, see M. V. Brewington, *Shipcarvers of North America* (1962; revised and reprinted, New York, 1972), fig. 23, p. 24, and Craven, *Sculpture in America*, figs. 1.24 and 1.25. For carvings attributed to John and Simeon Skillin, Jr., see Craven, figs. 1.17-1.21, 1.24.

24 Association Agreement, December 29, 1794, Pennsylvania Academy Archives.

25 *The Constitution and Bye-Laws of the Columbianum or American Academy of the Fine Arts*, adopted February 17, 1795, Pennsylvania Academy Archives. See also Papers Relating to the Early History of the Academy of Fine Arts of Philadelphia, Historical Society of Pennsylvania.

26 Other members of the Committee of Correspondence were John Stagg, Jr., and Charles Willson Peale. See letter of March 4 to Joshua Humphreys in *The Collected Papers of Charles Willson Peale and His Family*, ed. Lillian B. Miller, microfiche edition (Millwood, N.Y.: 1980), series II-A, card 19 [E11-12].

27 "The Exhibition of the Columbianum or American Academy of Painting, Sculpture &tc." (Philadelphia, 1795), copy in Historical Society of Pennsylvania.

28 Papers Relating to the Early History of the Academy of Fine Arts of Philadelphia, The Memoirs and Letters of Charles Willson Peale, p. 8, Historical Society of Pennsylvania.

29 See Charles Coleman Sellers, *Benjamin Franklin in Portraiture* (New Haven and London, 1962), pls. 16, 18.

30 For extracts from Peale's account of Wistar's involvement, see Charles Coleman Sellers, *Mr. Peale's Museum: Charles Willson Peale and the First Popular Museum of Natural Science and Art* (New York, 1980), pp. 123-58.

31 "The Autobiography of Charles Willson Peale," transcript by Horace Wells Sellers, *Collected Papers of Charles Willson Peale*, series II-C, card 19, p. 373.

32 *Minutes of Select and Common Councils, 1801–26*, R.S. 120.2, 120.3, City Hall Archives, Philadelphia.

33 See Minutes of the Board of Directors of the Pennsylvania Academy of the Fine Arts, 1805–34, Pennsylvania Academy Archives.

34 Board Minutes of the Society of Artists of the United States, May 28 and November 7, 1810, Pennsylvania Academy Archives.

35 Board Minutes of the Society of Artists, January 2, 1811. Rembrandt Peale was elected professor of painting, Benjamin Henry Latrobe, professor of Architecture, and George Murray, professor of engraving.

36 See *Preamble* and *The Constitution of the Society of Artists of the United States, Established at Philadelphia, May 1810* (Philadelphia, 1810), pp. 5, 9, 12, copy in Pennsylvania Academy Archives. The society wanted to establish an artist's relief fund, "a preference being always given to distressed members of the society, and their families."

37 See Board Minutes of the Pennsylvania Academy, 1810–1812, and Report of the Committee Appointed to Confer with the Committee of the Society of Artists on a plan for the union of the two institutions, December 16, 1811, Pennsylvania Academy Archives.

38 *The Democratic Press*, Philadelphia, December 11, 1811, p. 2.

39 Board Minutes of the Society of Artists, March 4, 1812.

40 Board Minutes of the Society of Artists, February 24, 1813.

41 Letter from William Rush, March 10, 1813, transcribed in Board Minutes of the Society of Artists, p. 107.

42 Letter from William Rush to Benjamin West, March 22, 1815, The New-York Historical Society.

43 Board Minutes of the Pennsylvania Academy, March 13, 1812.

44 Board Minutes of the Pennsylvania Academy, April 13, 1812. Other members were Robert Mills, Gideon Fairman, and Thomas Sully.

45 Report of Council of Academicians to Board of Directors regarding the Life-Academy, January 13, 1813, Pennsylvania Academy Archives.

46 For an excellent discussion of the yellow fever epidemics and Philadelphia Waterworks, see Nelson Manfred Blake, *Water for the Cities: A History of the Urban Water Supply Problem in the United States* (Syracuse, N.Y., 1956), particularly pp. 3-43 and 78-99.

47 Letter of William Rush, Esq., printed in "Report of the Committee of the Select and Common Councils of Philadelphia on the Navigation of the River Schuylkill" (Philadelphia, 1832).

48 Letter from Joshua Humphreys to the Honorable Adam Seybert(?), April 3, 1813, Joshua Humphreys Papers, Letter Book 3, 1800–35, p. 111, Historical Society of Pennsylvania.

49 William Chambers, *A Treatise on the Decorative Part of Civil Architecture* (1791; reprint, New York and London, 1968), p. 122.

50 Board Minutes of the Pennsylvania Academy, April 25, 1806.

51 These casts were made in Paris by Getti. *Catalogue of*

Statues, Busts, etc., in the Collection of the Pennsylvania Academy of the Fine Arts (Philadelphia, 1807), copy in Pennsylvania Academy Archives. For illustrations of these works, see Francis Haskell and Nicholas Penny, *Taste and the Antique* (New Haven and London, 1981).

52 It is unknown how many of his own works Rush painted. We know, for example, that he suggested several painters to Rembrandt Peale in Baltimore when he wanted his full-length statue of Washington painted [see 68]. George Swope painted Rush's allegorical pieces for the Fairmount Waterworks [96, 97] and the Hercules figurehead for the *Superb* [91].

53 Frances Trollope, *Domestic Manners of the Americans*, ed. Donald Smalley, (1832; reprint, New York, 1949), p. 262.

54 "In antique statues neo-classical artists saw not only 'noble simplicity and calm grandeur,' but, to quote Winckelmann . . . , 'precision of Contour, that characteristic distinction of the ancients.' " Hugh Honour, *Neo-Classicism* (Middlesex, England, 1968), p. 113.

55 Rush's religion is unknown. His father, Joseph, may have been Anglican since he was married in 1750 in Philadelphia's Christ Church (see Charles Henry Hary, "William Rush Sculptor and William Rush Publicist," *The Pennsylvania Magazine of History and Biography*, vol. 31 [1907], p. 382), which after the Revolution became part of the Protestant Episcopal Church. There is evidence that William Rush was Presbyterian: on October 29, 1846, his body, along with those of other family members, was moved to Woodlands Cemetery (Lot E, east ½″) in West Philadelphia from either the First Presbyterian burial grounds on Bank Street south of Market, or the Seventh Presbyterian burial grounds on Ranstead Court, west of Fourth Street, Burial Records, Woodlands Cemetery.

56 Abraham Ritter, *Philadelphia and Her Merchants as Constituted Fifty or Seventy Years Ago* (Philadelphia, 1860), p. 104.

57 For a concise explanation of Masonic symbols and their influence on American decorative arts and a general synopsis of the history of the Brotherhood in the United States, see Barbara Franco, *Masonic Symbols in American Decorative Arts*, exhibition catalogue (Lexington, Mass.: Scottish Rite Masonic Museum of Our National Heritage, 1976). See also Alan Gowans, "Freemasonry and the neoclassic style in America," *Antiques*, vol. 77 (February 1960), pp. 172-75.

58 Latrobe, "Anniversary Oration," p. 25.

59 Dunlap, I, p. 316.

60 Quoted in Marceau, p. 14.

61 Brewington, *Shipcarvers*, p. 163.

62 Organization Agreement, December 29, 1794, Pennsylvania Academy Archives.

63 Pauline A. Pinckney, *American Figureheads and Their Carvers* (New York, 1940), p. 199. For newspaper advertisement concerning Benjamin Rush's notice of two runaway apprentices, see *Dunlap's American Daily Advertiser*, Philadelphia, April 5, 1793, p. 3. (Note: Here Benjamin Rush's address is listed as 21 North Front Street.)

64 For example, see voucher dated June 14, 1792, for brig *Polly*, to Benjamin Rush "for one Scroal," *Girard Papers*, series 2, roll 164.

65 See Marceau, p. 66.

66 See Pinckney, pp. 80-81, and Brewington, *Shipcarvers*, p. 35. Marvin W. McFarland wrote to me that in 1797 John Brown carved a figurehead for Paul Bentalou of Baltimore. "The Rushes were evidently in the country because of the presence of yellow fever in town. John Brown was a second choice. There is correspondence about this matter."

67 The *Farmer's Museum, or Lay Preacher's Gazette*, Walpole, N.H., June 17, 1799, with a dateline New York, May 24, pp. 2-3, contains a description of the carvings on the *John Adams*. On p. 2: "Mr. Daniel N. Train, a young gentleman of genius abilities, late a pupil of Rush, the famous carver of Philadelphia, some time since arrived in this city, has lately completed the ornaments of the ship *Adams*. . . ."

68 Quoted in Pinckney, p. 70.

69 From the *Democratic Press*, July 14, 1840, quoted in Major William Stahle, *The Description of the Borough of Reading* (Reading, 1841), p. 42.

70 I am grateful to Peter Strickland, who is preparing an article on the Carpenter estate, for providing me with this information. The estate was torn down in 1898. See catalogue entry on John Rush and the Carpenter Estate.

71 Robert T. Trump, "Joseph B. Barry, Philadelphia Cabinetmaker," in *Philadelphia Furniture & Its Makers*, ed. John J. Snyder, Jr. (New York, 1975), pp. 94-98.

72 See William Macpherson Hornor, Jr., *Blue Book, Philadelphia Furniture, William Penn to George Washington* (1935; Washington, D.C., 1977), pp. 101, 109, 162, 212.

73 See Margaret Whinney, *Sculpture in Britain, 1530 to 1830* (Baltimore, 1964), pl. 130A.

74 Letter from Rush to West, March 22, 1815.

75 See Haskell and Penny, fig. 171, p. 322.

76 Latrobe, "Anniversary Oration."

77 Letter from Rush to West, March 22, 1815.

78 Rembrandt Peale, "Washington and his Portraits," in *Collected Papers of Charles Willson Peale*, series VI-B, card 19 [F11-20].

79 For discussion of Houdon's commercial methods, see H. H. Arnason, "Jean-Antoine Houdon (1741–1828)," in *Metamorphoses in Nineteenth-Century Sculpture*, ed. Jeanne L. Wasserman (Cambridge, Mass., 1975), pp. 57-62.

80 For discussion of influence of middle-class patronage on the visual arts, see Honour, *Neo-Classicism*, pp. 87-89.

81 Letter from Rush to West, March 22, 1815.

82 Dunlap, I, p. 315. According to Dunlap's diary, William Rush's son supplied him information. See "Diary of William Dunlap (1766–1839)," *Collections of The New-York Historical Society for the Year 1929*, 3 vols. (1929; reissued, New York, 1969), III, p. 799.

83 Quoted in Honour, *Neo-Classicism*, p. 83.

84 See *Report of the Watering Committee to the Select and Common Councils of the City of Philadelphia relative to the Dam at Fair Mount. Read and Adopted September 25, 1828* (Philadelphia, 1828); and *Report of the Committee of the Select and Common Councils of Philadelphia on the*

Navigation of the River Schuylkill (Philadelphia, 1832).

85 *The Philadelphia Gazette, and Daily Advertiser*, January 8, 1830, p. 2.

86 Membership List, 1824, Franklin Institute Archives.

87 See *First Annual Report of the Proceedings of the Franklin Institute of the State of Pennsylvania for the Promotion of the Mechanic Arts* (Philadelphia, 1825).

88 The third judge was John Gullen. (Thomas Sully was a judge on the "Paints and Colours" and the Fine Arts Committees.) *Report of the Second Annual Exhibition of the Franklin Institute of the State of Pennsylvania for the Promotion of the Mechanic Arts* (Philadelphia, 1825), p. 3.

89 See Minutes of the American Academy of Fine Arts, December 7, 1827, and Mary Bartlett Cowdrey, *American Academy of Fine Arts and American Art-Union*, 2 vols. (New York, 1953), "Exhibition Record," p. 317.

90 *United States' Gazette*, Philadelphia, October 27, 1830, p. 2.

91 *The Philadelphia Gazette, and Daily Advertiser*, July 20, 1830, p. 2. Of these buildings, only the design of John Haviland's 1824–25 Pennsylvania Institution for the Deaf and Dumb included the figures Rush described. Charles Michel, Abbé de L'Epée (1712–1789), and his follower Roch Ambroise Cucurron, Abbé Sicard (1742–1822), developed a communication system for deaf-mutes. There is no evidence these statues were ever installed, however.

The arcade on Walnut Street, also designed by Haviland, was built between 1826 and 1827. The Walnut Street Theatre was remodeled by Haviland in 1828. Christ Church, built 1727–44, is still standing on Second Street. None of Rush's proposals for statues in the niches of these buildings seems to have been realized.

THOMPSON, PUBLIC WORK

1 Henri Marceau, *William Rush 1756–1833: The First Native American Sculptor* (Philadelphia, 1937), p. 18.

2 Charles Coleman Sellers, "Mezzotint Prototypes of Colonial Portraiture: A Survey Based on the Research of Waldron Phoenix Belknap, Jr.," *The Art Quarterly*, vol. 20 (Winter 1957), pp. 407-68.

3 Jules David Prown, *John Singleton Copley: In America 1738–1774* (Cambridge, Mass., 1966), pp. 17-19. James Thomas Flexner, "Benjamin West's American Neo-Classicism," *The New-York Historical Society Quarterly*, vol. 36 (1952), pp. 5-41.

4 For an introduction and statistical record see Helen Park, *A List of Architectural Books Available in America Before the Revolution* (Los Angeles, 1973).

5 Marceau, pp. 10, 20-21.

6 For a history and bibliography of the Chestnut Street Theatre, see Brooks McNamara, "Chestnut Street, Federal Street, and the Haymarket," *The American Playhouse in the Eighteenth Century* (Cambridge, Mass., 1969), pp. 104-31.

Paired allegorical images of *Comedy* and *Tragedy* were common properties of the Georgian theater. Engravings of the Theatre Royal, Covent Garden, c. 1759 and 1763, record life-size figures of *Melpomene* and *Thalia*, elevated on bombé pedestals at either side of the proscenium. Cipriani painted a frontispiece or proscenium frame flanked by *Comedy* and *Tragedy* for the same theater in 1777. Henry Holland's elegantly decorated auditorium for the Drury Lane Theatre, 1791–94, also included life-size sculpture of *Comedy* and *Tragedy* on high pedestals on both sides of the proscenium. For reference to images of *Comedy* and *Tragedy* at these two royal patent theaters, see *The Theatre Royal, Drury Lane and The Royal Opera House, Covent Garden*, Survey of London, vol. 35 (London, 1970), pp. 54, 63, 65, 67, 88, 94, 101.

7 The Chestnut Street Theatre was popularly called "The Old Drury of Philadelphia." See James D. Reese, *The Old Drury of Philadelphia* (Philadelphia, 1932). For an illustration of Robert Adam's Drury Lane Theatre, see Survey of London, pl. 8.

8 See Harold Kirker, "The New Theater, Philadelphia, 1791–1792," *Journal of the Society of Architectural Historians*, vol. 22 (1963), pp. 36-37, and Kirker, *The Architecture of Charles Bulfinch* (Cambridge, Mass., 1969), pp. 66-73.

9 Kirker, "New Theater," p. 37.

10 *Dictionary of National Biography*, vol. 48 (London, 1896), pp. 215-16. Also, Survey of London, pp. 77, 89, 90.

11 *D.N.B.*, 52, pp. 406-07. Survey of London, p. 78n.

12 *D.N.B.*, 52, pp. 407-08. Survey of London, pp. 93-97.

13 *D.N.B.*, 9, p. 325. Survey of London, p. 56. Kirker in "The New Theater" (p. 37) confused Catton the elder with his son, Charles Catton (1756–1819), also a painter but not a Royal Academician. The latter emigrated to the U.S. in 1804.

14 *The Pennsylvania Gazette*, Philadelphia, June 20, 1792, p. 3.

15 McNamara, p. 105.

16 McNamara, p. 108.

17 Talbot Hamlin, *Benjamin Henry Latrobe* (New York, 1955), pp. 189-90.

18 Hamlin, p. 189.

19 George B. Tatum, *Penn's Great Town* (Philadelphia, 1961), pp. 61-62, 168-69.

20 A third relief panel by Jardella, an allegory of painting, was incorporated into the "Angel House" at Harmonville, Pennsylvania. Unlike *Drama* and *Music*, which were cut to a semicircular format by William Strickland when adapted to the Second Chestnut Street Theatre, 1820–22, *Painting* has retained its original rectangular shape. For an illustration, see Francis Burke Brandt and Henry Volkmar Gummere, *Byways and Boulevards in and about Historic Philadelphia* (Philadelphia, 1925), p. 132.

21 J. Thomas Scharf and Thompson Westcott, *History of Philadelphia, 1609–1884*, 3 vols. (Philadelphia, 1884), II, p. 973.

22 Hamlin, p. 267.

23 B. Henry Latrobe, "Anniversary Oration," *The Port Folio*, vol. 5 (1811), pp. 24-25.

24 *Poulson's American Daily Advertiser*, Philadelphia, April 2, 1808, p. 3.

25 James Greig, ed., *The Farington Diary, by Joseph Farington, R.A.*, 8 vols., (London, 1924), III, p. 182.

26 For illustrations of Rossi's *Comedy* and *Tragedy*, see Survey of London, pls. 49 and 51.

27 Scharf and Westcott, II, p. 973.

28 The sculpture was incorporated into niches in the facade of the Second Chestnut Street Theatre, 1820–22, by Latrobe's student William Strickland. See Agnes Addison Gilchrist, *William Strickland, Architect and Engineer, 1788–1854* (Philadelphia, 1950), pp. 60-61.

29 Hamlin, p. 267.

30 Hamlin, p. 267.

31 For information on Coade and Company I am grateful to the articles, correspondence, and discussion of Alison Kelly, London, whose forthcoming book on the subject should provide much new information about sculpture of the period. See Kelly, "Mrs. Coade's Stone," *The Connoisseur*, vol. 197 (January 1978), pp. 14-25. See also Rupert Gunnis, *Dictionary of British Sculptors, 1660–1851* (London, 1953), pp. 105-09.

32 Hamlin, p. 202.

33 B. Henry Latrobe, *View of the Practicality and Means of Supplying the City of Philadelphia with Wholesome Water, in a Letter to John Miller, Esquire, December 29th, 1798* (Philadelphia, 1799), p. 18.

34 *Remarks on a Second Publication of B. Henry Latrobe, engineer, Said to be Printed by Order of the Committee of Councils; and Distributed among the Members of the Legislature* (Philadelphia, 1799), p. 5.

35 Marceau, p. 16.

36 Quoted in David Sellin, "The First Pose: Howard Roberts, Thomas Eakins, and a Century of Philadelphia Nudes," *Bulletin: Philadelphia Museum of Art*, vol. 70 (Spring 1975), p. 5.

37 Sellin, p. 5.

38 For a history of the reputation of the *Celestial Venus*, see Francis Haskell and Nicholas Penny, *Taste and the Antique* (New Haven, 1981), pp. 320-21.

39 Gordon Hendricks, "Eakins' William Rush Carving His Allegorical Statue of the Schuylkill," *The Art Quarterly*, vol. 31, no. 4 (Winter 1968), pp. 382-404.

40 Marceau, pp. 26-27.

41 See, for example, Richardson, *Iconology*, fig. 89, *Propitious Augury*; fig. 191, *Pre-eminence*; or fig. 275, *Commerce*.

42 Richardson, pl. 18, no. 65.

43 Transcribed in Charles Coleman Sellers, "William Rush at Fairmount," in *Sculpture of a City: Philadelphia's Treasures in Bronze and Stone* (New York, 1974), p. 9.

44 Latrobe to William Jackson, November 1, 1809, Edward C. Carter, ed., *Microfiche Edition of the Papers of Benjamin Henry Latrobe* (Clifton, N.J., 1976).

45 D. Dodge Thompson, "The Attributes of William Penn: Mercy and Justice," in *Philadelphia: Three Centuries of American Art* (Philadelphia, 1976), p. 262.

46 Sellers, "Rush at Fairmount," p. 20.

47 *Second Annual Exhibition of the Society of the United States and the Pennsylvania Academy* (Philadelphia, 1812), p. 5.

48 For a history and bibliography of Lafayette's visit see Marian Klamkin, *The Return of Lafayette, 1824–1825* (New York, 1975).

49 "The Visit of General Lafayette," *The Port Folio*, vol. 18, no. 270 (October 1824), pp. 335-36.

50 John S. Morton, *A History of the Origin of the Appelation Keystone State* (Philadelphia, 1874).

51 Margaret Whinney, *Sculpture in Britain, 1530 to 1830* (Baltimore, 1964), p. 125.

52 Park, p. 39.

53 Edward M. Riley, "The Independence Hall Group," *Historic Philadelphia: From the Founding until the Early Nineteenth Century*, Transactions of the American Philosophical Society, vol. 43, part 1 (Philadelphia, 1953), pp. 7-42.

54 *Saturday Evening Post*, Philadelphia, vol. 8, no. 423 (September 5, 1829), p. 3.

55 For an outline of this tradition, see Haskell and Penny, pp. 272-73 and 310-11.

56 Whinney, p. 167.

57 Kelly, "Mrs. Coade's Stone," p. 16.

58 *Minutes of the Manhattan Company*, May 8, 1799: "W. Broome from the same Committee [Bylaws] reported that they had devised a common seal for the corporation the description of which is as follows 'Oceanus one of the sea gods sitting in a reclining position on a rising ground pouring water from an urn which forms a river and terminates in a lake, on the exerque will be inscribed *seal of the Manhattan Company*.' "

59 The watercolor of the Manhattan Reservoir was executed by G. P. Hall and dated 1825 (Davies Collection, The Museum of the City of New York). For illustration, see Jerry E. Patterson, *The City of New York: A History Illustrated from the Collections of The Museum of the City of New York* (New York, 1978), p. 99. Hall may have been working from memory in his rendering of *Oceanus*, because the Manhattan Company logo depicted the allegorical figure with head to left and feet to right.

60 Hamlin, p. 135.

61 For a history and bibliography of the project, see Dorinda Evans, "The Schuylkill Chained" and "The Schuylkill Freed," in *Philadelphia: Three Centuries of American Art*, pp. 262-64.

62 Marceau, pp. 57-58.

63 Sellers, "Rush at Fairmount," p. 11.

64 Transcribed in Sellers, "Rush at Fairmount," p. 11.

65 Scharf and Westcott, III, p. 1853, quoted in Marceau, p. 58.

66 Evans, p. 263

67 Evans, p. 263.

68 For a description and alternative illustration, see Tatum, *Penn's Great Town*, p. 162 and pl. 27.

69 For an illustration of a relevant engraved page from the Coade catalogue, see Kelly, p. 23.

70 For the history of the Montreal plaques, see Ida Darlington, "Frost and Damps have no effect," *Bank of Montreal Staff Magazine*, April 1965, pp. 2-6 and 44.

71 Wayne Craven, *Sculpture in America* (New York, 1968), p. 15.

72 Harriet Ropes Cabot, *Handbook of the Bostonian Society* (Boston, 1979), p. 55.

73 For an illustration of *Mercury* by Franzoni and Andrei, see Wilbur H. Hunter, Jr., "Salvage of 1810 Sculpture,"

Journal of the Society of Architectural Historians, vol. 14, no. 4 (December 1955), p. 27. For the exhibition of Godefroy's drawing, see *Third Annual Exhibition of the Columbian Society of Artists and the Pennsylvania Academy* (Philadelphia, 1813), p. 12.

GOODYEAR, PORTRAIT BUSTS

1 See, for instance, William H. Gerdts, *American Neo-Classic Sculpture: The Marble Resurrection* (New York, 1973), p. 12.
2 Wayne Craven, *Sculpture in America* (New York, 1968), p. 25.
3 William Dunlap, *History of the Rise and Progress of the Arts of Design in the United States* (New York, 1834), I, p. 315.
4 Dunlap, I, p. 315.
5 Henri Marceau, in *William Rush, 1756–1833: The First Native American Sculptor* (Philadelphia, 1937), pp. 49-50, dated these pieces c. 1816.
6 I am indebted to Virginia Naudé for providing me with technical information on the busts of *Elizabeth Rush* and *Mary Simpson Rush*. See Naudé, "Toolmarks and Fingerprints: A Technical Discussion."
7 I am indebted to Linda Bantel for this observation. See Bantel, "William Rush, Esq."
8 Charles Coleman Sellers, "Charles Willson Peale as Sculptor," *The American Art Journal*, vol. 2, no. 2 (Fall 1970), p. 8.
9 Sellers, "Peale as Sculptor," p. 8.
10 Ulysses Desportes, "Giuseppe Ceracchi in America and His Busts of George Washington," *The Art Quarterly*, vol. 26, no. 2 (Summer 1963), p. 148.
11 Sellers, "Peale as Sculptor," p. 12.
12 H. H. Arnason, *The Sculptures of Houdon* (New York, 1975), pp. 53-54, 58.
13 Dunlap, I, p. 315.
14 Letter from William Rush to Benjamin West, Philadelphia, March 12, 1815, New-York Historical Society. I am indebted to Linda Bantel for bringing this letter to my attention.
15 Rush to West, March 12, 1815.
16 Dunlap, I, p. 316.
17 Marceau, p. 35.
18 Desportes, p. 148.
19 In spite of its listing in the catalogue, the bust of *Benjamin Rush* was not included in the exhibition in deference to his family, as he had very recently died. It was first exhibited at the Academy in 1814.
20 William Rush to President James Madison, November 30, 1815, reprinted in Marceau, p. 43.
21 Marceau, p. 44.
22 *Poulson's American Daily Advertiser*, June 2, 1815, p. 3.

GERDTS, GENIUS OR ARTISAN?

1 For Shem Drowne, see Leroy L. Thwing, "Deacon Shem Drowne—Maker of Weather-vanes," *Early American Industries Association Chronicle*, vol. 2 (September 1937), pp. 1-2, 7; Esther C. Averill, "Early Weather-vanes Made in Many Styles and Forms," *American Collector*, vol. 2 (August 9, 1934), p. 7; and J. Rayner Whipple, "Old New England Weather Vanes," *Old Time New England*, vol. 31 (October 1940), p. 45. For the Skillins, see Mabel M. Swan, "A Revised Estimate of McIntire," *Antiques*, vol. 20 (December 1931), pp. 338-43; Homer Eaton Keyes, "Milton, Beverly, and Salem," *Antiques*, vol. 23 (April 1933), pp. 142-43; "John Skillin as Cabinetmaker," *Antiques*, vol. 26 (July 1934), p. 7; "Add to Skillins' Sculptures," *Antiques*, vol. 30 (July 1936), pp. 8-9; Leroy L. Thwing, "The Four Carving Skillins," *Antiques*, vol. 33 (June 1938), pp. 326-28; and Mabel M. Swan, "Simeon Skillin, Senior: The First American Sculptor," *Antiques*, vol. 46 (July 1944), p. 21. The bibliography on Patience Wright is extensive; the definitive study is by Charles Coleman Sellers, *Patience Wright: American Artist and Spy in George III's London* (Middletown, Conn., 1976), but it lacks a bibliography. Greenough, too, has been written about by many authors; the major study is Nathalia Wright, *Horatio Greenough: The First American Sculptor* (Philadelphia, 1963).
2 The major previous study of Rush, the catalogue of the Pennsylvania Museum of Art exhibition of 1937 by Henri Marceau, is entitled *William Rush 1756-1833: The First Native American Sculptor*.
3 For these earliest statues in America, see Fiske Kimball, "The Beginnings of Sculpture in Colonial America," *Art and Archaeology*, vol. 8 (May-June 1919), pp. 184-89. For Wilton's sculpture in America, see D. E. Huger Smith, "Wilton's Statue of Pitt," *South Carolina Historical Magazine*, vol. 15 (January 1914), pp. 18-38; *Southern Literary Journal and Monthly Magazine*, vol. 1 (January 1836), pp. 222-30; "Statue to William Pitt," *Magazine of American History*, vol. 7 (July 1881), p. 6, and "Some Account of the Statue of Lord Chatham which now stands in the Orphan House yard," *Magazine of American History*, vol. 8 (March 1882), pp. 214-20; Alexander J. Wall, "The Statues of King George III and the Honorable William Pitt Erected in New York City 1770," *New-York Historical Society Bulletin*, vol. 4 (July 1920), pp. 36-57, and "Account of the Statue of George III, Formerly Standing in the Bowling Green, New York," *New-York Historical Society Proceedings* (1844), pp. 168-75. For the definitive survey of American sculpture mentioning almost all the works discussed in this essay, see Wayne Craven, *Sculpture in America* (New York, 1968).
4 For the Houdon statue of Washington see Sherman McRae, *Washington: His Person as Represented by the Artists. The Houdon Statue, Its History and Value* (Richmond, 1873); "Historical Notes. The Houdon Statue of Washington," *South Carolina Historical Magazine*, vol. 8 (January 1907), pp. 42-46; Gilbert Chinard, "Houdon in America," *Historical Documents Institut Français de Washington*, cahier 4 (Baltimore and London, 1930);

and Charles Seymour, Jr., "Houdon's *Washington* at Mount Vernon Re-examined," *Gazette des Beaux-Arts*, 6th series, vol. 35 (March 1948), pp. 137-58.

5 For the Canova *Washington*, see Marshall DeLancey Haywood, "Canova's Statue of Washington," *South Atlantic Quarterly*, vol. 1 (July 1902), pp. 278-87; R.D.W. Connor, "Canova's Statue of Washington," *Publications of the North Carolina Historical Commission*, Bulletin no. 8, 1910; Philipp Fehl, "Thomas Appleton of Livorno and Canova's Statue of George Washington," *Festschrift für Ulrich Middeldorf* (1968), pp. 523-52; and "Canova's Washington," *Virginia Historical Society Occasional Papers*, no. 22 (April 1970), pp. 4-8.

6 The Chantrey *Washington* awaits a scholarly study. See the reference to it, and to Allston, in John Holland, *Memorials of Sir Francis Chantrey, R.A.* (Sheffield, [c. 1851]), pp. 287-88.

7 The bibliography on Ceracchi is extensive; the most significant articles on his American work are the following, all by Ulysses Desportes: "Giuseppe Ceracchi in America and His Busts of George Washington," *The Art Quarterly*, vol. 26 (Summer 1963), pp. 140-79; "Ceracchi's Design for a Monument," *The Art Quarterly*, vol. 27 (Autumn 1964), pp. 475-89; " 'Great men of America' in Roman Guise," *Antiques*, vol. 96 (July 1969), pp. 72-75.

8 The only study of the Italian sculptors in Washington is the somewhat inadequate dissertation by Kathleen Raben Castiello, "The Italian Sculptors of the United States Capitol: 1806–1834" (University of Michigan, 1975). See also Glenn Brown, *History of the University States Capitol* (Washington, D.C., 1900), and Charles E. Fairman, *Art and Artists of the Capitol of the United States of America* (Washington, D.C., 1927).

9 For Franzoni and Andrei, see Richard R. Borneman, "Franzoni and Andrei: Italian Sculptors in Baltimore, 1808," *William and Mary Quarterly*, 3rd series, vol. 10 (January 1953), pp. 108-11, and Wilbur H. Hunter, Jr., "Salvage of 1810 Sculpture," *Journal of the Society of Architectural Historians*, vol. 14 (December 1955), pp. 27-28. For Valaperta, see Alexander J. Wall, "Joseph Valaperta Sculptor," *New-York Historical Society Quarterly Bulletin*, vol. 11 (July 1927), pp. 53-56; for Capellano, see I. T. Frary, "The Sculptured Panels of Old St. Paul's Church, Baltimore," *Maryland Historical Magazine*, vol. 34 (March 1939), pp. 64-66; for Causici, see J. Jefferson Miller II, "Baltimore's Washington Monument" (masters thesis, University of Delaware, 1962); for Persico, see "An Italian Artist in Old Lancaster," *Papers Read before the Lancaster County Historical Society, Friday, March 8, 1912* (Lancaster, Pa., 1912).

10 For these, and other sculptural monuments in Philadelphia, see Fairmount Park Art Association, *Sculpture of a City: Philadelphia's Treasures in Bronze and Stone* (New York, 1974).

11 John Eckstein's career is documented really only for his European years, while Frederick Eckstein has been studied in regard to Cincinnati; see Ophia D. Smith, "Frederick Eckstein, the Father of Cincinnati Art," *Bulletin of the Historical and Philosophical Society of Ohio*, vol. 9 (August 1951), pp. 266-82.

12 For Peale's involvement with sculpture, see Charles Coleman Sellers, "Charles Willson Peale as Sculptor," *The American Art Journal*, vol. 2 (Fall 1970), pp. 5-12.

13 See *Historical Catalogue of the Paintings in the Philadelphia Museum* (Philadelphia, 1813), p. 48.

14 See Sellers, "Peale as Sculptor," pp. 9-12.

15 See by the present author, *American Neo-Classic Sculpture: The Marble Resurrection* (New York, 1973), especially pp. 19-21.

16 See Benjamin H. Latrobe, *Impressions Respecting New Orleans*, ed. with an introduction by Samuel Wilson, Jr. (New York, 1951), p. 102-05.

17 "Allegory in Art," *The Crayon*, vol. 3 (April 1856), p. 114.

18 William Dunlap, *A History of the Rise and Progress of the Arts of Design in the United States*, 3 vols. (1834; reprint, New York, 1965), I, p. 374. That it was Rush's son who supplied Dunlap with a notice on his father is confirmed in Dunlap's diary entry for June 27, 1833, see "Diary of William Dunlap (1766–1839)," *Collections of The New-York Historical Society for the Year 1929*, 3 vols. (1929; reissued, New York, 1969), III, p. 799.

19 Bill in the Philadelphia City Hall Archives, mentioned by Dorinda Evans in the exhibition catalogue *Philadelphia: Three Centuries of American Art* (Philadelphia Museum of Art, 1976), p. 263.

20 *The Port Folio*, 18, no. 270 (October 1824), pp. 335-36.

21 [William Tudor], "For the North-American Journal," *North American Review*, vol. 2 (December 1815), pp. 260-61.

22 Dunlap, I, p. 373, is the source for the information that Rush learned to model from Joseph Wright, about whom Dunlap received information from Wright's daughter; see "Diary of William Dunlap," III, pp. 802, 804. Otherwise, Charles Willson Peale might have taught clay modeling to Rush.

23 See "Z," "Sculpture and Sculptors in the United States," *American Monthly Magazine*, Boston, vol. 1 (May 1829), pp. 127-28.

24 Daniel Fanshaw, "The Exhibition of the National Academy of Design, 1827. The Second," *The United States Review and Literary Gazette*, vol. 2 (July 1827), p. 260.

25 Until the twentieth century, Rush's sculpture was exhibited only at the Pennsylvania Academy of the Fine Arts, except for the showing of his *Washington* bust at the 1876 Philadelphia Centennial. See Anna Wells Rutledge, ed., *Cumulative Record of Exhibition Catalogues: The Pennsylvania Academy of the Fine Arts, 1807–1870; The Society of Artists, 1800–1814; The Artists' Fund Society, 1835–1845*, Memoirs of the American Philosophical Society held at Philadelphia for Promoting Useful Knowledge, vol. 38 (1955), pp. 191-92.

26 Gratz collection, Historical Society of Pennsylvania.

27 Letter of March 22, 1815, New-York Historical Society.

28 For Augur, see the above mentioned article "Sculpture and Sculptors," pp. 130-31, and Ebenezer Baldwin, "The Fine Arts," *The American Historical Magazine*, vol. 1 (February 1836), pp. 41-53. In the twentieth century, see George Heard Hamilton, "Hezekiah Augur" (doctoral dissertation, Yale University, 1934), and his article

published in the *Bulletin of the Associates of Yale University*, vol. 8 (June 1938), pp. 70-72.

29 Thomas Hope, *Household Furniture and Interior Decoration* (London, 1807), quoted in David Irwin, *John Flaxman 1755–1826: Sculptor, Illustrator, Designer* (London, 1979), p. 187.

30 Marceau discussed possible sources drawn from *The Artist's Repository*, in the 1937 catalogue, pp. 10, 20-21; see also Charles Coleman Sellers, "William Rush at Fairmount," in *Sculpture of a City*, pp. 11-12; and Dorinda Evans in *Philadelphia: Three Centuries*, pp. 263-64. See also D. Dodge Thompson in *Philadelphia: Three Centuries*, p. 262, for the reference to the sources in James Gibbs's *Book of Architecture* (London, 1728), misprinted as William Gibbs's *Book of Adventure* (!).

31 For Wilson, see Mabel Munson Swan, "Ship Carvers of Newburyport," *Antiques*, vol. 48 (August 1945), pp. 78-81.

32 Craven, pp. 20-21.

33 See Clymer's discourse published in *The Port Folio*, n.s. vol. 3 (May 2, 1807), pp. 278-82, quoted from p. 279.

34 Review from the *American Daily Advertiser*, Philadelphia, reprinted in the Hudson, New York, *The Balance and State Journal*, vol. 1 (July 16, 1811), p. 229.

35 Benjamin H. Latrobe, "Anniversary Oration, Pronounced before The Society of Artists of the United States, by Appointment of the Society, On the Eighth of May, 1811," *The Port Folio*, vol. 5 (1811), appendix, pp. 1-32, quoted here from p. 24.

36 Latrobe, "Anniversary Oration," pp. 24-25.

37 *The Port Folio*, vol. 8 (August 1812), p. 145.

38 *The Port Folio*, n.s. vol. 2 (August 1813), p. 140.

39 George Murray, "Progress of the Fine Arts," *The Port Folio*, vol. 4 (September 1810), pp. 258-63. Republished by J. Meredith Neil, *The Pennsylvania Magazine of History and Biography*, vol. 93 (July 1969), pp. 412-16, under the mistaken assumption that Murray's address had never been printed. Murray's address preceded the aforementioned and quoted, better-known address by Latrobe, and was presented before the newly formed Society of Artists.

40 "Remarks on the Progress and Present State of the Fine Arts in the United States," *Analectic Magazine*, vol. 6 (November 1815), pp. 363-76.

41 These various printed discourses presented by "amateurs" or "Dilettanti," to use the term favored in the eighteenth and early nineteenth century to identify interested and talented laymen of taste concerned with the fine arts (and with no pejorative attendant to them, unlike current use of these terms), constitute one of the largest and most consistent body of contemporary art writing and criticism of the period, from the beginning of the century to the Civil War. Not unexpectedly, they are not without exaggerated rhetoric and nationalistic hyperbole—they were delivered, after all, as exhortations to artistic achievement—and they are somewhat repetitious, but they define many of the issues concerning men of culture of the times. The earliest ones were usually printed in local magazines after delivery but soon tended to be printed and issued as independent publications. Other separately published addresses of the period, similar in format but written by or in regard to such artists as Samuel F. B. Morse, John Trumbull, William Dunlap, and John Vanderlyn, tended to deal with narrower or more specific and more partisan issues.

42 Richard Ray, *An Address Delivered before The American Academy of the Fine Arts, November 17, 1825* (New York, 1825), p. 30. Ray's address included a frontispiece of what he and his generation considered sculptural supremacy, a depiction of the *Apollo Belvedere*, engraved by Asher B. Durand and eulogized at great length by Ray on pp. 23-24.

43 Fanshaw, p. 261.

44 "Sculpture and Sculptors," p. 131. Little has been published to date concerning John Frazee; the principal source concerned with his sculptural activities is his autobiography, in manuscript at the New Jersey Historical Society, excerpts published in *American Collector*, vol. 15 (September 1946), pp. 15-16, 23; (October 1946), pp. 10-11; (November 1946), pp. 12-14. This was previously published in the *North American Magazine*, vol. 5 (April 1835), pp. 395-403, and vol. 6 (July 1835), pp. 1-22. Unpublished are the masters thesis by Henry Bryan Caldwell, New York University, 1951, and the Ph.D. dissertation by Linda Hyman for the Graduate Faculty in History at the City University of New York, 1978.

45 Dunlap, I, p. 374.

46 Benson J. Lossing, *History of the Fine Arts* (New York, 1840), pp. 252-61, for American painting; Miss Ludlow, *Manual of the Fine Arts* (New York, 1850).

47 Pickering Dodge, *Sculpture: and the Plastic Arts* (Boston, 1850). Dodge discusses American sculpture, including Pre-Columbian art, in chapter 18, pp. 312-36. Dodge's previous volume was *The Art of Painting* (Boston, 1846), in which, again, the last chapter was devoted to American art. Dodge was the nephew of the Salem poet Henry Pickering, the patron of Thomas Cole and Washington Allston.

48 John Fanning Watson, *Annals of Philadelphia and Pennsylvania, in the Olden Time*, 3 vols. (Philadelphia, 1850), I, pp. 575-76, and II, p. 439. Watson's *Annals* was originally published in one volume in 1830. I have not attempted to compare his treatment of Rush in the successive early editions of the *Annals* since these were published during Watson's lifetime; he died in 1860.

49 Henry Theodore Tuckerman, *Book of the Artists, American Artist Life* (New York, 1867), p. 572.

50 Samuel Benjamin, "Sculpture in America," *Harper's New Monthly Magazine*, vol. 58 (April 1879), p. 668. Even here Benjamin wrote apologetically that "Rush worked only in wood or clay."

51 William J. Clark, *Great American Sculptures* (Philadelphia, 1878). Eakins's various William Rush paintings and sketches naturally figure in much of the voluminous literature on the artist, but the definitive article concerning the imagery is by Gordon Hendricks, "Eakins' William Rush Carving his Allegorical Statue of the Schuylkill," *The Art Quarterly*, vol. 31 (Winter 1968), pp. 383-404. Hendricks lists thirty-one works by Eakins on the theme.

52 *Catalogue of the First Exhibition Society of American Artists at Kurtz Gallery, New York* (New York, 1878), p. 5; Eakins offered the painting for sale for six hundred dollars.

53 The basic study of this phenomenon is Francis Haskell, "The Old Masters in Nineteenth Century Painting," *The Art Quarterly*, vol. 34 (Spring 1971), pp. 55-85. Haskell only deals with European artists, and it may be that there are comparatively few American examples. However, Elizabeth Evans has documented paintings by the American artist Edwin White, involving Giotto, Fra Angelico, Raphael, Michelangelo, Leonardo da Vinci, Vasari, Titian, Fra Bartolomeo, Van Dyck, Rubens, and Murillo, and White was certainly not unique in his interest in this fascinating pictorial sub-theme, though he may have been one of the most responsive of the Americans. I am indebted to Ms. Evans for her superb study of White's career prepared for a course in American History Painting at the City University Graduate School.

54 E. Leslie Gilliams, "A Philadelphia Sculptor," *Lippincott's Monthly Magazine*, vol. 52 (August 1893), pp. 249-53.

55 Wilfred Jordan, "William Rush: The Earliest Native-Born American Sculptor," *Art and Archaeology*, vol. 11 (June 1921), pp. 244-47.

56 Lorado Taft, "American Sculpture and Sculptors," *The Chautauquan*, vol. 22 (January 1896), pp. 387-95.

57 Lorado Taft, "Sculpture of the Nineteenth Century," in *The Fine Arts, A Course of University Lessons on Sculpture, Painting, Architecture and Decoration in both Their Principles and History* (Chicago, 1900), pp. 298-333; American sculpture treated on pp. 322-33.

58 Lorado Taft, *The History of American Sculpture* (1903; new edition, New York, 1925), pp. 20-24. Taft was not the only turn-of-the-century sculptor-writer to mention Rush; see also William Ordway Partridge, *The Technique of Sculpture* (Boston, 1895), for a cursory notice.

59 Adeline Adams, *The Spirit of American Sculpture* (New York, 1923), pp. 20-23.

60 Chandler Rathfon Post, *A History of European and American Sculpture from the Early Christian Period to the Present Day*, 2 vols. (Cambridge, Mass., 1921), II, p. 108.

61 See, for example, Sadakichi Hartmann, "Ecclesiastical Sculpture in America," *Catholic World*, vol. 77 (September 1903), pp. 760-67; Frank Owen Payne, "The Angel in American Sculpture," *Art and Archaeology*, vol. 11 (April 1921), pp. 155-61; Frank Owen Payne, "Some Noteworthy American Fountains," *The International Studio*, vol. 57 (January 1916), pp. 71-78.

62 In this period, for example, see Jenny Girton Walker, "The Ship Figure-head in America's History," *Daughters of the American Revolution Magazine*, vol. 61 (October, 1927), pp. 743-56; and Constance Lathrop, "A Vanishing Naval Tradition—the Figurehead," *United States Naval Institute Proceedings*, vol. 53 (November 1927), pp. 1166-77.

63 A. M. Nevill-Walpole, "American Wood Portraiture," *The Antiquarian*, vol. 12 (July 1929), pp. 27-29, 52; and Henry Branscombe, "Early American Wood Sculpture," *International Studio*, vol. 88 (October 1927), pp. 61-64.

64 Jordan, p. 247.

65 Not surprisingly, the exhibition of 1937 spawned several more articles on Rush, in addition to the exhibition catalogue. See "William Rush was First American Sculptor," *American Collector*, vol. 6 (March 1937), pp. 7-8, and Henri Marceau, "William Rush," *Pennsylvania Arts & Sciences*, vol. 2 (Spring 1937), pp. 19-23, in addition to reviews of the exhibition which appeared in both the art magazines and the general periodical press.

66 J. Meredith Neil, *Toward a National Taste: America's Quest for Aesthetic Independence* (Honolulu, 1975), pp. 104-05.

NAUDÉ, TOOLMARKS AND FINGERPRINTS

1 Regarding the wood statue of *George Washington* [68], Rush wrote to Benjamin West in London on March 12, 1815, "I intend it for a statue for any public place—and from which I expect to deliver Plaster casts, and probably some of Mettle—" (New-York Historical Society).

2 L. G. Carr Laughton, *Old Ship Figure Heads and Sterns* (1925; reprint, New York, 1973), pp. 19, 28.

3 F. Lewis Hinckley, *Directory of the Historic Cabinet Woods* (New York, 1960), pp. 116-17.

4 Committee on Water, Bills Received 1804–54, R.S. 120.43, City Hall Archives, Philadelphia.

5 Terminology here is taken from Lee H. Nelson, *Nail Chronology as an Aid to Dating Old Buildings*, American Association for State and Local History Technical Leaflet 48, vol. 24, no. 11 (November 1968). The term "brad" was used in Rush's time for nails without heads or nails with L- or T-shaped heads.

6 The first technical study (of which I am aware) made of Rush's wood sculpture was done by the late Walter J. Nitkiewicz of the National Park Service staff at Harpers Ferry, West Virginia, in 1971–73, when the wood *George Washington* was conserved. Nitkiewicz's report and photographs have been extremely helpful. His conclusions that Rush did not rely on glue and that he puttied joins before he nailed them together have been consistent with our findings.

7 See Nelson, *Nail Chronology*.

8 Henri Marceau, *William Rush 1756–1833: The First Native American Sculptor* (Philadelphia, 1937), p. 24.

9 "Gesso, in its broadest meaning, is any aqueous white priming or ground material that is used to prepare wooden supports for painting. . . ." Rutherford J. Gettens and George L. Stout, *Painting Materials* (1942; reprint, New York, 1966), p. 115. Rush used whiting ($CaCO_3$), probably in a varnish binder. See footnote 15.

10 Rush to James Madison, November 30, 1815, Historical Society of Pennsylvania.

11 Rush to Madison.

12 When preparing a log for sculpture, the artist must take into consideration that two types of cracks may develop (see fig. 68). The first type will appear on the outside: as dead wood ages cracks develop because shrinkage along each of the annual rings varies. The total shrinkage

of cells on the outer rings is greater than on the inner rings, and tension causes cell walls to collapse, resulting in a V-shaped crack. The top of the V is on the outside of the log, and the crack travels toward the inside. When the sculptor excavates his carving from the back, he essentially removes annual rings, thereby greatly reducing the difference in shrinkage between the remaining outermost and innermost rings.

The second type of crack occurs in the center of the log. The heartwood does not shrink markedly, but the surrounding sapwood responds to small losses of moisture by shrinking and pulling away from the center. Tension is released in one or more places forming heartchecks which travel outward. Removal of the heartwood decreases tension and thus measurably increases stability of the sculpture. See Robert L. Butler, *Wood for Wood-Carvers and Craftsmen, Source, Selection, Cutting, Treatment, Drying of Flitches, and Guidance in Their Use* (Cranbury, N.J., 1974).

13 Rush to John Rogers, Baltimore, May 23, 1816, Library Company of Philadelphia, quoted in part in the catalogue entry for *George Washington* [68].

14 Rush to Rogers.

15 Paint analysis was done by Walter C. McCrone Associates on a sample taken from *Samuel Morris*. Six layers were found: starting from the top, dirty varnish (or shellac); white (lead) paint layer, fine particles; off-white (lead) paint layer, fine and coarse particles; tan layer, whiting in a tan-colored medium, probably varnish or resin; whiting and some lead white pigment without binder; reddish resinous layer, presumably from the wood.

16 Hezekiah Reynolds, *Directions for House and Ship Painting* (New Haven, 1812; reprint, Worcester: American Antiquarian Society, 1978), p. 9. Reynold's birth and death dates, 1756 and 1833, correspond exactly with those of William Rush, and his publication came out the year that *Samuel Morris* was finished.

17 Research into this problem and the ensuing treatment was carried out in the summer of 1981 by Wendy Stayman at the Pennsylvania Academy on the figurehead *Peace* [29]. The object had been severely weather damaged and a great deal of paint had been lost. Insufficient traces of polychrome were found to form a meaningful decorative pattern. However, traces of lead white were found over a great deal of the figure, and since Rush was known to paint many of his sculptures white, the owners and conservator agreed to recreate a white surface although they did not rule out the possibility that the object might originally have been polychromed.

The wood was cleaned of modern paint, grime, and encrustations, and then sealed with Acryloid B 72. The surface was painted with Bocour Magna color, using white with small amounts of yellow ochre and ivory black pigments added to bring the color closer to that of *Samuel Morris*.

The paint was applied with a stippling technique which was found to best re-create the softened effect of aged paint and the coarse effect of paint applied with a brush. This technique also served to unify a weathered surface whose faults were much more noticeable under paint that had been applied evenly by spray and by brush in test areas. Stippling permitted maximum control of the visual effect from area to area and also required a minimal amount of paint.

Paint that was not obviously modern was not removed. Areas on the sculpture where original paint may be found under the B 72 and the Magna color are marked by the addition of a fluorescing material to the paint covering only those places. These spots are visible only in UV light and are documented with UV photographs. Wendy Stayman devised this plan so that original paint would remain in place for future scholars, making possible the collection of samples with minimal disturbance to the finished surface.

18 *Claypoole's American Daily Advertiser*, Philadelphia, June 5, 1799, quoted in Marceau, p. 73.

19 Rush to Madison, November 30, 1815.

20 William Dunlap, *A History of the Rise and Progress of the Arts of Design in the United States* (1834; reprint, Boston, 1918), I, p. 374.

21 "An Appreciation—by a Ship Carver," undated newspaper clipping in the scrapbook of Dr. William Rush Dunton, Jr., Philadelphia Museum of Art.

22 Committee on Water, Papers 1804–54, R.S. 120.42, City Hall Archives, Philadelphia.

23 Rush to Madison, November 30, 1815.

24 Quoted in Marceau, pp. 75-76.

25 "Lacing, the name of one of the pieces in the knee of the head, which runs up as high as the top of the hair bracket, and to which the figure is secured." R. Parsley, *The Shipbuilder's Repository; or, A Treatise on Marine Architecture* (London, 1788), p. 451. A glossary of technical terms is included on pp. 443-59.

26 David Clarke of Bristol, Rhode Island, witnessed the installation of one of his figureheads on the H.M.S. *Rose* in Lunenburg, Nova Scotia, in 1970, using a method said to be traditional there. The figure was set on a shelf that had been cut in the knee of the head, and the bracket at the back of the figurehead was secured to the lacing of the ship with ropes and a spike, as tightly as possible, after which the crevice between the two surfaces to be joined was evened out by sawing down the vertical join with a two-man crosscut saw. The figure was then released, the join cleaned, and the procedure repeated twice more after which the surfaces to be joined were flush. Guide holes for four ¾-in. bolts were drilled from the back. Where the surface of the figurehead was disturbed the holes were enlarged to 2-in. diameter to receive wood plugs which were glued and hammered into place after the bolts had been tightened with nuts front and back. The plugs were then carved and painted by the sculptor.

27 Harley J. McKee, FAIA, *Introduction to Early American Masonry, Stone, Brick, Mortar and Plaster* (Washington, D.C.: National Trust for Historic Preservation, 1973), p. 41.

28 John Larson, "The Conservation of Terracotta Sculpture," *The Conservator*, United Kingdom Institute for Conservation, no. 4 (1980), pp. 38-45.

29 Three samples of clay, from *Caspar Wistar*, the *Self-Portrait*, and *Lafayette*, were analyzed at the Center for Conservation and Technical Studies, Fogg Art Museum, Harvard University, by Eugene Farrell and Rich-

ard Newman. Their report of September 1981 includes a table which gives results of various tests. A Scanning Electron Microscope with X-ray Fluorescence Microprobe showed clay particles and Si, Al, K, Fe, and Ti. The major elements in an Emission Spectroscopy study were Si, Al, Fe, Ti, and Mg. Microscopy revealed quartz with clay and rutile rods in all three samples. The powder for *Wistar* and the *Self-Portrait* were both white; both contained hematite but the former in smaller amounts. Greater amounts of hematite were found in the *Lafayette* sample whose powder was pink. This sample also showed clay in sheath-like bundles. X-ray Diffraction showed quartz for all three samples with a few extra unidentified lines for the *Self-Portrait*. The report concludes, "The similarity in composition suggests that the clay in all three cases may be from the same or similar source. However, quantitative data on trace elements from a much larger number of samples would be required for such a conclusion to be drawn."

30 For a good description of the basic technique of clay sculpture see Jack C. Rich, *The Materials and Methods of Sculpture* (New York, 1947), pp. 23-51.

31 John H. Larson, "Carrier-Belleuse, A Technical Study of his Terracotta Sculpture," *French Sculpture 1780-1940*, exhibition catalogue (Somerset, England, and New York: Bruton Gallery, 1981).

32 Paint was removed at the Pennsylvania Academy in 1944 from the portraits of *Wright, Benjamin Rush, Physick, Wistar,* and *Lafayette*. Paint visible on the photograph of *Washington* in the 1937 exhibition catalogue has since

been removed. *Elizabeth Rush* was painted at one time but *Mary Rush* probably was not.

33 The identification of toolmarkings is one part of an important article on the examination and treatment of terracotta sculpture by John Larson at the Victoria and Albert Museum, London, referred to above, in note 28.

34 The plaster jabot had lost a considerable amount of mass and detail had been totally obliterated so that its impact as a design element was gone. It was released during conservation and saved but replaced by a jabot cast in plaster from the College of Physicians of Philadelphia cast. The collar tips were cast in plaster from the same model.

The missing collar tips on *Rush* and *Physick*, considerably smaller, were remodeled on the terracotta with polyfilla and polyfix, using whatever information was available on the terracotta itself and supplementing it with visual data from the plaster casts at the College of Physicians of Philadelphia, the Library Company of Philadelphia, and Pennsylvania Hospital for *Rush*, and for *Physick* from the plaster casts at the American Philosophical Society and the College of Physicians of Philadelphia. All the modeling of missing parts was done by Steven Pine.

35 Arthur Beale, "A Technical View of Nineteenth-Century Sculpture," *Metamorphoses in Nineteenth-Century Sculpture* (Cambridge, Mass., 1975), p. 54.

36 *Report of the Second Annual Exhibition of the Franklin Institute of the State of Pennsylvania for the Promotion of Mechanic Arts* (1825), no. 434.

INDEX OF WORKS BY WILLIAM RUSH

Allegorical Works

Agriculture, Market Street Bridge, Philadelphia [50]
Agriculture, Penn Street Bridge, Reading [74]
Allegory of the Schuylkill River *or* Water Nymph and Bittern [35]
Allegory of the Schuylkill River in Its Improved State [96]
Allegory of the Waterworks [97]
Charity [86]
Comedy [31]
Commerce, Custom House, Philadelphia [78]
Commerce, Market Street Bridge, Philadelphia [51]
Commerce, Penn Street Bridge, Reading [75]
Exhortation [52]
Faith [84]
Hope [85]
Justice [62]
Piety [70]
Praise [53]
Silence [87]
Tragedy [32]
Virtue [42]
Winter [45]
Wisdom [61]

Figureheads and other Ship Carvings

Benjamin Franklin, figurehead for the *Benjamin Franklin* [80]
Benjamin Franklin, figurehead for the *Franklin* [73]
Benjamin Rush, figurehead for the *Benjamin Rush* [72]
Captain John Smith, figurehead for the *Potomac* [89]
Columbus, figurehead, and trail boards and stern carvings, for the *Columbus* [77]
Commerce, figurehead for an English vessel [5]
Fingal, figurehead [36]
General Wade Hampton, figurehead [106]
Genius of the United States, figurehead for the *United States* [15]
George Washington, figurehead for the *General Washington* [4]
Goddess of Wisdom, figurehead for the *Congress* [22]
Helvetius, figurehead for the *Helvetius* [28]
Hercules, figurehead, and stern carvings, for the *Philadelphia* [24]
Hercules, figurehead for the *Superb* [91]
Hercules, figurehead design for the *Constitution* [14]
Hercules, figurehead, and stern carvings, designs for the *Pennsylvania* [93]

Indian, figurehead for the *North America* [44]
Indian Chief, figurehead for the *Algonquin* [95]
An Indian Orator, figurehead [108]
Indian Trader, figurehead for the *William Penn* [3]
John Adams, figurehead for the *John Adams* [23]
Liberty, figurehead for the *Liberty* [12]
Lion, figurehead [18]
Lion, figurehead [19]
Lion, figurehead, and stern carvings, designs for the *Crescent* [17]
Montezuma, figurehead [107]
Montesquieu, figurehead for the *Montesquieu* [30]
Nature, figurehead, and stern carvings, for the *Constellation* [20]
Peace, figurehead [29]
Revolution, figurehead for the *Chesapeake* [21]
River God, figurehead for the *Ganges* [10]
Rousseau, figurehead for the *Rousseau* [27]
Sir Walter Raleigh, figurehead for the *North Carolina* [81]
Voltaire, figurehead for the *Voltaire* [11]
William Penn, figurehead [109]
Female figurehead for the *Two Brothers* [9]
Figurehead for the *Ellen* [88]
Figurehead for the *Guerriere* [63]
Figurehead for the *Sally I* [8]
Figurehead for the *Sally II* [16]
Figurehead for a snow [13]
Figurehead for the *Two Brothers* [1]
Figurehead for an English vessel [6]
Quarter pieces for the *Good Friends* [26]

Miscellaneous Works

Anatomical Models [33]
Cherubim [82, 83]
Cherubim Encircled by a Glory [54]
Columbia [58]
Commemorative Statuette [34]
Crucifixion (St. Augustine's Church) [41]
Crucifix (St. Mary's Church) [47]
Eagle (PAFA) [37]
Eagle (St. John's Lutheran Church) [43]
Indian [7]
Mastodon Bones [25]
Mercury [99]
Mercury [100]
Mercury [101]
Plan for North East or Franklin Public Square, Philadelphia [92]
Plan for Penn Square [98]

Portraits

Bartram, William; wood bust [57]
A Citizen; wood bust [46]
Fox, Samuel M.; terracotta bust [67]
Franklin, Benjamin; wood bust [2]
Gentleman; terracotta bust [104]
Gentleman; clay bust [105]
Hanson, Alexander Contee; terracotta bust [69]
Jackson, Andrew; terracotta bust [79]
Jefferson, Thomas; plaster or terracotta (?) bust [103]
Lafayette, Marquis de; terracotta bust [94]
Linnaeus; wood bust [56]
Madison, James; plaster or terracotta (?) bust [102]
Morris, Samuel; wood bust [48]

Muhlenberg, Henry Ernest; wood bust [55]
Perry, Oliver Hazard; terracotta bust [64]
Physick, Philip Syng; terracotta bust [60]
Rush, Benjamin; terracotta bust [49]
Rush, Elizabeth; terracotta bust [39]
Rush, Mary Simpson; terracotta bust [40]
Scott, Winfield; terracotta bust [65]
Self-Portrait; terracotta bust [90]
Stansbury, Joseph; terracotta bust [66]
Thomson, Charles; terracotta bust [71]
Washington, George; terracotta bust [76]
Washington, George; full-length figure in wood [68]
Wistar, Caspar; terracotta bust [59]
Wright, Joseph; terracotta bust [38]

CHECKLIST OF THE EXHIBITION

William Rush

1. *Benjamin Franklin*, 1787   [2]
   Pine, 20¼ × 16¼ × 13 in. (51.4 × 41.3 × 33 cm.)
   Yale University Art Gallery, New Haven

2. *Peace*, c. 1805–10   [29]
   Figurehead for an unknown vessel
   Pine, painted, 70 × 24½ × 27½ in. (177.8 × 62.2 × 69.9 cm.), without base
   Mr. and Mrs. Gerald S. Lestz

3. *Comedy*, 1808   [31]
   Pine (originally painted), height without base 90½ in. (229.9 cm.)
   The Edwin Forrest Home, Philadelphia

4. *Tragedy*, 1808   [32]
   Pine (originally painted), height without base 90½ in. (229.9 cm.)
   The Edwin Forrest Home, Philadelphia

5. *Anatomical Models*, 1808–20   [33]
   Pine, leather, papier-mâché, polychrome; *Left temporal bone with inner ear structures* 21⅞ × 30 × 23 in. (55.6 × 76.2 × 58.4 cm.), *Right maxilla* 24⅝ × 25¼ × 16 in. (62.5 × 64.1 × 40.6 cm.)
   The Wistar Institute of Anatomy and Biology, Philadelphia

6. *Commemorative Statuette*, 1809   [34]
   Cherry, silver, and brass, 16 × 9½ × 4¼ in. (40.6 × 24.1 × 10.8 cm.)
   Incised on book, beneath left figure: Wm Rush Fect; engraved on silver plate, lower left: Rush sculptor; lower right: Kneass Eng
   Private collection

7. Head fragment of *Allegory of the Schuylkill River* or *Water Nymph and Bittern*, 1809   [35]
   Pine (originally painted), 10 × 9½ × 10 in. (25.4 × 24.1 × 25.4 cm.)
   Private collection

8. Posthumous full-length cast of *Allegory of the Schuylkill River* or *Water Nymph and Bittern*, 1872   [35]
   Bronze (originally not patinated artificially), 90¾ × 19⅛ × 34⁵⁄₁₆ in. (230.5 × 48.6 × 87.2 cm.)
   Incised, on base: Robert Wood & Co./Bronze Founders/Phila.
   The Fairmount Park Commission, Philadelphia

9. *Eagle*, c. 1810   [37]
   Pine, painted, 30⅜ × 32 × 12⅝ in. (77.2 × 81.3 × 32.1 cm.)
   Pennsylvania Academy of the Fine Arts, Philadelphia; Gift of Wilson Mitchell

10. *Joseph Wright*, c. 1810   [38]
    Terracotta, 19¾ × 16½ × 10 in. (50.2 × 41.9 × 25.4 cm.)
    Pennsylvania Academy of the Fine Arts, Philadelphia

11. *Elizabeth Rush*, c. 1810   [39]
    Terracotta, 12½ × 8¾ × 6½ in. (31.8 × 22.2 × 16.5 cm.)
    Philadelphia Museum of Art; Given by Dr. William Rush Dunton, Jr.

12. *Mary Simpson Rush*, c. 1810   [40]
    Terracotta, 13 × 9 × 7 in. (33 × 22.9 × 17.8 cm.)
    Philadelphia Museum of Art; Given by Dr. William Rush Dunton, Jr.

13. *Virtue*, c. 1810–20   [42]
    Wood, painted white, 70 × 24 × 24 in. (177.8 × 61 × 61 cm.)
    The Grand Lodge of Free and Accepted Masons of Pennsylvania, Philadelphia

14. *Eagle*, 1811   [43]
    Wood, painted, 63 × 65 in. (160 × 165.1 cm.)
    St. John's Lutheran Church, Philadelphia

15. *Winter*, c. 1811   [45]
    Pine (originally painted gray-white), height 28¹⁄₁₆ in. (71.3 cm.)
    The Brooklyn Museum; Dick S. Ramsay Fund

16. *Samuel Morris*, 1812   [48]
    Pine, painted white, 20½ × 19 × 12 in. (52.1 × 48.3 × 30.5 cm.)
    Incised, at center back: W^m· Rush/Fec^t
    The Schuylkill Fishing Company of the State in Schuylkill, Cornwells Heights, Pennsylvania

17. *Benjamin Rush*, 1812   [49]
    Terracotta, 18¾ × 15½ × 12½ in. (47.6 × 39.4 × 31.8 cm.)
    Pennsylvania Academy of the Fine Arts, Philadelphia
    PLASTER CASTS:

18. The Library Company of Philadelphia

19. The College of Physicians of Philadelphia
20. Pennsylvania Hospital, Philadelphia

21. *Exhortation*, 1812 [52]
 Pine, painted, 56 × 19 × 18 in. (142.2 × 48.3 × 45.7 cm.)
 St. Peter's Church, Philadelphia

22. *Praise*, 1812 [53]
 Pine, painted, 57½ × 24½ × 18 in. (146.1 × 62.2 × 45.7 cm.)
 St. Peter's Church, Philadelphia

23. *Cherubim Encircled by a Glory*, 1812 [54]
 Pine, painted, 20½ × 43 in. (52.1 × 109.2 cm.)
 St. Peter's Church, Philadelphia

24. *Linnaeus*, c. 1812 [56]
 Pine, painted white, 24¼ × 18½ × 12 in. (61.6 × 47 × 30.5 cm.), with base
 The Corcoran Gallery of Art, Washington, D.C.

25. *Caspar Wistar*, 1812–13 [59]
 Terracotta, 20 × 17 × 13½ in. (50.8 × 43.2 × 34.3 cm.)
 Pennsylvania Academy of the Fine Arts, Philadelphia
 PLASTER CASTS:
26. American Philosophical Society, Philadelphia
27. The College of Physicians of Philadelphia
28. Pennsylvania Hospital, Philadelphia

29. *Philip Syng Physick*, 1812–13 [60]
 Terracotta, 19 × 14¾ × 11¼ in. (48.3 × 37.5 × 28.6 cm.)
 Pennsylvania Academy of the Fine Arts, Philadelphia
 PLASTER CASTS:
30. American Philosophical Society, Philadelphia
31. The Library Company of Philadelphia
32. Robert Erwin Jones, M.D.
33. The College of Physicians of Philadelphia

34. *Wisdom*, after 1812–by 1824 [61]
 Pine (originally painted), 92¾ × 37 × 26 in. (235.6 × 94 × 66 cm.), with base
 The Fairmount Park Commission, Philadelphia

35. *Justice*, after 1812–by 1824 [62]
 Pine (originally painted), 93¼ × 38½ × 19¼ in. (236.9 × 97.8 × 48.9 cm.), with base
 The Fairmount Park Commission, Philadelphia

36. *Winfield Scott*, c. 1814–17 [65]
 Attributed to William Rush
 Plaster, painted white, 19⅞ × 21¾ × 14⅛ in. (50.5 × 55.2 × 35.9 cm.)
 National Portrait Gallery, Smithsonian Institution, Washington, D.C.

37. *George Washington*, 1815 [68]
 Pine, painted white, height 73 in. (185.4 cm.)

Independence National Historical Park Collection, Philadelphia

38. *Benjamin Rush*, c. 1815 [72]
 Figurehead for the *Benjamin Rush*
 Pine, 21½ × 18 × 14 in. (54.6 × 45.7 × 35.6 cm.)
 The Mariners Museum, Newport News, Virginia

39. *Benjamin Franklin*, c. 1815 [73]
 Figurehead for the *Franklin*
 Pine, painted white, 55½ × 27 × 22 in. (141 × 68.6 × 55.9 cm.)
 U.S. Naval Academy Museum, Annapolis, Maryland

40. *George Washington*, c. 1817 [76]
 Terracotta, 22½ × 20¼ × 14 in. (57.2 × 51.4 × 35.6 cm.)
 The Valley Forge Historical Society, Valley Forge, Pennsylvania
 PLASTER CAST:
41. The Art Museum, Princeton University, New Jersey; Purchased through the John MacLean Magie and Gertrude Magie Fund

42. *Andrew Jackson*, n.d. [79]
 Possibly after William Rush's bust of 1819
 Plaster, 28½ × 21 × 10 in. (72.4 × 53.3 × 25.4 cm.)
 Louisiana State Museum, New Orleans

43. *Cherubim*, 1820–21 [82]
 Wood, painted white, 48 × 56 in. (121.9 × 142.2 cm.)
 The Grand Lodge of Free and Accepted Masons of Pennsylvania, Philadelphia

44. *Cherubim*, 1820–21 [83]
 Wood, painted white, 48 × 56 in. (121.9 × 142.2 cm.)
 The Grand Lodge of Free and Accepted Masons of Pennsylvania, Philadelphia

45. *Faith*, 1820–21 [84]
 Wood, painted white, 26¾ × 58¾ × 12 in. (67.9 × 149.2 × 30.5 cm.)
 The Grand Lodge of Free and Accepted Masons of Pennsylvania, Philadelphia

46. *Hope*, 1820–21 [85]
 Wood, painted white, 32 × 64 × 14 in. (81.3 × 162.6 × 35.6 cm.)
 The Grand Lodge of Free and Accepted Masons of Pennsylvania, Philadelphia

47. *Charity*, 1820–21 [86]
 Wood, painted white, 37 × 69½ × 21 in. (94 × 176.5 × 53.3 cm.)
 The Grand Lodge of Free and Accepted Masons of Pennsylvania, Philadelphia

48. *Silence*, 1820–21 [87]
 Wood, painted white, 66 × 32 × 29 in.

(167.6 × 81.3 × 73.7 cm.)
The Grand Lodge of Free and Accepted Masons of Pennsylvania, Philadelphia

49. *Self-Portrait*, c. 1822   [90]
Terracotta, 15½ × 18 × 11 in. (39.4 × 45.7 × 27.9 cm.)
Pennsylvania Academy of the Fine Arts, Philadelphia

50. *Plan for North East or Franklin Public Square, Philadelphia*, 1824   [92]
Watercolor and pen and ink on paper, 14⅝ × 17¾ in. (37.1 × 45.1 cm.)
Inscribed, lower left: Coloured by Thoˢ Birch; lower right: Design'd & Drawn by Wᵐ Rush 1824
The Library Company of Philadelphia

51. *Design for Hercules Figurehead*, 1824   [93a]
Photograph of drawing
Inscribed, center bottom: D[rawn?] & [illegible] by Wᵐ Rush Philadᵃ Septʳ 14 1824
Whereabouts of drawing unknown; photograph taken from Pauline A. Pinckney, *American Figureheads and Their Carvers* (New York, 1940), pl. III

52. Stern plan for the *Pennsylvania*, 1824
Probably after William Rush   [93b]
Pen and ink on paper, 25 × 48 in. (63.5 × 121.9 cm.)
Inscribed, lower left: Ship of the Line Pennsylvania building at Philadelphia/ornamental part of the Stern designed & executed by William Rush Esqʳ of Phila in August 1824
The National Archives, Washington, D.C.

53. *Marquis de Lafayette*, 1824   [94]
Terracotta, 21¹⁵⁄₁₆ × 18¾ × 11⅛ in. (55.7 × 47.6 × 28.3 cm.)
Pennsylvania Academy of the Fine Arts, Philadelphia; Gift of Dr. William Rush Dunton, Jr.

54. *Allegory of the Schuylkill River in Its Improved State*, 1825   [96]
Spanish cedar, painted, 39⅜ × 87¼ × 26⁷⁄₁₆ in. (100 × 221.6 × 67.2 cm.)
The Fairmount Park Commission, Philadelphia

55. *Allegory of the Waterworks*, 1825   [97]
Spanish cedar, painted, 41³⁄₁₆ × 87¹⁄₁₆ × 30⁷⁄₁₆ in. (104.6 × 221.1 × 77.3 cm.)
The Fairmount Park Commission, Philadelphia

56. *Mercury*, 1828–29   [99]
Spanish cedar (originally painted), 44½ × 13 × 20 in. (113 × 33 × 50.8 cm.)
The Fairmount Park Commission, Philadelphia

57. *Mercury*, c. 1830   [100]
Pine, polychromed; height with base 49⅞ in. (126.7 cm.)

Museum and Library of Maryland History, The Maryland Historical Society, Baltimore; Gift of the Honorable A. J. Foble

John Rush (1782–1853)

58. *Goddess of Liberty*, c. 1840
Pine, painted white, 120½ × 44½ × 26 in. (306.1 × 113 × 66 cm.), without base
Berks County Historical Society, Reading, Pennsylvania

Possibly by John Rush

59. *David Rittenhouse*, n.d.
Pine, painted white, 24 × 17 × 10½ in. (61.0 × 43.2 × 26.7 cm.)
Pennsylvania Academy of the Fine Arts, Philadelphia

Thomas Birch (1779–1851)

60. *Preparation for War*, 1800
Engraving, 9⅛ × 11⁷⁄₁₆ in. (23.2 × 29.1 cm.)
The New-York Historical Society, New York City

61. Sketch of the *Franklin Figurehead*, c. 1815
Pen and ink on paper, 6¼ × 7⅛ in. (15.9 × 18.1 cm.)
The Historical Society of Pennsylvania, Philadelphia

John T. Bowen (active 1834–1856)

62. *A View of Fairmount Waterworks with Schuylkill in the Distance Taken from the Mount*, 1835
Lithograph, uncolored, 21¾ × 14⅝ in. (55.2 × 37.1 cm.)
The Library Company of Philadelphia

Charles Cassell

63. *Columbus* (sail plan of battleship), c. 1822
Pen and ink on paper, mounted on linen, 22¾ × 32¾ in. (57.8 × 83.2 cm.)
Signed, lower right: Charles Cassell
The Lenthall Collection, The Franklin Institute Science Museum, Philadelphia

Charles Dodge (1806–1886)

64. *Jeremiah Dodge*, c. 1825–30
Wood, painted, 27½ × 18 in. (69.9 × 45.7 cm.)
The New-York Historical Society, New York City

65. *Mrs. Charles Dodge*, c. 1830–40
Wood, painted white, 24⅝ × 15¾ in. (62.5 × 40 cm.)
The Brooklyn Museum; Dick S. Ramsay Fund

Thomas Doughty (1793–1856)

66. *View of the Waterworks on Schuylkill—Seen from the Top of Fair Mount*, 1826

Oil on canvas, 16¼ × 24 in. (41.3 × 61 cm.)
Private collection

Attributed to George Gilbert (active 1824–1831)

67. *Civic Arch for Lafayette*, 1824
Photograph of illustration in John Fanning Watson,
Annals of Philadelphia, in manuscript, II, p. 460
Inscribed, lower right: Gilbert
Courtesy of The Historical Society of Pennsylvania,
Philadelphia

Reuben S. Gilbert (active 1829–1849)

68. *The Interior of St. John's Church*, 1829
Watercolor on paper, 7⅛ × 11⅝ in. (18.1 ×
29.5 cm.)
Inscribed, lower left: 12, Jany. 1829; signed, lower
right: Reuben S. Gilbert
St. John's Lutheran Church, Philadelphia

Frederick Graff (1774–1847)

69. *Doorway to Mill House at Fair Mount*, n.d.
Pen and ink and watercolor on paper, 10¾ × 15 in.
(27.3 × 38.1 cm.)
The Frederick Graff Collection, The Franklin Institute Science Museum, Philadelphia

Nathaniel Hutton (active 1791–1832)

70. *Sail plan for the Frigate Philadelphia*, 1800
Pen and ink on paper, mounted on linen, 20⅛ × 29
in. (51.1 × 73.7 cm.)
Inscribed, lower right: Drawn by Nath¹ Hutton Junʳ,
May 16ᵗʰ 1800
The Lenthall Collection, The Franklin Institute Sci-
ence Museum, Philadelphia

D. J. Kennedy (active 1841–1871)

71. *Old Custom House*, 1871, after an 1834 sketch
by W. T. Small
Watercolor on paper, 9⅞ × 13⅜ in. (25.1 × 34
cm.)
Inscribed, lower right: D.J.K.; dated, lower left: 1871
The Historical Society of Pennsylvania, Philadelphia

John Lewis Krimmel (1789–1821)

72. *Fourth of July in Centre Square*, 1812
Oil on canvas, 23 × 28¾ in. (58.4 × 73 cm.)
Pennsylvania Academy of the Fine Arts, Philadelphia;
Academy Purchase from the Paul Beck Estate

George Lehman (died 1870)

73. *View of Fairmount*, 1833
Lithograph, uncolored, 9⁷⁄₁₆ × 12⁷⁄₁₆ in. (24 ×
31.6 cm.)
The Library Company of Philadelphia

Attributed to Samuel Lewis (active 1795–1817)

74. *The United States Frigate Dressed with the Colors of
Various Nations*, 1800–10
Oil on canvas, 12½ × 15¾ in. (31.8 × 40 cm.)
Warren Sturgis

Rembrandt Peale (1778–1860)

75. *Mastodon Skeleton*, 1801
Pen and ink on paper, 15¼ × 12¾ in. (38.7 ×
32.4 cm.)
American Philosophical Society Library, Philadelphia

Attributed to Rembrandt Peale

76. *William Rush*, before 1813
Oil on canvas, 23½ × 19½ in. (59.7 × 49.5 cm.)
Independence National Historical Park Collection,
Philadelphia

Titian Ramsay Peale (1799–1885)

77. *Interior of Peale's Museum*, 1822
Watercolor on paper, 14 × 20¾ in. (35.6 ×
52.7 cm.)
The Detroit Institute of Arts; Gift of the Founders
Society, The Director's Fund

John Perriman and J. W. Edy

78. *Perspective View of the Valiant*, London, 1791
Aquatint, colored, 20 × 21⅜ in. (50.8 × 54.3 cm.)
Inscribed, lower left: J. Perriman, delᵗ; lower right:
J. W. Edy, Fecit
The Mariners Museum, Newport News, Virginia

Jacob Petersen (1774–1854)

79. *The Ship Helvetius of Philadelphia comãndᵗ by Captⁿ
Adam Baush*, c. 1810
Watercolor on paper, 19³⁄₁₆ × 21¹⁄₁₆ in. (48.7 ×
53.5 cm.)
Signed, lower right: drawn af Jacob Petersen
J. Welles Henderson Collection, Philadelphia Mari-
time Museum

Max Rosenthal (1833–1918)

80. *Interior View of Independence Hall, Philadelphia*, 1856
Chromolithograph, 14½ × 18¾ in. (36.8 ×
47.6 cm.)
Independence National Historical Park Collection,
Philadelphia

Edward Savage (1761–1817)

81. *Constellation and L'Insurgent—The Chace*, 1799
Aquatint, 13⅞ × 20⅛ in. (35.2 × 51.1 cm.)
The New-York Historical Society, New York City
Irving S. Olds Collection

William Strickland (1787–1854)

82. *New Theatre, Chestnut Street*, 1808
Watercolor on paper, 25½ × 33½ in. (64.8 × 85.1 cm.)
Signed and dated, lower left: William Strickland pinx! 1808
Pennsylvania Academy of the Fine Arts, Philadelphia; Gift of Mr. and Mrs. William Jeanes

Attributed to Thomas Sully (1783–1872)

83. *Arms of Philadelphia*, c. 1824
Oil on canvas, 56¼ × 56 in. (142.9 × 142.2 cm.)
Independence National Historical Park Collection, Philadelphia

Artists unknown

84. *Stock Certificate for Chestnut Street Theatre*, 1791
Engraving, 11⅕ × 7⅗ in. (28 × 19.3 cm.)
The Historical Society of Pennsylvania, Philadelphia

85. *Figure of St. John*, c. 1795
Wood, painted white, life-size
The Lutheran Church of the Holy Trinity, Lancaster, Pennsylvania

86. *U.S. Frigate Philadelphia*, 1803–05
Watercolor on paper, 11⅝ × 15¼ in. (29.5 × 38.7 cm.)
The New-York Historical Society, New York City

87. *Broadside advertising Rush's statue of Washington*, 1815
9⅞ × 7½ in. (25.1 × 19.1 cm.)
The Historical Society of Pennsylvania, Philadelphia

88. *Music*, c. 1830
Pine, 37½ × 17¾ × 10½ in. (95.3 × 45.1 × 26.7 cm.)
The Historical Society of Pennsylvania, Philadelphia

89. *Design for Figurehead of Hercules*, c. 1837
Photostatic copy of pen and ink drawing on paper
Inscribed, lower right: "Pennsylvania"/Launched July 18ᵗʰ 1837
Courtesy of the National Archives, Washington, D.C.

GENEALOGY OF WILLIAM RUSH (1756–1833)

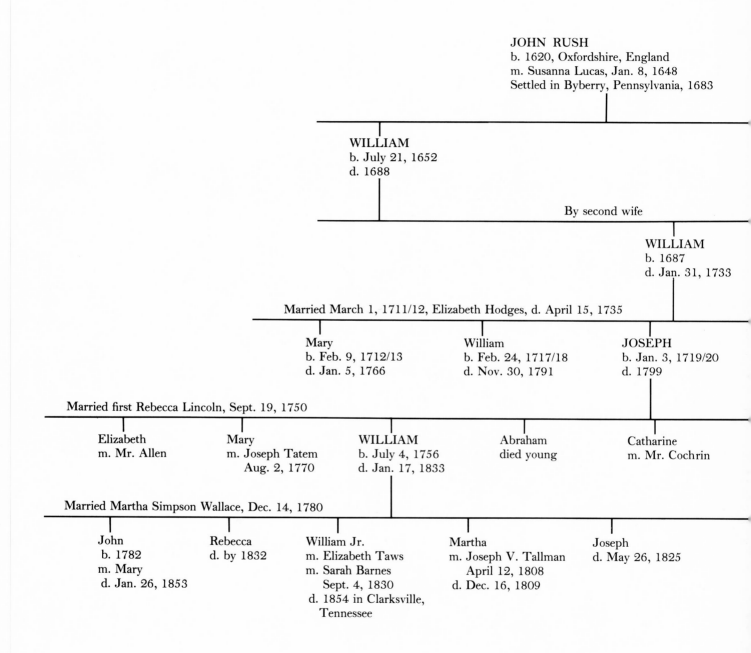

JOHN RUSH
b. 1620, Oxfordshire, England
m. Susanna Lucas, Jan. 8, 1648
Settled in Byberry, Pennsylvania, 1683

WILLIAM
b. July 21, 1652
d. 1688

By second wife

WILLIAM
b. 1687
d. Jan. 31, 1733

Married March 1, 1711/12, Elizabeth Hodges, d. April 15, 1735

Mary
b. Feb. 9, 1712/13
d. Jan. 5, 1766

William
b. Feb. 24, 1717/18
d. Nov. 30, 1791

JOSEPH
b. Jan. 3, 1719/20
d. 1799

Married first Rebecca Lincoln, Sept. 19, 1750

Elizabeth
m. Mr. Allen

Mary
m. Joseph Tatem
Aug. 2, 1770

WILLIAM
b. July 4, 1756
d. Jan. 17, 1833

Abraham
died young

Catharine
m. Mr. Cochrin

Married Martha Simpson Wallace, Dec. 14, 1780

John
b. 1782
m. Mary
d. Jan. 26, 1853

Rebecca
d. by 1832

William Jr.
m. Elizabeth Taws
m. Sarah Barnes
Sept. 4, 1830
d. 1854 in Clarksville,
Tennessee

Martha
m. Joseph V. Tallman
April 12, 1808
d. Dec. 16, 1809

Joseph
d. May 26, 1825

The genealogical chart is a revised version of the one which appeared in Henri Marceau's 1937 exhibition catalogue. The first two generations have been excerpted from Marceau's chart. Additions and corrections to subsequent generations are based on research of genealogical material, particularly wills, at the Historical Society of Pennsylvania.

Susan James-Gadzinski

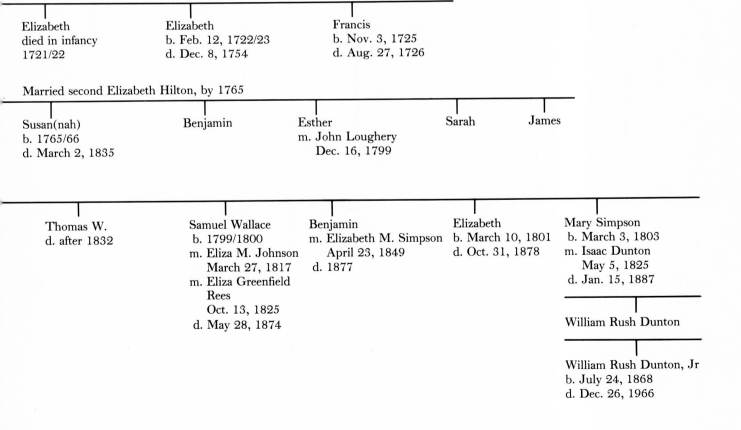

Elizabeth
died in infancy
1721/22

Elizabeth
b. Feb. 12, 1722/23
d. Dec. 8, 1754

Francis
b. Nov. 3, 1725
d. Aug. 27, 1726

Married second Elizabeth Hilton, by 1765

Susan(nah)
b. 1765/66
d. March 2, 1835

Benjamin

Esther
m. John Loughery
Dec. 16, 1799

Sarah

James

Thomas W.
d. after 1832

Samuel Wallace
b. 1799/1800
m. Eliza M. Johnson
March 27, 1817
m. Eliza Greenfield
Rees
Oct. 13, 1825
d. May 28, 1874

Benjamin
m. Elizabeth M. Simpson
April 23, 1849
d. 1877

Elizabeth
b. March 10, 1801
d. Oct. 31, 1878

Mary Simpson
b. March 3, 1803
m. Isaac Dunton
May 5, 1825
d. Jan. 15, 1887

William Rush Dunton

William Rush Dunton, Jr
b. July 24, 1868
d. Dec. 26, 1966

William Rush, American Sculptor

This book was designed by Klaus Gemming,
New Haven, Connecticut.

The typeface was first cast about 1796
in Philadelphia by Binny & Ronaldson.
In its recutting by Mergenthaler Linotype Company
it was named Monticello, since it was first used
for the fifty-volume *Papers of Thomas Jefferson*.
Princeton University Press set the text
in the new film version of Monticello.
Catalogue entry 79 includes a discussion
about James Ronaldson's background and his
involvement with William Rush's work.

The book was printed by Eastern Press, Inc.,
New Haven, Connecticut, on
Lustro Offset Enamel Dull paper,
manufactured by the S. D. Warren Company,
a division of the Scott Paper Company.

The binding is by Mueller Trade Bindery Corp.,
Middletown, Connecticut.

Pennsylvania Academy of the Fine Arts